BRITISH POETRY OF THE NINETEENTH CENTURY

Twayne's Critical History of Poetry Series
BRITISH LITERATURE

Alan Shucard, Editor
University of Wisconsin-Parkside

BRITISH POETRY OF THE NINETEENTH CENTURY

STEPHEN GURNEY
Bemidji State University

ICCC LIBRARY
Twayne Publishers · New York
Maxwell Macmillan Canada · Toronto
Maxwell Macmillan International · New York Oxford Singapore Sydney

Twayne Publishers
Macmillan Publishing Company
866 Third Avenue
New York, New York 10022

Maxwell Macmillan Canada, Inc.
1200 Eglinton Avenue East
Suite 200
Don Mills, Ontario M3C 3N1

Library of Congress Cataloging-in-Publication Data

Gurney, Stephen.
  British poetry of the nineteenth century/Stephen Gurney.
    p.   cm.—(Twayne's critical history of poetry series.
  British literature)
    Includes bibliographical references and index.
    ISBN 0-8057-8452-7
    1. English poetry—19th century—History and criticism.
  I. Title.   II. Series.
  PR451.G87   1993
  821'.809—dc20   93-19832
                                                             CIP

10 9 8 7 6 5 4 3 2 1

Printed in the United States of America

· *Contents* ·

· *Preface* ·

The following study of British poetry in the nineteenth century is intended to fill a vacuum in recent intellectual history. There are, of course, any number of literary histories that encompass the whole variety of literary genres and take as their domain the whole of British literature as it developed from the Roman occupation to the present. There have also been numerous specialized studies of nineteenth-century verse that trace the relationship between individual Romantics and Victorians or highlight some common theme that is modified as it passes from one poet to another. There has not, however, been a recent attempt to distill this impressive scholarship in the context of a broad historical survey that is neither too diffuse, and hence, superficial in its discussion of individual writers nor too concentrated and, hence, incomplete in its analysis of literary movements and periods. My purpose, here, is to achieve both a breadth of historical awareness—which will enable the reader to grasp a poet's relationship to his precursors, his peers, and the intellectual climate of his age—and to provide a knowledge of that poet's life and achievement that is more than merely perfunctory.

A critical assumption of this study is that, while the history of English letters constantly expands and changes, the study of the past has an intrinsic value inasmuch as it enables us to rise above the restrictive or reductive vantage point of our present moment. As Chesterton has observed, there is no more degrading slavery than being a child of one's age—or of any other age, for that matter. We are unable, however, to travel into the future, and hence to correct this deficiency, we must travel into the past. Thus Milton is not only of historical value insofar as some knowledge of his works is necessary to understand the reactions he engendered in Romantic poets like Blake and Shelley or feminists like the Brontës (and these writers in their Romantic revolutions or feminist revisions cannot be fully understood without appreciating their attitudes toward their precursors), but also for the foothold that he gives us outside the constricting circle of our age. For the themes he explores and the sensitivities he fosters are precisely those that our age may have forgotten—and that, therefore, we have the greatest need to hear and consider.

The worst we can do is flatter ourselves with the specious notion that the perceptions of our age have exploded or overridden the concerns of our ancestors. "Poets are the rock of defense of human nature," says Wordsworth. They appeal to what is "permanent, elementary, and enduring" in human experience and preserve the human spirit from the reductive theories of sophists, economists, and calculators, for whom the holiness of the heart's affections has little meaning or worth.

· *Acknowledgments* ·

As one in whose presence computers invariably short-circuit, I must first thank my secretary Nickie Petrowske for typing this entire manuscript and patiently sifting through numerous corrections, emendations, and afterthoughts. Nickie was also an invaluable source of support, encouragement, and intellectual stimulus.

I must also acknowledge the unfailing support of my editor, Alan Shucard. Not only did he respond to the several incarnations of this text with uncommon sensitivity and discrimination, he also sustained me through my task with his humor, empathy, and confidence in the worth of this project. And the same should be said of my department chair, Don Anderson, who equally lavished his time, attention, and understanding on a manuscript much improved by his editorial skills.

Thanks, too, are due to the Provost and Dean of Emmanuel College, Oxford—Dr. Terry Miethe and Rev. J. E. Jones—for inviting me to deliver a series of lectures at Emmanuel drawn from material in this book.

Finally, I should like to thank Dr. George A. Panichas, editor of *Modern Age,* for the inspiration of his example and the fidelity of his friendship.

· *Chronology* ·

1806   Elizabeth Barrett born.

1807   Wordsworth's *Poems in Two Volumes*. Byron's *Hours of Idleness*.

1809   Byron's *English Bards and Scotch Reviewers*. Alfred Tennyson born.

1810   Coleridge's *Lectures on Shakespeare*.

1812   Byron's *Childe Harold's Pilgrimage*, I and II. Robert Browning born.

1813   Byron's *The Giaour, The Bride of Abydos*. Shelley's *Queen Mab*.

1814   Wordsworth's *The Excursion*.

1815   Wordsworth's *The White Doe of Rylstone* and *Poems*. Byron's *Hebrew Melodies*.

1816   Coleridge's *Christabel* and *Kubla Khan*. Shelley's *Alastor*. Byron's *Childe Harold III*.

1817   Coleridge's *Sibylline Leaves* and *Biographia Literaria*. Byron's *Manfred*. Keats's *Poems*.

1818   Byron's *Childe Harold, IV* and *Beppo*. Keats's *Endymion*. Shelley's *The Revolt of Islam*. Mary Shelley's *Frankenstein*. Hazlitt's *Lectures on the English Poets*.

1819   Byron's *Don Juan, I and II*. Wordsworth's *Peter Bell*. Shelley's *Prometheus Unbound*. Arthur Hugh Clough born.

1820   Keats's *Lamia, Isabella, The Eve of St. Agnes and Other Poems*. John Clare's *Poems Descriptive of Rural Life*. John Keats dies.

1821   Byron's *Cain, Don Juan III–V*. Shelley's *Epipsychidion* and *Adonais*.

1822   Wordsworth's *Ecclesiastical Sketches*. Shelley's *The Triumph of Life*. Byron's *The Vision of Judgement*. Percy Bysshe Shelley dies. Matthew Arnold born.

1823   Byron's *Don Juan VI–XIV*. Coventry Patmore born.

1824   Byron's *Don Juan XV–XVI*. Lord Byron dies. Shelley's *Posthumous Poems*.

1827   John Clare's *The Shepherd's Calendar*. John Keble's *The Christian Year*. Wordsworth's *Poetical Works*, 5 vols. Coleridge's *Poetical Works*, 3 vols. William Blake dies.

Chronology

1828	George Meredith born. Dante Gabriel Rossetti born.
1830	Tennyson's *Poems, Chiefly Lyrical*. Christina Rossetti born.
1832	Tennyson's *Poems*. Oxford Movement begins.
1833	Robert Browning's *Paracelsus*.
1840	Robert Browning's *Sordello*. Thomas Hardy born.
1842	Tennyson's *Poems*. Browning's *Dramatic Lyrics*.
1844	Gerard Manley Hopkins born.
1845	Browning's *Dramatic Romances and Lyrics*.
1847	Tennyson's *The Princess*.
1848	Pre-Raphaelites organize.
1849	Arnold's *The Strayed Reveller*. Hartley Coleridge dies.
1850	Wordsworth's *The Prelude*. Tennyson's *In Memoriam*. Elizabeth Barrett Browning's *Sonnets from the Portuguese*.
1852	Arnold's *Empedocles on Aetna*.
1853	Arnold's *Poems*.
1855	Tennyson's *Maud*. Browning's *Men and Women*.
1857	E. B. Browning's *Aurora Leigh*.
1858	Arthur Hugh Clough's *Amours de Voyage*. William Morris's *Defense of Guinevere*.
1859	A. E. Housman born. Francis Thompson born.
1859–72	Tennyson's *Idylls of the King*.
1861	Dante Gabriel Rossetti's *Early Italian Poets*. Elizabeth Barrett Browning dies. Arthur Hugh Clough dies.
1862	Christina Rossetti's *Goblin Market*.
1864	Robert Browning's *Dramatis Personae*.
1865	Arnold's *Essays in Criticism*. John Henry Newman's *Dream of Gerontius*. Lewis Carroll's *Alice in Wonderland*. Algeron Charles Swinburne's *Atalanta in Calydon*. William Butler Yeats born. Arthur Symons born.
1866	Swinburne's *Poems and Ballads*.
1867	Arnold's *New Poems*. Morris's *Life and Death of Jason*. Lionel Johnson born. Ernest Dowson born.
1868–70	William Morris's *The Earthly Paradise*.

Chronology

1870   Dante Gabriel Rossetti's *Poems.*

1871   Swinburne's *Songs Before Sunrise.*

1873   Walter Pater's *The Renaissance.*

1875   Gerard Manley Hopkins's *Wreck of the Deutschland* (published 1918).

1877   Patmore's *Unknown Eros.*

1881   D. G. Rossetti's *Ballads and Sonnets.*

1882   Swinburne's *Tristram of Lyonesse.* Dante Gabriel Rossetti dies.

1888   Matthew Arnold dies.

1889   Yeats's *The Wanderings of Oisin.* Tennyson's *Demeter.* Robert Browning dies. Gerard Manley Hopkins dies.

1892   Arthur Symons's *Silhouettes.* Alfred Lord Tennyson dies.

1893   Francis Thompson, *Poems.*

1894   Arthur Symons's *London Nights.* Christina Rossetti dies.

1896   A. E. Housman's *A Shropshire Lad.* Ernest Dowson's *Verses.* Coventry Patmore dies. William Morris dies.

1897   Lionel Johnson's *Ireland and Other Poems.*

1898   Thomas Hardy's *Wessex Poems.*

1899   Yeats's *The Wind Among the Reeds.*

1900   Ernest Dowson dies.

1902   Lionel Johnson dies.

1907   Francis Thompson dies.

1909   Algernon Charles Swinburne dies.

1915   Hardy's *Satire of Circumstance.*

1918   Gerard Manley Hopkins's *Poems* published posthumously by Robert Bridges.

1922   Hardy's *Late Lyrics and Earlier.*

1928   Thomas Hardy dies.

1936   A. E. Housman dies.

1939   William Butler Yeats dies.

· ONE ·

The Romantic Ethos

When in 1770 the acknowledged father of English Romanticism, William Wordsworth, was born in the northwest corner of England known as the Lake District, the poetry of Great Britain was undergoing a fundamental change. The Augustan Age was on the verge of obsolescence. Pope, Swift, and Johnson would no longer dictate the terms of poetic composition or specify the nature of aesthetic response. Sophisticated wit, disciplined craftsmanship, the promulgation of moral and aesthetic standards regarded as paradigms of taste and conduct—these were the components of a neoclassical art that seemed increasingly remote from the turbulent decades that preceded the birth of the nineteenth century. In the age of Pope, poetry was above all a social art reflecting the topics of the day and concerned with the issues of the moment. Poets were not expected to indulge their private sentiments in lyrical effusions or to exploit their intimate experiences in rhapsodic confessions. To the contrary, their purpose was to crystallize, in language conspicuous for its clarity, balance, and poise, the inherited values of Christian civilization and classical antiquity—values they largely shared with a discriminating and educated audience. John Stuart Mill's later dictum that "eloquence is heard, poetry overheard" is a post-Romantic equation, the terms of which must be entirely reversed when considering the public and topical voice that characterizes the epistles, satires, and philosophic exordiums of poets in the generation from Pope to Johnson.

Poets of the eighteenth century regarded themselves as guardians and heirs of a spiritual tradition distilled from the collective wisdom of Western culture—a wisdom that throws the "vanity of human wishes," to cite the title of Johnson's celebrated poem, into satirical relief. In short, these poets consciously placed the foibles and idiosyncrasies of the individual and society in a perspective of cultural ideals and moral standards garnered from the sages of Greece and Rome or codified in the canons of the Christian church. Pope, Johnson, and Swift all adhere to a stable and hierarchic order of inherited values. And it is from the vantage of those values that they launch their darts at human folly and social corruption. Not surprisingly, satire is the most representative genre of the period. Like *The Vanity of Human Wishes*, Pope's *The Rape of the Lock* and *The Dunciad* are examples of the way in which the light of reason may be respectively beamed at individuals, couples, or societies to reveal their shortcomings and stimulate their regeneration. Poetry, in sum, was not a personal vision pursued in lonely isolation among the haunts of nature but a public address directed to urban sophisticates concerned about the quality of civilized life.

Prosodically, the most perfect form in which to compose this address proved for the Augustans to be the rhyming couplet—an idiom most closely associated with Dryden and exploited to its full expressive capacity by Pope. With its formal balance and elegant symmetry, the couplet is ideally adapted to the ironic muse. Thus Pope, in *The Rape of the Lock,* slyly exposes the tawdry values of a hypocritical society when his heroine, Belinda, denounces a suitor for surreptitiously clipping one of her ringlets:

> Not louder shrieks to pitying heaven are cast
> When husbands, or when lap dogs breath their last;
> Or when rich china vessels fallen from high
> In glittering dust, and painted fragments lie.[1]

The couplet's calibrated contrasts are shrewdly deployed by Pope. The deaths of husbands and of lap dogs, the breaking of china, and the loss of virginity are reduced to the same level. We conclude that in a world of appearances the one has no more importance than the other. But the couplet is an equally serviceable idiom for sounding epigrams and sagacious maxims. Thus Johnson's observation in *The Vanity of Human Wishes* on the dangers of wealth derives its categorical force from the couplet's stately movement and clinching rhymes: "Wealth heaped on wealth nor truth nor safety buys, / The dangers gather as the treasures rise."[2]

As is apparent from the foregoing citations, Johnson and Pope did not regard themselves as ethical revisionists or self-appointed prophets. "Man requires more frequently to be reminded than informed," writes Johnson as a way of recalling his readers to the graven tablets of tradition and authority. The purpose of poetry is not to explore some hitherto uncharted region of human consciousness like that traversed by Coleridge's ancient mariner or to challenge time-honored assumptions of decorum, duty, and taste, but rather to reinvoke the eternal verities in language of consummate polish and coruscating wit. Hence, as Pope avers in his *Essay on Criticism*, "True Wit is Nature to advantage dress'd / What oft was thought but ne'er so well expressed" (71). If the poet is to succeed in turning out established truths in comely verbal trim, he must not allow the circumstantial details of life to obscure the first principles and permanent values he is pledged to uphold. Nature in her complex multitudinous fecundity, must be "to advantage dress'd"—that is to say, trimmed of superfluities and methodized according to the canons of neoclassic judgment. Johnson endorses the same aesthetic in *Rasselas*: "The business of a poet ... is to examine not the individual but the species; to remark general properties and large appearances: he does not number the streaks of the tulip; or describe the different shades in the verdure of the forest. He is to exhibit in his portraits of nature such prominent and striking features as recall the original to every mind, and must neglect the minuter discriminations ..." (628).

Johnson's statement reveals the connection between the poetic technique of the Augustans and the metaphysics that informs their verse. This metaphysics derives from a belief in natural law. The Augustans subscribed, in short, to a universal scale of values vouchsafed to all peoples irrespective of particular creeds, forms of worship, and varieties of belief. For "the Almighty Cause," as Pope sententiously observes, "Acts not by partial but by general laws" (133). Poets, then, must bypass the merely local and particular and concentrate instead on standards of behavior and elements of style that have enduring relevance.

A belief, then, in reason as the divinely grounded and distinctively human faculty is the starting point for Augustan satire— since a correct scale of values is presupposed in any critique of the status quo. Because satire is preeminently concerned with social relations, the setting of Augustan poetry is chiefly urban and its purpose conspicuously pragmatic. Metaphysical speculation is generally eschewed. Dubious of enthusiasms unsanctioned by tradition and disruptive of order, the Augustan poets come down heavily on the side of restraint in evaluating both personal and public behavior.

But this belief in a general order—"Unerring Nature still divinely bright / One clear, unchanged, and Universal light" (Pope 65)—did not always have the most salutary effect on poetic diction, especially among Pope's followers. Certain locutions, for example, were deemed indecorous in a poem dedicated to classical principles of correctness and taste. In consequence, the Augustans often wrote in an artificial language that the Romantics would eventually reject as contrived and meretricious. When James Thomson in *The Seasons* refers to fish as "the finny tribe" or to chickens the "household feathery people," his language has departed so far from ordinary speech that it risks losing contact with both the linguistic patterns and the immediate sensations of the average reader. As Irving Babbit remarks with aphoristic flair, the Augustans sometimes "confused nobility of language with the language of the nobility."[3]

By the middle of the eighteenth century there had already begun, on the margins of English poetry, an undeclared but increasingly pervasive dissent from the mainstream of neoclassical taste. This dissent manifested itself on a popular level in the alternately ecstatic or mournful hymns of spiritual longing or contrition that the Wesleys and their new sect of Methodism inspired in such poets as William Cowper. In his celebrated *Dictionary*, Johnson defined enthusiasm as "a vain belief of divine favour." But notwithstanding the lackluster eye that Johnson cast on such "vain belief," a new note of confessional urgency and lyrical enthusiasm began to return in poets such as the Wartons, James Beattie, Edward Young, Christopher Smart, and, most arrestingly, William Collins and Thomas Gray. It is not altogether surprising that many of these poets, feeling out of touch with the spirit of the age, led a melancholic existence on the boundaries of the world of fashionable letters—as did Thomas Gray—or succumbed to periodic fits of mental alienation such as bedeviled Christopher Smart, William Cowper, and Thomas Chatterton. Chatterton, in fact, committed suicide at the age of eighteen and was consequently sainted by the next generation of writers as a martyr to romantic enthusiasm crushed by the insensate cruelty of an inhospitable world. For Wordsworth, in his lyric of poetic crisis, "Resolution and Independence," Chatterton became a cautionary figure, while Keats, in his letters, extols him as a model of pure and unaffected English prosody. Moreover, the dedication of Keats's *Endymion* is inscribed to the memory of this same hapless youth.

But is it Gray and Collins, above all, who most forcibly reveal the shift in poetic sensibility and technique that took place in the latter half of the eighteenth century. Witness, for example, the exquisite modulations of rhythm and sound in Collins's "Ode to Evening":

> If aught of Oaten Stop, or Pastoral Song
> May hope, chaste Eve, to soothe thy Modest Ear,
> > Like thy own brawling Springs,
> > Thy Springs, and dying Gales,
>
> O Nymph reserv'd, while now the bright-hair'd Sun
> Sits in yon western Tent, whose cloudy Skirts,
> > With Brede ethereal wove,
> > O'erhang his wavy Bed;
>
> . . . .
>
> Then lead, calm Vot'ress, where some sheety Lake,
> Cheers the lone Heath, or some time-hallow'd Pile,
> > Or up-land Fallows grey
> > Reflect its last cool gleams.
>
> But when chill blustring Winds, or driving Rain
> Forbid my willing feet, be mine the hut,
> > That from the Mountain's Side,
> > Views wilds, and swelling Floods,
>
> And Hamlets brown, and dim-discover'd Spires,
> And hears their simple Bell, and marks o'er all
> > Thy Dewy Fingers draw
> > The gradual dusky Veil.[4]

Perhaps the first thing to observe of Collins's ode is that nature is not merely a manicured backdrop for polite conversation, as it is in so many poems of the eighteenth century. Collins's nature already anticipates Wordsworth's—a refuge from the vain striving of corrupt worldlings and a temple for the free worship of dedicated spirits. The daylight world of common human enterprise is rejected in favor of twilight fancies and vagaries passing strange—a proto-Romantic preference that anticipates the ravishing vocal textures and vague nocturnal yearnings of Shelley's "To Night." A shift, too, is apparent in Collins's concern with the mysteries of the creative process rather than the rules of versification. Indeed the poem itself is largely concerned with the way in which the pulse and germ of life are imperceptively stilled into the modeled stasis of art. This process of poetic refinement and distillation is suggested through images of restive movement that give way to images of quiet repose. Thus, the *"brawling* springs of day" subside into evening's *"dying* gales," and the "bright-haired" sun relinquishes its glory on a "wavy bed" of clouds. And just as poetry arrests and gives permanent shape to life's fading joys and fugitive raptures, so the "last, cool gleams" of day in Collins's ode acquire an almost architectural permanence as they linger on some "time-hallowed pile" of Gothic vintage. These gleams, moreover, are the clear antecedents of those visionary gleams that Wordsworth both pursues and laments in his famous "Intimations Ode."

But Collins's ode is more than a poetic redaction of the classical adage "life is short, art is long"—it is an attempt to explore the very process of poetic transformation in a series of images organically drawn from the diaphanous weft of sunset. For in this poem twilight is to noon what art is to life. As the "dewy fingers" of Eve obscure the sharp outlines of day in a pastel wash of silver-toned harmonies, we recognize that this natural occurrence metaphorically expresses the way in which the imagination transforms the real world of action and movement into the ideal world of poetic form. Like the sheltered hut to which the poet will finally retreat, these forms provide a contemplative refuge from the "blustring rain" and "driving wind" of a sometimes threatening reality. Collins's poem deliberately counterpoints the "dewy freshness" of life against the "dusky veil" of art, and reminds us, in this regard, of Keats, who once described art as "might half slumb'ring on its own right arm."[5] The conflation of teeming life and waning energy characteristic of Collins's ode is also evident in Keats's "To Autumn," where "barrèd clouds" paradoxically *"bloom* the *soft-dying* day" (274). Moreover, Collins's *"Brede* ethereal" which draws its vaporous tracery across the sun reminds us of that "brede of marble men and maidens" (262) on Keats's urn whose arrested motions similarly denote the transubstantiation of life's torrid heats into art's frozen configurations.

In this astonishingly prophetic lyric Collins prefigures the principal characteristics of Romantic verse: a shift in emphasis from the poem as generalized statement or satiric commentary to a concern with the spiritual process that goes into the poem's making; a return to the lyric as the form in which the unalloyed essence of poetry itself is best distilled; a sense of language, heightened, to be sure, by expressive touches beyond the range of ordinary prose, but more attuned to the living voice of common speech; a reverence for nature as a matrix of mysterious and unfathomable forces; a tendency to make the poem a psychodrama that reflects the poet's own adventure in consciousness. Virtually all of the foregoing qualities are central to Wordsworth's definition of poetry in the "Preface" to *Lyrical Ballads*—a preface that transforms the sometimes diffident lyricism of a Gray or Collins into a Romantic manifesto that reverses the criteria of eighteenth-century aesthetics and brings the ballast of critical theory to the soaring flights of a new generation of poets.

William Blake was the first of the new generation to explicitly lament the impoverished condition of modern poetics in an age when the lofty examples of Milton, Shakespeare, and most especially the prophetic books of the Bible were neglected in favor of a poetry in which correctness on a narrow and less exalted plane of utterance had become more important than a visionary grandeur both daring and sublime. The "ancient melody" has "ceased," Blake laments, and the muses (those mythical embodiments of the human imagination) have been banished from a world where the divine radiance has been diminished to a mechanistic function in a clockwork cosmos. In an age of purblind rationalists who see only with, not through, the eye (that is to say, those for whom life is nothing more than the sum of its mechanical parts), poetry has lost its incantatory magic and visionary scope:

> Whether on chrystal rocks ye rove,
>   Beneath the bosom of the sea,
> Wand'ring in many a coral grove,
>   Fair Nine, forsaking Poetry!
>
> How have you left the ancient love
>   That bards of old enjoy'd in you!

> The languid strings, do scarcely move!
> The sound is forc'd, the notes are few![6]

Blake did not accept the notion, debated continuously throughout the eighteenth century, that the sublime pathos and prophetic richness of ancient poetry was a thing of the past. Nor could he believe that moderns must confine their efforts to the repetition of general truths or "moldy commonplaces," as the Romantic essayist Thomas De Quincey described the moral essays of Pope, in couplets laid out like a dead language.

Keats, too, decried the standardized perfection of neoclassic verse and its limited ability to express the complex rhythms of human emotion. In *Sleep and Poetry,* an early poem that charts the stages of his future poetic development, Keats indignantly asks:

> Is there so small a range
> In the present strength of manhood, that the high
> Imagination cannot freely fly
> As she was wont of old?
>
> . . . .
>
> . . . Yes, a schism
> Nursed by foppery and barbarism,
> Made great Apollo blush for this his land.
> Men were thought wise who could not understand
> His glories: with a puling infant's force
> They sway'd about upon a rocking horse
> And thought it Pegasus. . . .
>
> (55–56)

Keats alludes here to Pope's dictum from the *Essays on Criticism*: "The winged courser, like a generous horse / Shows most true mettle when you check his course" (65). But these checks for Keats, and for his friend and mentor, the essayist Leigh Hunt, became too facile and automatic in their polished but routine symmetries. Hunt is not altogether mistaken when in his essay "What is Poetry?" he points out the shortcomings of the heroic couplet as a medium for expressing the full range of human feeling. Citing a passage from *The Rape of the Lock*, he cannily notes its tendency to fall into a kind of mechanical seesaw, the "rocking horse" effect that Keats repudiates in *Sleep and Poetry*:

On her white breast—a sparkling cross she wore,
Which Jews might kiss—and infidels adore;
Her lively looks—a sprightly mind disclose,
Quick as her eyes—and as unfixed as those.
Favors to none—to all she smiles extends,
Oft she rejects—but never once offends;
Bright as the sun—her eyes the gazer's strike,
And like the sun—they shine on all alike.

(91)

Though Hunt has not sufficiently noted that the singsong meter here is in some ways the perfect verbal counterpart to a beauty that is itself mechanical and factitious, his example does serve to throw the distinctive versification of the Romantics into greater relief. Thus Coleridge in *Christabel*—an eerie poem of supernatural possession—modifies the octosyllabic couplet by counting stresses instead of syllables and achieves in style as well as subject matter what the Victorian critic Walter Pater defines as the quintessential Romantic note: "the addition of strangeness to beauty." When Coleridge describes the mossy oak under which Christabel confronts her future nemesis—the vampiric Lady Geraldine—the rhythm moves in perfect unison with the unfolding details:

There is not wind enough to twirl
The one red leaf, the last of its clan,
That dances as often as dance it can,
Hanging so light, and hanging so high,
On the topmost twig that looks up at the sky.[7]

The succession of spondees in "one red leaf" breaks up the regularity of the preceding iambic lines, thus emphasizing the starkness of the object that arrests the narrator's attention. The shift into dactyls in "Hanging so light and hanging so high" dexterously combines a falling meter with a rise in intonation—the long *i* of "light" and "high." This combination of rising sound and falling rhythm perfectly suggests an object that is at once delicately hanging and passively floating. The final upward soaring anapests oblige us to lift our gaze to that topmost twig where the leaf itself strains upward at the rising wind.

This is as good an example as may be found of organicism in Romantic poetry. The form, in short, is not imposed from without, but arises in organic union with the impulse that first quickens the act of composition in the poet's mind. When Keats writes in a letter to his publisher John Taylor "that if Poetry comes not as naturally as the Leaves to a tree it had better not come at all,"[8] or when Shelley declares in *A Defense of Poetry* (1821) that a "great statue or picture grows under the power of the artist as a child in the mother's womb,"[9] these organic or biological images are expressly chosen to suggest that the creative act is not a specialized mechanical function but a human redaction of that divine power which nourishes all things into life—from the lowliest plant to the loftiest manifestation of genius. Because, for the Romantics, a living poem has its roots deep in the significant soil of the poet's unconscious, form and content arise indissolubly from both the rules of written language and the demands of poetic vision. Thus, for Coleridge, "could a rule be given from without, poetry would cease to be poetry, and sink into a mechanical art.... The rules of imagination are themselves the very powers of growth and production. The words to which they are reducible, present only the outlines and external appearance of the fruit" (361–62).

It must be parenthetically observed, however, that the notion of organic form is not essentially alien to the finest examples of eighteenth-century verse. Pope's dexterous adaptation of the couplet to Romantic monodrama, philosophic discourse, acidulous satire, or lyric plangency is dazzling—and in the best sense of the word, organic. Despite his youthful petulance, Keats returned to Dryden as a model for his narrative poem "Lamia," while Byron continually held his contemporaries in contempt when compared with the Augustans. Blake had the perfect lyric gift but too often in his later works abandoned it out of a misplaced sense of prophetic afflatus. The windy oratory of *The Four Zoas,* so often harsh and formless, may be organic, but the growth chokes out both flower and fruit. The point is that in estimating the achievements of both neoclassic and Romantic verse, we must not, as Pater admonishes, place "one school of literary art against another," but cherish the best in the productions of each "against the stupidity which is dead to the substance, and the vulgarity which is dead to the form."[10]

Despite the foregoing qualifications, there is still some validity to Matthew Arnold's comparative estimate of neoclassic and Romantic verse: "the difference between genuine poetry," writes

Arnold in his essay on Thomas Gray, "and the poetry of Dryden, Pope, and all their school is briefly this: their poetry is conceived and composed in their wits, genuine poetry is conceived and composed in the soul."[11] While Arnold's judgment is somewhat overdrawn, his distinction has some warrant, as the following lines from Coleridge attest:

> Ah! from the soul itself must issue forth
> A light, a glory, a fair luminous cloud
> Enveloping the Earth—
>
> (114)

So writes Coleridge in praise of that quality which alone, according to Blake, goes into the making of a poet: the imagination. What reason is to the Augustans, the imagination is to the Romantics: "the vision and the faculty divine," as Wordsworth conceives it, which consecrates the poet's calling, rekindles the human spirit, and cleanses the doors of perception.

Romantic organicism is, then, not only a matter of technique—as with the Augustans, it is the verbal counterpart of a vision the roots of which are ontological. In other words, it grows out of a way of seeing the universe that contrasts forcibly with the ascendent empiricism of Enlightenment philosophers from Descartes in France to Locke in England. The Romantics rejected that intellectual tradition, which alienates the mind from the universe it beholds. Unlike Descartes, who divorces the world of intellect and value from the world of material extension and scientific measurement, or Locke, who regards the mind as essentially passive in the act of perception—a blank mirror upon which is inscribed the mass of impressions that reach our consciousness from the world outside—the Romantics saw themselves as healing the breach between the worlds of fact and fancy, imagination and reality. For Descartes and Hume, the mind fluctuates indeterminately between an empty cosmos despoiled of sanctity and a disengaged mind aloof from existence. For the Romantics, however, the mind and the world are an ontological unity—a unity that becomes apparent in moments of exceptional insight when the imagination throws a sacramental bridge between human consciousness and some ordinary object, revealing their hidden connections and divining their occult affinities. The moment of that poetic sacrament is the subject of Wordsworth's famous lines from his "prospectus" to *The Excursion*:

> Paradise, and groves
> Elysian, Fortunate Fields—like those of old
> Sought in the Atlantic Main—why should they be
> A history only of departed things,
> Or a mere fiction of what never was?
> For the discerning intellect of Man,
> When wedded to this goodly universe
> In love and holy passion, shall find these
> A simple produce of the common day.
> —I, long before that blissful hour arrives,
> Would chant, in lonely peace, the spousal verse
> Of this great consummation:—and, by words
> Which speak of nothing more than what we are,
> Would I arouse the sensual from their sleep
> Of Death, and win the vacant and the vain
> To noble raptures; while my voice proclaims
> How exquisitely the individual Mind
> . . . to the external World
> Is fitted:—and how exquisitely, too—
> Theme this but little heard of among men—
> The external World is fitted to the Mind;
> And the creation (by no lower name
> Can it be called) which they with blended might
> Accomplish:—this is our high argument.[12]

The knowledge derived from such a "creation" is a knowledge achieved through connaturality—that is to say, an intuitive apprehension of fundamental principles by which the knowing subject awakens to the depth of its inner substance and recognizes its relationship to the structure of Being. In that privileged moment of intuitive insight the poet not only discerns an inescapable correspondence between the mind of man and the goodly universe to which it is wedded, but also discovers the ground of Being upon which both are dependent.

This privileged moment, or "spot of time," as Wordsworth came to call it in *The Prelude*, is an instant of plenary grace that does not lift the poet above the everyday world of mundane existence, but repristinates that very world in the baptismal depths of the poetic imagination. This, moreover, is the moment, as Coleridge avers in his *Biographia Literaria* (1817), "which awakens the mind's attention from the lethargy of custom, and directs it to the loveliness and wonders of the world before us; an inexhaustible treasure, but for which, in consequence of the film of familiarity and selfish solicitude, we have eyes, yet see not, ears that hear not, and hearts that neither feel nor understand" (314).

For the Romantics, then, the imagination is not an idle faculty by which we dream ourselves into some never land of callow wish fulfillment. To the contrary, it is, in M. H. Abrams's classic analogy, a "lamp" that falls upon the multitudinous diversity of discrete particular phenomena and discovers their interrelations, so that like the bits of tesselated glass in a kaleidoscope, they coalesce into a coherent design that is at once an image of harmonious beauty and a token of transcendent order.

Instead of beginning, then, with a general or abstract order derived, in the manner of the Augustans, from authority and tradition, the Romantic poets dispose themselves to the rich diversity of the phenomenal world. It is in and through that diversity that they discover the unifying principle that in Shelley's words "wields the world with never wearied love, / Sustains it from beneath, and kindles it above."[13] It is this which enables the poet to perceive a particular grain of sand, a wildflower, an avian messenger (as, for example, Shelley's skylark or Keats's nightingale), a chance encounter (with say, an aging leech gatherer), or a work of art as a conduit charged with the concentrated essence of a transcendent reality. Which is to say, as does Coleridge in *The Statesman's Manual* (1816), that "a symbol ... is characterized above all by the translucence of the eternal in and through the temporal. It always partakes of the reality which it renders intelligible; and while it enunciates the whole, abides itself as a living part of that unity of which it is representative" (661).

This capacity to discover in the outward and tangible reality of things temporal the inward and spiritual grace of things eternal is given perhaps its most compendious expression by Blake:

> To see a World in a Grain of Sand
> And a Heaven in a Wild Flower,

> Hold infinity in the palm of your hand
> And Eternity in an hour.
>
> (431)

The pulse-beat of an artery that enables the poet to intuit the whole from the part and the universal in the particular is Blake's equivalent to Wordsworth's spot of time—a moment, that is to say, in which the many coalesce into one and the finite reveals the infinite. Blake's grain of sand is not merely one among a number of heterogeneous objects in a disconnected universe but a microcosm that distills the essence of the whole and takes us to the threshold of eternity.

The poem that provides a perspicuous instance of this visionary moment—a moment that transports us from the near, the familiar, and the distinct to the remote and the unknown—is perhaps the single most famous of Romantic lyrics, Wordsworth's "I wandered lonely as a cloud":

> I wandered lonely as a cloud
> That floats on high o'er vales and hills,
> When all at once I saw a crowd,
> A host, of golden daffodils;
> Beside the lake, beneath the trees,
> Fluttering and dancing in the breeze.
>
> Continuous as the stars that shine
> And twinkle on the milky way,
> They stretched in never-ending line
> Along the margin of a bay:
> Ten thousand saw I at a glance,
> Tossing their heads in sprightly dance.
>
> The waves beside them danced; but they
> Out-did the sparkling waves in glee:
> A poet could not be but gay,
> In such a jocund company:
> I gazed—and gazed—but little thought
> What wealth the show to me had brought.
>
> For oft, when on my couch I lie
> In vacant or in pensive mood,
> They flash upon that inward eye
> Which is the bliss of solitude;

And then my heart with pleasure fills,
And dances with the daffodils.

(311–12)

Apart from its intrinsic grace and verbal deftness, Wordsworth's poem is a representative instance of the Romantic lyric. These lyrics have generally a tripartite structure corresponding to traditional rites of initiation in which the novice is separated from familiar surroundings, transformed by a magical vision, and then returned to his original state. The speaker in these poems usually begins in a state of blank indifference or self-absorption; but his attention is then unpredictably seized by some object that grows increasingly radiant in meaning and significance. At length, the moment of transport passes, and the poet, rapt in the spell of his former state, gradually returns to the world of ordinary consciousness. His return, however, is leavened by the lingering enchantments of a vision that renews his sense of self-dedication or deepens his consciousness of ultimate realities. Indeed, this threefold movement is not only endemic to the Romantic lyric, it applies as well to many narrative poems—such as Coleridge's "The Rime of the Ancient Mariner" or Keats's "Eve of St. Agnes"—that enact psychodramas of similar proportions.

In Wordsworth's poem, the speaker is initially suspended "like a cloud" in a state of mental abstraction—unrelated to the world around him and indifferent to its multiform particulars. But the sudden appearance of the daffodils draws him back into the world of concrete shapes and living realities. In his first confused impression, the flowers are simply a crowd: that is to say, a random collection of discrete objects haphazardly thrown together. But as they kindle the poet's imagination, the daffodils are perceived as a "host"—in other words, a stately and august society of significant forms harmoniously arranged in a body suggestive of a "heavenly host." But "host" also suggests a eucharistic wafer, a real presence that heals the breach between the divine and the human, the actual and the ideal. And indeed, Wordsworth's poem may be construed as a secularized version of the Christian feast of communion. Moreover, as the poet's initial impression of the flowers deepens, the aimlessly "fluttering" blossoms come together in a gracious dance. And it is this dance that discloses to Wordsworth what David Perkins has called "the intercommunion of all things in an

· 15 ·

organic universe"—a communion that extends from the flowers at the poet's feet to the galaxy of distant stars. The revelation of this cosmic dance redeems the poet from his former isolation and, even as it fades, provides him with an experience that shall ramify endlessly into future years, revealing to the "inward eye" of memory levels of meaning exhaustless to contemplation. The images in the poem combine earth (flowers), air (clouds), water (lake), and fire (stars) in an alchemical spell that transforms the leaden weight of reality into the spun gold of poetic vision. The poet, in short, is no longer just a forthright honest craftsman, but a kind of priest transforming the unleavened bread of daily life into the visionary body of Romantic art.[14]

In Wordsworth's lyric, a "spontaneous overflow of powerful feelings" is followed by an "emotion recollected in tranquility." And indeed these phrases, from Wordsworth's "Preface" to *Lyrical Ballads*, designate the two interdependent elements of the Romantic lyric as it came to be practiced not only by Wordsworth but by a second generation of Romantic poets inspired by his example.

Faith, then, in the revelatory power of the human imagination is the salient characteristic of Romantic verse. For most of the Romantics, the imagination is a divining rod that searches out the hidden springs of spiritual power and leads to a reality that is ultimately sacred. This is not to say that the search was unaccompanied by doubts and misgivings and occasionally disavowals. "Was it a vision or a waking dream?" Keats asks of a nightingale's song that is symbolically akin to Wordsworth's daffodils. As his question implies, Keats is not altogether sure whether his vision is an authentic reality of independent substance or an emotional trance subconsciously self-induced. Keats's wistful ambivalence devolves, in Byron at any rate, into an almost automatic cynicism—what has been termed Romantic irony. But misgivings aside, the testimony of these poets weighs heavily in favor of the imagination as an authentic source of intuitive knowledge. "I am certain of nothing," writes Keats in a confident letter of 1817, "but the holiness of the Heart's affections and the truth of imagination—What the imagination seizes as Beauty must be Truth..." (36–37). And the least wavering of Romantic visionaries, William Blake, unequivocally states, "The world of imagination is the world of Eternity. It is the divine bosom into which we shall go after the death of the vegetated body. The world of the Imagination is infinite and Eternal, whereas the world of Generation, or Vegetation, is Finite and Temporal. There Exist in that Eternal World the Permanent Realities of Every Thing which we see reflected in this Vegetable Glass of Nature" (605). Similarly, Shelley in "Epipsychidion," that poem which aspires to the beatific vision whereby Dante was able to ascend from the love of a mortal girl to an ecstatic apprehension of the "Love which moves the planets and the other stars," declares that his love for Emilia Vivianni—a sixteen-year-old girl imprisoned in an Italian convent by her father—is itself analogous to the operations of the poetic imagination:

> Love is like understanding, that grows bright,
> Gazing on many truths; 'tis like thy light
> Imagination! which from the earth and sky,
> And from the depths of human fantasy,
> As from a thousand prisms and mirrors, fills
> The Universe with glorious beams, and kills
> Error, the worm, with many a sun-like arrow
> Of its reverberated lightning.
>
> (410)

Here, too, as in Wordsworth's lyric, the imagination enables the poet to perceive the "many truths" of a pluralistic universe as a series of anagogical mirrors illumined by a single refracted light—a light that, as Shelley writes in *A Defense of Poetry*, reveals "the very image of life ... in its eternal truth." But it is Coleridge who provides us with the most famous, one might almost say "notorious," definition of the poetic imagination—notorious not only by dint of its gnomic diction but also in its daring conflation of the divine and the human:

The primary imagination I hold to be the living power and prime agent of all human perception, and as a repetition in the finite mind of the eternal act of creation in the infinite I AM. It is essentially *vital*, even as all objects (*as* objects) are essentially fixed and dead. (313)

For Coleridge the imagination restores to our perception of the universe a sense of its living vitality—a vitality consubstantial with the life of its creator (whose enigmatic response to Moses concerning the nature of his identity was contained in the simple assertion "I AM"). It stands, moreover, in forcible contrast with the power of analysis that reduces objects to their constituent parts and betrays the spirit that animates and transfigures the whole. Implicit, too, in Coleridge's notion is the belief—more clearly enunciated in Blake—that the creation of the world is not something that took place once and for all in a hypothetical past, but is rather a continuous and ongoing process. This process requires the creative response of humanity to the *Lux Fiat* of the divine purpose. Thus Blake in his *Vision of the Last Judgement* replies to the question of an imaginary materialist interlocutor—"When the Sun rises do you not see a round disk of fire somewhat like a Guinea?" "O no no," writes Blake, "I see an Innumerable company of the Heavenly host crying 'Holy, Holy, Holy is the Lord God Almighty'" (617).

These celebrations of imaginative power carry with them an interesting corollary, namely, a renewed interest in the consciousness of childhood. In the eighteenth century, childhood was simply an awkward, troublesome, and intermediary stage in human development. For the Romantics, however, childhood is an emblem of that psychic and spiritual wholeness that is gradually lost in the compromises of adult existence. Because the child responds deeply and unself-consciously to the world around him, delighting in the exercise of his imaginative faculties and filling with his spirit the inanimate forms of nature, he becomes the type and emblem of the poet. For the poet, too, though with conscious effort and deliberate cultivation, remains fundamentally attuned to those deep instinctual springs from which the child draws his surplus of wonder and self-renewal. Hence it is that Wordsworth in his "Ode: Intimations of Immortality" addresses the child—in this instance, the six-year-old son of his close friend Coleridge—as a "Mighty prophet! Seer blest! / On whom those truths do rest, / Which we are toiling all our lives to find" (355); that Shelley in *Prometheus Unbound* prophetically proclaims the regeneration of the individual and society through the lips of a child, the spirit of the earth, born from the union of Prometheus and Asia; that even Byron, who in real life cynically placed his illegitimate daughter in a convent where she was largely forgotten, should open Canto III of *Childe Harold* with an invocation to his other, legitimate daughter, Ada (left behind and equally forgotten in England, though serviceable nonetheless as a symbol of the poet's lost innocence); that Keats in "There was a naughty boy," written for his younger sister Fanny, should describe in one of the finest children's poems of the nineteenth century the amblings and ramblings of his own rambunctious nonage; and that Blake in *Songs of Innocence* should give us what is simply the most beautiful and pure emblem of a child's unclouded world to be found in any literature, past or present.

All of this, however, has its darker side—as Blake well knew—especially given the massive exploitation of child labor in an age undergoing the first throes of the industrial revolution. The *Songs of Experience*, which Blake wrote a few years later, painfully reveal the way in which a state of innocence unnaturally protracted renders itself vulnerable to the most ruthless forces of a social economy based on the calculus of predatory competition. Similarly, Coleridge in "Dejection: An Ode," gives us a harrowing glimpse of the fate that awaits those—like Coleridge himself—who find it impossible to adapt to the exigencies and limitations of adult reality. This other tale, "less deep and loud," finds its fitting emblem in a

> . . . little child
> Upon a lonesome wild,
> Not far from home, but she hath lost her way:
> And now moans low in bitter grief and fear,
> And now screams loud, and hopes to make her mother hear.
> (116)

Wordsworth knew this dilemma too—the dilemma of suddenly awakening to an awareness that the child's unity of being and ignorance of death (a state tenderly enshrined in Wordsworth's early ballad "We are seven") inevitably gives way to self-division when the moral conscience awakens or the sheer necessity of having to earn one's living becomes inescapably pressing. Wordsworth, at least, as his poem "Resolution and Independence" suggests, was able to find a way out of this impasse. The leech gatherer who is the subject of this poem reveals that it is possible, even in poverty and physical decline, to retain a pristine response to the created glory of the universe.

Nostalgia for a lost innocence that is sometimes associated with the vanished paradise of childhood, or some golden age in an imagined past—Pericletian Athens and medieval Christendom being the two most favored periods—or the fresh, unpolluted vitality of nature untouched by human corruption reveals, then, another pervasive strain in Romantic art. But, in the end, it is neither childhood, nor an imagined golden age, nor even nature herself that the Romantic poet desires—these being, on closer scrutiny, but the counterfeits of an uncreated essence, a nameless something, a "light that never was on land or sea," which is the real object of Romantic longing—that "infinite indeterminate desire" for which Irving Babbit scolded the Romantics in his disapproving study *Rousseau and Romanticism*. But this desire has always had its partisans, not the least of whom is C. S. Lewis, who spoke of it as "the inconsolable secret which hurts so much that we take our revenge on it by calling it names like Nostalgia and Romanticism and Adolescence." It is the state Shelley describes in one of his last lyrics:

> I loved—oh, no, I mean not one of ye,
>   Or any earthly one, though ye are dear
> As human heart to human heart may be;
>   I loved, I know not what—but this low sphere
> And all that it contains, contains not thee,
>   Thou, whom, seen nowhere, I feel everywhere.
> From Heaven and Earth, and all that in them are
> Veiled art thou, like a . . .
>
> (658)

Significantly, the stanza was never completed—for, in truth, no simile is adequate to the compass of this desire. This is what T. E. Hulme and the early modern critics of the twentieth century meant when they referred to Romanticism as "spilt religion." But it is also possible to see this in another light. Thus D. G. James in his prodigiously capable study of the period advances the thesis that "Romanticism, after starting out with a strong antipathy to Christianity, came to acknowledge what Coleridge believed to be its necessity"[15]—that all the imaginative yearnings of the period resolve themselves most fully in the renewal of the Church of England which began in 1832 and came to be known as the Oxford Movement.

But the evolution of Romanticism into the historical and religious continuity of the Church of England is a tale that is best discussed in the context of the Victorian age. For in its early stages at any rate, Romanticism was not in the least amenable to the doctrines and discipline of the Christian faith. Indeed, the Romantic conception of human nature stands in forcible contrast with the church's position on original sin. For the majority of the Romantics the notion of original sin was itself a sin, distorting the uninhibited expression of human energy, creativity, and love. For the young Wordsworth, Coleridge, Blake, and Shelley, the church embodied an outworn and exploded system of metaphysics in which a distant and implacable God gave divine warrant to the repressive control by which priests and kings held in check what was superstitiously regarded as the expansive conceit of the unregenerate human will. But it was not the will that was unregenerate for the Romantics, it was the "mind-forg'd manacles" of a society devoted to preserving the vested interests of the ruling class and keeping the common man and woman in a state of demoralized subjection.

Perhaps no other episode in literary history more fully reveals the necessary and inescapable connections between life and art, literature and society, poetry and politics than does the period between 1789 and 1815—that is to say, between the fall of the Bastille and the defeat of Napoleon at Waterloo.

The French Revolution was the political and social counterpart of the Romantic movement. It was at once a consequence of and a reaction against the Age of Reason. Insofar as the Enlightenment encouraged people to estimate the viability of political institutions from the perspective of disabused reason, it played a major part in forming the conscience of the early revolutionaries. But when these new conceptions of society and human nature left the realm of speculation and entered the arena of human affairs, then the time was ripe for passion, energy, defiance, and rebellion—qualities that signal the demise of Augustan self-assurance and herald the advent of a new age.

The French Revolution was given its intellectual impetus by Jean Jacques Rousseau, whose manifesto of 1762, *The Social Contract*, begins with the ringing enunciation: "Man is born free but is everywhere in chains." If, in the past, human nature was regarded as a circumscribed well, stagnant and corrupt, without the inflow of those redeeming springs that sprang from the twofold source of church and state, then Rousseau (and the Romantics who inherited his spirit) regarded human nature as an irrepressible fountain of creative energy, stifled by false ideologies inimical to the full realization of man's potential—and woman's too, as Mary Wollstonecraft, in her feminist reply to Rousseau, *A Vindication of the Rights of Woman* (1792), was quick to assert. Remove the obstacles that generations of Christian orthodoxy and political oppression have imposed on humanity, and society will reconsolidate according to those generous impulses which are native to the human spirit. Rousseau's philosophical formulations entered the world of political action in 1789 when the Declaration of the Rights of Man was ratified at the National Assembly in Paris and the regime of Louis XIV felt the first of those reverberations that were to shatter the ancien régime and precipitate France into a reign of terror.

But in its initial stages at any rate the Revolution was full of promise, and the first generation of English Romantics responded to that promise with alacrity and enthusiasm. Wordsworth, who traveled to France for the express purpose of participating in the millennium, hailed the revolutionaries in words that have become part of the mythos of the period:

> For mighty were the auxiliars which then stood
> Upon our side, us who were strong in love!
> Bliss was it in that dawn to be alive,
> But to be young was very Heaven!
>
> . . . .
>
> Not favoured spots alone, but the whole Earth,
> The beauty wore of promise . . .
> (As at some moment might not be unfelt
> Among the bowers of Paradise itself).
>
> (203)

But Wordsworth's earthly paradise soon became a political inferno. Under the government of Robespierre, the revolutionaries turned against each other in a series of pogroms that sent the heads of suspected reactionaries rolling down the streets of Paris to the cheers of a bloodthirsty mob. Blake, safe in England, would celebrate the French uprising in the first of those prophetic books that have perhaps for the modern reader a ring of inflexible conviction that is dangerously fanatical—the lines of battle too easily drawn, the social ramifications blithely obscured in a fustian of visionary rant. Wordsworth, however, experienced these things at first hand and learned—surprisingly for someone already disposed to see humanity as being at home with "Infinitude and only there"—that a merely outward and external reconstruction of society can leave the darker recesses of the human heart untouched and untransformed. When Irving Babbit castigates the Romantic generation for extolling "the ascendency of imagination over judgment," for "throwing off the yoke of both Christian and classical discipline in the name of temperament" (21, 49), he is not just being a reactionary prig—at least when we consider the naive response of the first Romantics to the phenomenon of the French Revolution. But this is not the whole story. Wordsworth saw through the slogans of political ideologues and fanatics whose adherence to a rigid doctrine obscured their sense of human sympathy and personal responsibility. The September Massacres, at which the streets of Paris ran blood, prepared the way for a military dictatorship entirely contrary to the ideals of freedom, fraternity, and equality that inspired the early stages of the Revolution. When in 1804 Napoleon crowned himself emperor, Wordsworth's prophecy was fulfilled:

> But now, become oppressors in their turn,
> Frenchmen had changed a war of self-defense
> For one of conquest, losing sight of all
> Which they had struggled for.
>
> (204)

Despite Babbit's sweeping condemnation, the Romantic poets were quick learners. Wordsworth and Coleridge evolved into the distinctively British position that is best expressed by the poets' contemporary Edmund Burke in his *Reflections on the French Revolution* (1790). For Burke violent social upheaval constitutes a betrayal of the commonwealth—and is only permissible under circumstances of the most atrocious despotism. Revolution, in its concern with extending rights rather than acquiring virtues, becomes a formula for anarchy. In consequence, if society is to reform itself, according to Burke, it must do so in a spirit of ameliorism—building on its inherited social structures and modifying these in accordance with the twin desiderata of liberty and order. A society that forgets its spiritual patrimony in the pursuit of fashionable causes risks moral bankruptcy and political chaos. A true civil order, for Burke, is a living and organic confederation between the dead, the living, and the unborn. Wordsworth came to much the same conclusion. As he was to write in *The Prelude* regarding the upshot of his experience in France: "There is / One great society alone on earth: / The Noble living and the Noble dead" (206). In short, schemes of social renewal are only effective insofar as they are counterbalanced by a corresponding renewal of individual virtues. Governments may change, but the standards of human nobility remain the same.

Coleridge bears witness to this same process of political revisionism in his great peroration "France: An Ode." In response to the French invasion of Switzerland, Coleridge recants his youthful radicalism as inimical to the true spirit of freedom:

> Forgive me, Freedom! O forgive those dreams!
>   I hear thy voice, I hear thy loud lament,
>   From Bleak Helvetia's icy caverns sent
> I hear thy groans upon her blood-stained streams!
>
> (91)

Looking out from the edge of a cliff that fronts a massive tide of wind and wave, the poet declares that true freedom belongs only to those who find a foothold outside their age and aspire to a realm beyond the regimentation of the social ant-heap:

> Yes, while I stood and gazed, my temples bare,
> And shot my being through earth, sea, and air,
>   Possessing all things with intensest love,
>   O Liberty! my spirit felt thee there.
>
> (92)

In the same way, Byron, surveying the fields of Waterloo where Napoleon met his final defeat, implicitly contrasts the insensate ambition of the world-conqueror with the lofty aspirations of Childe Harold, the world-overcomer. And even Shelley, for whom the dawn of the French Revolution remained one of the great heroic moments in social history, observed in his "Preface" to *Prometheus Unbound* "that until the mind can love, and hope, and endure, reasoned principles of moral conduct are seeds cast upon the highway of life which the unconscious stranger tramples into dust" (203).

In extending the range of poetic expression, exploring the limits of human possibility, and suffering the repercussions of a revolutionary age, the Romantics stood at the forefront of human consciousness during a period of political upheaval and cultural transition. Without the shelter of traditional beliefs or the support of aristocratic patronage, they were obliged to reinvent the role of the artist and redefine the function of literature in an age when the value of poetry itself would be called into question by the disabused architects of postrevolutionary Europe. The world of modern industry, social utility, and political pragmatism that the Victorians inherited was already consolidating in the early decades of the nineteenth century. Shelley's belief that "poets are the unacknowledged legislators of the world" seemed increasingly quixotic to the hard-nosed utilitarians who were responsible for the reconstruction of Europe in the wake of the Napoleonic wars. In consequence, the Romantics strike for the first time in English poetry a note that is distinctively and disturbingly modern. If we are still, as David Perkins avers, in the tail of that comet known as Romanticism, an understanding of the dilemmas, both spiritual and aesthetic, that confronted these poets and the strategies they evolved to cope with them can better enable us to comprehend the desperation and confusion that mark the world of thought and letters in the benighted decades of our own century.

· TWO ·

William Blake

As the least compromising of Romantic visionaries, Blake is a scandal to the Christian and a stumbling block to the sceptic. Like the Christ of the Gospels, he frequently employs the language of paradox and hyperbole to explode the complacency of his listener. Despite his sympathy with the revolutionary writings of Voltaire and Rousseau, Blake's mystical sense of human destiny has no patience with those who confine their vision to finite boundaries of the natural world or the secular goals of social activism:

> Mock on, mock on, Voltaire, Rousseau,
>   Mock on, mock on; 'tis all in vain;
> You throw the dust against the wind
>   And the wind blows it back again.
>
> And every stone becomes a gem
>   Reflected in the beams divine;
> Blown back, they blind the mocking eye,
>   But still in Israel's paths they shine
>
> (418)

To Christians, however, who prefer a poor and threadbare otherworldliness to the drama and daring of human creativity, Blake can be equally pugnacious and abrupt: "Go, tell them that the Worship of God is honoring his gifts / In other men: & loving the greatest men best, each according / To his Genius, which is the Holy Ghost in Man; there is no other / God, than that God who is the intellectual fountain of humanity" (738). That Blake continued, even in the midst of such utterances, to think of himself as a Christian is only one contradiction among many that bedevil a student of his verse. Yet despite his disdain for passive instruction and his claims of oracular originality, there is good reason to see Blake as part of a heterodox but persistent tradition of Western mysticism that has always clung to the margins of institutional Christianity. This tradition, which goes back to the second century A.D., has been termed "gnosticism." The gnostic is one who regards both nature and the Bible as a coded spiritual message, the deciphering of which leads to a state of illumination wherein the individual's sense of personal identity is swallowed up in a consciousness of the divine reality. In this state one recognizes that one's own mind is not distinct from but actually part of the mind of the Creator. Not surprisingly, such a position was condemned by the early church, though it has enjoyed a periodic revival among those who suffer from illusions of the "inner light."

Did Blake thus suffer? To the dispassionate observer of his life and his works, there is no doubt that he did. Yet toward the end of his life, engaged in painting a series of illustrations to an edition of Dante, he seemed to recognize that the medieval Italian poet possessed what his own works sometimes lack, namely, what T. S. Eliot calls "a respect for impersonal reason, for common sense, for the objectivity of science. . . . What his genius required was a framework of accepted and traditional ideas which would have prevented him from indulging in a philosophy of his own, and concentrated his attention upon the problems of a poet."[1] In this regard, Blake's early works are the most purely poetic—both more accessible and aesthetically satisfying than his later troubled visions of gods and demons.

The problematic nature of Blake's Christianity—for he always insisted on the Christian sources of his inspiration—is traceable to the thirteenth-century Christian mystic Joachim of Flora. Joachim endeavored to move beyond the first two phases of divine revelation, enshrined respectively in the law of the Old Testament and the redemption of the New. Both Testaments being conspicuously silent on the subject of human creativity, Blake shares with Joachim a belief that a third testament is imminent and destined to supersede the previous two phases of God's self-disclosure. This third testament entails a revelation of God through the creative acts of humanity. In short, God is ultimately revealed in those representatives of humanity whose imaginative potency and spiritual vitality challenge the rest of us to discover the divine source of our own creative powers.

Accordingly, Blake has little patience with orthodox notions of a God who rewards the self-righteous prudence of the powerful, sanctions the unforgiving vendetta of the small-minded, and approves the desexualized morality of the ascetic. Blake refers to this God as "Nobodaddy" or "Urizen"—an intransigent enforcer of standardized morality, hypocritical religiosity, and state-sponsored oppression. At times, Blake seems to acknowledge no divinity apart from the "Four-fold Man," which is the poet's term for the perfectly self-integrated and irrepressibly self-actualized human being. Yet, in the final analysis, such a humanistic formula seems inadequate to comprehend the tormented spirituality of this poet. Even at his most defiant, there are moments in Blake's life and works graced by a naive sweetness that recalls the self-effacing sanctity of some early Christian saint. Alexander Gilchrist records an anecdote in his biography of Blake that gives us an instance of this naïveté. In response to the artistic difficulties that George Richmond, one of Blake's protégés, was experiencing for an unusually extended period, Blake turned to his wife, Catherine, and observed by way of commiseration, "It is just so with us, is it not, for weeks together, when the visions forsake us? What do we then, Kate?" She responded, "We kneel down and pray, Mr. Blake."[2] Throughout his career, Blake continued to kneel down and pray, even in those poems that elaborate a mythology distinctly at odds with conventional Christianity:

O Savior pour upon me thy spirit of meekness and love!
Annihilate the Selfhood in me; be thou all my life!
Guide thou my hand, which trembles exceedingly upon the rock of ages
While I write . . .

(623)

To the above words from Blake's epic, *Jerusalem,* may be added the following from *Milton*:

But, thou, O Lord,
Do with me as thou wilt! for I am nothing and vanity.
If thou chuse to elect a worm, it shall remove the mountains.

(502)

The writer of these lines cannot be construed simply as a precursor of Freud or Jung or the exponent of a self-contained humanism such as that which Harold Bloom or Northrope Frye elaborate in their studies of this poet. Thus, when Blake, on more than one occasion, proclaims that his poetry was dictated to him by invisible agents, Frye observes that this means that Blake's "inspiration often takes on a purpose of its own which appears independent of the will. . . ."[3] This may be true of most poets, but in Blake's case G. K. Chesterton seems nearer to the truth when he accepts Blake's statements at face value. Chesterton has no trouble accepting the reality of these invisible agents and imputes to them all the bogus spiritualism, tedious rhetoric, licentious ragings, and unorthodox beliefs that obscure the genuine Christian impulses in Blake's prophetic books. To Chesterton, in other words, these invisible agents were indeed the devils with whom Blake claimed that he trafficked.[4] As much as Blake might disagree with Chesterton on doctrinal matters, Blake would have preferred Chesterton's frank acceptance of the supernatural to the sophistry of literary critics like Bloom or Frye.

Indeed, any understanding of Blake must begin with a frank acceptance of the paranormal vision that was for this poet both a blessing and a curse. The visions began early—at the age of four, to be exact—when the boy saw the face of God pressed to his bedroom window. When he told his parents of a treeful of angels, he was roundly punished even though the religiosity of these London shopkeepers doubtless contributed to the precocious clairvoyance that was to distinguish their son. The atmosphere was distinctly Swedenborgian: Blake's family embraced the doctrine of the eighteenth-century Swedish mystic Emmanuel Swedenborg, for whom the world was a network of spiritual signatures, each having its ideal prototype in an imperishable realm of eternal essences. Indeed, Blake accepted Swedenborg's prophecy that the reign of that epoch when humanity should worship in spirit and truth would commence in 1757—as it turns out, the year of Blake's birth.

Blake began writing poetry at the age of twelve. Because of his artistic abilities, he was apprenticed by his parents to an engraver who set him to copying the Gothic images that adorn the interior of Westminister Abbey. As he worked, Blake began to fuse the arts of poetry and painting into illuminated engravings in which image, poem, and design reciprocally enhance our understanding of the whole. When Blake is read apart from this work, we get only a portion of his original intentions. The perfection of Blake's composition owes much to the example of the medieval missal; it was refined, according to Blake, under the telepathic supervision of his younger brother, Robert, whose death at the age of nineteen did not prevent him from remaining in constant touch with his elder brother.

At the age of twenty-four Blake married Catherine Boucher, an illiterate woman four years younger than he, who commiserated with the poet on hearing of his recent unrequited attachment to a young lady who caused him much suffering. Blake expressed his gratitude by way of marriage and taught Catherine to write, to draw, and even to see visions. Their mutual devotion has passed into legend. During a lifetime of obscurity and poverty, Catherine remained his constant support. Night after night, as the poet awoke from sleep in the throes of inspiration, Catherine would sit by his side and hold his hand as the room swarmed with the giant forms that Blake reproduced in the drawings that accompany his poems.

It is important to remember, however, that Blake wrote and painted without benefit of an audience and in consequence had no sounding board against which to check his obscurantist tendencies. His one public exhibition of art in 1809 was a complete failure; his poetry was regarded even by cognoscenti like the Hunt brothers (editors of *The Examiner* and friends of Keats and Shelley) as so much incoherent raving. He was not without sympathizers, such as Thomas Butts and John Hayley, who secured him commissions to decorate any number of objects from china plate to ladies' fans. But even these sympathizers Blake found burdensome, their material support being accompanied by a spiritual blindness to the visionary dimensions of his art. Derided, neglected, without an audience, and continually on the edge of poverty, Blake indefatigably labored to build a personal mythology that is now regarded as one of the authentic monuments of Romantic art. However one may lament the esoteric and eccentric nature of Blake's visions—for the mass of commentary on his more obscure writing is as contradictory, confused, and recalcitrant as the texts it purports to illumine—there is something heroic in all of Blake's works that challenges the worldly consciousness and disturbs the parochial mind.

He died at the age of sixty-nine, as unconventionally as he had lived. He broke into song—not a grim and lugubrious knell of mourning, but a joyous even earth-shaking hymn of ecstasy, interrupting his orisons at intervals to inform his wife that the words and music were not of his own making. Just before he died he rose from his bed, an expression of preternatural joy transfiguring his features. When he fell backward in death, those who stood around felt they had witnessed the death of a saint.

It is not surprising, when we turn from Blake's life to his art, to discover a body of work equally original and startling. Though one may discern the influence of Elizabethan and late Augustan models in the 1783 volume *Poetical Sketches*, the book as a whole is quite unlike anything created by Blake's contemporaries in the latter half of the eighteenth century. Its most arresting quality is its delicate verbal euphony. A matchless lyricism graces these early poems, which include four sensuous apostrophes to the seasons, as aromatic and sweetly cadenced as anything by Keats:

> O thou, who passest thro' our valleys in
> Thy strength, curb thy fierce steeds, allay the heat
> That flames from their large nostrils! Thou, O Summer,
> Oft pitched'st here thy golden tent, and oft
> Beneath our oaks has slept, while we beheld
> With joy thy ruddy limbs and flourishing hair.
>
> (1)

Blake's Summer, a lusty god eager to embrace the fecund, teeming earth, adumbrates that gratified desire which for Blake is true holiness: passionately alive and sensuously awake. Here, as elsewhere in Blake, lethargy, custom, timidity, and self-distrust are the enemies of life and happiness. Here, many of the poems celebrate the raptures, anticipated or enjoyed, of sexual union. In "To an Evening Star," the whispering sibilants and mild, mid-ranged vowels are a seductive music to accompany the ecstatic and reclusive abandon of the lover's bed:

> Thou fair-haired Angel of the evening,
> Now, whilst the sun rests on the mountains, light
> Thy bright torch of love: thy radiant crown
> Put on, and smile upon our evening bed!
>
> Smile on our loves: and, while thou drawest the
> Blue curtains of the sky, scatter thy silver dew

On every flower that shuts its sweet eyes
In timely sleep . . .

(3)

The verse itself seems to evanesce in twilit vapors by a device as simple as the unconventional placing of a weak article at the end of a line. The langorous state described in this poem would in Blake's full-blown mythology be designated as "Beulah." In Beulah the human spirit enjoys the renovating raptures of sexual bliss in an idyllic reprieve from the strenuous ardors of artistic or imaginative creation, though it is this latter creative state, subsequently christened "Jerusalem," that holds forth the highest opportunities for human growth. While "Jerusalem" transcends the sensuous paradise of "Beulah," "Ulro" threatens the innocent joys of sensuous revery. In "Ulro" the individual descends into a state of alienated introspection, one-dimensional naturalism, and selfish sensuality precisely because of his refusal to participate in the sacred workshop of imaginative creation. The speaker in Blake's panic-stricken "Mad Song," imprisoned in his own consciousness and longing for nothing less than insensibility as an escape from the raging desires that possess him, has become a mere specter of humanity confined in the isolated world of Ulro. The advanced student of Blake will recognize that many of this poet's most important themes are given their first tentative expression in the early unexampled lyrics that distinguish *Poetical Sketches*.

Poetical Sketches was followed in 1787 by *Songs of Innocence*. Of this volume it may justly be said that there is nothing like it in English literature. To render the state of childhood without puerility or condescension but with a profound sense of its mystery is a task everywhere exposed to the dangers of cloying sentimentality. Yet nothing could be less sentimental than this volume. Goodness, joy, faith, and love are proverbially far more difficult to express than sorrow, anguish, distrust, and doubt. But Blake does it without one false note. One could well cite the words of Jesus at the moment of his entry into Jerusalem as an epigraph to this work: "Out of the mouths of babes and sucklings thou hast perfected praise." Humble, reverent, joyous, patient, and disarmingly simple, *Songs of Innocence* presents a child's view of the kingdom of God. From its opening chant of ecstasy, "Piping down the valleys wild," to its ᶜ Christ's participation in the sorrows

's joy to all
'fant small,
ᵒf woe,
ᵕw too
(122)

...tes an harmonious faith in the consola-
...ᵢₒ promise. This is not to say that a certain irony
...grasp of childhood is lacking. To the contrary, the little
child who addresses a lamb in a perfect poetic redaction of an infant's prattle—"Little lamb who made thee/Dost thou know who
made thee?" (115)—is entirely unaware that, as with the Lamb of
God Himself, incarnation implies crucifixion, that this lamb, like
all emblems of innocence, is destined to suffer and be sacrificed in
a fallen world. Similarly, the little black boy cannot discern the fallacy in his mother's attempt to comfort him because of the preju-
dice aroused by the tincture of his skin. For the mother fails to
realize that if God is light, then it is the darker-skinned child who
has absorbed more of that light rather than the white child whose
superiority the mother tacitly assumes. Apart, however, from the
poem's attack on racism, it has also been read as a satire on that
life-denying puritanism that teaches a child to distrust the human
body rather than to delight in its God-given energies. A satirical intent also counterpoints the poignant innocence of the charity children in "Holy Thursday," for their docility and obedience allows
them to be exploited by the cruel and regimented morality of their
guardians. In the same way, Blake's poor, hapless chimney sweep
consoles himself with the promise of future felicity even as he is
victimized by a society that mercilessly overworks and abuses children. In spite of such terrible ironies in *Songs of Innocence*, the children's unconditional devotion to "Mercy, Pity, Peace, and Love"
embodies that optimum spiritual enlightenment that is at once a
corrective to and a judgment of the corrupt adult world.

The sense of God's indwelling presence and sustaining grace
that Blake expresses with such effortless conviction in these early
songs would continue to haunt his imagination, even as his themes

grew darker and his vision more disturbed. A portent
change in Blake's outlook is already discernible in The B
Thel (1790). To be sure, a residue of that spiritual refulgenc
characterized Songs of Innocence continues to pervade
ume, but Blake here has become more conscious of the
herent in willfully refusing to confront the darker
threatening aspects of existence. Thel is impoverish
stroyed precisely because of her timidity in the face of
dictions. Unwilling to accept the world of sexual ge
moral struggle, she flees back into the uncomplica
childhood. Her failure to accept the loss of innocenc
the challenge of experience leads to death-in-life: a
regarding fixation on the irretrievable raptures of a lost paradise.

Five years after *Songs of Innocence* Blake issued a complementary
volume that explores the nightmare world of social injustice, economic oppression, sexual torment, and religious hypocrisy. The
Songs of Experience are the disillusioned counterparts to the earlier
series of poems, revealing what Blake now calls "the two contrary
states of the human soul." Innocence is now equated with a spiritual passivity that actually encourages the forces of corruption and
dehumanization. The Christian ethos of the earlier poems no
longer squares with Blake's perception of human suffering. Indeed, conventional Christian piety is rejected as a callow fraud antagonistic to the dynamics of personal growth and social
regeneration. This is especially apparent for Blake in the church's
attitude toward sexuality. By repressing the sexual impulse, conventional piety distorts the relations between men and women. In
lieu of a free and open interchange of mutual joys, couples are condemned to grind in the mill of a sterile and undelighting copula-
tion—a situation that leads, for Blake, to the jealous entrapment of
another's will:

> Love seeketh only self to please
>   To bind another to its delight,
> Joys in another's loss of ease,
>   And builds a hell in heaven's despite.
>   (211)

Passionate love, forced underground, erupts in irrational and misdirected desires that both create and condemn the world of illicit

and mercenary sex. Superstition, fear, war, commerce, industry, and state religion collude, for Blake, in the suppression of human energy and the waste of human life. Every form of exploitation—sexual, social, economic, and military—is reducible to those "mind-forg'd manacles" that keep people intimidated in subjection to external authority.

> In every cry of every man
> In every infant's cry of fear
> In every voice, in every ban
> The mind-forg'd manacles I hear:
>
> How the chimney-sweeper's cry
> Every blackening church appals,
> And the hapless soldier's sigh
> Runs in blood down palace-walls.
> (216)

The only way out of this situation for Blake is to unleash the prophetic wrath of the reformer and artist. This wrath is Blake's "Tyger"—the most famous poem from the collection, and one that looks forward to the spiritual warfare that Blake would continue to wage against the unenlightened despots of his age. Paradoxically, the Tyger both embodies and transcends the numerous evils that Blake discerns in society and nature. The ingenuous catechism of the child speaker in "The Lamb" is matched here by a perception of explosive forces unamenable to the simple-minded faith of the true believer. But if the Tyger personifies the imponderable enigma of evil itself—of the apparent discrepancy between the notion of a compassionate and all-powerful God and the reality of human suffering—it also personifies that aspect of the divine being which is customarily thought of and reviled as satanic. But active and rebellious energy are necessary to life itself, according to Blake. Humanity can choose to stare at these dread forces, benumbed by fear and apprehension—as does the speaker in Blake's poem—or can actively integrate this energy into the reformer's zeal, the lover's passion, and the artist's dream.

In any case, the "Tyger" and the "Lamb" are crucial to an understanding of Blake, for they embody those internal tensions that are endemic to the divine life itself. For Blake, it is necessary to worship God with both one's "good" and "evil" impulses. Surrender to God, as personified in the lamb, always exists in creative tension with rebellion against God. Even for God the process of creation, as Blake understands it, is difficult: for it involves a withdrawal of omnipotence so that free creatures may flourish in independence and self-determination. Yet if this independence is not to deteriorate into pure self-will, it must be counterbalanced by an awareness that man's creative energy ultimately derives from and is dependent on the creative energy of God. Blake's "Tyger" is the inescapable by-product of a creative universe that is really creative— whose denizens, in other words, are not merely resigned in a mechanical and automatic way to God's will. And yet without the "Lamb" who knows that "in His will is our peace," the primal energies and creative impulses of the "Tyger" would become empty and self-destructive.

What happened to change Blake from the inspired rhapsodist of childhood to the defiant iconoclast and indignant rebel? In the 1790s Blake received a commission to illustrate a volume intended to expose the brutal atrocities associated with the slave trade. He was obliged to draw in graphic detail the unspeakable tortures inflicted upon the victims of this socially approved evil. We can well imagine how the tenderhearted singer of *Songs of Innocence* responded to these revelations of human depravity. But what about the doctrine of free love, which seems to obsess Blake at this stage of his career? How does this square with the poet's ostensible allegiance to the gospel message? For, if anything, Blake is even more outspoken about this eccentric notion of human relations in *The Marriage of Heaven and Hell* (1790) than he is about social injustices like the slave trade.

The Marriage is, in part, an attempt to revise the Christian understanding of God as expressed, for example, by Milton in *Paradise Lost* (1667)—perhaps the most widely read piece of literature in eighteenth-century England apart from the Bible. Blake was not the only Romantic to battle with Milton, though he was the first to claim that Satan is the real unsung hero of the poem. For Blake, Milton's Satan is not distinct from but actually a part of the divine being. His wrathful energy, like that of Blake's Tyger, is conducive to the full efflorescence and creative renewal of the human spirit. "He who desires but acts not breeds pestilence" (151), Blake writes in a representative aphorism from this work, which consistently defies conventional morality. The problem, however, is that

Blake's gospel of unrestrained desire is just as one-sided as the antiseptic puritanism against which he is reacting.

It is important to emphasize, however, that Blake remained a purely theoretical libertine, although on one occasion he did attempt to put his theories into practice by advising Catherine that he intended to introduce a concubine into their domestic arrangements. As it turns out, this was none other than Mary Wollstonecraft, author of the feminist manifesto *A Vindication of the Rights of Women* (1792). When his wife wept by way of response, he abandoned the notion and acted upon that sage utterance in *The Marriage of Heaven and Hell* that underlines the essential humanity of its author: "The most sublime act is to set another before you" (151). In this one sentence Blake puts aside his deviant notions of a new, divinely inspired ethic and falls back upon fundamental Christian charity. And no one, apart from the Christ of the Gospels, has stated that principle more forcibly than Blake: "Mutual forgiveness of each vice / These are the gates of paradise" (761). Who knows? Perhaps Chesterton was right and Blake's vision was deliberately obfuscated by demonic forces. How else does one explain the unprecedented combination of moral lucidity and wrongheaded truculence in this poet's works? In any case, Blake's married life with Catherine is a living refutation of the doctrine so daringly advanced in *The Marriage*. Through mutual forbearance, fidelity, and love they ripened into a palmary example of the sacrament that Blake so often attacks.

The next phase of Blake's development is the one that has commanded the most attention from modern commentators. This involves the engraved prophetic writings in which Blake endeavors to develop a coherent mythology based upon his understanding of human nature. The inspiration for these books is traceable to two sources, the Bible and the poems of Ossian (1761–1763)—an apparent compilation of ancient Celtic myths and legends collated by the eighteenth-century Scotsman, James Macpherson, who tricked the public into accepting the veracity of his scholarly claims. The fact is that he dreamed up these so-called sagas in a style that reflects what the eighteenth century thought a primitive legend should sound like. The style is windy, rhetorical, bombastic, and inflated; and its influence on Blake is less than salutary from a strictly prosodic point of view. Much of the ranting and roaring that disfigures page after page of Blake's prophetic books derives not only from his psychic conflicts and spiritual crises but also from the influence of a style that occasionally rises to levels of grandeur but more often sinks into quagmires of bathos. (One recalls, in this regard, the response of Samuel Johnson to an assembly of Macpherson's defenders who asked, as Boswell records, if "any man in the modern age could have written such poems?" "Yes, sir," Johnson replied, "many men, many women, and many children.")[5]

If Macpherson provided Blake with a poetic example of some dubiety, the same cannot be said of the majestic cadences of the King James Bible, frequently echoed by Blake to great effect. Beyond the verbal echoes, the Bible provided Blake with an example of myth-making on the large scale that his imagination required. The trouble, however, is that Blake's attempt to legitimize his radical mythos of creative freedom by assimilating it to the Judeo-Christian tradition only exacerbates the unwieldy incoherence of his vision. Blake's Jesus, for example, is no longer the historical Jesus of the Gospels, come to fulfill the law, but rather a symbol of emancipated humanity freed from the burden of moral constraint.

But the problem of articulating a coherent epic vision in an age when the verities of dogmatic faith were being replaced by the hypotheses of scientific theory is a dilemma universal to the generation of Romantic poets. No one has stated this dilemma more succinctly than Jacques Maritain: "The effort of a poet to create new metaphysical myths of his own invention, for the sake of his work as a poet, is self-contradictory, since, having made them, he cannot believe in them."[6] The point is that genuine myth grows out of an actual historical event subject to refinement and interpretation by generations of believers whose collective experience of this event creates, by slow degrees, a consensus of authority and faith around a body of dogmas, beliefs, and factual claims. As much as Blake rejects the notion that his works belong to the inferior and secondary plane of allegory as opposed to the primary and transcendent plane of vision, his mythic books are, in fact, allegorical. Time and again Blake is obliged to disrupt his whirling, disconnected narratives and explain in simple terms that his characters are meant to be construed as projections of intrapsychic forces—in short, that they are allegorical impersonations of mental states. One has only to turn to Homer, Virgil, Dante, or

Milton—poets fortunate enough to live in ages that gave them myths ready-made for dramatic development—to see the difference between a poet who is in control, both intellectually and artistically, of his material, and a poet who is losing control of compulsive images that frequently overwhelm his powers of communication.

Blake elaborated his myths in a series of books that extend from *The Book of Urizen* (1794) to *The Four Zoas* (1797), *Milton* (1808), and *Jerusalem* (1818). The latter three are regarded as his most strenuous attempt to work out the convoluted story of humankind's fall and redemption. For it is nothing less than this grand biblical myth that Blake interprets according to his own idiosyncratic lights. Though it is impossible in an historical survey to elucidate the complex nature of this vision, the following outline may suggest something of its complexity and daring.

Blake's myth is embodied in a group of sinewy characters with jaw-breaking cognomens who represent the divided powers and capacities of a single fragmented mind that has lost its psychic and spiritual equilibrium. This mind is "Albion," the original self-integrated human being whose division and breakdown are in part a consequence of the material bias of the modern world. The ascendant empiricism of modern science has reduced existence to that which is verifiably certain according to the standards of measurement and observation. The prophet, visionary, and reformer are thrown into exile, and the dead letter of legalism, scientism, and custom has triumphed over the living spirit of freedom, love, and creativity. In one of his crisp and incredibly concentrated aphorisms, Blake prays, ". . . May God us keep / From single vision and from Newton's sleep" (818). When "single vision"—the establishment of empirical fact or the weight of moral prohibition—becomes the sole criterion for judging truth or regulating human relations, the inevitable outcome for Blake is the death of the imagination, the decay of hope, the failure of love, and the decline of art. Spiritual health is the capacity to balance and keep in dynamic play the multiple levels of human intellection, feeling, and understanding. Hence it is important that humanity's warring faculties be reintegrated in a cooperative embrace that affirms the irreducible integrity of the human form divine, that is, made in the image of God and animated by the spirit of brotherhood, forgiveness, and love. In a word, the hegemony of Urizen, who represents for Blake both reason and restraint, as well as the orthodox image of God, must give way to a division of powers among the Four-Fold Man. When Los (imagination), Orc (emotion), and Tharmas (instinct) are accorded their proper role in the economy of human nature, then creation itself will be restored to its original pristine splendor and humanity will recognize its own God-like capacities.

While it is clear that Blake rejects the reductive naturalism of his day, it is by no means certain that his poetry brings us any closer to what is traditionally understood by the term "God." According to Martin Buber, "the great images of God fashioned by mankind are born not of imagination but of real encounters with real divine power and glory."[7] But for Blake the imagination is God, and in consequence there can be no encounter of the kind Buber describes. Blake's gnostic vision of a regenerate humanity has no need, it seems, for a divine mediator or a suffering Savior, and yet this same poet tells us "we are put on earth a little space / That we may learn to bear the beams of love" (125), a phrase that echoes in the mind like a mantra and seems in perfect accord with a Christian understanding of human growth. There is no getting around the fact that Blake is one of the greatest enigmas in English literature.

But whether it is by a trick of fate or a divine joke at Blake's expense, there is one lyric from the prophetic books that has rightfully attained a renown independent of its function as a preface to *Milton*. In fact, it might legitimately be called the unofficial national anthem of England, being sung, in the beautiful setting by Sir Hubert Parry, more often in that country than "Rule Britannia," its official counterpart. That it is sung by average churchgoers and ordinary citizens untroubled by Blake's hallucinated visions and dissident beliefs, reveals that at his best Blake may be appreciated without the learned tomes of the commentators or the superior airs of the initiate. Its point of departure is the long-standing English legend that Jesus once visited ancient Britain in company with Joseph of Arimathea. Ascending the chariot of Ezekiel, Blake anticipates the Savior's return to an England unspoiled by the "dark Satanic Mills" of the factory system (or the distorted theology of traditional chrisendom, as some interpreters would have it), and awakened from the sleep of the sensual and the proud. Perhaps none of Blake's shorter lyrics better distills the concentrated

essence of his poetic vision or more urgently expresses the apocalyptic thrust of his prophetic zeal:

> And did those feet in ancient time
> Walk upon England's mountains green?
> And was the holy lamb of God
> On England's pleasant pastures seen?
>
> And did the Countenance Divine
> Shine forth upon our clouded hills?
> And was Jerusalem builded here,
> Among these dark Satanic Mills?
>
> Bring me my Bow of burning gold:
> Bring me my arrows of desire:
> Bring me my spear: O clouds unfold!
> Bring me my chariot of fire!
>
> I will not cease from Mental Fight,
> Nor shall my sword sleep in my hand,
> Till we have built Jerusalem
> In England's green & pleasant land.
>
> (480–81)

· THREE ·

Wordsworth and Coleridge

In his marginal annotations to Wordsworth's poems, William
Blake reproves what he takes to be a failure of imagination in this
poet of nature and natural piety: "I see in Wordsworth the Natural
Man rising up against the Spiritual Man continually, and then he is
No Poet but a Heathen Philosopher at Enmity against all true Po-
etry or Inspiration" (782).

Blake's unqualified rejection of Wordsworth's genius reveals,
however, the very elements in Wordsworth that make him more
impressively self-adjusted and clear-sighted than Blake. These involve a sober and humble awareness of the natural universe as an
objective fact in which we live and move and have our being. Far,
however, from paralyzing Wordsworth as Blake suggests, it is precisely this awareness which gives his verse its special quality of
hard-won and dearly purchased calm: a serenity wrung from an
acceptance of human limits even as those limits suggest a spiritual
order beyond the contradictions of mortal existence. If Blake, to
paraphrase some remarks of G. K. Chesterton, wishes to get the
heavens into his head by eradicating the distinction between the
divine and the human, then Wordsworth wishes to get his head
into the heavens by celebrating nature as a source of spiritual enlightenment.

This is not to say that Wordsworth is a nature poet in the common acceptation of that term. The massive weight of the material
universe does not stifle his creative powers; to the contrary, it activates them. "An auxiliar light," the poet writes, "Came from my
mind, which on the setting sun / Bestowed new splendor" (137).
Natural objects are of value for Wordsworth in exact proportion as
they excite the imagination to shoot beyond them. But even in such
moments the poet never forgets the qualitative distinction between
"the primal source / of all illumination" and "the transitory Being
that beheld / [the] Vision" (232).

The Victorian poet Matthew Arnold, who as a child was a neighbor of Wordsworth's near Rydal Mount, best describes this delicate balance of visionary grandeur and spiritual humility in the poet's verse. With "His eyes on Nature's plan," Arnold declares, he "Neither made man too much a God, / Nor God too much a man."[1] While Blake repudiates the objective and external universe as an impediment to imaginative fulfillment, Wordsworth regards nature as "the nurse, / The guide, the guardian of my heart" (92). The office of nature, in this regard, is twofold: it reveals to Wordsworth the extent of his biological ties to the whole of existence, and it gradually weans him from those ties by stimulating visions of a spiritual realm beyond the encroachments of age and death. "Insensibly subdued / to settled quiet," as Wordsworth writes in "Animal Tranquility and Decay," the mind is composed by sorrow, loss, and decline, to the contemplation of those permanent realities that lie beyond the flux of sensuous existence.

Among the many passages in Wordsworth's verse that take us to the threshold of such contemplation, especially notable is an episode from *The Excursion* (1814) that describes the youth of the "Wanderer"—an itinerant moralist on the theme of human transience who represents a phase of Wordsworth's own development midway between "the Solitary," a spiritual bankrupt brooding of the trauma of revolutionary France, and "The Pastor," a rural clergyman who has assimilated Wordsworth's natural piety into the calendar worship of the Christian year.

Even as a child herding sheep in the mountains, the Wanderer rose above the daily round of animal husbandry and caught a glimpse of that far-off happiness that ravishes the soul. Once, observing the massing of cloud forms from the perspective of a mountain headland, he was granted a vision of decisive importance for his future development:

> . . . Far and wide the clouds were touched,
> And in their silent faces could be read
> Unutterable love. Sound needed none,
> Nor any voice of joy; his spirit drank
> The spectacle: sensation, soul, and form,
> All melted into him; they swallowed up
> His animal being, in them did he live,
> And by them did he live; they were his life.

In such access of mind, in such high hour
Of visitation from the living God,
Thought was not; in enjoyment it expired.
No thanks he breathed, he proffered no request,
Rapt into still communion that transcends
The imperfect offices of prayer and praise,
His mind was a thanksgiving to the power
That made him; it was blessedness and love.

(413)

This is the authentic Wordsworthian note: a spirit of meditation so intense that it passes beyond the material forms which summoned it into being. Wordsworth, especially susceptible to these impressions and intuitions in his boyhood, returns to them again and again as a source of replenishment and renewal in his later years. In "There was a boy," for instance, Wordsworth describes his own experience as a child sporting among the islands of Winander. At nightfall, he would imitate the sound of hooting owls and thus set off a train of echoes among the distant hills. But so often in Wordsworth the child's willful disturbance of nature's stillness or conscious delight in his own physical energy is followed by a recoil of reverential awe in which his own identity is absorbed by the greater powers that encompass him. And hence when the dying echoes are followed by a pregnant silence, the boy is suddenly aware of his relationship to the whole of creation:

... And, when there came a pause
Of silence such as baffled his best skill:
Then sometimes, in that silence, while he hung
Listening, a gentle shock of mild surprise
Has carried far into his heart the voice
Of mountain-torrents; or the visible scene
Would enter unawares into his mind
With all its solemn imagery, its rocks,
Its woods, and that uncertain heaven received
Into the bosom of the steady lake.

(111)

Of these lines, Coleridge observed that if he had come upon them in a desert wilderness he should instantly have shouted

"Wordsworth!"—their character and tone being unmistakable. Especially unmistakable is that intuition which is the central sustaining element in Wordsworth's verse—an intuition of being itself as an immaterial essence, an abiding reality that both inheres in and yet rises immeasurably beyond the finite particulars of the material world. In this regard, Wordsworth was endowed with an almost preternatural sensitivity to the metaphysics of things. Indeed, an awareness of ultimate realities entered his mind with the same alacrity with which the twilit sky in "There was a boy" is absorbed into the mirror of the mountain lake.

As a youth Wordsworth did not endeavor to categorize these realities according to the formulas of philosophy or faith—though in later years he felt that their meaning could be retrospectively elucidated in the context of Christian worship. But by that time the primal intuitions that nourished his genius had largely departed.

The record of Wordsworth's growth under the pressure of these intuitions is described in *The Prelude*—a blank verse epic that dispenses with the mythological machinery of the past to concentrate on the poet's own development from childhood to maturity. The true hero of this epic, begun in 1805 and continually polished until its publication in 1850, the year of Wordsworth's death, is the poet himself, tracing in the incidents of his own life that thread of meaning which the traditional institutions of church and state seemed incapable of providing in an age dedicated to throwing off the rags of past oppression.

In a real sense, the other "hero" of *The Prelude* is the Lake District of England; for it was here among the common sheep farmers, peasants, and local artisans that Wordsworth derived his sense of our elemental ties to the natural order and the way in which those ties simultaneously raise us to the heavens even as they root us in the earth. It is the natural piety expressed by Wordsworth's skylark: "Type of the wise who soar, but never roam; / True to the kindred points of Heaven and Home" (643).

Here, to the undisturbed recesses of these lakes, tarns, and crags, Wordsworth—after a brief period of self-division in Cambridge and revolutionary France—returned to imbibe the inexpressible peace which invests even his most harrowing accounts of rural hardship in the face of nature's imperturbable laws. "Fair seed time had my soul, and I grew up / Fostered alike by beauty and by fear" (128). Thus Wordsworth describes the way in which nature ministered to his growing consciousness, exacting from him, even in boyhood, a religious responsibility in the reception of the most simple gifts. (Indeed, a cardinal tenet of Wordsworth's verse is the belief that the life lived in conscious dependence on seasonal change and natural law builds more character and fosters more poetry than the life of the urban dweller, distracted by the fashionable trends of the city. Because in rural life "the passions of men are incorporated with the beautiful and permanent forms of nature," as Wordsworth writes in his "Preface" to *Lyrical Ballads*, both the speech and the sentiments of the unsophisticated countryman are more susceptible to poetic transformation and lyrical treatment than are the conventional notions of the rootless cosmopolitan.)

The coalescence, then, of beauty and fear, of awe tinged with penitential overtones—as if in contrition for those occasions when the poet denied his dependence on nature's primal source—is what chiefly distinguishes Wordsworth's experience among the mountains and lakes of his native district. This is apparent in three boyhood episodes from *The Prelude* in which the child's capacity of spiritual surrender to the magnitude of the created universe is accompanied by vague misgivings of personal unworthiness. On one of these occasions, Wordsworth stole an unattended boat and ventured midway out on a lake near Patterdale, delighting in the moonlit solitude and the success of his undetected prank. Impelled by the fury of the boy's energetic strokes, the boat shoots in the direction of a precipice that rises perpendicularly from the water's edge. The shadow of its walls, projecting from behind the boy and casting the boat in shadow, is so sudden and unexpected that it grips the child with panic awe. He contrives to return safely to shore—but on his way home he is haunted by the shadow of some unconditional power, "a dim and undetermined sense of unknown modes of being," which occupies his mind for days. On another similar occasion, the boy joins a group of his comrades to pilfer nest eggs among the mountain crags. A sudden gust of wind imperils his grip and he hangs, suspended, in precarious balance above the vales below:

> Oh! when I have hung
> Above the raven's nest, by knots of grass
> And half-inch fissures in the slippery rock

> When others heeded not, he heard the South
> Make subterraneous music, like the noise
> Of bagpipers on distant highland hills.
>
> (238–39)

He may not possess Wordsworth's remarkable facility of rhythmic utterance, but those last lines show that Michael too has been vouchsafed a vision of nature's exhaustless mystery and ineffable depth. Like Abraham and Sara, Michael and his wife are blessed in their later years with the birth of a child on whom they lavish all their tenderness and devotion and through whom their sense of living contact with the human generations is sustained. Wordsworth is at his best in describing the filial bond between parent and child as Michael, the most sensitive and nurturing of fathers, instructs the boy Luke in the daily rounds of animal husbandry. When foreclosure is threatened, Michael protests in vain against the boy's resolution to compensate his parents' love by working off their debts in the distant city. In a ritual gesture of farewell, Michael and Luke meet at an unfinished sheep fence of the kind that cross and recross the Cumberland mountains from base to top, built of carefully positioned slate by generations of toiling shepherds. In an act that symbolizes the sacred covenant of the generations, Luke and his father lay a cornerstone for one of these fences, linking by that simple act, the past and present, old life and new, parent and child.

But Luke is destroyed by the temptations of the city, and his parents suffer a moral loss worse than any material deprivation. The poem concludes with moving simplicity, all the more eloquent in its understated empathy and deliberate restraint. Wordsworth leaves us with the image of Michael, habitually repairing to the abandoned sheepfold to silently mourn for his lost child:

> Among the rocks
> He went, and still looked up to sun and cloud,
> And listened to the wind; and, as before,
> Performed all kinds of labour for his sheep,
> And for his land, his small inheritance.
> And to that hollow dell from time to time
> Did he repair, to build the fold of which
> His flock had need. 'Tis not forgotten yet
> The pity which was then in every heart

> For the old Man—and 'tis believed by all
> That many and many a day he hither went,
> And never lifted up a single stone.
>
> (244)

That last line, which Matthew Arnold singled out for special praise, distills all the unuttered sorrow of the stoical old shepherd, even as it expresses that "visionary dreariness" (210) which so often invests Wordsworth's description of human struggle in a universe of arresting but unresponsive beauty. The very dreariness of the unfinished sheepfold stands as an emblem of human endurance pointing, like the soaring crags that circle Michael's dwelling, to a source of comfort and dim hope beyond the broken world of mortal suffering.

If *The Prelude*, "Tintern Abbey," and the "Ode: Intimations of Immortality" reveal Wordsworth at his most stately and orotund, then the *Lyrical Ballads* of 1798 and 1800 reveal a poet who has studied with self-effacing attention the common joys and sorrows of ordinary human beings. The simple language is in perfect accord with the unpretentious character of his themes.

After the French Revolution, Wordsworth discovered that most human ills cannot be resolved by ideological nostrums or rationalized in the regions of abstract speculation. Suffering, grief, and loss are not problems susceptible to technical solution but mysteries to be lived through with patient endurance and deepening empathy. Though these experiences can crush, they can also exult and tranquilize—disclosing depths of visionary dreariness that point to "something evermore about to be." Hence, in the concluding poem to the 1800 edition of *Lyrical Ballads*, "Poet's Epitaph," Wordsworth describes those qualities that distinguish the poet from statesmen, statisticians, anatomists, lawyers—in short, those who would subvert the integrity of the human spirit by treating individuals as grist for the mill of abstract theory or economic calculation:

> Art thou a Statist in the van
> Of public conflicts trained and bred?
> —First learn to love one living man;
> *Then* may'st thou think upon the dead.
>
> (113)

The poet's ability to identify with everything and everyone—from a dispossessed beggar or a gatherer of leeches to an unwed mother or an abandoned child—makes him, as Wordsworth avers in his "Preface" to these ballads, "the rock of defense for human nature."

One of the most moving tributes ever paid to Wordsworth's "healing power" is that of John Stuart Mill, the son of Wordsworth's contemporary James Mill and the famous exponent of utilitarianism who preached the greatest good for the greatest number. James Mill's notion of good, however, was limited to material comfort, and, accordingly, his conception of human nature reposed on the belief that people are motivated exclusively by the pursuit of pleasure and the circumvention of pain. As a social activist James Mill accomplished much good, but he raised his son in the belief that logical analysis is the sole criterion by which to measure the worth of institutional policies and individual pursuits. By his early twenties, however, John Stuart Mill was burdened by a sense of emotional bankruptcy and spiritual emptiness. Life seemed a mere aggregation of mechanical forces grinding the individual into the dust. From this state of moral and emotional impoverishment he was rescued by Wordsworth. For it was Wordsworth who made him feel "that there was real permanent happiness in tranquil contemplation. Wordsworth taught me this, not only without turning from, but with a greatly increased interest in the common feelings and common destiny of human beings."[3]

But long before John Stuart Mill discovered in Wordsworth a counterpoise to the soulless rationalism of his age, another young man only three years Wordsworth's junior, found in this same poet the polestar of his own literary ambitions and a potential helpmate in the realization of them. This, of course, was Samuel Taylor Coleridge, whose own spiritual evolution synchronized remarkably with that of the elder poet whose aspirations seemed coincident with his own.

By the age of twenty-five Coleridge had gone through his own disillusioning contact with contemporary materialist philosophies. Although he did not travel to France, he was won over by Robert Southey—another Lake Poet whose exotic epics of improbable adventure are largely forgotten—to translate the failed ideals of the French Revolution to the more hospitable climate of America. He accordingly married Southey's sister-in-law, Sara Fricker, a woman of unimaginative temper who was nevertheless near at hand, related to his fellow enthusiast, and willing to try out the experiment of communal living on the banks of the Susquehanna. In the event, the whole project fell through and Coleridge found himself united in a less than supportive marriage. By this time, too, he had outgrown his youthful iconoclasm and started searching for a means of reconciling the poetic imagination with the axioms of the Christian faith. "My mind feels as if it ached to behold and know something great, something one and indivisible," he wrote.

The example of his father, a gentle-hearted preacher who died when Samuel was nine years old, became forcible again. Indeed, his father's death opened a psychic wound in Coleridge's nature that never fully healed. Subject to psychosomatic illness since childhood, he had become dependent on opium, a palliative whose addictive properties were not fully known in Coleridge's day. The use of this drug reinforced Coleridge's temperamental dreaminess, his need to lose himself in the contemplation of cloudy and consoling abstractions. Indeed, Coleridge spent much of his life in the endeavor to connect the fragmentary, multiple, and disassociated truths of both scientific and liberal studies into one universal, all-embracing, and transcendent truth that revealed the fundamental unity of all knowledge. In this grandiose effort Coleridge, not surprisingly, failed. "My mind," he writes, "had been habituated *to the Vast* and I never regarded my senses as in any way the criteria of my belief" (503). Well, *the Vast* is notoriously recalcitrant to systematic exposition.

But though Coleridge failed to create the kind of systematic theology that would conduce to the reintegration of knowledge in the modern age, he did prepare the ground for at least a tentative harmony by adjudicating between the rival claims of science and faith. Recognizing that faith is not a matter of assent in empirical propositions but rather a personal and intellectual commitment to the values dramatized in the life and death of Christ, Coleridge prefigured the kind of Christian existentialism that transcends the opposing claims of scientific objectivity and biblical fundamentalism. His influence on the Oxford Movement—that attempt to revitalize the English Church from the perspective of such a sacramental faith—is indisputable.[4]

But what has all this to do with Coleridge's poetry? The fact is that the bulk of Coleridge's writings are discursive and philosophical. Virtually all of the poetry by which he is remembered was conceived between 1796 and 1798—the years of his intimate association with William and Dorothy Wordsworth. By 1806, Coleridge had separated from his wife, was far gone in dependence on opium, and had lost the capacity to sustain a long-term poetic flight. But despite the paucity of his output, his poetry is one of the glories of the age. Moreover, it was not Coleridge alone who benefited from his relation with Wordsworth. The influence was reciprocal in terms of both form and content. It was Coleridge in his early conversation poems who provided Wordsworth with an example of a blank verse unburdened by the wooden rhythms of neoclassical poets and, hence, amenable to the accents of domestic intimacy. It was Coleridge, too, who first expressed in poetry that mystic sense of a sacramental life uniting nature and successive generations of humanity in a bond of mutual dependence and love.

In many ways Coleridge is the most lovable of English poets. He could scale visionary heights, as in "Kubla Khan"—perhaps the most romantic of Romantic lyrics—but his habitual tone, at least in the conversation poems addressed to his friends and relatives, is that of a humble, childlike spirit aware of his own shortcomings and delighted to be a part of the human family. He is not averse, either, to appearing all-too-human in his mortal fallibilities. In "The Aeolian Harp," he accepts the judicious reprobations of his wife, Sara, on the subject of his unorthodox nature worship, and in "This Lime-Tree Bower, My Prison," he describes the rather awkward circumstance of being laid up with a burnt foot as a result of a cooking accident on the day he intended to join William, Dorothy, and the Romantic essayist Charles Lamb on a bucolic stroll to the seashore.

"The Aeolian Harp" provides us with a gracious entrance into the world of these conversation poems. Addressed to Sara Fricker in the days before their mutual incompatibility, it begins in the circumscribed powers of their cottage in Somerset. As in Wordsworth's "I wandered lonely as a cloud," the poet's immediate surroundings are transformed as a fitful breeze animates the strings of a Grecian wind harp—a symbol of poetic inspiration responding to invisible currents of spiritual energy in the universe and modifying these in accordance with the human arts of harmony and measure.

An Aeolian harp, however, has not a consoling timbre. Its eerie, high-pitched wail evokes the coldness of interstellar space. But to the youthful Coleridge its otherworldly tremulations are magically evocative of things beyond the world of ordinary consciousness. And hence it is that the poem moves from the seen to the unseen, the real to the imaginary:

> And now its strings
> Boldlier swept, the long sequacious notes
> Over delicious surges sink and rise,
> Such a soft floating witchery of sound
> As twilight Elfins make, when they at eve
> Voyage on gentle gales from Fairy-land,
> Where Melodies round honey-dropping flowers
> Footless and wild like birds of Paradise,
> Nor pause, nor perch, hovering on untamed wing.
>
> (28)

Wordsworth described Coleridge as an "epicure of sound." The foregoing lines are surely an illustration of this—especially the way in which Coleridge has revitalized the idiom of blank verse. Instead of imitating the mannerisms of Milton like the early poets of the eighteenth century, Coleridge realizes that the effect of iambic pentameter is largely owing to a subtle interplay between the expectation of metrical regularity and the natural pauses of spoken utterance. In this way the rhythm is unobtrusively suggested through the instinctive pauses of human speech. When we add to this the complex patterns of assonance and alliteration that Coleridge has deftly orchestrated into a measure of unexampled euphony, it must be allowed that the poet was uncommonly attuned to the modalities of musical language.

But in "The Aeolian Harp" these "elfin melodies" do more than rinse the ear—they lead the poet to an all-embracing vision of reality, an awareness of a single life unsearchable in its essence though known through the palpable forms of nature that it nourishes and sustains:

> O the one Life within us and abroad,
> Which meets all motion and becomes its soul,
> A light in sound, a sound-like power in light,
> Rhythm in all thought, and joyance everywhere—

Methinks, it should have been impossible
Not to love all things in a world so filled:
Where the breeze warbles, and the mute still air
Is Music slumbering on her instrument.

(28)

For Coleridge, even the silences of nature are but musical rests in a continuous symphony of divine praise. The synesthetic correlations between light and sound suggest a world of hidden correspondences not only among the human senses but between those senses and a spiritual dimension which is intuited through them. Coleridge anticipates by three years that "sense sublime / Of something far more deeply interfused" (91) which graces Wordsworth's reflections near the ruins of Tintern Abbey.

Illustrating that tripartite pattern—separation, initiation, and return—which is endemic to Romantic verse, Coleridge concludes his poem in the bowered cottage where his vision of universal harmony initially bloomed. Realizing, moreover, that the vision itself is beyond the understanding of any mortal—even a Romantic poet—Coleridge accepts the gentle misgivings of his wife, Sara, who suggests that plenary visions notwithstanding, the human race remains unaccountably apostate to its own highest impulses. The conclusion has been read by some as a somewhat craven anticlimax, symptomatic of the self-recriminations that were to bedevil Coleridge's career as a poet. A preferred reading, however, would claim that such simple human modesty gives the poem greater weight and authority. The poet's spiritual tact in acknowledging his own limitations is delicately balanced against the sacramental vision that enables him to rise above those limits.

Coleridge's greatest achievement in this mode of meditative revery is "Frost at Midnight"—the most tenderly domestic of Romantic lyrics, which nevertheless achieves a certain grandeur all the more convincing for its humble roots in a father's prayers by his sleeping child. The poet sits by his cottage fire, conscious at once of the cold night air without and the warmth of human intimacy within. His attempt to discover some underlying affinity between the natural world of ice and cold and the human world of care and kinship is apparent in the poem's opening line: "The Frost performs its secret ministry, / Unhelped by any wind." With masterful verbal economy Coleridge calls forth a whole world of wintry desolation, while the phrase "secret ministry" suggests some hidden connection between the poet's broodings over past and future and a seasonal phenomenon apparently removed from such human preoccupations. The word "ministry" here is especially evocative, typical of Coleridge's verbal wizardry—his ability, in brief, to invest even the most ordinary of occurrences with uncanny connotations and suggestive undercurrents. The full significance of that moment, when the drop of water from the eaves crystallizes into a stalactite of seamless ice is not, however, revealed until the poem's conclusion. Instead, the poet's attention is absorbed in the contemplation of his sleeping child, Hartley, and the spurt of the hissing grate from which a tongue of flame intermittently rises. In Coleridge's day, these sudden disturbances of a hearth fire were regarded superstitiously as a portent of a coming visitor. The poet is thus led back into memories of his own childhood when, a lonely boarder in a London schoolhouse, he similarily gazed at the sputtering grate, hoping for the arrival of some friendly face from his distant Devonshire home.

As the poet travels back in time, a basic identity is established between his own dreaming childhood and the infant slumbers of the child who now dreams beside him. But the poet's fixation on the past gives way to the present reality of his paternal responsibilities. Meditating on his child's future, he prays that, contrary to his own lonely and isolated childhood, his boy shall dwell in a world open to the beneficent eye of nature and grow into an awareness of that one life which consecrates all things. Such growth is organically related to the orderly development of the revolving seasons, which Coleridge evokes in the last verse paragraph. A fundamental kinship is thus established between the revolutions of the natural world and the successive stages of human life. The inner world of human values and the outer world of natural laws coalesce, just as the apparent opposites of frost and fire come together in a poem that recognizes the mutual kinship of all things in an organic universe. Finally, the poet returns to the opening image by way of a prayer for the young Hartley. Coleridge anticipates a future in which the boy, like his father before him, shall ripen into an understanding of nature's infinite depth and numinous power—a power of such potency that even in the dead of winter it can wring magic and mystery from the most commonplace events, as when, for example,

> ... the eave drops fall
> Heard only in the trances of the blast,
> Or if the secret ministry of Frost
> Shall hang them up in silent icicles,
> Quietly shining to the quiet Moon.
>
> (89)

The air of gracious benediction that breathes from this final image remains something of a mystery. But its metaphorical relationship to the spiritual and psychological process the poem enacts is increasingly clear. This process avows that fidelity and loyalty are the essence of fatherhood—a fidelity between parent and child, past and present, remembering and nurturing, human growth and seasonal change. The frost is a symbol of the human family bound together in a sacramental bond that preserves the spiritual patrimony of the past and fosters the infant promise of the future. The eave-drops, or "minute drops" as they are sometimes called in England, clearly suggest the steady passage of time; but the frost that binds them together into a single continuous sheath represents the unbroken continuum of human generations, united in sustaining love and irradiating that "one life" which they receive from a source beyond themselves and give back, like the moon's reflected light, to the power to which they owe their being.

If "Frost at Midnight" discovers the sacramental unity of life in the context of domestic revery, then "Kubla Khan" storms the heavens in an aggressive quest for occult knowledge. In this heterodox poem, Coleridge, like Blake before him, insists on the creative autonomy of the human imagination. Indeed, the poet's authority in "Kubla Khan" is established independently of conventional religion or traditional worship, and the poem as a whole tacitly challenges the belief that the mind of the Maker is qualitatively distinct from the power of the human imagination. Coleridge endeavored to obviate this challenge to traditional Christianity by claiming that the poem was a by-product of a drug-induced hallucination, but the fact is that the poem possesses a thematic coherence which belies the notion that it was a random gathering of unconscious impressions.

Its ostensible subject is the creation of the architectural and horticultural paradise of Xanadu by the ancient Mogul conqueror Kubla Khan. But Coleridge's Khan is nothing less than the "Infinite I AM" and his creation nothing less than the creation of the world. The river Alph, which flows through the verdant paradise of Xanadu, takes us from the first to the last letters of the alphabet, from Alpha to Omega, the beginning to the end, with Khan himself appropriately poised, like the letter *K*, midway between. The river cuts through a teeming wilderness of proliferating natural forms, and the imagery, rich in sexual connotations, suggests a cosmos sustained through generational cycles of desire and decay. But this river, which rises between the two hypothetical eternities of birth and death, between "caverns measureless to man" and a "sunless sea" of inscrutable darkness and unknown depth, is counterbalanced by a magical dome that rises above its vaporous windings and hangs suspended in midair—a miraculous cupola composed of seeming opposites, fire and ice, from which the Khan can behold the progress of the river beneath, from its primeval origins to its predestined end.

After summoning this symbolist paradise, the poet himself emerges in the final stanza—a seer rapt in the spell of this visionary landscape. If he could only sustain in perpetuity the vision of this dome, the whole of existence would be transfigured, swallowed up in the ecstatic triumph of a knowledge that encompasses all history and resolves all discord. Like the divine being who presumably beholds all time not as a succession of passing moments but as a pattern in which the past, the present, and the future are perceived simultaneously, the poet too would be able to rise above the sequential flow of human existence and discover the everlasting principle that reconciles apparent opposites, compensates individual loss, and bridges tracts of time and space. It is toward such a privileged station that the poet aspires:

> I would build that dome in air,
> That sunny dome! those caves of ice!
> And all who heard should see them there,
> And all should cry, Beware! Beware!
> His flashing eyes, his floating hair!
> Weave a circle round him thrice,
> And close your eyes with holy dread,
> For he on honey-dew hath fed,
> And drunk the milk of Paradise.
>
> (103–104)

That final image of the inspired bard not only recalls Wordsworth's description of Coleridge as "The rapt one of the god-like forehead," it also raises the question of the legitimacy of the vision that the poem enshrines. Is this attempt to contravene the spatio-temporal boundaries of mortal life and attain parity with the "Infinite I AM" a species of Romantic satanism in which the poet, like the fallen archangel, has aspired beyond his appointed place in the scheme of creation? Is the closing exhortation to "Beware! Beware!" a warning to those whose narrow and self-centered lives risk shipwreck in the regions of the sublime, or a timely admonition to the poet himself who tempts divine retribution for reaching beyond the laws of human limits—those laws, for example, which Pope expressed as follows:

> In Pride, in reasoning Pride, our error lies;
> All quit their sphere, and rush into the skies.
> Pride still is aiming at the blest abodes,
> Men would be Angels, Angels would be Gods.
> Aspiring to be Gods, if Angels fell,
> Aspiring to be Angels, Men rebel.
> And who but wishes to invert the laws
> Of ORDER, sins agains th' Eternal Cause.
>
> (132–33)

Pope's admonition to the overweening intellect reveals the ambiguity of Coleridge's search for poetic or occult knowledge. And this ambiguity is central, as well, to Coleridge's most commanding achievement, "The Rime of the Ancient Mariner."

In looking back on his collaboration with Wordsworth on that watershed publication in the history of English poetry—the *Lyrical Ballads* of 1798—Coleridge describes in his *Biographia Literaria* how both poets endeavored to use a language closer to common speech and a poetic form—such as the ballad—that arose spontaneously from the soul of the folk and the soil of the past. Despite these common concerns, however, their contributions to the 1798 volume were conditioned by opposing but complementary considerations. "My endeavors," writes Coleridge, "should be directed to persons and characters supernatural, or at least romantic; [and] . . . to procure for these shadows of imagination that willing suspension of disbelief . . . which constitutes poetic faith . . . Mr. Wordsworth, on the other hand, was . . . to give the charm of novelty to things of every day . . ." (314).

But "The Ancient Mariner" is more, very much more, than an attempt to titillate the reader with specious thrills and ghostly doings. It is a parable of metaphysical loss and spiritual crisis, but a parable that never sacrifices the sheer excitement of nautical adventure to the themes of guilt, retribution, and conversion that the story inescapably suggests. In a word, the undercurrents of meaning never overwhelm a surface richly evocative of the salt spray and the open sea.

Though an extended narrative, the poem adheres to the tripartite pattern of the Romantic lyric. We begin in port amid the familiar surroundings of civilized society—the church, a marriage feast, and a lighthouse (representing, perhaps, the feeble ray of human reason in a universe composed of incomprehensible forces). Arresting a wedding guest on his way to church, the Mariner weaves a tale of human treachery and betrayal that takes us to the remotest wastes of the South Pole:

> The fair breeze blew, the white foam flew,
> The furrow followed free;
> We were the first that ever burst
> Into that silent sea.
>
> (50)

The Mariner's sudden gratuitous slaying of an albatross—a bird of good omen vaguely associated with the world of moral order and Christian hope—precipitates the vessel into these hitherto unexplored depths of marine wilderness. And in these depths, the Mariner discovers nothing less than the inviolable sanctity of the moral law he has unconscionably flouted. Whether the voyage be construed as the arrogance of the human will charting its own course in a universe stripped of objective values or an insensate and perverse desire to declare one's independence from the inherited ethos of Christian civilization, the Mariner is condemned to experience (in a way that is prophetic of modern literature and philosophy) the silence or, as Nietzsche would have it, the death of God:

> Alone, alone, all, all alone,
> Alone on a wide wide sea!

> And never a saint took pity on
> My soul in agony.
>
> (54)

The poem is full of suggestive horror and eerie effects, from the nightmare ship *Life-in-Death* whose wraithlike denizens play dice for the Mariner's soul, to the spectral resuscitation of the dead crew members whose bloodcurdling stare is strangely premonitory of the eyes of prisoners dehumanized in the camps of Auschwitz and Buchenwald:[5]

> All stood together on the deck,
> For a charnel-dungeon fitter:
> All fixed on me their stony eyes
> That in the Moon did glitter.
>
> (60)

The emptiness in those eyes expresses Coleridge's horror at the thought of a universe in which the divine radiance has been extinguished. After a series of harrowing ordeals, the Mariner is, at length, brought back to his point of origin to be shriven by a hermit for his willful separation from the human community. Yet the poem leaves us with many disturbing questions.

There is, for example, the question of the Mariner's conversion. In a crucial moment that determines his future redemption (if such it may be called), the Mariner unconsciously repents his willful assassination of the bird in an access of involuntary prayer. He is suddenly and unaccountably overwhelmed by the beauty of the water-snakes—forms from which he at first recoiled in nauseous repudiation of a universe writhing with a hostile and disgustingly prolific life. With a sudden and unpremeditated shift in perspective, all this is changed:

> Oh happy living things! no tongue
> Their beauty might declare:
> A spring of love gushed from my heart,
> And I blessed them unaware.
>
> (55)

But this moment of grace, as gratuitous as the impulse that led the Mariner to kill the bird, does not bring about a decisive change in the Mariner's sufferings. To the contrary, his isolation deepens. Even after a series of penitential experiences through which he is presumably purged and reconciled with God and humanity, he is driven by a nameless, gnawing species of remorse that gives him no rest. He is obliged to repeat again and yet again his inexpiable tale of spiritual apostasy:

> O Wedding-Guest! this soul hath been
> Alone on a wide wide sea:
> So lonely 'twas, that God himself
> Scarce seemed there to be.
>
> (65)

Clearly the Mariner has violated the cosmic order that Coleridge celebrates in "The Aeolian Harp" and "Frost at Midnight"—that order which comprehends the human generations in a sacramental bond and reveals the world of nature as the handiwork of God. But having repented his sin, why should the Mariner be remorselessly haunted by his former profanation?

The concluding moral, which Coleridge later adjudged as being too explicit—

> He prayeth best, who loveth best
> All things both great and small;
> For the dear God who loveth us,
> He made and loveth all.
>
> (65)

—may not fully satisfy the complex and contradictory nature of the Mariner's experiences, yet it is undeniably a moral to which the Mariner has earned the right—since it expresses, after all, the only healing alternative to the metaphysical wound that afflicts the Mariner's consciousness.

Critics have naturally associated the Mariner's dilemma with that of Coleridge himself. The demon vessel *Life-in-Death* that haunts the Mariner in part 3 of the poem may be taken as a person-ification of that mental state against which Coleridge was fighting a losing battle. It is, moreover, the state described in one of the finest irregular odes in the English language—"Dejection," written in 1802 after Coleridge heard Wordsworth read aloud the first sketches of his own Pindaric ode: "Intimations of Immortality from Recollections of Early Childhood."

Both odes are records of spiritual crises that are remarkably similar, notwithstanding the differences in the resolution of either poem. In Wordsworth's case the crisis was in part a consequence of growing up. It might almost be said that he was victimized by a childhood too rich in imaginative enjoyment and poetic rapture. In "Tintern Abbey," Wordsworth, as we have seen, endeavored to integrate these childhood raptures into the expanding perspectives of adult awareness—finding for a time, at least, "abundant recompense" for the loss of childhood magic in the philosophic vistas opened up by mature reflection. But the poem ends on a note of wistful yearning, as the poet turns to his sister Dorothy and beholds in her that spirit of undiminished wonder in the presence of natural beauty that the poet himself could now enjoy only in retrospect.

Despite the philosophic assurance of "Tintern Abbey," Wordsworth obviously felt the need to reestablish a vital link with his former self—since the very thing that made him a poet, namely, a deep instinctual response to the mystery of being and the beauty of nature, was essential to his continued vitality as a writer. Hence in "To the Cuckoo" (1802), the poet denies the loss of imaginative vision described in "Tintern Abbey" and claims that even as an adult his susceptibilities to natural magic have not in the least diminished:

> And I can listen to thee yet;
> Can lie upon the plain
> And listen, till I do beget
> That golden time again.
>
> O blessed Bird! the earth we pace
> Again appears to be
> An unsubstantial, fairy place
> That is fit home for Thee.
>
> (311)

But that "golden time"—namely, the period in Wordsworth's childhood when the whole of nature seemed animate with companionable presences and unknown modes of being—was clearly receding from his grasp. And it is this awareness that engendered the greatest and most influential of Romantic odes, "Intimations of Immortality."

But it was not the loss of childhood magic alone that brought about this crisis. Wordsworth was also distressed by the clear evidence of Coleridge's own increasing debility, brought on by the wreck of his marriage and the abuse of opium. But even greater than the decline of his closest friend or the pathos of retreating youth was the complex fusion of conflicting emotions that centered on his marriage to Mary Hutchinson on 4 October 1802 and the concomitant need to redefine his relationship with Dorothy. On more than one occasion, Wordsworth had memorialized Dorothy in his verse; but perhaps the most moving tribute to his sister is contained in these lines from "The Recluse" (1800):

> Mine eyes did ne'er
> Fix on a lovely object, nor my mind
> Take pleasure in the midst of happy thoughts,
> But either she whom now I have, who now
> Divides with me this loved abode, was there
> Or not far off. Where'er my footsteps turned,
> Her voice was like a hidden Bird that sang.
> The thought of her was like a flash of light,
> Or an unseen companionship, a breath
> Of fragrance independent of the wind.
>
> (223)

Wordsworth's relationship with Dorothy was unusually intense, and although it never devolved into anything illicit, it could not but be troubling to a man as scrupulous of moral probity as was Wordsworth. Is a hint of these scruples apparent in the "Lucy" poems, whose real-life prototype remains something of a mystery—if she is not altogether a poetic confabulation? In these moving ballads composed between 1799 and 1801, Wordsworth describes the first anxieties a lover feels at the thought of his beloved's mortality, his grief at her actual death, and his attempt to intuit her spirit as a force diffused among the manifold forms of nature. Is Lucy's death and subsequent transfiguration into a spirit of natural piety an attempt by Wordsworth to distance himself from the overwhelming pull of an affection too dangerous to cultivate? We can only conjecture. Yet Dorothy's journals bear ample witness to the mutual delight these siblings felt in their walks among the mountains of Grasmere. Often on returning to Dove Cottage they would sit entranced in mutual sympathy—silent, unmoving, under a spell: "After we came in we sate in silence by the window—I on a chair and William with his head on my shoulder. We were deep in silence and love, a blessed hour."[6]

This condition was almost too exquisitely tender to sustain. His recent marriage, the decline of Coleridge, mixed emotions about Dorothy, and the fear of imaginative dessication all contributed, then, to the composition of the "Immortality Ode." The rise and fall of its swelling cadences are like a poetic seismograph tracing with delicate precision the dimensions of a crisis that is not finally resolved until the poem's end. By finally accepting the inevitability of age and loss and death, the poet achieves a calm that is not mere resignation but a winning through to a firmer faith and more steadfast spirit:

> What though the radiance which was once so bright
> Be now forever taken from my sight,
>   Though nothing can bring back the hour
>   Of splendour in the grass, of glory in the flower;
>   We will grieve not, rather find
>   Strength in what remains behind;
>   In the primal sympathy
>   Which having been, must ever be;
>   In the soothing thoughts that spring
>   Out of human suffering;
> In the Faith that looks through death
> In years that bring the philosophic mind.
>
> (356)

The poem begins as an inconsolable dirge but ends on a note just short of triumph. Listening to Wordsworth's recital of this poem, Coleridge was emboldened to confront his own related crisis, though he was obliged to confess that, unlike Wordsworth, he lacked the resources to transmute his loss into an occasion for rebirth. The reasons for this lack are in part due to Coleridge's inveterate habit of philosophic abstraction. Not content with dramatizing human dilemmas or finding a counterpoise to his perplexities in the bosom of nature, Coleridge was committed to what Keats called "an irritable reaching after fact and reason." Less self-conscious than Coleridge, Wordsworth found in nature and familial responsibilities ample matter for meditation, commitment, and purpose. Accordingly, he was able to survive his crisis and go on writing poetry, of less importance, to be sure, but still resonant on occasion with some of the old magic. "A deep despair hath humanized my soul," Wordsworth wrote in his elegy to his brother John, whose drowning at sea leveled another blow at the poet's youthful optimism and natural piety. But the humanizing effect of shared sorrows always, for Wordsworth, superseded the accompanying despair of lost illusions. After *The Excursion* of 1814, Wordsworth was only periodically graced with visitations of poetic power, though he continued to write sonnets with the facility he brought to the best of his youthful efforts in this idiom: "The world is too much with us," "It is a beauteous evening calm and free," or "Earth has not anything to show more fair." Wordsworth, in fact, was the principal rejuvenator of the sonnet form, fallen into neglect since the ages of Shakespeare and Milton, though destined for renewal by the Victorians largely through the example of Wordsworth.

Coleridge, however, was pretty much finished as a poet after "Dejection: An Ode" (1802). The poem is addressed to Wordsworth's sister-in-law, Sara Hutchinson, for whom Coleridge had conceived an unrequited passion. This passion prompted a flood of poetry that the poet was obliged, out of deference to his wife, to suppress or disguise. Doubtless the fact that the sources of his inspiration were such that he could not reveal them in public further contributed to the stifling of his creative powers. In any case, like the innocent Christabel, the subject of his unfinished ballad set in the Middle Ages, Coleridge discovered that by opening himself to love, beauty, and the sacred—the themes of his great conversation poems—he rendered himself simultaneously vulnerable to the disequilibrium of a love that neither his friends nor his public would forgive or condone. The imagination that formerly enabled Coleridge to perceive the world as "A new Earth and new Heaven, / Undreamt of by the sensual and the proud" (115) has become stillborn; and the joy the poet once felt at beholding a universe baptized in the depth of the creative unconscious has become "void, dark, and drear" (113).

Moreover, the attempt to compensate this loss through metaphysical speculation is unavailing—a poor substitute for "that light, that glory, that fair luminous mist" that once issued from the poet's soul and bathed the world in unexampled splendor. The Aeolian lute that formerly disclosed the fundamental affinity between the mind and nature, now gives forth "a scream / Of agony by torture lengthened out . . ." (115). This is Coleridge's dark night of the soul—a personal and lyrical expression of that cosmic homelessness the Mariner knew on the becalmed seas of the polar south.

While Coleridge may have died as a poet, his conceptual powers remained as formidable as ever—inspiring the second generation of Romantic poets to see beyond the mechanistic spirit of eighteenth-century rationalism and to further explore the uncharted reaches of that poetic landscape which Coleridge and his friend Wordsworth were the first to discover. The presence of these two giants continued to loom large in the poetry of the nineteenth century. In the 1888 edition of *Essays in Criticism*, the Victorian poet Matthew Arnold denominated Wordsworth the third greatest poet in the English language after Shakespeare and Milton, while the influence of Coleridge's philosophic and critical writings continues to this day in the domains of both literary theory and Christian apologetics.

· FOUR ·

Byron and Shelley

Disinherited sons of the ruling class, rebels against the code of conventional values, fellow exiles driven from England by courtroom scandals and the sting of social obloquy, Byron and Shelley were the notorious exponents of the Romantic spirit in the generation after Wordsworth and Coleridge. Following their almost simultaneous estrangement from England in 1816, they mutually benefited from the friendship and stimulus that grew from their common dedication to poetry. And yet they are poets of entirely different stamps. Worldly, cynical, torn by the contradictory extremes of Promethean aspiration and rueful disenchantment, Byron is a poet of dichotomous extremes, capable, at once, of reckless idealism and corrosive satire, rhetorical grandeur and deflating deadpan. Shelley, too, could adapt his poetic gift to a variety of moods and genres, from the familiar and conversational ease of *Julian and Maddalo* and the stately pomp of *Prometheus Unbound* to the sprightly playfulness of *The Witch of Atlas* and the Dantesque gravity of *The Triumph of Life*. But in Shelley's case this facility of varied expression is a consequence of aesthetic tact and ordonnance—in a word, the cunning incarnation of his thematic material in a verbal form perfectly adapted to the spirit that it embodies. In point of sheer craftsmanship, Shelley, according to Wordsworth, was the most accomplished of the Romantic school. But Shelley's accomplishments, for all their variety, are the expressions of a spirit far more homogeneous than Byron's. This homogeneity derives from Shelley's consistent engagement with the issues of abstract metaphysics.

To Shelley these were not the intangible nothings that the worldly-wise dismiss with blank indifference. To the contrary, they were of ultimate and inescapable importance, the very crux of human aspiration, and perhaps the only goods worthy of contemplation and pursuit. While Shelley had his moments of Byronic skepticism regarding the efficacy of this pursuit and the existence of these intangibles, he could not forbear in poem after poem to trace the fugitive essence of that unseen power "whose taste," as the poet wrote, "Makes this cold common hell, our life, a doom / As glorious as a fiery martyrdom" (411).

Byron, more brutally conscious of the discrepancy between the loftiness of human desire and the vanity of mortal life, sought relief in sensual dissipation and self-protective wit. Shelley, on the other hand, was a steadfast exponent of ideals dedicated to the regeneration of the human spirit and the search for abiding verities. Doubtless, Byron found in Shelley's poetry an expression of his own latent though tattered idealism, while Shelley saw in the works of Byron a declaration of his own repressed misgivings and doubts. In any case, their alliance—for they remained friends despite personal disagreements and temperamental differences—was highly propitious for both. After Shelley's death, at the age of twenty-nine, Byron became even more cynical and, in an effort at self-distraction, conceived the quixotic scheme of aiding the Greeks in their war against Turkish oppression. The scheme ended at Missolonghi, where Byron died at the age of thirty-six.

Byron's life has generated more critical commentary perhaps than his poetry. More than any of his contemporaries, Byron succeeded in identifying himself in the popular imagination with the incarnate spirit of Romanticism. His "inheritance of storms,"[1] as he termed it in an epistle to his half-sister and lover, Augusta Leigh, refers to an aristocratic lineage peopled by characters as colorful as those in the poet's oriental tales. Byron's father, who earned the sobriquet "Mad Jack" by dint of his wild behavior, was the son of "Foulweather Jack" Byron—a one-time naval officer whose nautical adventures ended, so it was said, in mutiny or shipwreck. Byron waggishly refers to this legend in his masterpiece *Don Juan*, when following the shipwreck of his hero, he wryly observes, ". . . his hardships were comparative / To those related in my grand-dad's 'Narrative'" (676). Part of his grand-dad's narrative involved a dispute with Byron's uncle, "Wicked" Lord Byron of Newstead Abbey, childless himself and possessed of inveterate hatred for his seafaring brother. When the "Wicked Lord" died, the estate, or what was left of it, passed into the hands of "Foulweather Jack." From thence it finally devolved upon the poet—but not before he had suffered many indignities as a child who bore the full brunt of his mother's resentment at being betrayed and abandoned by the poet's father, who led a dissolute life and died a premature death in France.

Byron was the offspring of his father's second marriage to Catherine Gordon of Gight, a rich though overweight noblewoman who promised to compensate Mad Jack for having squandered much of his inheritance following the breakup of his first marriage. Byron was brought up by the irascible and volatile Catherine, assisted by a Calvinist nurse who solaced her young charge with the consoling reflection that the clubfoot with which he was born was a mark of Satan and an unmistakable sign of his predestined damnation. This strangely twisted woman also gave the boy a premature taste of the life of the senses. But with the death of his father and grandfather, Byron came into the inheritance of Newstead and eventually, after attending Eton and Cambridge, took his seat in the House of Lords. While Byron invariably stood on ceremony when it came to questions of rank and privilege, his speeches in Parliament were distinguished by a compassionate concern for the plight of the working classes—just one of the contradictions endemic to this most contradictory of characters.

To compensate for his clubfoot, Byron became an expert marksman, horseman, and swimmer, and like the Greek hero Leander of old, actually swam the Hellespont. He was also, by all accounts, a man of uncommon physical beauty. "That beautiful pale face will be my destiny," wrote Lady Caroline Lamb, the wife of the future adviser to Queen Victoria. Though only one among Byron's amorous train, she was not the least colorful—slitting her wrists in lovelorn pique at Byron's infidelities and then retiring to the country to write the story of her affair, which Byron himself later reviewed in concentrated rhyme, "I read 'Glenarvon' too by Caro Lamb: / God damn!"

The legend of Byron and Byronism outgrew the fame of his poetry, and he did everything he could to enhance it. He drank out of a skull from one of his ancestors whom he had dug up at Newstead in order to make his head into a cup. He toured the Middle East and came back with a bundle of swashbuckling tales of pirates, adventurers, and aristocratic rogues whose criminal doings smacked of the nobility of Robin Hood and were perpetrated in any case to assuage the inconsolable sorrows of their ravaged hearts. This combination of Byronic swagger and Byronic gloom became all the fashion (even the young Keats picked it up for a thankfully brief spell)—and to the women of his age it proved irresistible.

But the chef d'oeuvre of Byron's continental tour was the first two cantos of *Childe Harold's Pilgrimage* (1812). With the publication of these Byron became overnight a household word. No one had succeeded as skillfully as he at putting his finger on the pulse-beat of an age. The cynicism of post-Napoleonic Europe, the despair of human arrangements and sense of failed ideals—the loss, in short, of those Romantic dreams that fired the French revolutionists—had thrown the younger generation back upon itself in a brooding search for vanished certitudes. But there were none, only an aching void at heart and the search for amatory compensation in Romantic love. But this too proved to be illusory, and hence the unceasing alternation of satiate desire, self-disgust, and rekindled aspiration. These are the essential characteristics of Byron's *Childe Harold*, at least in his earlier incarnations. In expressing the complex truth about himself, Byron had seized upon the spirit of the age.

The truth of Byron, however, was even more complex than that, though it would be several years before he acquired the skill and versatility to express the whole range of his complex personality in verse. In the meantime, he had grown weary of indiscriminate desire and succumbed to the advances of Lady Annabella Milbank, a mathematician and moralist who regarded the poet as a prime specimen upon which to impose her stringent code of eugenics. The marriage lasted a year, produced one daughter, and brought to a head the rumors that had been circulating about Byron's liaison with his half-sister, Augusta Leigh. Henceforth Byron was excluded from polite circles. Ostracized by his own class, Byron shook off the dust of England and traveled first to Switzerland (where he met Shelley, Mary Wollstonecraft Godwin, and Shelley's future sister-in-law, Claire Clairmont, who promptly got herself pregnant with Byron's child). He finally settled in Italy, preferring Venice as the appropriate backdrop for a life of histrionic exploits. He became the sometime lover of an Italian countess, Teresa Guiccioli, whose husband seemed willing to put up with the affair—at least until he learned that Byron was smuggling weaponry to Greek revolutionaries out of his basement.

After Shelley's death by drowning in 1822, Byron, though engaged without a sign of flagging on that masterpiece of irrepressible wit and energy *Don Juan*, decided to take a more active role in Greek politics. With a piratical friend, Edward Trelawny, he sailed in company with mercenaries to the isles of Greece. But the glory of battle was not to be his. Dying of dysentery in Missolonghi, one of his last observations on the subject of divine judgment was unrepentantly Byronic: "Shall I sue for mercy? Come, come, no weakness! Let's be a man to the last."[2]

Byron's earliest volume, *The Hours of Idleness*, published in 1807, is largely juvenilia. There is a pleasing facility about the volume, but the jog-trot dactylic rhythms that predominate lack the distinction of Shelley's more subtly crafted music. One poem, however, which hymns the bleak beauty of Scotland's Loch Na Garr, has a genuine ring and impetuous roll that sweeps the reader along in its ecstatic celebration of the wild and desolate: "Round Loch Na Garr while the stormy mist gathers, / Winter presides in his cold icy car: / Clouds there encircle the forms of my fathers; / That dwell in the tempests of dark Loch Na Garr" (29). Exploiting the exotic color of his Scottish heritage, Byron already paints himself as outcast and exile, only at home among the mountains, which reflect the sublimity of his independent spirit. To be sure, the pose is crudely obvious, but it adumbrates an important dimension of the future Childe Harold. The critics, however, were unedified by the performance and responded with crushing scorn. In consequence, Byron retaliated with his own criticism in pentameter couplets, "English Bards and Scotch Reviewers" (1810)—a literary lampoon that first revealed Byron's penchant for Augustan satire and his affinity with the world of Dryden, Johnson, and Pope. While never achieving the compact craftsmanship of his neoclassic predecessors or rising to height of satirical brilliance that elevates *The Dunciad*, for example, onto the plane of prophecy, the poem shoots its darts with accuracy, poise, and comic wit. Many of Byron's victims have been forgotten, but we can still relish his jibes at Wordsworth, Coleridge, and especially Southey, whom Byron pursued with mischievous gusto throughout his career.

Two Byrons thus emerge as early as 1810: the disconsolate lyricist only at home among the wilds of nature or at the feet of beauty, and the disabused man-of-the-world sardonically deflating the pretensions of the self-important and the second-rate. The cynical cosmopolitan emerges for a moment in "English Bards," then pretty much withdraws into the privacy of Byron's racy and ribald correspondence. Not until *Don Juan* would Byron find a way to integrate the poetically divided halves of his double consciousness. In the meantime, there was much to be gained financially from exploiting the mythos of the morose lord haunted by nameless transgressions and inexpiable sorrows. Though Byron was the most read, talked about, and influential of nineteenth-century English poets on the European continent, his uncertain status among English critics is in part traceable to the slapdash exuberance of his verse (a quality that does not lend itself to close textual analysis). But more than this, the vexed question of the poet's sincerity led to charges of disingenuousness that made him less than satisfactory to the earnest Victorians of the next generation. Still, he was extolled by Matthew Arnold for the qualities of "sincerity and strength,"[3] and no less a critic than T. S. Eliot, closer to our day, has applauded the poet's honesty: "With his charlatanism, he has also unusual frankness ... with his humbug and self-deception he has also a reckless raffish honesty."[4]

The earlier incarnations of Byron's poetic personae are, however, too theatrical in the main for modern taste. The series of swashbuckling verse-tales from *The Giaour* (1813) to *The Island* (1823), whose heroes all wear the same mask of melancholy weltschmerz, are largely forgotten except by students of the genre. The same attitudinizing makes *Childe Harold*, with its stilted back-glances in the direction of eighteenth-century Spenserians, equally meretricious. But these efforts were not entirely negligible. From the tales Byron mastered the arts of anecdote and narrative that would serve their turn in that consummate masterpiece *Don Juan*, while the themes of alienation and exile, the quest for glory and the fall of empires would be tapped with greater felicity in the lyrical outpourings of 1816.

For by 1816 *Childe Harold* was not just a mask put on for the opera ball of poetic melodrama, but an alter ego whose lineaments bore an increasing likeness to the poet himself. Following the breakup of his marriage Byron was indeed the remorseful exile whom he had celebrated somewhat factitiously in his earlier poems. The remorse was less a consequence of having flouted conventional behavior than it was a result of yielding to those conventions that the poet heartily despised. For Byron this meant exile from his sister, Augusta Leigh. Retreating to the Swiss Alps, Byron, like Blake before him, enunciated an ethic that anticipates the amoralism of the Nietzschean superman. As Manfred, one of Childe Harold's aliases, puts it rather rudely to a Swiss shepherd who saves him from suicide: "Patience and patience! Hence—that word was made / For brutes of burthen, not for birds of prey; / Preach it to mortals of a dust like thine,— / I am not of thy order" (395). This Byronic bird of prey, an object of dread to ordinary mortals, is gifted with a surprisingly mellifluous voice, for the poems of Byron composed in Switzerland at this time—the third canto of *Childe Harold, Manfred,* the "Epistles" to Augusta—are among the most successful and moving of his lyrical utterances. Whatever personal reasons may have contributed to this, there is no doubt that Shelley—whose influence became seminal at this time—was especially auspicious to the Byronic muse.

The pseudogothic trappings that disfigure the first two cantos of *Childe Harold* are absent in *Childe Harold III* and *IV,* which we may discuss here as a unit even though the last canto was completed two years later in Italy. The split between pious narrator and naughty "childe" that is maintained in the first two books is here replaced by a straightforward lyricism that collapses the distinction between the poet and his personae. The Spenserian stanzas are executed with a new speed and grace that has little in common with either Spenser or his Augustan imitators. Especially effective is the concluding alexandrine, which unfolds like the roll of a drum or the last fading chord of a symphony.

The poem as a whole is dominated by one big theme: the disparity between human wishes and mortal limits. For Byron the most cherished ideals of love, beauty, nobility, and truth painfully highlight the sordid actualities of our fugitive lives. The entire production is steeped in the doldrums of disillusion. But the disillusion is frequently transformed by Byron into a dashing act of heroic defiance. A thunderstorm among the Alps can thus become a sounding board to the poet's Promethean passions:

> Sky, mountains, rivers, winds, lake, lightnings! ye!
> With night, and clouds, and thunder, and a soul
> To make these felt and feeling, well may be
> Things that have made me watchful; the far roll
> Of your departing voices, is the knoll
> Of what in me is sleepless,—if I rest.

> But where of ye, O tempests! is the goal?
> Are ye like those within the human breast?
> Or do ye find, at length, like eagles, some high nest?

> Could I embody and unbosom now
> That which is most within me,—could I wreak
> My thoughts upon expression, and thus throw
> Soul, heart, mind, passions, and feelings, strong or weak,
> All that I would have sought, and all I seek,
> Bear, know, feel, and yet breathe—into *one* word,
> And that one word were Lightning, I would speak;
> But as it is, I live and die unheard,
> With a most voiceless thought, sheathing it as a sword.
>
> (223)

Such poetry is hard to resist. To be sure, when examined closely, the stanzas are full of generalized emotion and indistinct imagery, but the pacing of the verse is impeccable. We can feel those eagle wings expanding in the long alexandrine of the first stanza and partake of their gradual ascent as the long vowels rise to a higher pitch and the line lengthens out in soaring flight. And the second stanza, with its series of periodic clauses rising to a climax on the resounding plosive "speak," carries us along with irresistible force, until in the last two lines the cathartic outburst subsides into stoic resignation and deliberate constraint. The concluding swagger with which Byron flings the sword of articulate aspiration back into the scabbard of voiceless despair is irresistible. In the very act of sheathing his eloquence Byron's showmanship is at its most daring; we cannot but admire the brazen ploy with which he tricks his reader into believing that the poet's sullen silence masks thoughts too unutterably splendid and inexpressively profound to submit to the limits of language.

Apart, however, from the histrionics, the stanza also reveals the crux of Byron's dilemma. While he cannot forbear to aspire in the direction of some ideal realm adequate to the compass of his longings, he is no less convinced of the futility of such aspirations. Like Wordsworth, Byron would pass beyond the outward and visible universe into some realm of transcendent and limitless beatitude; unlike Wordsworth, Byron is convinced such impulses are self-deceiving and unrealistic. In consequence, he remains permanently polarized between two incommensurates: the supernal world of supposititious ideals and the sublunary world of sad realities. Between these dichotomous extremes Byron alternates frenetically, until he sinks—agonized but stoical, despondent but defiant—into a pessimism that is the obverse side of star-bound perfection. In Canto III, Byron endeavors to lose himself in the enchanting recesses of the Alpine wilderness, but unlike Wordsworth, who genuinely forgets himself among the majestic forms of nature, Byron never quite lets us forget how exquisitely refined his spirit must be to experience such elevating moments and traumatic letdowns. Moreover, Byron is not humbled by being brought into contact with nature—as Wordsworth invariably is—but it is nature that is humbled by being brought into contact with Byron. Nature does not offer the poet an antidote to the introspective turmoil of his passions as it does Wordsworth; rather it is the only setting cosmic enough in scope to accommodate and express the sublime energy of those passions.

The fourth canto of *Childe Harold* moves from the Swiss Alps to the ruins of classical antiquity. The scene is changed to Italy: "Italia! oh Italia! thou who hast / The fatal gift of beauty" (233). The "Bridge of Sighs," the dying gladiator, the Venetian twilight, the marbles of ancient Rome, the grotto of Egeria, the Mediterranean Sea—things, in short, of vast expanse and timeless grandeur—these and these alone are adequate emblems of the poet's indomitable spirit. This is the poetry of melodrama, larger than life and verging on parody. The Grotto of Egeria is an especially revelatory instance of the Byronic syndrome. This shrine, dedicated to an ideal vision of unearthly beauty, only serves to underscore "the nympholepsy of [that] fond despair" (242) which racks the poet's heart. The *OED* defines "nympholepsy" as "a state of rapture supposed to be inspired by nymphs, hence, an ecstasy or frenzy of emotion especially inspired by something unattainable." For this ailment, however, there is no nostrum:

> Oh, Love! no inhabitant of earth thou art—
> An unseen seraph, we believe in thee,—
> A faith whose martyrs are the broken heart,—
> But never yet hath seen, nor e'er shall see
> The naked eye, thy form, as it should be;
> The mind hath made thee, as it peopled heaven,

Even with its own desiring phantasy,
And to a thought such shape and image given,
As haunts the unquench'd soul—parched, wearied, wrung, and riven.
(243)

The verse constantly skirts the edge of satire in its unrestrained ardors and surcharged emotions—but it proved irresistible to Byron's contemporaries and can still hurl us into the stars today. This is the aspect of Byron that the poets, composers, and painters of nineteenth-century Europe saw fit to emulate and admire.

Byron composed *Manfred* at the same time as the third canto of *Childe Harold*. Not surprisingly, the heroes share the same characteristics. Like Mary Shelley's Dr. Frankenstein, who was modeled in part on both Byron and Shelley, Manfred is a Faustian seeker of forbidden and occult knowledge. He repudiates his mortal status and earthly dust and, like Dr. Frankenstein, aspires to a state of pure or at least ersatz divinity. In a fine piece of metaphysical paradox, the French theologian Simone Weil observes that "if we forgive God for the crime of having created us finite, God will forgive us for the crime of being finite."[5] But Byron's Manfred will not forgive the "crime," nor will he acquiesce in the indignity of being "Half dust, half deity, unlike unfit / To sink or soar" (393).

In *Manfred* Byron deliberately titillates his readers with autobiographical insinuations of incest between Manfred and his deceased sister Astarte, whom he summons at one point from the dead in a necromantic spell defiant of both man and God. In the end Manfred dies, asserting the autonomy of his matchless spirit—but his defiance, like much of Byron's defiance in this period, strikes us as empty and unconvincing. Its individualist isolation is sterile and self-regarding, and in the end it contrasts unfavorably with the metaphysical rebellion of a writer of our age like Camus, whose philosophic formula, "I rebel, therefore *we* exist," shows a sense of solidarity with human suffering largely absent in Byron. Like Camus's metaphysical rebel, Byron too arraigns the universe for developing the incongruous mix of that creature called man—whose suffering is more intense in proportion as his spirit is more developed. But in Byron this rebellion does not translate into sympathy for the ordinary and oppressed, as it does with Camus. Byron is chiefly concerned with his own emancipation and his own uniqueness. It is observable, too, that the principal characteristics of the

Byronic hero—those by which he claims his superiority to his fellow men and his exemption from the rules of conventional behavior—would be regarded in another age, say the medieval Christian, as signs of distinction to be sure, but distinction of a diabolic rather than exemplary order. The incessant self-communings are a mark of acedia—that moody, morose melancholy contemptuous of earthly limits and divine laws. Byron, fully aware of this, played the satanic role to the hilt.

There are, however, two poems of this period pitched in a subtler and more intimate key. The first is the "Epistle to Augusta," which, along with a handful of lyrics from *Hebrew Melodies* (1815), such as the ubiquitous "She walks in beauty," must be credited as among the most successful of Byron's shorter poems. The address to Augusta deliberately evokes Wordsworth's address to Dorothy in "Tintern Abbey," and indeed much of the poem echoes the sentiments and situations in Wordsworth's lyric. But the differences are more telling. Byron, for instance, cannot find in the Swiss Alps that natural counterpoise to human suffering that Wordsworth peacefully imbibes in the Wye Valley. And, of course, his estrangement from Augusta contains undertones of incestuous longing that are never allowed to surface in Wordsworth:

> My Sister! my sweet Sister! if a name
> Dearer and purer were, it should be thine;
> Mountains and seas divide us, but I claim
> No tears, but tenderness to answer mine:
> Go where I will, to me thou art the same—
> A loved regret which I would not resign.
> There yet are two things in my destiny,—
> A world to roam through, and a home with thee.
>
> (90)

The poem is disarmingly disingenuous—especially for Byron. And the fact that he honored Augusta's request by not publishing it in his lifetime shows that for once, at least, the poet was unwilling to convert his sentiments into stock on the literary marketplace.

One other poem from the summer of 1816 deserves consideration—*The Prisoner of Chillon*. Its ostensible subject is the heroic defiance and subsequent imprisonment of the patriot François Bonivard and his two brothers in the dungeons of Chillon on Lake

Geneva. But Byron converts this apparent paean to the spirit of liberty into an elaborate parable of the human condition. For the incarceration of Bonivard epitomizes for Byron the desperation of the human plight. The seven pillars to which the prisoners are chained represent the seven ages of man, and the inability of the brothers to comfort one another underscores the essential isolation of the human heart. The "living grave" of the dungeon is a metaphor of that death-in-life which characterizes an existence toiling under the conscious weight of its predestined end.

Byron explicitly rejects the Wordsworthian belief in salvation through nature when a bird alights at the dungeon grate and cheers Bonivard with the delirious dream that it is the soul of his dead brother. Like Wordsworth's daffodils, the song of the bird seems to offer the prisoner an opportunity for self-transcendence. But it departs with cruel suddenness, and Bonivard is left "twice so doubly lone, / Lone as a corse within its shroud, / Lone as a solitary cloud" (340). Bonivard's epiphany ends where Wordsworth's begins, "lonely as a cloud / That floats on high o'er vales and hills." Instead of mediating divine visions, Byron's nature cruelly mocks the desperate credulity of enchained humankind. This is Romantic existentialism, and Byron's parable has the same significance for his age that Camus's *Myth of Sisyphus* has for ours. But Byron saves the ultimate irony for last. When Bonivard is finally freed—the only of the brothers to survive—he regains his freedom with a sigh: "My very chains and I grew friends, / So much a long communion tends / To make us what we are" (340). Bonivard may have lost his physical chains, but the chains that bind us to age, death, and loss are inexorable. In *The Prisoner of Chillon* Byron gives an objective and impersonal authority to those themes that *Childe Harold* expresses with confessional passion.[6]

But the preceding analysis of Byron's poetic career is less than half of the picture. While Byron would certainly be remembered if he had ceased to write in 1818, he would not have been deemed, by Matthew Arnold, the greatest poet of the Romantic Age after Wordsworth; nor would he be ranked as second only to Shakespeare by one of the Bard's most able critics in our day, G. Wilson Knight. For when Byron took off in 1818 on the subject of Don Juan, he found both a poetic form and a colloquial idiom elastic enough to accommodate the complex and often contradictory levels of his many-sided genius. Although *Don Juan* is a terribly self-indulgent poem, the self it indulges is irresistibly fascinating and immensely entertaining. It is the work of a born raconteur whose vivid anecdotes and penetrating observations we would not miss for the world. "I rattle on exactly as I'd talk / With anybody in a ride or walk," (834) observes Byron of the numerous digressions that diversify his tale.

Byron's Don is neither the dissolute rake of Spanish legend nor the tragic amorist of Mozart's opera; to the contrary, he is a generous-hearted and vulnerable pretty boy, more often seduced than seducing. He is of little intrinsic interest in himself, but as a provoker of authorial commentary he is indispensable. For, as every student of Byron knows, the real hero of *Don Juan* is the narrator, whose capricious wit and satirical innuendos punctuate the misadventures of Juan with humorous though devastating asides on social hypocrisy and human self-deception. Indeed, apart from the asides, the narrative is relatively thin.

Don Juan (pronounced to rhyme with *ruin*) is a gracious youth sent packing by his master following an affair with Donna Inez—a family friend married to a man many years her senior. When their affair is discovered, Donna Inez is placed in a convent by her husband and Juan is sent on a voyage by his mother. The ensuing shipwreck is one of the great set pieces in the poem—revealing another, less edifying side of nature than that which Wordsworth contemplates in the sheltered recesses of the Cumberland range. Grotesquely, the survivors are obliged to draw lots—torn rudely from strips of Donna Inez's last love letter to Juan—to determine who shall be sacrificed to keep the others from starving. So much for the beneficence of nature and the enchantments of love. Juan is finally cast ashore on a pirate island where he is nursed by Haidee, the captain's daughter, in a romantic interlude that mixes the tender with the sardonic. When Papa returns, Juan is sold into slavery. He is exhibited on the Turkish slave mart, where he catches the eye of a sultana who smuggles him into her service in the disguise of a female attendant—an indignity at which Juan fumes. But not for long—the ribaldry is cut short by an invasion of Russian troops with whom Juan join forces. The invasion prompts Byron to one of the most scathing attacks on the wastefulness of war to be found in English poetry: "'Let there be light'" said God, and there was light!" / 'Let there be blood' says man, and there's a sea!" (748). When Juan rescues an orphaned Muslim girl and becomes her protector, his heroism brings him to the attention of Catherine the Great, and he is accordingly sent to Russia, where he becomes—inevitably—the Empress' lover. Eventually, after Catherine sends him to England on a diplomatic mission, Juan becomes the center of intrigue and rivalry among three English noblewomen who vie for his favors. Throughout the poem's installments, Byron promises hundreds of cantos more by way of response to censorious critics who regard his efforts as immoral. But the poem was cut short by Byron's death.

Don Juan is first and foremost a gigantic spoof. The narrator's quicksilver changes of mood and emotion are exhilaratingly irreverent. Stanza after stanza builds to what appears to be a grandiose flourish of Romantic sentiment, but each time the whole structure comes crashing to a fall in a verbal equivalent of the banana-peel joke. This tactic is reinforced by the ottava rima stanza—a perfect medium for Byron's iconoclastic wit. With its tumbling roll of periodic rhymes (ababab) cut suddenly short by the deflating deadpan of the closing couplet, Byron found the perfect medium for his disabused look at marriage, war, fashion, the boast of heraldry, and the pomp of power. As the poet remarks with an accepting shrug, "the sad truth which hovers o'er my desk / Turns what was once romantic to burlesque" (699).

Don Juan most often recalls the picaresque novels of the eighteenth-century—especially Fielding's *Tom Jones.* Indeed, the poem as a whole hearkens back to Augustan satire, but with one signal and essentially Romantic difference. The disrobing of human vanities by writers such as Pope, Swift, or Johnson was empowered by a perception of enduring standards against which moral deviations could be measured. But Byron's exposure of human follies calls upon no standard other than that of the poet's own uncompromising and comprehensive nature. Though his defiance is leavened with laughter, it is still the defiance of a Manfred or Childe Harold whose nature is so rich, complex, varied, and dynamic that it sees through and repudiates the staid conventions, secondhand sentiments, and narrow-minded prejudices that hold the majority of his fellows in thrall. Byron's satire proceeds from the perceived superiority of the poet's nature, not from an established code of conduct or values.

Still, the changes that have taken place in the Byronic personae may be gauged by placing the following stanza from *Don Juan* on the illusory nature of love next to the stanza formerly cited from Childe Harold, "O Love no inhabitant of earth thou art!" While *Childe Harold* wails over this circumstance in accents of inconsolable grief, the narrator of *Don Juan* is more wryly philosophical:

> Love bears within its breast the very germ
>   Of change; and how should this be otherwise?
> That violent things more quickly find a term
>   Is shown through nature's whole analogies;
> And how should the most fierce of all be firm?
>   Would you have endless lightning in the skies?
> Methinks Love's very title says enough:
>   How should "the *tender* passion" e'er be *tough*?
>
> (831)

Byron's italicized epithets make it somewhat unclear whether we are talking about the throes of love or sides of beef. In any case, humorous acceptance has replaced Promethean defiance—though the poem never ceases to surprise, and on occasion the rueful melancholy of the old Childe Harold will surface. *Don Juan* is fatalism with a smile—but behind the bracing facade, one can detect a nihilistic undercurrent that skirts the borders of despair.

It was against this fatalism and despair that Percy Bysshe Shelley dedicated his poetic career. No poet of the Romantic movement was more enamored of ideas or more grounded in classical learning. Shelley's scholarly endowments were immense. He was adept in seven languages; his erudition was as formidable as his gift of lyrical expression. His translations of Homer, Plato, Euripides, Goethe, Calderon, and Dante make us wish that had been granted another lifetime to render the bulk of the world's classics into English—his instinctive feel for Dante being especially arresting. But since he was granted less than half a lifetime, Shelley sometimes lacked what Samuel Johnson calls "judgment" (though this was coming, nay, already had come, in his last extended efforts, *Adonais* and *The Triumph of Life*). At the early stages of his career, however, Shelley did not always perceive the contradictions inherent in his peculiar poetic mix. This mix initially involved an inflammatory rhetoric based on the revolutionary principles of that proto-Marxist philosopher William Godwin, whose *Political Justice* preached the abolition of private property, the virtues of free love, the benefits of a vegetarian diet, the overthrow of state-sponsored religion, and the general emancipation of the working masses. The philosophic underpinnings of this creed are materialistic and necessitarian. Blame for the world's evil is largely ascribed to a superstitious notion of deity and an unequal distribution of the world's goods. Shelley picked up on the necessitarian doctrine in his first year at University College, Oxford, when he indited "The Necessity of Atheism" and had the temerity to distribute it among the heads of Oxford's various colleges. Expecting a rational response to his arguments, he was instead summarily expelled—much to the dismay of his father, who expected the boy to enter Parliament. Shelley had other ideas, such as preaching revolution to the Irish and sending incendiary missives aloft in hot-air balloons filled with gases manufactured from the chemical apparatus in his own amateur laboratory.

But Shelley's vision of social utopia was predicated on the politics of nonviolence, and his aspirations, for all their affinity to those of William Godwin, Thomas Paine, and other rational skeptics of the revolutionary age, have more in common with the visionary politics of Virgil's fourth eclogue or the prophecies of Isaiah regarding the millennium of peace and happiness when the lion shall lie down with the lamb. Shelley, in short, was a seer; and despite his faith in the inexhaustible goodness of human nature, his utopian visions were millenarian and apocalyptic. It is this mix of revolutionary politics and sidereal perfection that makes his early poems an often incongruous farrago of contradictions.

Thus *Queen Mab* (1813), which enjoyed a wide circulation among nineteenth-century socialist circles, purports to be a paradisical vision of postrevolutionary Europe disclosed to Ianthe, the poem's heroine, in a dream. But the vision is delivered by the fairy Mab—not the sort of company usually kept by disgruntled radicals. And the fairy's speculations on death as some sort of divine transfiguration seem strangely out of place in a poem whose premises are grounded in necessitarian and materialist doctrines of human felicity. Similarly, *The Revolt of Islam* (1818) concludes with Laon and Cythna, those long-suffering martyrs to the cause of freedom and justice, being conducted in a magical boat to some postmortal paradise where they shall preside as patron saints to social altruists crucified in the cause of civil liberty. As with *Queen Mab*, Shelley's social criticism and secular concerns seems incommensurate with the gossamer imagery and otherworldly scenarios that compete with the ostensible subject matter of these poems.

Between *Queen Mab* and *The Revolt of Islam* Shelley wrote another poem of some length. Though the atmosphere of *Alastor* (1816) is pantheistic rather than Christian, the quest to which the protagonist is committed has more in common with the medieval dream vision than the reductive philosophy to which Shelley nominally subscribed. *Alastor* is, in fact, the first of Shelley's attempts to follow to their wellsprings those overflowing fountains of beauty, hope, love, and joy whose effects are apparent in works of imaginative genius and acts of self-sacrificing virtue, but whose essence remains enigmatic and inaccessible to human comprehension. *Alastor* represents that side of Shelley that keenly responded to the philosophy of Plato and rapturously extolled the *Paradiso* of Dante as "a hymn of everlasting love." Despite his repudiation of institutional religion, Shelley, as George Santayana remarks, "was also removed from any ordinary atheism by his truly speculative sense for eternity."[7] It is the "speculative sense for eternity" that impels the visionary in *Alastor* to abandon all human comforts in the search for an absolute that is ultimately sacred.

Critics have noted Shelley's ambivalence toward his hero, whose quest takes the form of a metaphorical voyage in a frail vessel down a winding river to discover the secret wellsprings of life and thought. He is guided in his quest by the lovely apparition of a disembodied maiden whose "voice was like the voice of his own soul/ Heard in the calm of thought" (18). She is at once an emblem of that intellectual beauty on whose trace the poet is driven and a personification of the imaginative faculty that awakens the poet's nostalgia for that nameless something which the "Preface" describes as "all of wonderful, wise, or beautiful, which the poet, the philosopher, or the lover could depicture" (14). She is, in short, the first of Shelley's female incarnations of eternal spirit—an image of the human soul freed from the burdens of mortality and a conduit through whom the principle of everlasting love issues into the regions of this world. We shall see her again as Asia in *Prometheus Unbound*, Emily in *Epipsychidion*, Urania in *Adonais*, the lady with the green thumb in *The Sensitive Plant*, and finally the goddess who kindles the dormant aspirations of the youthful Rousseau in *The Triumph of Life*.

But her pursuit in *Alastor* leads, paradoxically, to the protagonist's ruin. It has been frequently noted that the "Preface" to *Alastor* censures a quest that detaches its partisans from the solid body of average humanity, while the poem itself—or, at least, the poem's narrator—involuntarily succumbs to the allure of the youth's idealism. The conclusion is most revealing. Though the youth expires in a quest that is evidently vain and unproductive, the narrator applauds his efforts despite their indisputable futility. The quest, to be sure, is chimerical and the youth destroyed; but this very fusion of magnanimity and folly, lofty sentiment and self-defeating credulity ultimately transfigures the very world the youth has abandoned. The mere psychological fact that a few choice spirits in each generation are impelled to pursue such a quest irretrievably alters our sense of reality. Though the absolutes of beauty, grace, and truth remain a mere hypothesis, and the fate of those who dedicate their lives to these absolutes appears unencouraging, there is a residue of glory that radiates from their very defeat—and it is this that fundamentally alters our perception of ourselves and the universe we inhabit: "Nature's vast frame, the web of human things, / Birth and the grave, that are not as they were" (30).

A year after *Alastor,* Shelley composed two lyrics that continue the search for the hidden sources of human thought. For Shelley, this search is sometimes so intense that it passes at its highest reaches into a kind of mystic and unpremeditated orison. The "Hymn to Intellectual Beauty" (1816) is one of these. The poem posits the existence of a transcendental power that the poet vainly seeks to confirm on the plane of rational demonstration. And yet this "Spirit of Beauty, that dost consecrate / With thine own hues all thou dost shine upon / of human thought or form . . ." (526) can no more be disproved than it can be validated. In a world of metaphysical incertitudes, it remains an unsubstantiated vagary, intuitively present though tantalizingly out of reach. The images Shelley evokes to characterize this Spirit are as fleeting, evanescent, and unpredictable as the Spirit itself: moonbeams, clouds in starlight, dying music, rainbows, the onset of spring. "Doubt, chance, and mutability" are the only indisputable constants, but despite this disheartening conclusion and the poem's rejection of a naive supernaturalism—"No voice from some sublimer world

hath ever / To sage or poet these responses given" (526)—the lyricist concludes with a hope that these indeterminate glimpses of
"an unseen power that floats though unseen among us" will crystallize, at length, into an assured conviction giving support and
serenity to his future years:

> The day becomes more solemn and serene
>> When noon is past—there is a harmony
>> In autumn, and a lustre in its sky
> Which through the summer is not heard or seen,
> As if it could not be, as if it had not been!
>> Thus let thy power which like the truth
>> Of nature on my passive youth
> Descended, to my onward life supply
>> Its calm—to one who worships thee
> And every form containing thee . . .
>
> (528)

It is no wonder that C. S. Lewis wrote of this poet, "there is
something holier about the atheism of a Shelley than about the the-
ism of a Paley."[8] Paley was the eighteenth-century deist whose natural theology Shelley endeavored to refute in "The Necessity of
Atheism." Clearly, for Lewis, Shelley's troubled but irrepressible
intuition of intellectual beauty was more compatible with the spirit
of genuine faith than Paley's impersonal syllogisms and complacent theological formulaes.

"Mont Blanc" is a companion piece to "Intellectual Beauty," similarly positing the existence of a supreme power enthroned behind
the shifting flux of the Swiss valley of Arve. But as in the "Hymn,"
the source of that teeming wilderness of life and death, glory and
desolation, predatory fauna and opulent flora remains "Remote,
serene, and inaccessible," like the silent peak of Mont Blanc, which
majestically rises from the Alpine valley below. No voice speaks to
Shelley from this mountain, like the fabled voice that thundered
from the top of Sinai. The poet endeavors to rise above the world of
material phenomena, as later his skylark will do: in "a legion of
wild thoughts, whose wandering wings / Now float above [the
mountain's base]" (529). But his only discovery is the myth-making
faculty of the human mind—that faculty which seeks, as Shelley
wrote in a letter, "to see the manifestation of something beyond the

present and tangible object." Shelley's dilemma is that of the mystic who cannot bring himself to believe in the truth of revealed religion. In consequence, the existence of that power which rolls through the Arve and kindles the poet's mind with conjectures of possible divinity remains hypothetical—unconfirmed by human experience and unmeasured by scientific means. Yet as "Mont Blanc" implies, humanity is most true to itself when it embroiders the silent surface of the material universe with the hieroglyphics of myth, poetry, and, yes, praise. Mont Blanc is an inscrutable cipher, a tabula rasa upon which, in an inversion of Locke's epistemology, the poet projects his own tentative theorems of divine power. But the mountain remains silent, like the vast power behind the shows of things that it suggests. Upon the "vacancy" of this perplexing universe the poet disburdens his metaphysical postulates as a saving alternative to despair.

A philosophic skeptic dedicated to the improvement of the human lot and an uncompromising visionary seeking to confirm, in a world beyond the senses, the nebulous visions that ravish his soul, Shelley, in *Prometheus Unbound* (1820), successfully integrated the two sides of his complex nature in a poem Yeats described as one of the sacred books of the world. Its sacredness may be arguable, but as a mythopoeic expression of the Romantic spirit it must be regarded as one of the few successful long poems of the nineteenth century. Its success may be measured in part by its having eclipsed or at least modified our perception of Aeschylus's *Prometheus Bound* to the point that we can no longer think of it without Shelley's belated sequel. With *Prometheus*, the unripe ethos of Shelley's revolutionary politics evolves into a complex anatomy of the human psyche. "What a difference," observes Kierkegaard, "between youthfully desiring to change the whole world and then discovering that it is oneself that is to be changed."[9] In *Prometheus* Shelley is still beset by "a passion for reforming the world," but this passion is now applied to interior psychology and a recognition that change must be from the inside out. Even the most liberal of governments and advanced of societies remain moribund unless the men and women who constitute its polis are themselves spiritually awake. *Prometheus Unbound* is the drama of that awakening. Virtually all of the characters, with the exception of the somewhat shadowy Demogorgon, are fragmented particles of a single divided mind seeking reintegration and rebirth. The key word of the drama is "unite."

Shelley's drama reverses, of course, the assumptions of Aeschylus. Prometheus, as the "Preface" proclaims, is "the type of the highest perfection of moral and intellectual nature, impelled by the purest and truest motives to the best and noblest ends" (201). Jupiter is a nonentity, which is to say that he is nothing more than a projection onto the cosmos of human fears, anxieties, and self-contempt writ large. His earthly incarnations include all oppressive governments and sectarian bigotries. Prometheus is thus enthralled by a being of his own creation. His earlier curse upon Jupiter simply perpetuates the despotic reign against which Prometheus struggles. But hatred, Shelley implies, is the worst tyranny of all. It is this curse that keeps the Titan enchained. By recalling the curse and responding to oppression with patience, forbearance, forgiveness, and love, Prometheus is finally triumphant.

But there is work to be done besides the dethronement of Jupiter. For this, Prometheus's banished spouse, Asia, is required. For it is Asia who endeavors to discover the moral and spiritual roots of Prometheus's defiance, to trace to its source that demand for justice and mercy which emancipates Prometheus from the disfiguring authority of Jupiter. Prometheus's rebellion, in short, is predicated on the existence of a higher heaven against which Jupiter's reign is implicitly judged. The Titan's rejection of revenge is thus complemented in Act II by Asia's quest, in the realm of Demogorgon, for the authentic sources of that moral law by which the Jupiters of the world are ultimately measured.[10]

In the cave of Demogorgon—the personification of that shadowy power which Shelley formerly intuited at the peak of Mont Blanc—Asia learns of a spiritual principle enthroned beyond the world of appearances and the workings of natural law. Demogorgon's replies to Asia are elliptical and enigmatic, for the "deep truth is imageless" and, hence, can only be suggested by metaphor and symbol: "What to bid speak / Fate, Time, Occasion, Chance, and Change? To these / All things are subject but eternal love" (234). Reborn through contact with Demogorgon, Asia is the purified emblem of the human imagination in the same way that Prometheus, in his exchange of forgiveness for revenge, is the emblem of the purified human will. As in *Alastor*, Asia's purification involves a metaphorical voyage on a winding river that leads the regenerated soul back to its primal origins and pristine beginnings:

> My soul is an enchanted boat,
>   Which, like a sleeping swan, doth float
> Upon the silver waves of thy sweet singing;
>   And thine doth like an angel sit
>   Beside the helm conducting it
> Whilst all the winds with melody are ringing.
>   It seems to float ever, for ever,
>   Upon that many winding river,
>   Between mountains, woods, abysses,
>   A paradise of wildernesses!
> Till, like one in slumber bound,
> Borne to the ocean, I float down, around,
> Into a sea profound, of ever-spreading sound.
>   (237–38)

Acts III and especially IV are given over to a description and celebration of the new dispensation in a series of lyrics that burst across the page like fireworks, a succession of dazzling pyrotechnics that, in C. S. Lewis's words, seem composed of "air and fire" and produce a sensation as of "Untrammelled, reckless speed through pellucid spaces which make us imagine while we are reading it that we have somehow left our bodies behind."[11] The celebration is brought to an end by the appearance of Demogorgon, who utters both a benediction and a warning. The rush of anapests, dactyls, and tumbling syncopated varieties of metrical rhythm comes to a standstill, while the deep organ tones of Demogorgon's stately iambics rise from the very depths of being:

> To suffer woes which hope thinks infinite;
>   To forgive wrongs darker than death or night;
> To defy Power, which seems omnipotent;
> To love, and bear; to hope till Hope creates
>   From its own wreck the think it contemplates;
> Neither to change, nor falter, nor repent;
> This, like thy glory, Titan, is to be
> Good, great and joyous, beautiful and free;
> This is alone Life, Joy, Empire and Victory.
>   (264)

After *Prometheus Unbound*, Shelley's poetry is increasingly dedicated to the pursuit of Demogorgon—in short, to the intuition and adoration of that ground of being which Demogorgon vaguely shadows forth. In *Epipsychidion* (1821), for example, Shelley attempts, on the plane of personal confession and idealized biography, to discover through the mediating love of Emilia Viviani that ultimate reality which is likewise mediated to Prometheus through the ministrations of Asia. The poem is full of Dantesque echoes and begins with a free translation from *La Vita Nuova* by way of warning to unenlightened readers who may misconceive the poet's intentions or regard them as morally suspect. The warning notwithstanding, it must be admitted that the poem—though rising to levels of lyrical beauty worthy of Dante—often muddles the boundaries between physical desire and spiritual illumination. This is a common Romantic fallacy, which we shall see repeated in the Victorian poet Dante Gabriel Rossetti—though perhaps Rossetti is finally a little more honest than Shelley about these matters. But with *Epipsychidion* Shelley does begin to explore, if not resolve, the contradictions implicit in his scheme of things. The contradictions were both philosophical and personal. On the personal level, it is fair to say that Shelley's love life was something of a mess—even by contemporary standards. In the poem Shelley dignifies this mess through a series of astronomical images that represent the various women in his life.

Following his expulsion from Oxford, Shelley had run off with Harriet Westbrook, a sixteen-year-old classmate of Shelley's sisters who had come into contact with the poet's works and wrote to him expressing her sympathy for his vision of redeemed humanity. But she also hinted of suicide as the only refuge for the persecutions she sustained in consequence of being radicalized by the poet. Shelley quixotically intervened and the two were married. From this union a pair of children were born, and Harriet became more insistent that her husband reconcile with his father so that they could live in the aristocratic comfort that Shelley's lineage warranted. But the poet was intransigent and began to repent his impulsive chivalries. He found sympathy in the home of William Godwin—the radical philosopher who had fired his youth—and, at length, met Godwin's daughter, Mary Wollstonecraft-Godwin. Mary's mother, the illustrious champion of women's rights, Mary Wollstonecraft, had died when Mary was a child. In the churchyard where she was buried, Shelley declared his love for this daughter of double genius. But despite his advocacy of free love in *Political Justice,* Godwin, on learning of the affair, expelled Shelley from his house. Nothing daunted, Shelley and Mary eloped to the continent. Harriet committed suicide, and Shelley returned to claim his children. But his father-in-law contested the poet's parental fitness in the British courts, and the children were placed in a foster home. Shelley departed from England with Mary in 1816, and after a brief stay in Switzerland with Byron, settled in Italy, "the paradise of exiles." Mary was every bit the poet's equal intellectually, but as her novel *Frankenstein* reveals, she had many misgivings about Shelley's idealized conceptions of human nature. The loss of several children to illness and disease plunged Mary into increasing gloom; and Shelley, in need of sympathy and estranged from Mary, began a platonic flirtation with a young girl imprisoned in an Italian convent.

Emilia Vivianni is celebrated in *Epipsychidion* as a Dantesque mediary between the divine and the human. Drawing on literary imagery from *The Song of Songs* and the works of Dante, Shelley describes the stages of a pilgrimage that has brought him, through Emily, to a contemplation of beauty itself, single and indivisible, an eternal essence that abides beyond the world of spatio-temporal shadows and things that ripen and decay. In the end, the Dantesque springs of Shelley's lyric eventually triumph over the repressed sensualism of the poem's undercurrents. In the concluding section, the poet conceives of an island where he and Emily shall ascend to an awareness of that abiding One which overcomes mortal distinctions and individual differences:

> Let us become the overhanging day,
> The living soul of the Elysian isle,
> Conscious, inseparable, one. Meanwhile
> We two will rise, and sit, and walk together.
> Under the roof of blue Ionian weather,
> And wander in the meadows, or ascend
> The mossy mountains, where the blue heavens bend
> With lightest winds, to touch their paramour;
> Or linger, where the pebble-paven shore,
> Under the quick, faint kisses of the sea
> Trembles and sparkles as with ecstasy,—

Possessing and possessed by all that is
Within that calm circumference of bliss . . .

(417–18)

In *Epipsychidion*, as George Santayana shrewdly remarks, Shelley "shatters the world to bits, but only to build it nearer to his heart's desire, only to make out of its colored fragments some more Elysian home for love, or some more dazzling symbol for that infinite beauty which is the need—the profound, aching, imperative need—of the human soul."[12]

This is the crux of Shelley's dilemma. Committed since his youth to a necessitarian philosophy that denies the reality of metaphysical axioms, Shelley at the same time feels the need, the "profound, aching, imperative need" to discover some objective and impersonal source for those moral visions and immortal longings to which this world's circumstances seem unequal. Shelley asks, "What were virtue, love, patriotism, friendship—what were the scenery of this beautiful universe which we inhabit; what were our consolations on this side of the grave—and what were our aspirations beyond it, if poetry did not ascend to bring light and fire from those eternal regions where the owl-winged faculty of calculation dare never soar?"[13]

Epipsychidion concludes with the tacit acknowledgement that the love of which Emily had been the conduit, remains, on this side of paradise, a fugitive, uncertain, and infrequent guest. Its loss is bitter, but as the postscript avers, "Love's very pain is sweet, / But its reward is in the world divine / Which, if not here, it builds beyond the grave" (418–19).

Within a few months of the composition of *Epipsychidion*, the death of the young English poet John Keats provided Shelley with the opportunity to again "bring light from those eternal regions" to which the poet instinctively aspired. *Adonais* (1821) is the most distinguished of Shelley's extended poems. Its architectonics are nothing short of dazzling. The poet weaves together a complex series of images associated with fire and moisture, heat and cold, flowers and stars, light and darkness, time and eternity, as the salient facts of Keats's poetic career are assimilated to the Greek myth of the dying vegetation god. Drawing on the Greek bucolic poets Bion and Moschus for inspiration, Shelley departs from their assumptions in one important respect. The Adonis of Bion's lament is mourned by an earthly Venus representing the cyclical patterns of life and death in nature. In Shelley's poem Adonis becomes Adonais—the extra vowel giving the name a mournful plangency appropriate to an elegy, and suggesting, by the same stroke, the transcendental origins of earthly life. Remove the final consonant, and Adonais reveals his sonship to the principle of everlasting life that Hebrew scripture reverently forbears to utter except by indirection—the *Adonai* or Lord of ineffable name. By the poem's conclusion it becomes apparent why Shelley's deceased poet is mourned by Urania, the goddess of astronomy, rather than Venus. The principle that impelled Keats to remodel the world according to the lights of his poetic vision is immutable. Its extinction is only apparent, like that of the stars whose radiance is obscured by the atmospheric mists of early morning. At the poem's conclusion the mists of earthly life are swept away and the starlike radiance of Adonais is perceived in its changeless essence—a fixed star in the firmament of infinity:

> The splendours of the firmament of time
> May be eclipsed, but are extinguished not;
> Like stars to their appointed height they climb,
> And death is a low mist which cannot blot
> The brightness it may veil.
>
> (436)

In the poem's most famous stanza, Hebrew and Platonic elements intertwine as the atmosphere of mortal life is compared to a "dome of many-coloured glass" behind which abides that ultimate One "whose smile kindles the universe" (438).

But the conclusion leaves us with certain misgivings. At some point in the poem's unfolding metaphysics, the search for an ultimate reality devolves into something less salutary—a death wish that reveals an unripe petulance, an immaturity of vision that still clings to the works of this gifted but youthful poet and tempts him to spurn the created structures of being for glorious shipwreck on the shoals of eternity:

> The breath whose might I have invoked in song
> Descends on me; my spirit's bark is driven
> Far from the shore, far from the trembling throng
> Whose sails were never to the tempest given;

The massy earth and sphered skies are riven!
I am born darkly, fearfully, afar;
Whilst, burning through the inmost veil of Heaven,
The soul of Adonais, like a star,
Beacons from the abode where the Eternal are.

(438–39)

That last stanza explicitly alludes to Shelley's great lyric of 1818, "Ode to the West Wind," where in a series of breathless, rapid stanzas in the difficult Italian meter of terza rima, the poet assumed the identity of the ancient vegetation god with whom Keats is associated in *Adonais*. In the earlier ode, Shelley regards this myth of the dying and resurrecting corn god as a true emblem of human growth and change—life itself being a series of initiatory deaths and rebirths into deepening levels of consciousness and humanity. In the ode this process is cyclical and recurrent—"O, Wind, / If Winter comes, can Spring be far behind?" (574)—and operates simultaneously in the life and death of empires, the phases of individual life, and the revolution of the seasons. In *Adonais*, however, this naturalistic framework is supplanted by an ultimate and irrevocable apocalypse. Like the skylark whose song, in Shelley's celebrated lyric, is

Keen as are the arrows
Of that silver sphere,
Whose intense lamp narrows
In the white dawn clear
Until we hardly see—we feel that it is there,

(597)

so the morning star of Keats's immortal spirit, though apparently quenched by the spreading light of dawn, still persists—an "intense lamp" whose ever-living radiance is obscured but not destroyed by the prismatic mists of our mortal day.[14]

In *A Defence of Poetry*, Shelley proclaims that poetry "strips the veil of familiarity from the world, and lays bare the naked and sleeping beauty, which is the spirit of its forms." So Shelley in *Adonais* intuits beyond the veils of thought and sense that ultimate reality to which *Adonais* has returned. But can a mortal being survive the vision thus unveiled? At one point in *Adonais*, Shelley compares himself to Actaeon, the mythic huntsman who had gazed unwittingly on the naked beauty of Diana. For this sacrilege he was changed by the goddess into a stag, while her nymphs, metamorphosed into hounds, dragged him to his death. In the same way, Shelley's visionary propensities could not but exacerbate his sense of earthly ills and human limits. "The consequence," as Santayana observes, "was that Shelley, having a nature ... tender, passionate, and moral, was exposed to early and continual suffering. . . . If to the irrepressible gushing of life from within we add the suffering and horror that continually checked it, we shall have in hand, I think, the chief elements of his genius."[15]

Shelley's last poem, the unfinished *Triumph of Life* (1822), is devoted to an anatomy of that "suffering and horror" which he saw in the world around him. It is the most sober and disillusioned of Shelley's works and develops with a gravity and restraint that are a kind of literary breakthrough. Yeats observed that Shelley "lacked a vision of evil" and, in consequence, did not attain to that greatness which belongs to poets of more comprehensive vision. But *The Triumph of Life* brings Shelley to the threshold of such greatness. Its vision of human life is frank, uncompromising, disabused; and the tercets in which it is composed are, as T. S. Eliot remarked, as close an approximation as we have in English to the majestic gravity and economical speed of Dante. Dantesque, too, is the image of human suffering that Shelley beholds in a dream-vision like that of *The Divine Comedy*. And just as Dante is hosted through hell by the Latin poet Virgil, so Shelley is hosted through his modern nightmare of spiritual lostness by the representative man of the Romantic age: Jean Jacques Rousseau. Shelley's tragic awareness of the way in which the visionary gleam of youthful idealism is gradually destroyed by the compromises, betrayals, and disloyalties of so-called maturity is far removed from the Godwinian belief in human perfectibility that enchanted the poet in his adolescence. Despite Rousseau's youthful vision of a radiant goddess—the personification of that "visionary gleam" whose passing Wordsworth laments in the "Immortality Ode"—he cannot constrain himself from joining the mad procession of greedy, appetitive, and discontented worldlings driven to distraction by the promises and betrayals of earthly existence. This procession of broken spirits and disfigured forms follows in the wake of a triumphal chariot drawn by a nebulous being of uncertain shape. The chariot represents the counterfeit joys and parodistic pleasures life holds forth, and the shapes that trail behind are the dehumanized specters of those who have betrayed their deepest selves in the pursuit of vanities:

> Old men and women foully disarrayed,
> Shake their gray hairs in the insulting wind,
>
> And follow in the dance, with limbs decayed,
> Seeking to reach the light which leaves them still
> Farther behind and deeper in the shade.
>
> (507)

In the whole of human history only two privileged beings are exempt from this brutalizing procession: Socrates and Jesus Christ. Though it is hazardous to venture an interpretation of a poem left incomplete by the poet's death, it seems clear that Shelley was subjecting his earlier visions of regenerate humanity to mature revaluation. For Rousseau's vision of the disfiguring chariot follows almost instantaneously upon his drinking from the proffered cup of that goddess who is the last of Shelley's incarnations of intellectual beauty. The only explanation for this is so startling that it reverses the assumptions which Mary Shelley first articulated regarding her husband's works and which most critics have subsequently endorsed, namely, that "Shelley believed that mankind had only to will there would be no evil and there would be none" (267). But in *The Triumph of Life* not only the vision but the desire of evil is directly consequent upon Rousseau's draining the cup held forth by that "Shape all light" whose "half-extinguished beam / Through the sick day in which we wake to weep / Glimmers, forever sought, forever lost" (512–14). What does this episode suggest but that human nature is such that its loftiest visions of surpassing loveliness and moral good activate the perverse desire to deface, to destroy, to profane those visions?

In this way humanity is free, though haunted by its former longings, to pursue self-interest and self-gratification, even to its own undoing. Such a realization implies a reversal of those assumptions that had formerly determined Shelley's philosophic outlook—a reversal that reveals, perhaps, the extent to which Shelley's reading of Dante and the Gospels in their original languages was beginning to modify his worldview. But this is conjecture. And the question

with which the poem abruptly ends, "'Then what is life?'" I cried,"
remains unanswered.

Shelley died in 1822 when his sailboat, the *Ariel*, went down in a
storm eerily prefigured in the concluding stanza of *Adonais*: "my
spirit's bark is driven / Far from the shore, far from the trembling
throng / Whose sails were never to the tempest given" (438–39).
Mary lived to see her only surviving son, Sir Percy Florence, inherit
the Shelley estate and settle into the life of an English landowner
untroubled by the perturbations of genius. Sir Percy's wife, Lady
Jane Shelley, was an indefatigable champion of the poet's memory.
Mary never remarried; her principal work, after *Frankenstein*, is the
complete edition of Shelley's poems, to which she added copious
notes on the poet's life and thought. These notes carry on a kind of
posthumous debate with the spirit of the dead poet and sound
what for many readers is a valid criticism of his works—namely,
their tendency toward the "wildly fanciful ... discarding human
interest and passion, to revel in the fantastic ideas that his imagination suggested" (382). But the instinctive bias of Shelley's nature
inclined precisely in the direction that Mary faulted as vague and
insubstantial. If it is true that Shelley sometimes leaves the world
and the common reader behind, it must also be allowed, as George
Santayana observes, that "his abstraction from half of life, or from
nine-tenths of it was perhaps necessary if silence and space were
to be won in his mind for its own upwelling, ecstatic harmonies.
The world we have always with us, but such spirits we have not
always."[16]

· FIVE ·

John Keats

Keats had the briefest life of the major Romantic poets, expiring in Rome at the age of twenty-five after months of remorseless suffering. Yet in terms of moral strength, spiritual maturity, and sheer human wisdom, Keats is in many ways the ripest, most sympathetic, and warmly approachable of the Romantic poets. Keenly responsive to mortal beauty and sensuous delight, Keats was also the only poet, as Camus observed, who could touch pain with his fingertips. He has neither Shelley's illusions about human perfectibility nor Byron's cynical disgust at human limits. He is more completely the poet than Coleridge, whose early gift was sacrificed on the altar of abstract speculation, and more comprehensively human than Wordsworth, whose spirit prematurely withdrew into the fortress of a rigid stoicism. And he is altogether devoid of that eccentric religiosity which makes Blake, at his worst, something of a crank. Artistically dedicated and humanly modest, Keats is that unusual poet whose character is as commanding as his verse and whose spirit is as genuine as his utterance. He has been most often compared with Shakespeare in the breadth of his humanity and the bloom of his language. "Shakespeare," he said, "led a life of Allegory; his works are the comments on it" (*Letters*, 218). This typically Keatsian observation, in its stress on the relation between experience and wisdom, life and art, is equally pertinent to Keats himself.

Keats was born in 1795 in a room above the *Swan and Hoop*, a London livery stable owned by the poet's grandparents, William and Mary Jennings. The stable was largely run by Thomas Keats, a hired hand of cockney background who had eloped with the Jennings' daughter, Fanny. He proved, in the event, to be dependable and diligent, assiduously cultivating the family business and conscientiously concerned about the welfare of his wife and children. John was the eldest of these, followed by George, Tom, and

Fanny. For the first nine years of his life, John Keats lived in the security of domestic happiness and family comfort. The poet's father did all he could to ensure the well-being of his children, scraping and saving to send the boys to Enfield Academy, a progressive school where John flourished both academically and athletically. The athletics were largely chivalric. Though short, Keats was a burly, broad-chested lad who took it upon himself to protect slighter boys from the school bullies. He struck up a friendship with Charles Cowden Clark, the headmaster's son and one of the first to recognize Keats's latent genius.

But this idyllic nonage was short-lived and came crashing to a close in the poet's ninth year. Within a period of months both his parents were lost to him. His father died of a concussion suffered in a riding accident, and his mother—vulnerable, affectionate, uncommonly beautiful, and possessed of a warm sensibility—was seduced, several months later, by a fortune hunter, William Rawlings, whom she subsequently married. For several years Fanny Keats disappeared from the lives of her children; what happened in the interim is anyone's guess. She returned, however, to her mother's home, ravaged by sickness and near to death, when John was fourteen years old. This twofold loss was the great trauma of Keats's childhood, and yet he bravely assumed the role of nurturer and surrogate parent to his younger siblings. Moreover, when his mother returned, he supervised her care and nursed her through her final illness. His mother's death plunged Keats into a fit of depression, which he largely combatted through the use of his fists; the number of school fights he became involved in at Enfield at this time was legendary. Yet with the support and encouragement of Cowden Clark, he also completed a prose translation of Virgil's *Aeneid* for which he won a school prize. He devoured Lempriere's *Classical Dictionary*, delighting in the legends of Greek antiquity that, as Cowden Clark later affirmed, he could recite from Lempriere by heart. Later, in his "Preface" to *Endymion* (1818), Keats would humbly proclaim, "I hope I have not at too late a day touched the beautiful mythology of Greece, and dulled its brightness . . ." (64). Subsequent generations would confirm that far from dulling it, Keats's poetry endowed these myths with a splendor and radiance that equaled and at times surpassed their classical prototypes.

John Keats

Following his mother's death, Keats pledged himself to a career in medicine. The training began early—much earlier than it does today—and according to a system of apprenticeship. At sixteen Keats entered the family of a London surgeon, experiencing at first hand the myriad brutalizing afflictions to which human flesh is heir. And given the primitive state of medicine in the early nineteenth century, the absence of anesthetics and the neglect of sanitation, these experiences could be unspeakably harrowing. It is possible to trace the suffering of the fallen Titans in Keats's aborted epic of 1820, "Hyperion," back to the surgery cases in which he participated at Guy's Hospital:

> . . . the brawniest in assault,
> Were pent in regions of laborious breath;
> Dungeon'd in opaque element, to keep
> Their clenched teeth still clench'd, and all their limbs
> Lock'd up like veins of metal, crampt and screw'd;
> Without a motion, save of their big hearts
> Heaving in pain, and horribly convuls'd
> With sanguine feverous boiling gurge of pulse.
>
> (289)

Keats's early exposure to aspects of human experience from which many are spared until maturer years accounts in part for their precocious wisdom and spiritual tact of his verse. Disabused from childhood upward of illusions about human felicity, Keats is yet the most felicitous of poets in the opulence of his language and the depth of his sensibility.

As a counterpoise to his grueling internship at Guy's Hospital, Keats would customarily spend his evenings with Charles Cowden Clark, with whom he shared a mutual love of English literature. On one of these evenings, Clark brought home an Elizabethan translation of *The Odyssey* by Shakespeare's contemporary, George Chapman. Keats's response to this find was delivered the next day in the form of a sonnet, "On First Looking into Chapman's Homer." Its ostensible subject is the Chapman translation, but Chapman is virtually forgotten as the poet becomes an explorer in "the realms of gold," or a rapt astronomer gazing at the heavens as "as new planet swims into his ken" (45). By the last lines of the sestet, he stands in "wild surmise" with Cortez on the edge of the Pacific, gazing on leagues of unfathomable ocean. The poet, in short, has become an explorer of heaven and earth; by the poem's conclusion it is fully apparent that this is not merely a panegyric on Chapman's translation but a declaration of artistic intent and poetic dedication. Keats, in fact, had determined to suspend, for the present, his medical studies, hoping instead to make himself a worthy heir of Spenser, Shakespeare, and Wordsworth. "Chapman's Homer" was published by Leigh Hunt in *The Examiner*, and Keats soon found himself a member of the Hunt circle, where his personal modesty, incomparable talent, and genius for friendship earned him the affection and respect of London's foremost cognoscenti.

Keats, at this time, was living with his brothers in Hampstead, but within a year both were lost to him. George, who married in 1818, left England to seek his fortune in America, and Tom, with whom Keats felt a special bond, died of the consumption which would claim the poet himself two years later. Keats nursed Tom dutifully during his last illness; when his brother died, Keats moved into a neoclassic villa in Hampstead Heath owned by his friend Charles Brown. The house was divided into two quarters, in one of which lived Fanny Brawne, the girl to whom Keats had become engaged during 1818. This was clearly a crucial year for the poet. The reviewers continued hostile to his efforts, while his engagement to Fanny mercilessly synchronized with the death of Tom. It is not, therefore, surprising that the poems of December 1818 to September 1819 should be largely concerned with the fugitive nature of mortal joy.

Keats's last volume—one of the single most important collections of poetry from any period in English literature—appeared in July of 1820. (It is this volume, incidentally, that was found in Shelley's coat pocket when his body washed ashore several days after the wreck of the *Ariel*.) But despite the promise of favorable reviews, the poet was by this time deathly ill. Fanny and her mother invited him to recuperate in their home, but Keats, not wishing to put his fiancée through the grief that he had twice sustained in nursing his own dying loved ones, demurred, and persuaded his friends that a year's convalescence in Italy would conduce to his recovery. But when he departed from England with his friend, the painter Joseph Severn, he knew it was a final farewell. Keats died in February 1821 in a Roman apartment—now a shrine to his memory—overlooking the Spanish steps.

Given the brevity of Keats's life and the darker realities that, from childhood upward, he was obliged to face, it is not altogether surprising that he developed as a poet with incredible speed. The six years he devoted to the craft of verse are a breathless succession of spiritual transformations and literary breakthroughs, a progressive deepening of thought and expression that only rare poets achieve at the end of a normal lifetime. And the achievement is all the more commanding when measured against the false starts, foppish affectations, tentative gestures, and inchoate fragments of his first youthful volume of 1817. Much of that volume follows the rather loose, gushy, and confectionery diction of Leigh Hunt; the swooning raptures and aesthetic titillations give some warrant to Yeats's rather unbalanced image of the young Keats as a youth with "his face pressed to a sweet shop window." The previously cited sonnet "On Chapman's Homer" obviously transcends this category, but even the two considerable achievements of the 1817 volume—"I stood tip-toe" and "Sleep and Poetry"—are rather too rife with mawkish rhapsodizings. "I stood tip-toe," written in sometimes flaccid rhyming couplets, owes a great deal to the example of Hunt's *Story of Rimini,* a line of which serves as an epigram to the poem: "Places of nestling green for Poets made." The conception of poetry advanced here, as Hunt's line suggests, is escapist and regressive—a bowered consciousness withdrawn into a recessed world of sensuous luxuries. The poem is a disconnected tableau of natural and mythological descriptions thrown together associatively and without any apparent connection. "What next?" asks Keats at one point, obviously uncertain of where to turn. What follows is a bouquet of floral delectations: "A tuft of evening primroses, / O'er which the mind may hover as it dozes; / But that 'tis ever startled by the leap / Of buds into ripe flowers."

Just as we are about to write off these pleasantries as too cloying and deliquescent, Keats startles us with a burst of energy that deliberately pits a passive abandonment to sensuous reverie against an awareness of life as growth, vitality, and movement: "the *leap* / Of buds into ripe flowers" (7). And it is between these two images or aspects of natural growth—passive receptivity and strenuous exertion—that Keats, in his early poetry, remains precariously poised. Despite its many shortcomings, felicities do abound, not the least of which is the image of "the moon lifting her silver rim / Above a cloud, and with a gradual swim / coming into the blue with all her light" (7). The pace of the verse cannily monitors the moon's journey with an almost preternatural sensitivity.

At this point Keats endeavors to move the poem from sensuous description to poetic myth, as the moon recalls the story of Diana and Endymion. But this myth is stillborn even it is enunciated, and the poem drifts back into a "pillowy silkiness" in which "the soul is lost in pleasant smotherings." Completely unexpected, however, is the poem's concluding image. Wishing for the capacity to capture in contemporary verse the spirit of Greek mythology, Keats suddenly switches from an apostrophe to the moon goddess to the image of a sickbed from which arises a suffering woman miraculously healed:

> The breezes were ethereal and pure
> And crept through half closed lattices to cure
> The languid sick: it cool'd their fevered sleep,
> And soothed them into slumbers full and deep.
> Soon they awoke clear eyed: nor burnt with thirsting,
> Nor with hot fingers, nor with temples bursting:
> And springing up, they met the wond'ring sight
> Of their dear friends nigh foolish with delight;
> Who feel their arms, and breasts, and kiss and stare,
> And on their placid foreheads part the hair.
>
> (11)

Biographers have been quick to link this passage with Keats's unconscious recollections of his dying mother. And this concluding flourish of wish fulfillment, which brings to the fore the world of pain, suffering, and hardship that the bulk of the poem conspicuously excludes, reveals a fundamental rift in the poet's conception of his craft. On the one hand, poetry is regarded as a kind of bucolic holiday in the regions of mythic fancy, but opposed to this and threatening to overwhelm it is a more sober conception of the art as a means of grasping and penetrating the human predicament. Keats ends by asking, "Was there a poet born?" For the twenty-one-year-old poet, the answer is still in suspension.

The other extended poem in the 1817 volume, "Sleep and Poetry," continues, albeit on a more conscious and sophisticated level, the aesthetic debate implicit in "I stood tiptoe." As the title implies, poetry, like sleep, has its source deep in the instinctual springs of the poet's subconscious. But while sleep may give rise to hypnagogic images, it is an insubstantial foundation upon which to erect the noblest scaffolding in verse. Keats continues to vacillate here between the dreaming unproblematic innocence of appetites unburdened by moral conflict and a sobering apprehension of those poetic and human reaches that await mature exploration. Suspended, in short, between "the realm ... / Of Flora and old Pan" (53)—of mythic innocence unperplexed by adult anxieties, and "the agonies, the strife of human hearts" (54), that is to say, a tragic awareness of the disparity between human aspiration and mortal possibility, Keats again refuses to take the plunge, fearing that "a sense of real things" might, "like a muddy stream ... bear along / My soul to nothingness" (55). The poet falls back into his favorite dream of wish fulfillment, catching "the white-handed nymphs in shady places / To woo sweet kisses from averted faces" (54). But at the last the insufficiency of this regimen for a poet who aspires to follow the path of Virgil from rustic delights to epic power is tacitly recognized. Referring, in the poem's last line, to the catalog of sweets he has just finished stringing loosely together, the poet as it were claps the volume shut, and in peremptory tones dismisses this last exercise in adolescent reverie: "howsoever they be done, / I leave them as a father does his son" (61). Despite the foregoing qualifications, it must still be urged that the 1817 volume contains poetry of remarkable beauty and exquisite craftsmanship. It is mainly in the context of Keats's later achievements that its shortcomings become fully apparent. And while the youthful poet is still rapt in the spell of many callow illusions, they should not be perfunctorily condemned—especially by those whose minds are so dull and hearts so barren that they have never had any illusions to begin with.

Despite the apparent closure with which Keats abandons the "realm of Flora and Old Pan" in "Sleep and Poetry," his next major poem, *Endymion* (1818), based on the Greek legend of a shepherd boy enamored of the moon goddess, is still ambivalent in its direction and uncertain in its structure. Keats regarded the poem as in part an exercise to determine whether he was able to "make

4000 lines of one bare circumstance and fill them with Poetry"
(*Letters*, 27). The result is a prolixity of images so dense and rich
in their sensuous realization that they virtually crowd out the
themes that the poet was intent on exploring and confuse the structure in a maze of tangled overgrowth. Several things, however, are
clear. This is a coming-of-age poem in which a young novitiate,
Endymion, goes through a series of ritual passages that require
him to recognize and assimilate the complex demands that an
awareness of death, sexuality, and the sacred impose on human
consciousness. Keats might have chosen the lines from Heraclitus
which T. S. Eliot places at the head of *Four Quartets* as an epigraph
to his poem—"The way up is the way down"—for that, in a nut-
shell, is what Endymion is obliged to learn. Nowhere is this stated
more clearly than in the impressive proem that opens the piece:

> A thing of beauty is a joy for ever:
> Its loveliness increases; it will never
> Pass into nothingness; but still will keep
> A bower quiet for us, and a sleep
> Full of sweet dreams, and health and quiet breathing.
> Therefore, on every morrow, are we wreathing
> A flowery band to bind us to the earth,
> Spite of despondence, of the inhuman dearth
> Of noble natures, of the gloomy days,
> Of all the unhealthy and o'er-darkened ways
> Made for our searching ...
>
> (65)

As this passage denotes, beauty is like a plant that both roots
us in the earth and inspires us to rise above it. In a letter written
during the composition of *Endymion*, Keats avers that "what the
Imagination seizes as Beauty must be truth," and goes so far as to
speculate that our sense of beauty both prefigures and fulfills itself
in a hereafter where "happiness [shall be] repeated in a finer tone."
He believes in "nothing but the holiness of the Heart's affections
and the truth of Imagination" (*Letters*, 36–37). The imaginative perception of beauty is at once transcendent and immanent, rooting us
deeper in the world of natural growth even as it discloses a
glimpse of splendors beyond the ordinary range of human perception. The first book of *Endymion* describes the awakenings of this
percipience in the shepherd prince. And the symbol of that awak-

ening is Diana, the moon goddess, who is, at once, transcendent beauty and the goddess who presides over the cycles of life and death in nature. The "Hymn of Pan," uttered by the shepherds who gather to celebrate the seasonal cycle of growth and fruition, is the centerpiece of Book I. Despite Wordsworth's supercilious summation of the hymn as "a pretty piece of paganism," it is, in fact, a genuinely sacramental utterance that expresses a natural piety in the presence of nature's irrepressible bounty:

> O THOU, whose mighty palace roof doth hang
> From jagged trunks, and overshadoweth
> Eternal whispers, glooms, the birth, life, death
> Of unseen flowers in heavy peacefulness;
> Who lov'st to see the hamadryads dress
> Their ruffled locks where meeting hazels darken;
> And through whole solemn hours dost sit, and hearken
> The dreary melody of bedded reeds—
> In desolate places, where dank moisture breeds
> The pipy hemlock to strange overgrowth . . .
>
> (71–72)

If Pan presides over the ferment of nature's genes, he also leads his votaries to an awareness of realities that transcend the spatio-temporal limits of mortal life: "Be still the unimaginable lodge / For solitary thinkings; such as dodge / conception to the very bourn of heaven . . ." (73). Following this hymn, Endymion discloses to his sister, Peona, that he has been visited by an immortal. In consequence, he can never return to the unself-conscious innocence of the pastoral world celebrated in the "Hymn to Pan" but must remain in perpetual disquiet until the advent of such another visitation. His disclosure culminates in a meditation on beauty that leads platonically up the ladder of sensuous life, from nature to art, from art to friendship, and from friendship to Love itself—an abiding essence, imperishable and everlasting. The meditation is an outgrowth of Diana's or Cynthia's love, and, thus far, the lines of Endymion's development are pretty clear. But with Book II, Keats begins to lose his sense of direction. The moon goddess is alternately a symbol of "the eternal Being, the Principle of Beauty in all things" (*Letters*, 85), and at other times a frankly voluptuous and uninhibited seductress whose lips are "slippery blisses," to quote the howler that is invariably cited to illustrate the youthful excesses of the fledgling poet. Endymion, moreover, becomes increasingly impatient with anything less than a protracted love night with his lunar mistress. Indeed, Cynthia is eventually obliged to awaken him from the voluptuary enthrallments that she herself is so adroit at providing: "Endymion: woe! woe! is grief contain'd / In the very deeps of pleasure" (121). For the student of Keats this moment is of signal importance, for it adumbrates briefly that tragic sense of life that was to preoccupy increasingly the mature poet. What is more, it functions in the poem as a counterpoise to Endymion's jejune notion of beauty as an imaginative escape from the pressures and demands of existence.

Endymion is thus obliged in Books II and III to reassess his notion of felicity and grace and to discover that our happiest moments are the source of our deepest regrets. Thus in Books II and III, Endymion confronts, in the image of Venus and Adonis and the tale of Glaucus and Circe, a parody of his quest for ideal beauty. The quest itself may decline, if its votaries are not sufficient vigilant, into a kind of self-regarding eroticism, which is pretty much what happens to the hapless Adonis who lies, a thrall to Venus, in a state of suspended animation presided over by watchful cupids. Similarly, Glaucus, in Book III, in his over-eager yearning for eternal beauty has mistaken Circe for his beloved water-nymph, Scylla. As a result, he is cursed by Circe with eternal life without eternal youth—a fitting punishment for a mortal whose love of beauty resulted in a repudiation of common humanity. Endymion finally frees Glaucus from his curse and successfully reunites him with Scylla. During these ordeals Cynthia has been absent, and by Book IV the shepherd prince, disabused of youthful illusions, is dangerously close to despair. Notwithstanding his efforts on behalf of others, he sees nothing in the world to compensate for the lost raptures of waning adolescence. In this "lowliness of heart" Endymion is suddenly arrested by the song of a dark-haired maiden, the burden of which affirms that joy and sorrow, pleasure and pain, celebration and mourning are inextricably intertwined:

> O Sorrow,
> Why dost borrow
> The natural hue of health, from vermeil lips?

John Keats

> To give maiden blushes
> To the white rose bushes?
> Or is't thy dewy hand the daisy tips?
>
> (163)

Though somewhat rambling and prolix, the theme anticipates the measured Shakespearean harmonies of Keats's lyric masterpiece, "Ode on Melancholy." The maiden goes on to reveal that like Endymion she, too, sought relief from the burden of mortal limits through intoxicating diversions. The sense of human suffering was muted for her in the train of Bacchus, whose approach had been heralded by "silver thrills / From kissing cymbals" (164). That last image with its synesthetic combination of sound, touch, and color is but one instance among many of the felicities that abound in this uneven but ravishingly sensuous poem.[1] As it turns out, the maiden is none other than the golden-haired Cynthia in disguise, bringing Endymion to that dialectical moment when the quest for beauty evolves into an acceptance of life's contradictions. But such an acceptance does not come easily, and Endymion is obliged to spend some time in the "Cave of Quietude," a kind of pagan dark night of the soul, where he reflects on the transitory nature of mortal joy:

> There lies a den,
> Beyond the seeming confines of the space
> Made for the soul to wander in and trace
> Its own existence, of remotest glooms.
> Dark regions are around it, where the tombs
> Of buried griefs the spirit sees, but scarce
> One hour doth linger weeping, for the pierce
> Of new-born woe it feels more inly smart.
>
> (174)

Disenthralled and disenchanted, Endymion awakes from this passage and turns against his former conceptions of love and beauty:

> I have clung
> To nothing, lov'd a nothing, nothing seen
> Of felt but a great dream! O I have been
> Presumptuous against love, against the sky,

> Against all elements, against the tie
> Of mortals each to each, against the blooms
> Of flowers, rush of rivers, and the tombs
> Of heroes gone!
>
> (177)

The poem concludes, however, with an unexpected apotheosis. The Indian maiden metamorphoses into the golden-haired Cynthia and, before the worshipful eyes of Peona, Endymion's sister, departs with her shepherd Prince back into the world of Flora and Old Pan. The weakness of the conclusion derives from Keats's own ambivalence about the relations between myth and history, the ideal and the real, or, to use his own cognomens, beauty and truth.

Like the Victorians after him (and Keats, if he had lived, would have been foremost among their number), the poet is greatly concerned about imaginative and human survival in a world where the consoling myths and comforting rituals of the past have dissolved under the corrosives of modern skepticism and historical relativity. The apotheosis of the Indian maiden is an attempt to resolve this dilemma by positing a notion of the beautiful and the sacred that grows out of the world of change and process even as it transforms that world with authentic inklings of possible sublimity. If *Endymion* fails to satisfy, the failure is traceable to the poet's own uncertainty about the function of the imagination in the overall economy of human life. As the poet himself stated in the "Preface" to this poem, "the imagination of a boy is healthy, and the mature imagination of a man is healthy; but there is a space of life between, in which the soul is in a ferment, the character undecided, the ambition thick-sighted: thence proceeds mawkishness . . ." (64). What is astonishing, however, is that Keats's "mawkishness" was so short-lived. With the completion of *Endymion* on 28 November 1817, Keats, with a little more than three years to live, completes his poetic novitiate and begins to compose works of such authoritative power and consummate artistry that critics have had to go back to Shakespeare to find comparisons worthy of their company.[2] It is a miracle in cultural history analogous to the last symphonies of Mozart, which came with equal alacrity and unprecedented splendor in the last year of the composer's life.

The change in Keats's sensibility becomes initially apparent in a verse letter addressed to his friend and fellow poet, John Hamilton

Reynolds. It begins by basically taking back the premise upon which "Sleep and Poetry" reposes. Instead of dreams being an ana- logue of the creative act, they are described here as an incongruous combination of the day's impressions: "Old Socrates a-tying his cravat, / And Hazlitt [the Romantic essayist] playing with Miss Edgewood's Cat" (485). In lieu of a gorgeous landscape glowing in golden tints by Claude or Titian, Keats's dreams are troubled by a mixture of distracting and grotesque images: "O that our dream- ings all of sleep or wake / Would all their colours from the Sunset take; / From something of material sublime, / Rather than shadow our own soul's day-time / In the dark void of night/ (486). Keats's inability to create an autonomous world of imaginative pleasures leads him to an awareness of realities that are not amenable to Ro- mantic idealization. As a consequence his "Imagination brought / Beyond its proper bound, yet still confined,—/ Lost in a sort of Purgatory blind, / Cannot refer to any standard law / Of either earth or heaven" (486). This is the state of mind that we associate with the Victorian poets, wandering between an old world of sac- erdotal values and supernatural supports and a new world of de- terministic forces and impersonal laws. When Keats goes on to describe the kind of vision that befell him as he sat on a knoll over- looking the ocean, we begin to sense an anxiety that is virtually Darwinian: "I saw / Too far into the sea, where every maw / The greater on the less feeds evermore.—/ But I saw too distinct into the core / Of an eternal fierce destruction, / . . . The Shark at savage prey—the hawk at pounce, / The gentle Robin, like a pard or ounce, / Ravening a worm . . ." (487).

The discrepancy between Keats's earlier poetry of naive wish fulfillment and his growing awareness of an "eternal fierce de- struction" at the heart of things is the subject of his next narrative poem, "Isabella or the Pot of Basil." The poem inspired two bril- liant paintings among that group of artists who in 1848, under the leadership of the poet and painter Dante Gabriel Rossetti, denomi- nated themselves "Pre-Raphaelites," by dint of their medieval sub- ject matter and conscious alienation from the ethos of modern industrialism. Keats is clearly a progenitor of this movement, and as "Isabella" shows, a poet who anticipated many of the themes and anxieties that were to preoccupy the next generation of poets. Composed in ottava rima and based on a story of Boccaccio's,

"Isabella" seems a pretty crude tale, indeed, something of a pot-boiler in its sensationalistic mix of the tender and the macabre, love and violence. But Isabella anticipates all those Victorian ladies from Tennyson's "Lady of Shalott" to Rossetti's "Blessed Damozel" who pine away in a self-enclosed world of unavailing fancies. She is, in short, an emblem of the poetic imagination consciously choosing illusion and self-deception in a universe where survival, as Keats wrote in one of his letters, requires "that a man should have the fine point of his soul taken off . . ." (*Letters*, 40).

This story is briefly thus: Isabella is the only daughter in a family of merchants who have consolidated their wealth through brutal exploitation and slave labor. (The economic context of the poem is itself a startling change from Keats's idyllic bowers.) The heroine's brothers discover a clandestine love between Isabella and Lorenzo, the family servant. Determined that their sister should marry a rich merchant, they murder Lorenzo in a wood. But his ghost appears to Isabella and she accordingly sets forth with her servingwoman to the site of the execution. They exhume the body and decapitate it. Isabella, driven to distraction, implants Lorenzo's head in a pot of basil that she assiduously waters with her tears. Her brothers, alarmed by her strange obsession, break open the vase, discover the grotesque evidence, and flee in fear of persecution. Isabella, bereft of her only comfort, devolves into madness and dies. Pretty silly stuff, one might think. But then Keats partly thinks so, too. Alternating between plangent lyricism and arch self-mockery, the poem explores the tensions between imagination and reality, and even anticipates—in the figure of the funerary urn—the subject matter of Keats's lyric masterpiece "Ode on a Grecian Urn."

The paradox of the poem is this: Isabella's endeavor to beautify death by preserving the head of her beloved in a vessel whose lovely surface belies its putrefying contents is emblematic of the Romantic poet who confronts the unpalatable truth of that "eternal fierce destruction" which feeds on our loftiest dreams and then ameliorates that truth by creating necessary but insubstantial fictions that make life more bearable. Keats, in short, is beginning to question the efficacy of the human imagination as an authentic source of spiritual understanding and is worried that such a faith may, after all, be a delusion that leads to the neurotic escapism of Isabella. In "Sleep and Poetry" Keats had written, "they shall be accounted poet kings / Who simply tell the most heart-easing things" (58). But the degree of edification to be derived from the "heart-easing" discourse of a poet is dependent on the honesty with which he or she confronts the truth of a sometimes horrible reality. If he buries his head in the sand or, for that matter, in a basil pot, he is liable to be dismissed as a mere speechifier and sentimentalist.[3] This is, however, the last poem that shows the indecisiveness and mawkishness of the early style; henceforth, Keats is, to use his own words, "committed to the extreme," that is to say, to an honest, forthright, and unflinching confrontation with "the agony / The strife of human hearts." If it is still possible to create beauty out of this, then such a beauty must be purged of all that is specious and delusional. Beginning with "Hyperion" and continuing with the odes, this terrible beauty is born.

"Hyperion" resurrects the pagan myth of a lost golden age in order to test how far, in the absence of consoling sacraments and ritual comforts, the modern poets may go in creating a coherent and edifying myth for his age. For the fall of the sun-god Hyperion is nothing less than the fall of the youthful Keats into an awareness of human misery, heartbreak, pain, and oppression. The poem endeavors to face this suffering headlong and test whether it is possible to derive beauty from that suffering without denying its unspeakable ravages or violating the demands of truth. This was not an academic question for Keats, for his work on the poem coincided with the decline and death of his younger brother Tom, whom Keats dutifully nursed throughout the composition of "Hyperion." "I wish I could say Tom was any better," he writes to a friend; "his identity presses upon me all day.... I am obliged to write, and plunge into abstract images and ease myself of his countenance, his voice, and feebleness.... if I think of fame of poetry it seems a crime to me, yet I must do so or suffer" (*Letters*, 153). Keats's personal conundrum translates in the poem into the moral agonies of the dispossessed sun-god, who in part represents the naive sensuousness of the poet's early verse. But a poetry of pure sensation is unable to survive a real assent in human suffering:

> O dreams of day and night!
> O monstrous forms! O effigies of pain!
> O spectres busy in a cold, cold gloom!

John Keats

O lank-eared Phantoms of black-weeded pools!
Why do I know ye? why have I seen ye? why
Is my eternal essence thus distraught
To see and to behold these horrors new?
Saturn is fallen, am I too to fall?
Am I to leave this haven of my rest,
This cradle of my glory, this soft clime,
This calm luxuriance of blissful light,
These crystalline pavilions, and pure fanes,
Of all my lucent empire? It is left
Deserted, void, nor any haunt of mine.
The blaze, the splendour, and the symmetry
I cannot see—but darkness, death and darkness.

(284)

This is a grand Miltonic passage; and indeed "Hyperion" derives its stylistic ambience from Milton's example. It is this that made Keats, in part, dissatisfied with the poem. It goes about too self-consciously on poetic stilts. But there was another reason why he finally abandoned it. The hope that abstract knowledge, embodied in the new sun-god, Apollo, might somehow compensate for the loss of an instinctive sacramentalism went too much against the poet's grain. For Hyperion's palace is a repository of ancient mythologies and religious wisdom, adorned with "hieroglyphics old / . . . Now lost, save what we find on remnants huge / Of stone, or marble swart, their import gone, / Their wisdom long since fled" (285). In short, Hyperion's crumbling demesnes are a storehouse of that mythopoeic consciousness which responds to and embodies in temporal images those authentic religious impulses that express humanity's sense of the sacred. Apollo, Hyperion's dispossessor, is born into a world of historical fact unredeemed by religious authority. His purpose is to create poetry out of this fact by putting it in the perspective of some intellectual scheme that renders it transparent to human understanding. But Apollo's transfiguration at the poem's conclusion seems gratuitous and unmerited, and the hope that the acquisition of knowledge would somehow ease the pain of human loss was essentially wishful thinking. This was not to be Keats's way. Moreover, Keats's dismay at the disagreeables of existence—or, more specifically, the premature death of his brother, Tom—was not to be so easily overcome. Keats's letter of 3 May 1818 to John Hamilton Reynolds indicates, however, the direction his genius would take:

I compare human life to a Mansion of Many Apartments, two of which I can only describe, the doors of the rest being shut upon me—The first we step into we call the infant or thoughtless chamber, in which we remain as long as we do not think—We remain there a long while and notwithstanding the doors of the second chamber remain wide open, showing a bright appearance, we care not to hasten to it; but are at length imperceptibly impelled by the awakening of the thinking principle within us—we no sooner get into the second chamber, which I shall call the chamber of maiden-thought, then we become intoxicated with the light and the atmosphere, we see nothing but pleasant wonders, and think of delaying there forever in delight: However, among the effects this breathing is father of is that tremendous one of sharpening one's vision into the heart and nature of Man—of convincing ones [sic] nerves that the World is full of misery and heartbreak, pain, sickness, and oppression—whereby this chamber of maiden thought becomes gradually darken'd and at the same time on all sides of it many doors are set open—but all dark—all leading to dark passages—We see not the balance of good and evil. We are in a mist. *We* are now in that state—We feel the "burden of the Mystery."

(*LETTERS*, 95)

With "The Eve of St. Agnes," written as an engagement present to Fanny Brawne, Keats abandons the pure cerebration of Apollo's response to the human dilemma, and takes us to the threshold of those "dark passages" described in the letter to Reynolds. This is Keats at his best—warm, human, richly expressive, ravishingly sensuous and yet disarmingly honest. It is hard to believe that the stanza in which the poem is composed—the Spenserian—is the same that Shelley used in *Adonais*. Shelley's lines are swift, translucent, coruscating, incorporeal; Keats's lines are weighty, measured, colorful, and solid. Set in a medieval world of romance, the poem would become another source of inspiration to the Pre-Raphaelite painters. Its plot is simple and straightforward with conscious borrowings from Shakespeare's *Romeo and Juliet*, though unlike the drama, Keats's ending is happy.

Playing with the medieval superstition that a young virgin on retiring after a day of fast will have dreams of her future spouse, Keats weaves an elaborate symbolic design that traces the steps whereby Porphyro, Madeleine's lover, enters his beloved's castle during a feast of more than ordinary vulgarity; evades the watchful and hostile eyes of Madeleine's dissipated kinsman; succeeds, with the help of Angela, an old servingwoman, to gain access to Madeleine's bedchamber; tricks his semiconscious paramour into believing that he is part of her dream; and then escapes with Madeleine to a secure castle "o'er the southern moors." The poem turns on what has become a familiar Keatsian theme, the relationship of romance to reality, fact to fancy, beauty to truth. Madeleine is at once an authentic witness to "the holiness of the heart's affections and the Truth of Imagination," and the potential victim of a threadbare illusion, for it is her unconditional belief in the tidings of St. Agnes that enables Porphyro to ravish her in her trance. When Madeleine awakes in a half-sleep and addresses her lover as if still in dream—"Oh leave me not in this eternal woe / For if thou diest, my Love, I know not where to go"—Porphyro takes advantage of her credulity and consummates his desires on his unsuspecting lover:

> Beyond a mortal man impassion'd far
> At these voluptuous accents, he arose,
> Ethereal, flush'd, and like a throbbing star
> Seen mid the sapphire heaven's deep repose;
> Into her dream he melted, as the rose
> Blendeth its odour with the violet,—
> Solution sweet.
>
> (252)

Keats is thus exploring the ways in which the imagination can leave one vulnerable to exploitation but also—as the poem's happy ending proves—enable one to reconstruct reality according to those fictions that give human life its splendor, beauty, nobility, and pathos. Twentieth-century critics have perhaps been too one-sided in their estimate of this poem, viewing Madeleine as a victim of wishful thinking or patriarchal aggression. Keats, however, seems to recognize that joy and happiness are possible only if we are willing to be open and vulnerable to experience—even if, by the same token, that openness exposes us to betrayal and deception. In any case, the poem is deliberately ambiguous and turns on the opposition of contrary images that counterpoint a harsh and threatening reality with a warm and believing humanism. Thus

Madeleine's warm bedchamber is surrounded by the crippling cold of St. Agnes Eve as the credulous aspiring youth of the lovers is opposed to both the austere and gloomy asceticism of the Beadsman and Angela, and the purblind, drunken sensuality of the bloated revelers. Images of warmth and cold, gold and silver, music and statutary, flesh and spirit are consciously contraposed throughout the poem as a means of highlighting these essential dichotomies. Moreover, Porphyro's progress through Madeleine's castle to his lady's bedchamber and then, accompanied by his lover, to the hostile world beyond is a virtual equivalent to the "Mansion of Many Apartments" that Keats described in his letter to Reynolds. The lovers escape, but the dark passages await them, and the poem stands like a frescoed sanctuary in which Keats takes a last deep breath before he too follows the lovers into the storm.

With the "Ode on Melancholy" and "La Belle Dame Sans Merci," Keats convinces his "nerves that the World is full of Misery and Heartbreak, Pain, Sickness, and Oppression" (Letters, 95). These masterpieces are complementary statements on a single theme, namely, the way in which suffering and illumination, joy and sorrow, loss and gain, are inseparably interwoven in human life. The "Ode on Melancholy" may be taken as Keats's credo, for it provides a criterion that enables us to grasp the significance of the other odes. And these odes, in their complex matching of cadence and content, form and feeling, inevitably recall the most compelling of Shakespeare's mature soliloquies. The "Ode on Melancholy" is not, as one might suspect from the title, an endorsement of doleful deliberations. To the contrary, it rejects the fashionably desolate reflections prevalent in eighteenth-century odes on country churchyards and moldering gravestones. In the first stanza all the traditional paraphernalia of melancholy are evoked only to be dismissed as ways of circumventing an awareness that the ode, as a whole, resolutely confronts, in a word, the tragic sense of life. To dull one's mind with drugs or dampen one's spirits with gloom is to be less than fully alive or complexly human.

For the paradox of the poem is this: in proportion as one renders oneself susceptible to joy, happiness, pleasure, and love, so, by the same stroke, one has also rendered oneself vulnerable to the inevitable loss and suffering that shadow these mortal delights. Keats does not argue that we should avoid commitments, withhold affection, or mortify our senses as a means of palliating this grief;

rather, he urges us to taste experience to the full, even though like
the honey of the flower that chemically evolves into the sting of the
bee, these experiences of delight and joy are destined ultimately to
stab us. The last stanza in which Melancholy, or the tragic sense of
life, is personified as a priestess inhabiting a sacred shrine, best describes this excruciating but unavoidable process:

> She dwells with Beauty—Beauty that must die;
>> And Joy, whose hand is ever at his lips
> Bidding adieu; and aching Pleasure nigh,
>> Turning to Poison while the bee-mouth sips:
> Ay, in the very temple of Delight
>> Veil'd Melancholy has her sovran shrine.
>>> Though seen of none save him whose strenuous tongue
> Can burst joy's grape against his palate fine . . .
>
> (275)

How quintessentially Keatsian that last gustatory image, for true
wisdom to Keats is not merely an act of abstract intellection but an
awareness that, like a bursting grape, suffuses the whole being and
penetrates the entire man. Keats's penchant for images of touch
and taste are, to be sure, part of this poet's hypersensuous temperament; but more, like the psalmist who urges us "to taste and
see," they denote an attitude toward life in which nothing in our
complex human makeup is withheld out of fear or suppressed out
of anxiety. To embrace those lovely things that time will take away
may lead to suffering, but as the liturgical imagery denotes, this
suffering is perhaps the most salutary way in which to achieve human authenticity.

If in the "Ode on Melancholy," Keats humbly accepts the contradictions of mortal joy, then "La Belle Dame Sans Merci," which re-
casts the same theme in ballad form, is more troubled and uneasy
in its embrace of the human dilemma. For the Knight in this ballad,
who is initiated by the enigmatic lady of the poem's title into the
organic relations of joy and sorrow, is unable to sustain that awareness without being cruelly afflicted and irretrievably traumatized.
"La Belle Dame" is another version of the priestess in the "Ode on
Melancholy," and the Knight's rite of passage leads him to a perception of the way in which love, despite moments of unalloyed
bliss, leads naturally and ineluctably to a perception of time and

history. On the simplest level, this may be construed as an awareness that sex has consequences, for the "Pale Kings and Princes"
who intrude on the paradisical "elfin grot" of the poem's bewitching "fairy child," bring to the fore a tragic awareness of what follows from her embrace—in brief, the whole complex entanglement
of human history in its insensate antagonisms and bruising cross-
purposes. By shortening the last line of the traditional ballad
stanza, Keats creates a metrical parallel to the Knight's rude awakening. The abruptness with which each stanza terminates drives
home the knight's disorientation and despair:

> And this is why I sojourn here
>   Alone and palely loitering.
> Though the sedge has wither'd from the lake,
>   And no birds sing—
>
> (443)

Keats continued to have misgivings about the wisdom of the
"Ode on Melancholy"—misgivings that carry over into the sequence of odes that followed in the spring of 1819. Like the Knight
of "La Belle Dame," he too is suspended between the fairy realm
of the wild-eyed enchantress (which may be construed as an emblem of Keats's earlier poetry of unself-conscious sensation) and
the "Pale Kings" and "warriors" (who represent, perhaps, the
tragic sense of human destiny that the poet could no longer keep
at bay).

By far the most famous of these lyrics of 1819 is the "Ode on a
Grecian Urn." Inspired by a visit to the British Museum to observe
the recent acquisition by Lord Elgin of the ancient marbles that formerly adorned the Parthenon at Athens, the "Ode on a Grecian
Urn" is a concentrated statement of aesthetic purpose that inquires
into the ultimate meaning and function of art in the economy of
human civilization. The first stanza essentially restates the classic
definition of poetry or art articulated first by Aristotle and later by
Sir Philip Sidney. The philosopher, according to both Sidney and
Aristotle, is concerned with the "bare rule," the abstract notion, the
general or universal Truth, with a capital *T* singular; in consequence, he is liable to circumvent altogether the concrete world of
living particulars. The historian is, conversely, so buried in a heap
of multitudinous details that he is prone to lose his sense of what is

enduring or universal in human experience. Only the "peerless poet," according to Sidney, simultaneously seizes the general in the particular, so that in Aristotle's words, "Poetry is a more philosophical and a higher thing than history." Hence, Keats's urn is a "foster-child of silence and slow time," blending together the general and the particular, myth and history, the transcendent and the immanent in a complex fusion of the timeless with the transient. While depicting on its painted surface the "mad pursuit" and "struggle to escape" of mortals locked into the dialectic of attraction and repulsion, desire and repletion, the urn nevertheless remains an "unravish'd bride of quietness" (260) attuned to a stillness and a silence beyond the frenetic whirl of human passion. As a "sylvan historian," it fuses a sense of eternity with a sense of time, combining "deities" and "mortals," gods and men in a complex dance that lifts earth to heaven and brings the divine down to the human.[4]

The first stanza is relatively straightforward and unproblematic, but in the second and third stanzas the speaker becomes obsessively enthralled by the perennial beauty of the images that adorn the urn. He wishes that he, too, could arrest the passage of time and enjoy just such an everlasting bliss as the young lovers, the youthful singer, and the ever-blooming trees tantalizingly suggest. Though destined to remain forever frozen in a gesture of unfulfilled desire, they at least will never experience the bitter aftermath of mortal joy. The reader realizes at this point that the poem's speaker is precisely endeavoring to forestall that tragic knowledge that "leaves a heart high-sorrowful" in the "Ode on Melancholy." But the phrase "high-sorrowful" compels us to reflect on those aspects of mature experience that the figures on the urn can never feel.

Accordingly, in the fourth stanza, a new scene appears on the urn's revolving surface—a scene of religious sacrifice, a "pious morn" of burnt offerings on behalf of those departed folk who can never return. (At this point we may conjecture that, like Isabella's basil pot, this is doubtless a funerary urn intended to hold the ashes of the dead.) Art is thus finally seen not as an escape from reality into an imaginary realm of immortal youth, but a response to that reality and a revelation of another, even higher reality. The world of mortal loss and suffering is thus transfigured and made bearable by dint of those myths and rituals—of which art is an expression—that aspire beyond the world of the senses and speak in "the spirit ditties of no tone."

By the last stanza, the speaker no longer wishes to join the figures on the urn to escape the human burden, for it is precisely by shouldering that burden that the imagination is activated and the holiness of the heart's affections issues in the creation of poetry, myth, and religious observance. The concluding avowal that "Beauty is Truth, Truth Beauty" does not mean that life is always and everywhere uplifting. To the contrary, it is by recognizing and facing the eternal fierce destruction suggested in the sacrifice of the fourth stanza that human energies are roused to their noblest efforts on behalf of suffering humanity. The capacity of art to palliate suffering lies in its revelation, as Keats observes in one of his letters, of some "electric fire in human nature tending to purify—so that among these human creatures there is continually some new birth of new heroism" (*Letters*, 229). Art is "a friend to man" insofar as it reveals this heroism, even in the face of loss and hardship and despite the inexorable wasting of human generations.

Keats's definition of art is largely derived from Shakespeare, especially *King Lear*—a play that mercilessly probes the baseness of human action and the tragedy of human life. But it is precisely in *King Lear*, as Keats wrote in one of his letters, that we discover that "the excellence of . . . Art is its intensity, capable of making all disagreeables evaporate, from their being in close relationship with Beauty and Truth" (*Letters*, 42). The "disagreeables" constitute the truth of what is base, ignoble, and gratuitously wounding in human experience; the "Beauty" is the heroic effort and self-sacrificing love that these experiences can draw forth. The transformation of Lear and Gloucester through suffering, the loyalty of Cordelia, the Fool, Kent, and Edgar, ultimately triumph in our imaginations over the evil circumstances that call their virtues forth; hence it is that the "momentous depth of speculation" excited by such heroism "buries the repulsiveness" (*Letters*, 42) of treachery and suffering surrounding it and leads us to a perception of those "unheard melodies" that bespeak the redeeming value of the human struggle and sweeten the asperity of mortal loss.

Despite the collocation of Beauty and Truth in the "Ode on a Grecian Urn," Keats had not fully overcome the temptation to leave the struggle behind and reject the concrete world of precious but perishable relationships. If the static world of sculpture or painting is the principal art that controls the meditations in "Ode on a Grecian Urn," then music with its bittersweet oscillations from major to minor, its yearning for the tonic resolution of chromatic dissonances, becomes the principal focus of "Ode to a Nightingale." This is one of the richest and most densely layered poems in the English language, and perhaps as near to perfection as any mortal utterance can come. From the vertiginous plunge of its opening lines to its wistful, ambivalent conclusion, it is the purest example of poetic wizardry in the Romantic age. The poem commences after an experience so excruciatingly rich in its felicity that the poet is plunged by sheer contrast into a state that borders on insensibility:

> My heart aches, and a drowsy numbness pains
>   My sense, as though of hemlock I had drunk,
> Or emptied some dull opiate to the drains
>   One minute past and Lethe-wards had sunk.
>   (257)

The downward fall of the opening dactyl, the cluster of low vowels and nasal consonants that verbally reproduce the feel of swollen tissues, the solemn roll of the stately iambics, all contribute to the poem's remarkable effect.

But what is it that has precipitated this state of radical loss and mourning? As in the "Ode on Melancholy" it is not sorrow per se that makes us aware of the tragic sense of life, but happiness—and the richer, more complete, and transfiguring that happiness, the more poignant, irreparable, and lacerating the loss when it is withdrawn. For the speaker has been "too happy in thine happiness"—the happiness, that is to say, of a nightingale whose "full-throated" song seems, for a moment, to partake of or enunciate an unearthly beauty. In the next two stanzas the speaker endeavors to return to that experience, but the methods he proposes as a way of restoring that joy become, in essence, a betrayal of his former experience. For wine or drugs—which the speaker here considers as a way of modifying his grief—would be but an artificial paradise consciously self-induced rather than an unpremeditated moment of spontaneous insight. Indeed, by the third stanza, the speaker realizes the inefficacy of wine or drugs as a means of release and begins to soberly detail the mortal anxieties that the nightingale's song has paradoxically thrown into greater relief: "the weariness, the fever, and the fret / Here, where men sit and hear each other groan, / . . . Where youth grows pale, and spectre-thin, and dies" (258). The tacit allusion to Tom's death makes that last line especially poignant to students of Keats's life.

The poem thus far expresses the speaker's attempt to circumvent the awareness that is crucial to the "Ode on Melancholy," to find and arrest an unconditional joy beyond the world of growth and process, and to reject the burden of the human condition for the refuge of an ideal but possibly illusory bliss. As the fourth stanza indicates, the nightingale inhabits a realm of shadowless light while the speaker is pavilioned by the boughs of a dark beech grove where "there is no light / Save what from heaven is with the breezes blown / Through verdurous glooms and winding mossy ways." But humanity cannot subsist in a state of shadowless light, of pure and unconditional joy, and the desire to achieve such a state can easily devolve into a death wish: the ultimate means of escaping from the human dilemma. As the poet, in the fifth stanza, traces the fugitive song of the bird through the deepening shadows of the beech grove, he is inescapably reminded of the world of growth and process where the springtime whiteness of the hawthorn must yield to the rich experiential reds of the late season musk rose and "the murmurous haunt of flies on summer eves"— in short, to the imminent advent of decline and death.

So paralyzing is this suggestion that in the sixth stanza the poet construes death itself as a release from these contradictions and a possible avenue of approach to the ideal world disclosed in the nightingale's song. But the death wish is forestalled as the poet reflects that there is no explicit revelation which guarantees that death itself is anything more than nothingness and insensibility. The shock administered by that thought enables the speaker to step back from his dilemma and see his situation as paradigmatic of the human lot. As the seventh stanza would have it, humankind is ambiguously suspended between "hungry generations" that follow one another to the grave, and inklings of eternity—such as those portended in the nightingale's music—which leaven that awareness with compensating myths that open a "magic casement" on the human situation.

But the word "forlorn" echoes into the commencement of the last stanza as the nightingale's song subsides and the speaker finds himself alone facing the dilemmas that activated the preceding series of ruminations. Though nothing is finally resolved, the speaker has clearly come to accept the contradictions and ambiguities of existence that in the first stanza he could not confront without the need to escape. As the song fades, the speaker asks, "Was it a vision, or a waking dream? / Fled is that music:—Do I wake or sleep?" (260). Unable to ascertain the respective degrees of wish fulfillment, self-delusion, or authentic revelation implicit in the nightingale's song, the poet ends in a state of wistful uncertainty, rapt in a spell that puzzles the will and eludes his understanding. In one of his letters, Keats describes himself as "straining at particles of light in the midst of a great darkness" (*Letters*, 230). And elsewhere he defines the only attitude appropriate to a being like man, who must remain, in the final analysis, ignorant of what things really are in their intrinsic essence. He called such an attitude "negative capability," and meant by this a capacity to subsist in uncertainty, doubt, and indeterminancy without "irritably reaching after fact and reason" (*Letters*, 43). The humility of such a stance is given its poetic expression in the concluding stanza of "Ode to a Nightingale."[5]

The odes were chiefly written in the spring of 1819, yet by late summer and autumn of that year, Keats returned to the themes that originally perplexed him in "Hyperion" and recast the poem as "The Fall of Hyperion," choosing Dante rather than Milton as his principal precursor and model. In "The Fall of Hyperion," the poet himself takes the place of Apollo, undergoing on his own pulses the process of transformation that the young sun-god had only partially realized. The poem begins with a Dantesque dream vision in which the poet stumbles upon a ravaged garden associated with all those prelapsarian groves that haunt the mythologies of Jerusalem and Athens. The poet comes upon the remains of an abandoned meal; perceiving "a cool vessel of transparent juice" (510), he drains its contents and is suddenly transported to an august temple that stands on the threshold of a desolate shore and faces west. The movement from east to west, dawn to dusk clearly adumbrates the stages of human life. As in a nightmare, the poet struggles up a series of enormous steps at the top of which appears the figure of a veiled goddess.

The goddess, who is a variant of the priestess who presides over the shrine of "Melancholy," accuses the poet of escapism and wishful thinking, thus rousing him to a defense of his vocation and an apology for his art. Repudiating all notions of poetry that fall short of the tragic wisdom that only the greatest poets have attained, "sure," the poet replies to his accuser who berates him for using his craft as a means of evading reality, "sure a poet is a sage; / A humanist, Physician to all men" (514). Having satisfied Moneta, the goddess of tragic wisdom, of his sincerity and having honorably exculpated his profession from the charge of both egoism and self-indulgence, he is granted a vision of reality that only a poet of the caliber of Dante or Shakespeare or Wordsworth is ultimately vouchsafed. As she withdraws her veil, the poet looks into her eyes and sees

> . . . a wan face,
> Not pin'd by human sorrows, but bright-blanch'd
> By an immortal sickness which kills not;
> It works a constant change, which happy death
> Can put no end to; deathwards progressing
> To no death was that visage; it had pass'd
> The lily and the snow; and beyond these
> I must not think now, though I saw that face.
>
> (516)

One need not be oppressively Freudian to connect this description with the specter of Keats's dying mother; the connection is obvious and simple, as it was doubtless to the poet, and reflects on nothing beyond itself. But Moneta's face also recalls the countenance of Shakespeare's Cordelia, who bears witness to human suffering even as she takes upon herself the redeeming function of scapegoat and suffering servant. The description of Moneta at once looks back to the agonized expression of Christ on the cross and forward to an existential apprehension of human misery unleavened by the counterpoising grace of God's sacrifice.[6]

It is, in short, an image of human suffering sustained without the remedial intervention of a divine mediator. This is a poet facing the demythologized wasteland of the modern age. Can beauty still be wrung from the truth of this comfortless perspective? As the poet's gaze penetrates Moneta's eyes, he perceives the vision of the fallen Titans adumbrated in the first "Hyperion"—a fall that is now nothing less than the loss of those sacramental and healing myths that formerly made human existence bearable. But just when Keats seems to strike an attitude that anticipates certain aspects of Victorian and even modern poetry—the kind of grim and disillusioned stoicism that we associate with Arnold or Hardy—he confesses that a world devoid of otherworldly comforts and reconciling myths is unamenable to poetic transformation, to the possibility, in other words of distilling beauty—even a tragic beauty—from the unredeemable suffering that is too often the truth. "Without stay or prop / But my own weak mortality, I bore / The load of this eternal quietude" (519). For Keats, this is the quietude of God's silence where to the imponderable questions raised by the gratuity of human torment "No God, no Demon of severe response, / Deigns to reply from Heaven or from Hell" (470). With an honesty and ingenuousness that are the hallmark of this poet, Keats confesses his inability to transform his perception of tragic loss into anything that even remotely approximates to the edifying, the beautiful, the poetic:

> Oftentimes I pray'd
> Intense, that Death would take me from the vale
> And all its burthens—Gasping with despair
> Of change, hour after hour I curs'd myself;
>
> (519)

For Keats, the ordeal of contemplating this brave new world of broken mythologies and spiritual bankruptcy was too paralyzing to sustain. Accordingly, like the first version of "Hyperion," the poem remains a splendid, suggestive fragment. But its fragmentary nature may also be attributed to the strides that, even in the last months of his life, this poet was continuing to make.

By September of 1819, Keats had given up on "The Fall of Hyperion"—not only because its message was so disheartening but also because he had grown beyond it. His final poetic utterance, "To Autumn," is a benediction of such warmth, radiance, and concentrated wisdom that it seems impossible the poet could have written it during some of the darkest hours he was to know. Yet such is the case. In spite of growing symptoms that his medical training could not fail to diagnose, money worries consequent on a generous loan to his impoverished brother and sister-in-law in America, nagging concerns as to how he would support himself and Fanny should his next volume fail, and mounting anxieties that his poetic efforts were fated to oblivion, Keats produced what is perhaps the most serene, self-assured, and deeply reverent ode in the English language.

One of the ways in which Keats endeavored to come to terms with a "world of pains and troubles" had been posited, or better, hypothesized in a letter to his brother and sister-in-law. Rejecting all notions of human perfectibility within temporal or mundane contexts as pipe dreams, Keats accepts suffering, loss, and death as the necessary concomitants of mortal life. Yet it is precisely such an acceptance that quickens the "spiritual yeast" in the souls of men to "battle with circumstance"—a battle that for Keats, eventuates in the creation of a self-conscious identity. We begin, Keats hypothesizes, as impersonal "sparks of God," abstract "intelligences" without the distinguishing attributes of individual existence. The world is thus a "Vale of Soul-Making," "a place where the heart must feel and suffer in a thousand diverse ways" so as to acquire the individuating stamp of human character. The way in which the individual responds to those myriad contingencies that "school an intelligence and make it a soul" determines the quality and character of that individual's life (*Letters*, 249–51). It is this process of soul creation that redeems or, at the least, renders bearable a world in which the heart may suffer and feel in a thousand diverse ways. Without adverting to this theory or, indeed, digressing, however briefly, from an arable landscape teeming with the earth's tangible fruits, Keats in the ode "To Autumn" subtly insinuates that the world is indeed a "Vale of Soul-Making" in which, to use Shakespeare's arresting phrase from *King Lear*, "ripeness is all."

In the most recent book-length study of the odes, Helen Vendler observes that "until the 'Ode to Autumn' Keats perpetually sheltered himself in bowers or sanctuaries. The supersession of flowers by fruit and the resolve to enter into the open fields of the reaped furrow thus become heroic compositional choices—a recognition of inescapable sacrificial process as part of life and a generous adoption of the whole world—not a sequestered portion of it—as the territory of growth and art."[7]

Unlike the earlier odes where the poet is cut off from an imagined or artificial ideal of fadeless beauty, "To Autumn" has its roots in a dimension that precedes the sundering of being into subjects and objects. In short, the ode "To Autumn" lays bare the underlying structure of being itself as the horizon within which created beings ripen into individual identities. The acceptance of this process gives the ode a remarkable air of serenity, detachment, *Gelassenheit*—to use here the virtually untranslatable German locution that suggests, at once, humility, patience, receptivity, openness, even ecstasy. It is a serenity that comes from a simple acquiescence in the transitoriness of all things mortal.

Keats's sense of natural fruition is nicely balanced between contrasting images of fulfillment and loss. The sheer abundance of the season is carried in a series of tactile verbs that communicate impressions of weight and mass. Thus autumn is a force that "bend[s] with apples the moss'd cottage-trees," "Fill[s] all fruit with ripeness to the core," "Swell[s] the gourd, and plump[s] the hazel shells / With a sweet kernel," "Set[s] budding more, / And still more, later flowers for the bees," and "O'er-brim[s]" the "clammy cells" of "summer" (273).

But there is also loss. If autumn's "hook / Spares the next swath and all its twined flowers" (274), it also urges things toward a finality that ends in "mists"—the inevitable counterpart of "mellow fruitfulness." Autumn's consummation—its bringing of beings into ripeness—inescapably predicates the acceptance of time, change, and death. These contrasting aspects of the season are symmetrically balanced throughout the poem: the *"bloom"* of the clouds is colored by the "soft-*dying* day," while the "stubble plains" are touched by the sunset with a *"rosy* hue" (274). The suggestions of life distilled and sweetness extracted organically pass into a sense of valediction and farewell. The auditory images of the last stanza gradually attenuate as the "wailful choir" / of "gnats" and the "loud-bleat" of the "lambs" give way to the shrill concert of the "hedge-crickets," the high whistle of the "red breast," and the faint trills of the "gathering swallows" (274). Keats's ode takes us to the threshold of silence where, beyond these voices, there is peace.

In retrospect, Keats may be seen not only as the poet in whom the Romantic age reached its highest level of expressive power and spiritual insight, but also as a forerunner of the age that was to follow. If the rising arc of Romanticism ascends to the pinnacle of Keats's poetry, then the Victorians may legitimately be said to de-scend from that Olympian height. This is not intended as pejorative; it was literally impossible, after Darwin, Marx, and the so-called higher biblical criticism of the mid-nineteenth century, to wear the poetic mantle with the same commanding authority that makes the Romantics so exotic and in some ways so remote. For despite their occasional misgivings, the Romantic poets were largely sustained by the Renaissance belief that "man is the measure of all things"—a belief which would appear increasingly untenable in the wake of Darwin's evolutionary theories, Marx's dialectical materialism, and the deconstruction of sacred texts launched by the German biblical critics. But of all the Romantics, it was Keats who anticipated this change the most and whose example—both stylistic and thematic—seemed most pertinent to the next generation of poets. To slightly alter Walter E. Houghton's statement, "To look into [Keats's] mind is to see some primary sources of the [Victorian] mind."[8]

· SIX ·

The Victorian Ethos

The early deaths of Keats and Shelley, the decline of Coleridge's poetic powers, and the increasing rigidity of the aging Wordsworth created something of a vacuum in English poetry between 1824 and 1832—that is to say, between the death of Byron and the appearance of Tennyson's *Poems, Chiefly Lyrical*. In this atmosphere of change, transition, and uncertainty, a legion of minor poets did mount, shine, evaporate, and fall. Suspended between the dying splendors of a defunct Romanticism and the alienated vision of the Victorians, these poets, who included Thomas Beddoes, George Darley, John Clare, Thomas Hood, and Hartley Coleridge (son of the illustrious Samuel Taylor), lived under the shadow of their great Romantic predecessors and were destined to be eclipsed by their Victorian heirs. Their discipleship to the Romantics shows clearly through their verse. Thus John Clare, though a poet of considerable acuity in his observation of natural phenomena, remains a minor follower of Wordsworth, and Hood, though original in his comic and satirical poems, is on the whole a second-rate imitator of Keats. While the lingering fires of Romanticism smoulder in their verse with a certain pungency and poignancy, they are generally wanting in the confidence and self-command necessary to carry through a large poetic design, and conspicuously lacking in the energy required to sustain an extended "criticism of life," the quality that Matthew Arnold ascribes to the first rank of poets.

The fate of Hartley Coleridge, who as a child was the recipient of both his father's and Wordsworth's poetic benedictions, may be taken to typify the wayward lot of this lost generation of British poets. Even more abstracted and impractical than his father, Hartley was dismissed from Oxford for general dissipation and besottedness. Though kind and tenderhearted he was incapable of looking after himself—a duty that devolved upon his godfather, William Wordsworth, next to whom Hartley lies buried in Grasmere cemetery. Much of Hartley's difficulty doubtless stemmed from his sense of abandonment by a father whose undisciplined will and philosophic abstraction left him ill-equipped to sustain the responsibilities of parenthood. "Yet can I not but mourn because he died / That was my father, should have been my guide," writes the adult Hartley in a sonnet to the father whose paternal reveries in "Frost at Midnight" take on a peculiar irony when seen from the retrospect of the son's career. (For the elder poet's prophecy that his babe would "wander like a breeze" was fulfilled in a manner Samuel Taylor Coleridge would live to regret.) But with Hartley—and this is what makes him premonitory of the great Victorians who were to succeed him—the lament for his father's absence imperceptibly blends with the image of a deity whose word no longer resonates, whose rod no longer checks and reproves.

Perhaps no poem in the relatively arid interregnum between the last installment of *Don Juan* and the first major works of Tennyson and Browning better anticipates the peculiar spirit and ethos of the Victorian age than Hartley's "The Deserted Church: A prophecy, the fulfillment of which the writer never wishes to see." For in this poem Hartley anticipates one of the chief misfortunes perpetually lamented by the Victorian poets—the loss of a stable system of values and beliefs that could give meaning and purpose to the human enterprise. The Romantics were either hostile to or had largely done without the apparatus of organized religion. For them imaginative insight had replaced religious belief. But Coleridge and Wordsworth eventually recanted this early faith and turned, in their later years, toward a very specific manifestation of Christianity, namely, the Anglican Church. And indeed that church was destined for renewal in the 1830s through the theological and poetic efforts of John Keble, Isaac Williams, and John Henry Newman, the principal exponents of the Oxford Movement.

Opposed to the spirit of an age increasingly enthralled by an ascendant materialism, the Tractarians, as they were also called, endeavored to integrate the churchless sacramentalism of the Romantics into the continuity of Christian worship. This marriage of poetry and religion was defended by Newman in his essay on Aristotle's *Poetics*:

With Christians, a poetical view of things is a duty,—we are bid to colour all things with the hues of faith, to see a Divine meaning in every event,

and a superhuman tendency.... It may be added, that the virtues peculiarly Christian are especially poetical—meekness, gentleness, compassion, contentment, modesty, not to mention the devotional virtues;
whereas the ruder and more ordinary feelings are the instruments of
rhetoric more justly than poetry—anger, indignation, emulation, martial
spirit and love of independence.[1]

Newman's attempt to restore poetry to its ancient privilege in the
church was not, however, universally accepted. As the century
waned, religion, demythologized and attacked, was increasingly
relegated to a branch of ethics, while poetry began to arrogate to itself, as Arnold prophesied in his seminal essay "The Study of Poetry," the privileges and authority formerly bestowed on religion.
In "The Deserted Church" Hartley anticipates this process of cultural fragmentation and breakdown. Entering an abandoned
church long fallen into ruin, the poet describes the moldering remnants of this desecrated temple. A single bell, intermittently knell-
ing, signals the ruin of a faith that seems to have departed from the
modern age. It is a premonition of things to come. For the poetry of
the Victorians is primarily concerned, as J. R. Watson observes,
"with loss, the loss of loved ones, of loved places, of youth, of a belief in God."[2]

When the Victorian critic Walter Pater spoke of "that inexhaustible discontent, langour, and homesickness, the chords of
which ring all through our modern literature,"[3] he was referring
precisely to that sense of loss which Watson sees as endemic to the
age. The Victorians were certainly not the first to feel a sense of dis-
continuity with a more stable and reassuring past. The Reforma-
tion, for example, was rife with spiritual anxieties precipitated by
the breakup of Western Christendom. But the Victorians felt themselves and the values they cherished attacked on a number of intellectual fronts, which left them exhausted, dismayed, and anxious—and they were not altogether wrong in sensing that this attack was qualitatively distinct from anything that had happened
before. The attacks came from geologists, historians, philosophers,
theologians, political theorists, and biologists who, despite the het-
erogeneity of their disciplines, were more or less homogeneous in
the positivism of their convictions.

Many of the most cherished assumptions about humanity's
place in the economy of the universe were called into question dur-

ing the Victorian period. The assault began on both the political and scientific fronts in 1832, when the passage of the Reform Bill by Parliament made it possible for dissenters from the Church of England to run for national election. This resulted in the suppression of five Irish bishoprics by fiat of secular authority. The question of whether the Anglican communion, whose fortunes had been tied since the time of Henry VIII to the vagaries of British government, had any independent claim as an apostolic body descending from Christ's original disciples was thus reopened in a particularly galling and uncomfortable way for its professing members. At the same time, Sir Charles Lyell's *Principles of Geology* exploded the biblical account of creation—an account further called into question by Darwin's theories of natural selection and Marx's theories of economic determinism. Marx was responding to the social ills of an empire that also preoccupied the minds of England's foremost belletrists and poets: Carlyle, Ruskin, Arnold, and William Morris (the Pre-Raphaelite poet who personally took care of Marx's daughter following her father's death). The dramatic rise in population, Britain's radical shift from an agrarian to an industrial economy, the untold number of impoverished, brutalized, and exploited workers who concentrated in the new manufacturing cities of the North Midlands and led lives of unspeakable squalor and deprivation—these were but a few of the changes that challenged the conscience of Victorian England.

In Germany, the rise of a new school of historical critics began to question the veracity of biblical texts. David Strauss's *Life of Christ,* translated into English by the Victorian novelist George Eliot, dismissed the miraculous claims of the Gospels as pious exaggerations without a shred of historical evidence. In consequence, people were forced to revaluate old beliefs, to doubt discredited traditions, to revise social policies, to change moral valuations.

The upshot of all this was that man was increasingly regarded as a naked ape—a mere compendium of mechanical, social, and biological parts whose destiny was limited by mortal contingencies and whose happiness was found in material well-being. The traditional domains of literary discourse and aspiration were derided or debunked as relics of the past with little or no relevance to the network of industrial civilization that was transforming the face of England and ushering in the age of modern capitalism. The one term that best describes the new intellectual climate is "utilitarian"—a philosophy of practical and unenchanted realism that values all things according to the tangible benefits they are able to produce. The father of this philosophy, James Mill, argued that poetry has no more value than push-pin—a popular nineteenth century parlor game—if push-pin is what gives people satisfaction. The revered Aristotelian idea that there are certain achievements—in art, philosophy, or literature—intrinsically worthy of our praise, and that the purpose of education is to train us to like those things we ought to like and to hold in subordinate esteem or downright contempt those objects or actions that violate an objective order of conduct or beauty, is thus completely repudiated by Mill. (Ironically, Mill's philosophy of self-complacent materialism was devastatingly refuted by his own son, John Stuart Mill, who rebelled against the soulless mechanism of his father's views and encapsulated that rebellion in one irresistible sentence: "It is better to be a dissatisfied Socrates than a satisfied pig.")

But it was James Mill whose views were ascendant in the Victorian age. A tendency to equate the quality of civilized life with the rise or fall in the gross national product, a belief in the steady and irreversible progress of the species, a grimly austere work ethic inimical to imaginative enthusiasms and poetic vagaries—all were pervasive characteristics of the age during which England became the undisputed world power. Not surprisingly, the majority of Victorian writers found it difficult to hold to Romantic claims of the oracular poet or to compete, in terms of cultural centrality and significance, with the new technical advances unleashed by the industrial revolution. The notorious Crystal Palace, erected in 1851 to celebrate England's sense of national importance, was in essence a temple devoted to the idolatrous worship of material wealth—what Carlyle termed the "Gospel of Mammon." The use of iron as a building material, the scarring of England by a vast network of railways, the invention of photography and the telegraph, the discovery of anesthetics and the establishment of public education—all were among the mixed bag of technical innovations and cultural changes that developed during the century on an unprecedented scale. Like the advancing rails of a lengthening train-line, the effect of all this was to leave the past and the accumulated wealth of its spiritual patrimony in an ever-receding distance.

Increasingly marginalized and diffident of their task, poets retreated, as did the early Tennyson and the Pre-Raphaelites, into a medieval dream-world, or combatively reaffirmed the primacy of the spirit—as did Browning in his monologues or Arnold in his prose. But the story is more complex than this, for the Victorians were themselves divided and contradictory. Though they worshipped Mammon—the deity of industrial capitalism—they still prized their poets. They enjoyed being lectured and hectored by those eloquent Jeremiahs who spoke in plangent tones of England's spiritual decline: Carlyle, Ruskin, Arnold, and Newman. And they celebrated their poets as no poets have been celebrated before or since. Tennyson, with the publication of *In Memoriam* (1850), became a national institution—a role deepened and extended by the *Idylls of the King* (1859–1885), among the most widely read and highly popular of Victorian poems. But the most popular Victorian poet of all—though little heard of today—was John Keble, one of the original founders of the Oxford Movement, whose lyrics of devotional accompaniment to *The Book of Common Prayer*, entitled *The Christian Year*, satisfied an appetite for consolation that became more acute as the sense of spiritual disinheritance grew throughout the century. Indeed, at the height of its popularity, *The Christian Year* was owned by one out of every sixty persons in Britain alone.[4] This would perhaps be roughly proportionate today to the percentage of Americans owning VCRs.

Yet the burden of *The Christian Year* is that man does not live by bread alone and that true fulfillment and joy are more readily to be found in self-denial and transcendence than in the instant gratification of the ego or the senses: "The trivial round, the common task, / Would furnish all we ought ask; / Room to deny ourselves; a road / To bring us daily nearer God." No one would claim that this is great poetry, but against Keble's religious sentiments, our own mass ethic of consumerism and self-indulgence surely demonstrates a decline in spiritual vision that should keep us from assuming supercilious airs toward Tractarian verse. Moreover, despite the growing skepticism of Britain's intelligentsia and the relentless demoralization of her working masses, the Victorian age produced two of the greatest devotional poets in the history of English literature—Christina Rossetti and Gerard Manley Hopkins. It was still possible in the middle and late nineteenth century for a poet to speak about original sin, the need for atonement, and the hope for redemption without being regarded as eccentric, obscurantist, priggish, stupid, or reactionary. Today, of course, the opposite is the case.

But neither Hopkins nor Rossetti nor Keble fully represent the anguish that the majority of Victorian poets felt in apprehending a universe devoid of divine assurances. For Arnold, Tennyson, and even the generally affirmative Browning, the objective and external world of faith had disappeared. If one examines the devotional verse of the seventeenth century, it becomes immediately apparent that the individual's struggle to conform to the tenets of the divine will occur in a universe where that will is preeminent and indisputable. When George Herbert in "Love" hesitates to enter the presence of God, his hesitation does not call into doubt the priority of that presence or that love. If he is estranged from God, it is a consequence of his own self-will reacting against a command that is prior to any act of individual apostasy: "Love bade me welcome: yet my soul drew back, / Guilty of dust and sin...."[5] Love here comes first and remains constant despite the "dust and sin" of the poet. He may draw back out of diffidence or shame or fear, but his withdrawal leaves the world of faith untroubled and intact.

In the Victorian age this situation is reversed; the objective and external world of faith is no more. In its place there is the iron and fatalistic necessity bequeathed to the poet by modern science, political theory, and cultural relativism. If the poet is to achieve faith, it must be done by first detaching himself from this world and finding in the depths of his own subjectivity that divine radiance and light which is no longer recognized by the makers of modern thought. The situation of George Herbert is thus entirely reversed, and hence the doubts, misgivings, and anxieties that bedevil Victorian professions of religious faith. One finds this even in the nonsense poetry of the period—especially in Lewis Carroll, who in *Alice in Wonderland* (1865) parodies the divine hymns of Isaac Watts by turning them into fables of Darwinian survival. Hence when Alice endeavors to reorient herself in the mad world of Wonderland by quoting a childhood hymn—

> How doth the little busy bee
> Improve each shining hour
> And gather honey all the day
> From every opening flower.

In works of labour or of skill
I would be busy too.
For Satan finds some mischief still
For idle hand to do

—it comes out all wrong. Instead of reestablishing the eternal verity of this catechistic nursery rhyme, Carroll transmogrifies Watt's hymn into a dark comment on a world where survival reduces to eating or being eaten:

How doth the little crocodile
   Improve his shining tail,
And pour the waters of the Nile
   On every golden scale.

How cheerfully he seems to grin,
   How neatly spreads his claws,
And welcomes little fishes in,
   With gently smiling jaws.[6]

Lewis Carroll was, of course, the pseudonym of Charles Dodgson, who, as professor of mathematics at Christ Church College, Oxford, was one of the hosts for the famous Oxford debate between Bishop Wilberforce and Thomas Huxley on the respective claims of evolution and creationism. That his own faith was disturbed by this issue is apparent again in *The Hunting of the Snark* (1876)—a mock quest poem in which a grotesque group of misfits whose names all begin with the letter *B* (as in "To be or not to be") search for an ultimate reality that turns out to be a mere chimera— or worse, the nothingness and death that are intrinsic to all things mortal. Thus the Baker, who has finally caught up with this amphibious beast who represents the whole of humankind's hopes and fears, discovers that his uncle's dying words regarding the quest for the absolute are true:

But oh, beamish nephew, beware of the day
   If your snark be a Boojum! For then
You will softly and suddenly vanish away,
   And never be met with again.[7]

Carroll's "Boojum"—a compendium of "Boo" and perhaps "Fe Fi
Fo Fum," not to mention "Boogeyman," has replaced the God of
Abraham, Isaac, and Jacob.

Yet, like most Victorians, Carroll was very much divided regarding matters of doubt and faith. The very Alice books that subvert
traditional notions of a divine reality nevertheless conclude with
"an Easter Greeting" to the children who delight in Alice's adventures:

The Easter sun will rise on you, dear child, feeling your life in every limb,
and eager to rush out into the fresh morning air—and many an Easter day
will come and go, before it finds you feeble and gray-headed, creeping
wearily out to bask once more in the sunlight—but it is good, even now, to
think sometimes of that great morning when the 'Sun of Righteousness
shall rise with healing in his wings.'(249)

The seditious adventures of Carroll's Alice are thus enshrined in a
parenthesis of piety—but it is a piety that works against the nightmare world of wonderland where a mad queen screams, "Off with
his head," and the predatory teeth of the Cheshire cat hover men-
acingly over its denizens. Carroll's inner divisions illustrate a
salient trait of Victorian poetry—what Arnold designates as "the
dialogue of the mind with itself"[8] and Tennyson dramatizes in an
interior monologue like "The Two Voices." This incessant debate
between the respective claims of doubt and faith is recurrent and
obsessive in Victorian poetry.

Not all poets, however, were as traumatized as Tennyson by the
so-called death of God. The notion of a universe arranged according to a structure of fixed hierarchies from greatest to least, from
the divine to the human, gave way to a belief in a naturalistic life-
force celebrated by poets like George Meredith and Algernon
Swinburne. With Swinburne, in especial, we behold a recrudes-
cence of pagan goddess-worship, since the goddess with her biological ties to the cycles of the moon, the waxing and waning of
the seasons, and the whole operation of Eros and Thanatos in
the realm of sexual reproduction, seems a fitting personification
of the life-force in a largely post-Christian age. Swinburne's sometimes bizarre and amoral celebration of the goddess has its counter
part today in certain quarters where the denigration of Judeo-
Christian principles is accompanied by a fashionable devotion to

Ashtoreth—though mention is never made of the child sacrifice central to this ancient Babylonian cult. Barbara G. Walker in *The Woman's Encyclopedia of Myths and Secrets* observes, "Astarte-Ashtoreth was transformed into a devil by Christian writers, who automatically assumed that any deity mentioned in the Bible other than Yahweh was one of the denizens of hell." Christine Downing also attacks the faith of ancient Israel for denigrating Ashtoreth. Worship of the goddess has thus sometimes become a form of anti-semitism. When Jeremiah in the old testament rails against Ashtoreth, he decries the child sacrifice which some Hebrews during the Babylonian captivity began to practice as well. Mass graves of children have been unearthed at the ancient shrines of Ashtoreth.[9] In any case, Swinburne deliberately set out to shock his contemporaries, for the Victorians could be inordinately squeamish when it came to the subject of sex—almost as squeamish as we are in acknowledging that triumverate of Platonic virtues, the True, the Good, and the Beautiful.

Historians are wont to explain this squeamishness by appealing to sociological categories. The rising middle class, which had made its wealth through the exploitation of the brutalized masses, found that hard work and industry could be sustained to greater material advantage if the distractions of eros were kept to a minimum. Moreover, the Victorian cult of chastity was a way through which the new monied classes could achieve a sense of self-respect on the basis of something more lofty than material prosperity. There may be some truth to this, but like all mechanical explanations of human motives, this truth is at best partial and one-sided. For there is in Victorian poetry that which can only be described in traditional terms as the tension between the way of affirmation and the way of negation: in other words, the everlasting tension between the sensuous beauty of created things and the supersensuous beauty of uncreated being. As it turns out, the Victorians were not entirely post-Christian after all. For the need to temper an awareness of material bounty with a recognition of its transcendent origins is a recurrent source of conflict in the poems of Hopkins, Browning, Christina Rossetti, and Tennyson. Moreover, such a conflict between the desires of the creature and the claims of the Creator has its roots in both Platonic and Christian traditions and cannot be dismissed as a mere manifestation of Victorian prudery. Our contemporary blindness to this conflict makes us far more anomalous than the Victorians who, after all, shared this concern with the principal poets and thinkers from classical antiquity to the Age of Reason.

Still, as Rollo May observes, "The Victorian person sought to have love without falling into sex; the modern person seeks to have sex without falling in love."[10] As a general desideratum, the first part of Rollo May's formula was, of course, impracticable and un-manageable even for the Victorians. At its worst, such an attitude created the hypocrisy that has resulted, by way of reaction, in the amoralism of our own age. This hypocrisy is evident in the fact that while the Victorians shed copious tears over "a fallen woman" such as Little Emily in Dickens's *David Copperfield,* the city of London provided support in the 1850s for over eight thousand prostitutes. One Victorian poet at least, Dante Gabriel Rossetti, saw through the double standard, recognizing, as Alicia Craig Faxton puts it, that "for every fallen woman there must be a fallen man."[11] In a dramatic monologue entitled "Jenny," Rossetti's speaker addresses his words to a prostitute whose services he had initially sought before realizing that such a coupling would violate his own vestigial sense of integrity: "Yet Jenny, looking long at you / The woman almost fades from view / A cipher of man's changeless sum / Of lust, past, present, and to come."[12] In his private life Rossetti was not always as exemplary as his speaker; but as his friend Hall Caine once observed, the plight of the streetwalker "often affected him to tears," and "it was not unusual for Rossetti to drop all the coins in his pocket into the lap of a woman begging or sleeping in the street."[13] Some critics suggest, moreover, that Rossetti recognized an affinity between the poet, who as Hamlet observes "must like a whore unpack his heart with words," and the prostitute, who similarly exploits human emotion for aesthetic or at least sensory effects.

Be that as it may, Rossetti's sister, Christina, presents us with a more salutary instance of the Victorian tendency to seek love without falling into sex. Christina Rossetti's *Monna Innominata* is a sequence of love poems inspired by the Dantesque conviction that "all that man vainly desires here below is perfectly realized in God. We have all those impossible desires within us as a mark of our destination, and they are good for us provided we no longer hope to fulfill them."[14] The thirteenth lyric in this most poignant and in-spired of Victorian sonnet sequences expresses this with exquisite tact and matchless grace:

> If I could trust mine own self with your fate,
>   Shall I not rather trust it in God's hand?
>   Without whose Will one lily doth not stand,
> Nor sparrow fall at his appointed date;
>   Who numbereth the innumerable sand,
> Who weighs the wind and water with a weight,
> To Whom the world is neither small nor great,
>   Whose knowledge foreknew every plan we planned.
> Searching my heart for all that touches you,
>   I find there only love and love's good will
> Helpless to help and impotent to do,
>   Of understanding dull, of sight most dim;
>   And therefore I commend you back to Him
> Whose love your love's capacity can fill.[15]

Betty S. Flowers would have us believe that a sonnet like the foregoing illustrates Christina's tendency to use religion as a way of achieving personal autonomy. By commending her beloved back to God, she effectually frees herself from having to be answer-able to a man. What these critics are saying, then, is that Christina's religion is only of value insofar as it enables the poet to pursue her avocations without being bothered by male importunities—since religion was one of the few activities that a Victorian woman could pursue without calling down the censure of her contemporaries. While there may be a degree of psychological insight in such a no-tion, this interpretation violates the integrity of Christina's faith and trivializes matters that for her were of ultimate concern. In treating Christina's religion—the very center and focus of her life—as a mere subterfuge for personal "empowerment," these crit-ics deny Christina's ability to understand her own motives or to choose her own course.

For it was not personal empowerment that Christina sought in the devotional life, but rather an awareness of realities that would enable her to transcend the nagging importunities of the self. Per-haps the most notorious interpretive distortion of Christina's po-etry is to be found in a critic whose genuine insights have been distorted by a strong ideological bias. Discussing "The Lowest

Place," Rossetti's lyric of religious self-abnegation in the presence of God's overwhelming otherness, Dolores Rosenblum in her essay, "Christina Rossetti and Poetic Sequence" pronounces Rossetti's sentiments as "notorious" from a "feminist perspective." But not to worry, however; for what Rossetti really and subversively desires in seeking the "lowest place" is to put herself above all her earthly brethren—especially men—since the "the lowest in heaven is infinitely higher than the highest place on earth." In short, Rossetti's lyric of self-effacing adoration becomes a strategic ploy for outwitting her masculine counterparts. Not only is this reading a misrepresentation of Christina's Christian muse, it is a disfigurement of this poet's genuine perception of human dependence on a divine being—a dependence that embraces both genders and has no truck with invidious, backbiting comparisons between the sexes. In their uncharitable construal of Christina's writings, this "feminist" reading distorts the poetry and misrepresents the poet. Indeed, such readings underscore the truth that great art provides a standard that judges the critic even as the critic assumes that he or she is judging the art.

But the mention of a poet like Christina Rossetti calls up another aspect of Victorian poetry that is largely unprecedented in literary history, namely, the growth of a poetry by and about women that is implicitly and legitimately feminist in its themes and situations. The novel, of course, had been the domain of women since the eighteenth century—a domain extended in the Victorian age by the illustrious achievements of George Eliot, the Brontë sisters, Elizabeth Gaskell, and Mrs. Humphrey Ward. But in the middle of the nineteenth century two women poets of major rank—Elizabeth Barrett Browning and Christina Rossetti—began to explore issues associated with the whole question of female creative identity in a patriarchal culture. Christina repudiated the title of feminist and adhered forcibly to the Christian tradition. But in a poem like "Goblin Market" she eloquently dramatizes the plight of the female artist who must risk her very selfhood by daring to enter a world of letters hitherto controlled by male assumptions and sensibilities. Similarly, Elizabeth Barrett, in her blank-verse novel of female emancipation and artistic growth, *Aurora Leigh* (1856), dramatizes the struggle of her heroine to achieve creative autonomy and personal integrity in a world controlled by sex-role stereotypes.

Yet both Christina Rossetti and Elizabeth Barrett seem to have anticipated, absorbed, and gone beyond much contemporary feminism. This is conspicuously apparent in their love poetry, which declares the need for and recognition of a male other as a complementary pole to their own being. To be sure, parity between the sexes is a crucial concern—but it is a parity that comes from either gender's cognizance of a divine life that unites both in a spirit of mutual subordination and trust. A modern feminist poet like Adrienne Rich tells us again and again in her poetry that she loves herself—which is, one may suppose, better than not loving anything. But Christina Rossetti and Elizabeth Barrett, as the *Monna Innominata* sequence and the *Sonnets from the Portuguese* make clear, ring all the beautiful changes of that love which is centered on devotion to another. The contemporary feminist's insistence on her own inviolable self-sufficiency would be construed by Christina as a conspicuous instance of "Pride"—a theological defect that has always characterized the male of the species and that is now fast becoming the salient attribute of much feminist literary criticism as well.

If, in the Victorian Age, the relations between the sexes were becoming ever more confused and confusing, it is nothing compared to the ubiquitous bewilderment brought on by the proliferation of knowledge, information, and detail detached from any comprehensive or commanding view of human nature or spiritual purpose. This phenomenon is technically reflected in the fact that Victorian poetry has a density of specific detail, often microscopically precise, which is so diverse and prodigal that it threatens to overwhelm the poet's sense of hierarchy, order, and coherence. What, for example, is all this grotesque flora doing in a love poem by Browning that purports to trace a good minute of mutual unreserve between a man and a woman?

> Oh the sense of the yellow mountain-flowers,
>   And thorny balls, each three in one,
> The chestnuts throw on our path in showers!
>   For the drop of the woodland fruit's begun,
> These early November hours,
>
> That crimson the creeper's leaf across
>   Like a splash of blood, intense, abrupt,
> O'er a shield else gold from rim to boss,

And lay it for show on the fairy-cupped
Elf-needled mat of moss,

By the rose-flesh mushrooms, undivulged
   Last evening—nay, in today's first dew
Yon sudden coral nipple bulged,
   Where a freaked fawn-coloured flaky crew
Of toadstools peep indulged.[16]

It is not only the toadstools that are "freaked" in this poem—so is the reader who cannot figure out what all these prolific forms of fecundating matter have to do with two lovers strolling down a woodland path.

The Victorian eye for detail is a subject Carol T. Christ has astutely explored in her seminal study *The Finer Optic*. According to Christ, the principal element that unifies the diverse achievement of the Victorians is a concern with the respective relations between the One and the many, the universal and the particular, the infinite and the finite. The heavy weight of detail in Victorian poetry fails, for Christ, to coalesce fully into a transparent image that reflects some underlying pattern or design, a providential order that binds the diverse phenomena of experience into a coherent whole. As Christ observes, "the Victorians lost the transcendental sense of nature that allowed the Romantics to perceive significance in the most minute grain of sand. They, therefore, came to perceive nature as a collection of disparate particular forms with nothing to offer but the experience of their own sensations."[17] Shelley's "Skylark" is thus no longer perceived by Thomas Hardy as a conduit through which a divine reality overflows into the world, but a ball of dust circling with other balls of dust in a universe without aim or direction:

Somewhere afield there something lies
In Earth's oblivious eyeless trust
That moved a poet to prophecies—
A pinch of unseen, unguarded dust:

The dust of the lark that Shelley heard,
And made immortal through times to be;—
Though it only lived like another bird,
And knew not its immortality.[18]

Hardy's disillusioned assessment of Shelley's poem is tempered, as is almost all Victorian verse, by an aching nostalgia for the lost enchantments that the age could no longer embrace. Thus, in a poem like "The Oxen," Hardy wishes to share the immemorial belief that on Christmas Eve, at the stroke of twelve, farmyard animals everywhere kneel in homage to the incarnate Savior. Though a gross superstition that the poet can no longer accept, he cannot forbear to cast a lingering glance backward at a time when such a belief could be piously entertained:

> So far a fancy few would weave
>   In these years! Yet, I feel,
> If someone said on Christmas Eve
>   'Come, see the oxen kneel
>
> In the lonely barton by younder coomb
>   Our childhood used to know,'
> I should go with him in the gloom,
>   Hoping it might be so.
>
> (468)

Hardy, here, is caught, in Arnold's famous phrase, "between two worlds, one dead, / The other powerless to be born" (302). Like Arnold, who found in the sacramental life of the monks of the Grand Chartreuse a communal ideal he both envied and rejected, Hardy too is unable to embrace a sacramental past or to give his assent to an impoverished present.

The same dilemma pervades Browning's poem "Saul," where the mental affliction of the Hebrew warrior expresses the damned vacillating state of the Victorian believer. As a committed Christian, however, Browning finds in the spiritual hymns of the young David an anodyne to Saul's perplexities. For as David contemplates the wreck of his former friend, he discovers in his own heart the desire to enter vicariously into the sufferings of Israel's stricken king. In a moment of visionary afflatus, this desire becomes a touchstone and an index of the heavenly nature that implanted it there:

> Do I find love so full in my nature, God's ultimate gift,
> That I doubt his own love can compete with it? Here,

the parts shift?
Here, the creature surpass the Creator,—the end,
what Began?
Would I fain in my impotent yearning do all
for this man,
And dare doubt he alone shall not help him,
who yet alone can?

(728)

Apart from Browning's brilliant recreations of human character in his innovative and daringly colloquial series of dramatic monologues, it was sentiments such as these that endeared him to the Victorian audience who found in his poetry an edifying alternative to their own disquietudes and fears.

But despite Browning's stiff upper lip and aspiring sentiments, the visionary gleam was on the wane in this age of post-Romantic limits, political conservatism, and domestic retreat. The first fine careless rapture of a Blake or Shelley—their epiphanic insights, holistic readings of human destiny, and transfiguring visions of a renovated universe—gave way to the slow and perhaps necessary declension of these visions to the exigencies and contradictions of workaday existence. Less strenuous in spiritual demand, more prudent in political possibility, and possibly more attuned to the actual limits of human nature, the Victorians lost the confidence that enabled the Romantics to judge the whole of human existence or experience a sense of oneness with the whole of reality. The increasing recalcitrance and complexity of the phenomenal world were no longer susceptible to imaginative synthesis or amenable to an all-embracing vision of reality. In consequence, the Victorian poets were obliged to diminish their expectations, accept human limits, and find some point of rapprochement with the quotidian world of common humanity. But this does not make their verse less interesting. Quite the contrary. It is the honesty with which they own up to the necessary disillusion that all individuals experience when they awake one day to the reality that the aspirations of youth need to be tempered by the limitations of maturity, which gives their verse its peculiar tension and appeal.

This transition has been memorably characterized by one critic as "the retrenchment of infinity."[19] Such a retrenchment is manifest in the efforts of Victorian poets to straddle that high literary fence between the unbounded hopes, expansive desires, and visionary schemes of the early Romantics and the tamed expectations, equable passions, and neo-Burkean politics of their literary progeny. In short, like the eighteenth-century British statesman, Edmund Burke, the Victorians believed that political action should sustain a sense of local identity, a feeling for continuity, a respect for community, and an awareness of practical possibility over any abstract or visionary scheme that might promote violent upheaval or cultural dislocation. One sees this especially in the novels of Trollope. Moreover, Carlyle's frequently cited exhortation to "Close thy Byron; open thy Goethe" is an instance of the new emphasis on the practical and sociocentric as opposed to the visionary and egocentric. Hence, one finds in much of the love poetry of the period, a reintegration of the Augustan emphasis on decorum, taste, and normative values into the highly colored world of romantic exoticism. Instead of Shelley's *Epipsychydion,* in which the lovers virtually explode in the insensate pursuit of eros, we have the cozy domesticity of Browning's "By the Fireside," the uxorious ditties of Coventry Patmore's *The Angel in the House,* or the cautionary wisdom of Arnold's guilt-ridden retelling of the legend of Tristran and Iseult. By the same token, one of the principal themes of Tennyson's *Idylls of the King* is the disruptive and chaotic role of passion in a civilized community that centers on the values of loyalty and marital commitment. Byronic restlessness is thus neutralized in the commonplace world of domestic arrangements and moral standards. The sublime yields to the scenic, revolution to retrenchment, romantic love to a benevolent matriarchy, the expansion of desire to the comforts of the hearth.

In the last two decades of the nineteenth century, however, these mini-paradises began to show their cracks. They are seen as precarious, at best, and thus give way, in the poets of the nineties, to a new disillusion more bitter and brooding than that of the post-Napoleonic period, precisely because by the end of the century the collapse of belief in any system of salvation, either personal or collective, became increasingly ubiquitous. This is especially apparent in the poets of the fin de siècle Rhymers Club, most of whose members died prematurely from burning the proverbial candle at both ends. The most representative poet of this circle, Ernest Dowson, described by his associates as a demoralized

Keats, struck the keynote of fin de siècle decadence in a poem like "Dregs":

> The fire is out, and spent the warmth thereof,
> (This is the end of every song man sings!)
> The golden wine is drunk, the dregs remain,
> Bitter as wormwood and as salt as pain;
> And health and hope have gone the way of love
> Into the drear oblivion of lost things.
> Ghosts go along with us until the end;
> This was a mistress, this, perhaps, a friend.
> With pale, indifferent eyes, we sit and wait
> For the dropt curtain and the closing gate:
> This is the end of all the songs man sings.[20]

When Dowson wrote that he was only thirty-two years old. He was dead a year later. Tennyson, whose poetic career was an endeavor to reunite the respective claims of morality and aesthetics in an indissoluble whole was scandalized by the sensuality, license, and cynicism of these younger poets:

> Authors—essayists, atheist, novelist, realist, rhymester,
>   play your part,
> Paint the moral shame of nature with the living hues of
>   art.
> Rip your brothers' vices open, strip your own foul passions
>   bare;
> Down with Reticence, down with Reverence—forward—
>   naked—let them stare.
>
> . . . .
>
> Set the maiden fancies wallowing in the troughs of Zolaism—
> Forward, forward, ay and backward, downward too
>   into the abysm.[21]

For the contemporary reader, Tennyson's lines could just as well apply to the 1990s as the 1890s. Many of these minor poets whom Tennyson excoriated were led, largely by the example of Newman, to the threshold of Catholicism. It must be noted, however, that the attraction of the faith was for many of these poets more aesthetic and ritualistic that it was spiritual or conversionary. As Chesterton observed not altogether fairly of Ruskin, they admired every part of the cathedral except the altar.[22]

Indeed, the last decade of the Victorian period brings to the fore a dichotomy that runs throughout the century; it is, moreover, a dichotomy unprecedented in the history of art and can be ascribed to the rise of a secular industrial state utterly unhaunted by the metaphysics of things. This dichotomy involves a fundamental rift between the artist and his audience, and a subsequent valorization of art as an autonomous entity answerable to nothing outside of itself. In his early verse, Tennyson had expressed this desire to retreat into a palace of art, a wholly artificial dream-world in defiance of the soulless mechanization of modern society. "The Lady of Shalott," one of Tennyson's most exquisite lyrics, precisely dramatizes such a resolution. But Tennyson was troubled by this tendency and endeavored, as did Browning and Arnold, to subordinate his sense of craft to the larger social, moral, and religious issues that art had formerly addressed in the past. This conflict between the poet's artistic conscience—which demands absolute fidelity to the requirements of his poetic vision—and what may be termed a "social" or "moral" conscience, which compels the poet to recognize that he is not an isolated and incommensurate being totally untouched by the society in which he lives and the readers for whom he writes, had never been as acute or disastrous as it was during this age of material expansion.

The reasons for this rift may be traced to the growing number of self-complacent "philistines," to use Matthew Arnolds' term, whose pursuit of economic advantage left them indifferent to the sense of beauty, ungraced by immortal longings, and contemptuous of the creative imagination. These attitudes were not only characteristic of the new captains of industry but also of the new educational bureaucrats. These hucksters of mass education wanted to abolish the classics of Western thought and literature. The idea of forming a student's character through the intensive study of both the Greek and Hebraic sources of Western civilization gave way to a practical and utilitarian concern with the vocational, the empirical, and the factual. Dickens is not completely exaggerating in *Hard Times* when an instructor at the McChockumchild school impresses his colleagues with the importance of "... Facts. Teach these boys and girls nothing but Facts. Facts alone are wanted in life. Plant nothing else, and root out everything else. You can only form the minds of reasoning animals upon Facts: nothing *else* will ever be of any service to them."[23]

The retreat of poets from this demoralizing situation is nowhere more apparent than in the group of writers and artists who centered around that polymath of creative genius, Dante Gabriel Rossetti, and christened themselves "Pre-Raphaelites." Inspired by the social and artistic theories of John Ruskin, the Pre-Raphaelites endeavored to transform Victorian culture from the perspective of a medieval ideal based on an organic notion of art's relationship to religion and society. Apart from being an art critic, Ruskin was the first great ecologist who saw in the industrial pollution of England's skies a symptom and a portent of divine disfavor. Humanity's repudiation of that divine stewardship with which it is entrusted, the increasing substitution of wealth for life, and the way in which the principle of competition and gain was fast replacing the principle of service and love were all symptomatic, for Ruskin, of a fundamental betrayal of life. The Pre-Raphaelite devotion to the art of the Middle Ages was inspired by Ruskin's example—especially that seminal essay "The Nature of Gothic," in which the medieval cathedral becomes an architectural expression of a communal order based on the highest values of service, love, and individual creativity—and an opposing emblem to the dark satanic mills that were ravaging and uprooting England's green and pleasant land. The Pre-Raphaelites initially hoped to restore to modern life and technical society some of the grace, style, enchantment, and hieratic dignity of pre-Renaissance Christendom.

But, in the last resort, the lofty ambitions of these artists could not square with their egalitarian and socialist sympathies. The result was that instead of transforming the lives of the laboring classes, their works and household crafts became exclusively affordable to the rich. Their prophetic and programmatic zeal soon devolved into a patina of painterly effects and extravagant illusions that hid rather than harrowed the hell of modern industrial society. This contradiction is especially evident in the life and works of William Morris, whose lyrics of poetic escapism into remote never lands of ancient mythology contrast forcibly with his intransigent Marxism and materialist ideology. The conflict was shrewdly and humorously noted by the young William Butler Yeats, who attended a gathering of socialists at Morris's house and marveled at the contrast between Rossetti's paintings of dreamy-eyed maidens in medieval garb that adorned the walls, and the gruff, inflammatory, and acrimonious politics that dominated the conversation.[24]

But if Morris tried to bring together political realism and far-flung poetics, both his escapist literary work and his medieval dream-visions reveal a stance of increasing hostility toward a populace that seemed to have lost both its spiritual roots and aesthetic sensibilities. In consequence, poetry became something of a cult—cherished for its own sake and cut adrift from its former moorings in the worlds of faith, patriotism, or morality. Needless to say, we moderns are the heirs of this anomalous situation. When Matthew Arnold wrote "Ah, two desires toss about / The poet's feverish blood / One drives him to the world without / And one to solitude" (309), he was describing what he elsewhere denominates as the "poetrylessness" of the age—a poetrylessness in part attributable to the individual's immersion in an anonymous collectivity or retreat into a sterile isolation. A sense of community based on the mutual adherence of its members to a reality both sacred and unconditional had largely disappeared. In the absence of shared mythologies, the poet was left with little to explore but the vagaries of his own emotional life or the wounds of his bewildered and restless spirit.

In their thematic concerns and aesthetic problems, the Victorians are in every way our immediate ancestors. Born into an age that seemed discontinuous with the inherited ethos of humanity's past, their poets speak to us in terms that are familiarly modern. And yet despite certain technical innovations, their verse continues to chime in the recognized but ever-renewable accents of English poetry from Spenser to Milton to Keats to Morris. They had not yet lost that indispensable sense of beauty without which poetry forfeits its claim to excellence and becomes nothing more—as we see too often at present—than the half-articulate self-communings or unintelligible fantasies of the verbally deaf and artistically inept. T. S. Eliot observed of Tennyson that "he lived in a world that was acutely time-conscious ... a great many things were happening, railways were being built, discoveries were being made, the face of the world was changing. It was a time busy in keeping up to date. It had for the most part, no hold on things, on permanent truths about Man and God and life and death."[25] In this world, according to Eliot, Tennyson—the representative Victorian poet par excellence—had "nothing to which to hold fast except his unique and unerring feeling for the sound of words." What Eliot said of Tennyson's age is perhaps even more pertinent to our own. But there is one difference. "The sound of words" for which the Victorian poets had so refined an ear has all but disappeared in our age—so that the one redeeming element that Eliot discerns in that period of spiritual lostness and confusion, for us no longer obtains. As we look back at the Victorians across the great divides of two world wars and a contemporary artistic and cultural scene in which every aberration of human behavior and every expression of shameless appetite are defended as "art," we cannot but feel the sobering accuracy of Simone Weil's searing observation: "We must certainly have committed crimes which have made us accursed, since we have lost all the poetry of the universe."[26]

· SEVEN ·

Tennyson and the Brownings

In his series of caricatures of the Victorian poets entitled *Rossetti and His Circle,* Max Beerbohm has a particularly telling spoof of Alfred Lord Tennyson. Posing for a portrait bust by the Pre-Raphaelite sculptor Thomas Woolner, Tennyson, with noble features and leonine head, sits in conscious self-command in the forefront of the cartoon. His wife, Emily, in the background approaches the hirsute, besmocked sculptor and timidly inquires, "You know, Mr. Woolner, I'm one of the most un-meddlesome of women; but—when (I'm only asking), when do you begin modelling his halo?"[1]

Unlike Keats, who was possessed of what one critic describes as a "seraphic humility," Tennyson took himself with the utmost seriousness. And so did the Victorian reading public, despite some early bad reviews of the 1832 volume *Poems Chiefly Lyrical.* Tennyson could be a humorless, petty, self-regarding man, dependent upon external praise to a degree that even his admirers found astonishing. His infamous quip to Benjamin Jowett, headmaster of Balliol College, Oxford, is a case in point. Sipping sherry and reading from his manuscripts in the don's sitting room, Tennyson, on being admonished by Jowett that his poems required much in the way of improvement, responded in high dudgeon: "If it comes to that, Master, the sherry you gave us at luncheon today was positively filthy."

But despite his social indiscretions and personal insecurities, Tennyson's creative achievement arises, like Dostoyevski's, from a "burning furnace of doubt" about the whole meaning and purpose of the human enterprise. The keynote of this poetry is disquietude. For like the Russian's novels, Tennyson's works are everywhere haunted by the fear of what Samuel Beckett describes as "the absolute absence of the Absolute."

The circumstances of the poet's life certainly contributed to this disquietude. Despite the idyllic surroundings of his Lincolnshire home, the poet and his family were in a state of perpetual anxiety regarding the unpredictable outbreaks of the father, George Tennyson, the local rector whose smouldering passions and resentments were fueled by bouts of alcoholic abuse. Having been dispossessed by the poet's grandfather—a man of great wealth who left the family patrimony to his younger son, Charles—George Tennyson was obliged to enter the church, a calling for which he felt little inclination. The poet's mother, though herself much afflicted, was a source of strength and consolation to her children. Yet George Tennyson, who died at the early age of fifty-two, was genuinely mourned by Alfred. Like his siblings, Tennyson was acutely susceptible to nervous conditions throughout his life—a residue, no doubt, from his anxious childhood.

But if the rectory was often a source of domestic torment, the venerable churchyard and the surrounding country with its rolling sandhills sloping down to the sea was the breeding ground of Tennyson's poetry. He is the landscape painter par excellence in English literature; and these landscapes—brooding, vaporous, mournful, and full of longing—invoke a state of mind that we think of as quintessentially Tennysonian:

> Tears, idle tears, I know not what they mean,
> Tears from the depth of some divine despair
> Rise in the heart and gather to the eyes,
> In looking on the happy Autumn-fields,
> And thinking of the days that are no more.
>
> Fresh as the first beam glittering on a sail,
> That brings our friends up from the underworld,
> Sad as the last which reddens over one
> That sinks with all we love below the verge
> So sad, so fresh, the days that are no more.
>
> Ah, sad and strange as in dark summer dawns
> The earliest pipe of half-awakened birds
> To dying ears, when unto dying eyes
> The casement slowly grows a glimmering square;
> So sad, so strange, the days that are no more.

Dear as remember'd kisses after death,
And sweet as those by hopeless fancy feign'd
On lips that are for others; deep as love,
Deep as first love, and wild with all regret;
O Death in Life, the days that are no more.

(134)

This lyric from the 1850 volume *The Princess* is Tennyson at his most characteristic. And like so many Victorian poems, it both evokes and distances itself from the preceding generation of Romantic poets. The celebration of orderly growth and ripeness that one finds, for instance, in Keats's "To Autumn" has here passed into an awareness that ripeness is not all, but rather, as one critic notes, "a passing moment in a cycle."[2] Far from affirming the poet's oneness with this cycle, "Tears, Idle Tears" explicitly emphasizes the speaker's estrangement from the fruit of those "happy autumn fields," which offer no anodyne to the poet's grief. Significantly, this poem, which was initially written in response to the death of Tennyson's closest friend, Arthur Hallam, is set in the vicinity of Cleveland Churchyard where Hallam was buried. The site is but a few miles from Tintern Abbey. And it is the proximity of that medieval ruin, which resonates so deeply in Wordsworth's "Lines" of 1798, that underscores the peculiarly Victorian state of mind that is Tennyson's.

For Wordsworth's ability to intuit "a sense sublime of something far more deeply interfused" that bridges the gap between the suffering mind and the restorative powers of nature is here replaced by a sense of utter alienation from a cosmos indifferent to human needs. "The happy Autumn Fields," which reach their completion in an annual cycle of ripeness and decay, offer no consolation to the speaker, whose consciousness hopelessly yearns toward a finite moment in an irretrievable past. The exquisite pathos of this situation derives from and is exacerbated by a remorseless quirk of human psychology: the fact, namely, that the mind is subject to involuntary fits of memory so intense that a moment from the past can suddenly overwhelm and drown out the present. Our surrounding circumstances and immediate situations thus appear less real and less alive than those bygone moments which we associate with security, happiness, or meaning. Yet for all that, they are gone, and except in memory or art will never come again. The result, as the speaker well knows in Tennyson's poem, is to leave one in a zone of timeless indeterminancy, a "death in life" in which the present is less substantial than a past that, for all its vividness, is extinct and irrevocable.

This is the poem's great paradox—a paradox reinforced by images that function as analogues to this painful double consciousness.[3] Thus the dying man who listens at dawn to the half-awakened birds is more alert and awake (like the days that are no more) as he strains to hear the last sound that he shall presumably ever hear, than the birds whose tentative pipings emerge from a heavy sleep. The deepness and wildness of the poet's regret is conditioned by his awareness that the past is and must remain out of reach, despite the disturbing alacrity with which it rises into consciousness and effaces the present moment.

In articulating these sentiments, Tennyson was both responding to and rebelling against the mercantile spirit of the age. The rebellion is apparent in the expression of a grief that is not amenable to technical solution. There is little utility in indulging sentiments that suggest areas of human want that are not responsive to economic expansion or a rise in the gross national product. But insofar as this want remained as a repressed dimension of the Victorian psyche, Tennyson had his partisans among readers who could not but question the efficacy of a civilization whose emphasis upon external machinery threatened to still or silence those immaterial longings that sophists, economists, and calculators deny at the risk of their own impoverishment.

Yet being a child of his age, Tennyson was divided against himself. This division is apparent in the dublety with which the poet contemplates the mawkish, self-regarding sorrows of the unrequited lover in "Locksley Hall." After much elaborate bemoaning of his rejection by the turncoat, "shallow-hearted" Amy, the speaker at length consoles himself with the thought that these are great times to be alive—and even greater times lie ahead, rife with the wonders of technical advance:

> For I dipt into the future, far as human eye could see,
> Saw the Vision of the worlds and all the wonder that would be;
>
> Saw the heavens fill with commerce, argosies of magic sails,
> Pilots of the purple twilight, dropping down with costly bales;

Heard the heavens fill with shouting, and their rain'd a ghastly dew
From the nations' airy navies grappling in the central blue;

Far along the world-wide whisper of the south-wind rushing warm,
With the standards of the peoples plunging thro' the thunderstorm,

Till the war-drum throbb'd no longer, and the battle-flags were furl'd
In the Parliament of Men, the Federation of the world.

(93)

In this ecstatic anticipation of Comte's "religion of humanity" there
is no time for tears, idle tears. For Tennyson, here, has captured the
image of a world imagined by the Victorian positivist, Auguste
Comte, in which humanity, having dispensed with the notion of
God, worships nothing higher than its own technical ingenuity and
social engineering. In "Locksley Hall" Tennyson gives memorable
expression to a common Victorian delusion: a belief in the inevitable march of human progress. "The great error of all the nineteenth century," writes Simone Weil, "was to believe that by
walking straight ahead one had mounted into the air." The fragility
of Tennyson's adherence to this belief is evident, however, in
"Locksley Hall Sixty Years Later," where the spectacle of material
progress inspires the poet with deep misgivings about its equation
with human progress.

Many of Tennyson's early poems reflect the divided sensibilities
of a poet who spoke in two voices about an expansionist empire
devoted to a measurable, computable, and quantifiable good. This
split is especially apparent in "Ulysses," a dramatic monologue in
magisterial blank verse that gives with one hand what it takes
away with the other. Tennyson's King—restless, yearning, unfulfilled, strangely driven—looks with disdain on the complacent,
humdrum existence of his people, his son, and his kingdom.
Goaded by an imperious pressure to find some magical and remote
region of wonders and knowledge and heroic struggle, he repudiates both the civic and domestic virtues in his longing for an intangible glory:

> Come my friends,
> 'Tis not too late to seek a newer world.
> Push off, and sitting well in order smite
> The sounding furrows; for my purpose holds
> To sail beyond the sunset, and the paths

Of all the western stars, until I die.
It may be that the gulfs will wash us down;
It may be we shall touch the Happy Isles,
And see the great Achilles, whom we knew.
Tho' much is taken, much abides; and tho'
We are not now that strength which in old days
Moved earth and heaven, that which we are, we are,—
One equal temper of heroic hearts,
Made weak by time and fate, but strong in will
To strive, to seek, to find, and not to yield.

(89)

These lines are at once an urgent summons to strive onward and upward, and an expression of escapism and irresponsibility. The sonorous series of infinitive phrases that concludes this grandly euphonious utterance can easily mask the fact that Ulysses is simply avoiding the daily tasks and workaday problems of civic administration and domestic routine. Tennyson has, paradoxically, given forcible expression to Victorian notions of struggle, toil, and progress even as he expresses his own regressive nostaliga for an age of lost myths and visionary gleams. When Ulysses cries, "Some work of noble note, may yet be done, / Not unbecoming men that strove with Gods" (89), he is expressing Tennyson's own sense of belatedness, of arriving on the literary scene immediately after an immense wave of creative energy has broken and withdrawn— though its clash echoes still in those heaven-storming lyrics of the great Romantics.

Tennyson's inability to sustain the faith of the Romantics in the imagination as an organ of spiritual perception is reflected in "Tithonus," a dramatic monologue that is something of a pendant to "Ulysses." The speaker in the poem is the mortal of Greek legend who fell in love with Eos, goddess of the dawn. Though vouchsafed the gift of eternal life, Tithonus discovers that his paramour has failed to grant the complementary gift of eternal youth; in consequence, Tithonus grows older and more wizened while Eos remains forever panting and forever young. The plangent opening lines with their long, low vowels, heavy nasal consonants, and steady, drumming iambics are a Tennysonian trademark. For in terms of sheer euphony and oratund eloquence, Tennyson is virtually matchless among English poets. Tithonus's longing to return to the mortal world of natural growth, decline, and death is con-

summately expressed in the mournful, plaintive music of these
moving lines:

> The woods decay, the woods decay and fall,
> The vapors weep their burthen to the ground,
> Man comes and tills the field and lies beneath
> And after many a summer dies the swan.
>
> (89)

Tithonus's exemption from this natural cycle is sharply underscored by the grammatical inversion of the fifth line where the
direct object pronoun, "Me" appearing unconventionally at the beginning of the sentence gives structural emphasis to the speaker's
sense of his own isolation: "Me only cruel immortality / Con-
sumes; I wither slowly in thine arms, / Here at the quiet limit of the
world" (89).

Tennyson transforms this classical myth into a parable on the
tension between life and art, reality and imagination. Like the previous generation of Romantic poets, Tithonus aspires to an ideal
and timeless beauty, suggested here in the fresh and changeless aspect of Eos, goddess of a perpetual dawn. But the poetry in which
these aspirations are enshrined in all their original fervor only
serves, like Eos herself, to mock the mortal poet who, unlike his art,
is subject to the wasting process of age and decline. The Romantics
were often able to resolve this dilemma by regarding their poetry
as a means of apprehending a fixed and changeless order beyond
the world of mortal limits. But for Tennyson such aspirations simply strand the poet on a reef of fruitless longing. The Victorians
could no longer be certain that art was indeed a conduit of a higher
reality; perhaps the poet nursing such claims was ultimately de-
priving himself of the only satisfactions that life affords, namely,
those which leaven the ordinary world of mortal accidents and natural laws. Tennyson's diffidence as a poet caught between the Romantic world of infinite desire and the Victorian world of rational
skepticism is poignantly suggested in Tithonus's indeterminate
state.

In his early poems Tennyson is often tempted to escape this
"damned vacillating state" in the bowers of a refined aestheticism in which art is used as a kind of drug to dull the remorseless
call of reality. "The Lotus Eaters," "The Palace of Art," and "The

Lady of Shalott" are all expressions of this poetic retreat. Yet these poems are more complex than this formula would suggest; for even here Tennyson worries over the probity of such a withdrawal and transforms the very impulse to escape into a cautionary tale of the dangers that attend the artist who breaks faith with his kind. "The Lady of Shalott" is the most suggestive of these poems. Tennyson's indebtedness to Keats is everywhere apparent in its sensuous coloring and medieval atmosphere. And insofar as Keats's poetry was also a seedbed of visual images for the Pre-Raphaelites, it is not at all surprising that painters such as Holman Hunt and John Waterhouse should have been equally drawn to "The Lady of Shalott" as subject matter for their most celebrated canvases. Tennyson's self-exiled lady, who perceives reality at second remove in the mirrored images of a room atop a Gothic tower, is an emblem of the poetic imagination reflecting, refining, and remolding the flux of mortal contingency into the permanence of crafted art. The lilies in her garden—symbols of beauty and purity—contrast forcibly with the fruit-laden barges that circle her island on their way to Camelot. The lady, in short, is an embodiment of the contemplative life. Moreover, her ancestry derives, in part, from Shelley's image of poetic inspiration in "To a Skylark," where

> ... a high-born maiden
>   In a palace tower,
> Soothing her love-laden
>   Soul in secret hour
>   With music sweet as love which overflows her bower
>   (597)

is one of a series of images representing the poet "hidden in the light of thought."

But Tennyson's maiden is tempted to forego her isolation when her mirror suddenly flashes with the bold, dazzling image of Sir Lancelot. The scintillating brilliance of the mail-clad knight is a superlative example of Tennyson's incomparable skill as a word-painter:

> The gemmy bridle glittered free,
> Like to some branch of stars we see
> Hung in the golden galaxy.

The bridle bells rang merrily
   As he rode down to Camelot;
And from his blazon'd baldric slung
A mighty silver bugle hung,
And as he rode his armor rung,
   Beside remote Shalott.

(28)

Like Wordsworth's daffodils, Lancelot's bridle is compared to a galaxy of distant stars. The image suggests the possibility that the real world, as manifest in the brilliance and energy of Lancelot, is not unredeemably hostile to poetic vision but, to the contrary, the very source of the artist's awareness of life as a grand system of spiritual correspondences. The "gemmy bridle" is thus a microcosm of the energy that moves the planets and the other stars and therefore poses no threat to the inspiration of the Lady. But when Tennyson's maiden endeavors to leave her island, and find inspiration in the real world of human enterprise, the mirror cracks and she is borne in a shallop to Camelot, where she expires on the threshold of Arthur's court. The unanswered question is whether her death is an indictment of a Camelot whose false glitter is inimical to the cultivation of authentic poetry, or whether her protracted withdrawal has destroyed her ability to face and transform into art the sometimes harrowing circumstances of a cold reality. The Lady's dilemma is an appropriate emblem of the Victorian artist in an age of commercial competition. Repulsed by its hollowness and yet attracted by its success, the poet becomes uncertain of his survival in a society dedicated to the gospel of mammon. Tennyson's ambiguity regarding the spirit of his age is reflected in the claustral confines of his early verse and his need to move beyond the self-reflexive syndrome of the modern artist. With *In Memoriam* Tennyson achieved the goal he so deeply cherished: to speak not only to a cadre of hypersensitive aesthetes but to an audience of the widest possible range regarding the ultimate questions and concerns of suffering humanity.

Begun shortly after the premature death of Arthur Hallam (Tennyson's closest friend at Cambridge and the betrothed of his sister, Emily), the poem eventually effloresced into a series of introspective lyrics marking the spiritual stations of Tennyson's grief over a period of fourteen years. It is, moreover, a compendium of Victorian concerns about personal survival, evolutionary theory, and the Christian faith. It is also, as T. S. Eliot astutely noted, "the concentrated diary of a man confessing himself."[4] The extent to which Tennyson was able to diagnose and even assuage the spiritual perplexities of the Victorian reading public is apparent in the widespread popularity accorded *In Memoriam* at its publication in 1850—a popularity sealed, at Prince Albert's instigation, by Tennyson's appointment as poet laureate following the death of Wordsworth. And when Albert died in 1861, *In Memoriam* became, after the Bible, a principal source of consolation to Queen Victoria.

Why did the poem achieve so universal an appeal? The reason may be partly traced to the skill with which Tennyson subsumes his troubled broodings within the consoling measures and pious conventions of the traditional hymn.[5] The use of repetitious phrasing, for example, in which the first line of four successive stanzas begins with the adjuration "Be near me . . .," adds a gloss of reassuring familiarity to reflections that are anything but consoling in themselves:

> Be near me when the sensuous frame
> Is rack'd with pangs that conquer trust;
> And Time, a maniac scattering dust,
> And Life, a Fury slinging Flame.
>
> (175)

These vivid depictions of physical decay and mental anguish are hardly the property of the traditional hymn. And despite the use of the octosyllabic quatrain, which is a common feature of the sung hymn, Tennyson has modified the rhyme scheme from *abab* to *abba*—a modification that verbally mirrors the action of a mind in debate with itself, turning in, around, and out, in a series of open-ended speculations.

Do the successive stanzas record a series of episodic and self-contained reflections, or is there a larger structure to the poem that comprehends the individual parts? Despite the discrete nature of the several lyrics, a larger pattern may be discerned as the poem extends over a period of three springs and three Christmases during which the poet is imperceptibly weaned from his sorrow and gradually restored to the vital forces of life and nature that surround him.

One of the arresting features of Tennyson's poem is the seemingly exhaustless versatility of the *In Memoriam* stanza. Plaintive lyricism, bitter lament, scientific disquisition, philosophic discursiveness, personal reminiscence, occult communings, haunting landscapes that function as correlatives of the poet's mind—these are but a portion of those currents and crosscurrents that give the poem its emotional weight and musical complexity. The length, depth, and value of the poem to the Victorian period requires a book-length study. The following brief observations can only suggest the range and depth of this indispensable elegy.

The initial stages of the poet's grief are akin to paralysis. The poet wonders whether the revered theological notion that suffering and loss somehow promote the growth of the spirit is anything more than a pious rationalization for ills that have no ultimate purpose. Shock and numbness are thus the principal burden of the poem's early sections. When Tennyson revisits Hallam's house, incredulous that his friend will not appear to greet him at the threshold, the poem moves from cold light to the deepest darkness with the realization that this absence is irretrievable:

> Dark House, by which once more I stand
>   Here in the long unlovely street,
>   Doors, where my heart was used to beat
> So quickly, waiting for a hand.
>
> A hand that can be clasp'd no more—
>   Behold me, for I cannot sleep,
>   And like a guilty thing I creep
> At earliest morning to the door.
>
> He is not here; but far away
>   The noise of life begins again,
>   And ghastly through the drizzling rain
> On the bald street breaks the blank day.
>   (165)

The allusion to Hamlet's ghost in "like a guilty thing" becomes all the more startling when we realize that the phrase applies to the poet and not the deceased. In *Hamlet* the ghost starts "like a guilty thing" at the commencement of dawn. But here the speaker is the "guilty thing," suggesting that the best portion of the poet's life has died with the deceased and that what now remains, like the ghost of Hamlet's father, is largely posthumous.[6] When one adds to this resonant allusion the breathtaking cluster of sighing sibilants, harsh plosives, and low, hollow vowels in the last stanza, one realizes that this is poetry of the highest technical order.

At length, the poet's dazed incredulity gives way to an internal debate on the issues of doubt and faith. Sections 31 through 34 are a concentrated extract of this debate. Adverting to the supposed resurrection of Lazarus, Tennyson wonders if Mary's simple un-tormented faith, as her gaze "Roves from the living brother's face / And rests upon the Life indeed" (171), can possibly speak to a Victorian believer whose trust, two thousand years after the fact, has been undermined by biblical scholars who have come to question the veracity of Christ's miracles. As belief in the process of natural selection threatens to displace confidence in the world as a divine creation, the universe the poet beholds becomes increasingly alien—a work of beauty, to be sure, but beauty without aim, direction, or conscience:

> This round of green, this orb of flame,
>   Fantastic beauty; such as lurks
>   In some wild poet, when he works
> Without a conscience or an aim.
>
> What then were God to such as I?
>   (171)

"What then were God?"—that is the question the poet in his fruitless interrogations of providence poses again and again. But there are some answers, or at least hypotheses, that the poem tentatively suggests or cautiously posits. Thus in the forty-fourth section, the poet meditates on the process whereby a self-conscious identity is gradually built up over a long, difficult period of personal growth. Why should this elaborate, complex process be enacted at all if the final product is destined to ultimate extinction? Surely, the poet conjectures, the world is a valley of soul-making, as Keats would have it, and, therefore,

> This use may lie in blood and breath
>   Which else were fruitless of their due,

> Had man to learn himself anew
> Beyond the second birth of death.
>   (174)

Notwithstanding this momentary resolution, the poet is again overcome with skepticism and disbelief. Thus, stanzas 56 and 57 enunciate the Darwinian theory of natural selection. Nature is indeed "red in tooth and claw," and like the dinosaurs whose fate is read in fossilized stone, the human race will itself undergo eventual petrification in a universe of death. If this, then, is the final truth, then human beings, in Tennyson's estimate, are the most anomalous of living creatures. Other animals, as far as we know, suffer no aspirations beyond the immediate circle of their appetites. Once these are sated they are perfectly content. But human beings, whose highest endowment is to cherish and propitiate a belief in justice, a sense of beauty, and a hope for eternal life, are nothing more than nature's laughingstocks—hopelessly maladjusted in a world where the non-ethic of crass survival mocks the loftiness of our illusions and the pathos of our creeds:

> . . a monster then, a dream,
> A discord. Dragons of the prime,
> That tare each other in the slime.
> Were mellow music match'd with him.
>
> O life as futile, then, as frail!
>   O for thy voice to soothe and bless!
>   What hope of answer, or redress?
> Behind the veil, behind the veil.
>   (176)

As that last line suggests, Tennyson's nagging questions will only be answered, if at all, in a state beyond death.

But *In Memoriam* does not exclusively record these internal debates. There are moments of pure lyric grace that provide periodic relief and at least temporary resolution of the poet's conflicts. Thus, in the second spring after Hallam's death, the poet is involuntarily touched by the beauty of the season:

> Sweet after showers, ambrosial air,
>   That rollest from the gorgeous gloom

> Of evening, over break and bloom
> And meadow, slowly breathing bare
>
> The round of space, and rapt below
>   Thro' all the dewy-tassel'd wood,
>   And shadowing down the hornéd flood
> In ripples, fan my brows and blow
>
> The fever from my cheek, and sigh
>   The full new life that feeds thy breath
>   Throughout my Frame, till Doubt and Death,
> Ill brethren, let the fancy fly
>
> From belt to belt of crimson seas
>   On leagues of odor streaming far,
>   To where in yonder orient star
> A hundred spirits whisper "Peace."
>
> (183–84)

Atmospheric word-painting has never reached a higher pitch in English poetry. The breezy open vowels, rolling liquids, and whispering sibilants form a bewitching mass of tangled sweetness in which the poet's response to the advent of spring finds its perfect counterpart in euphonius sound. If a madman, as G. K. Chesterton observes, is someone who has lost everything except his reason, then Tennyson, at his point, recovers everything through the discovery that reason by itself is incapable of proving the deepest intuitions of the human spirit. For it is this unexpected intrusion of beauty that suspends the futile racing of the poet's mind and opens his spirit to sources of renewal that logic, by itself, can neither grasp nor admit.

Despite the ephemeral nature of these privileged moments, Tennyson's recovery grows more assured and more sustained. In another episode of equivalent grace, Tennyson evokes a garden party at Somersby where several of Hallam's bereaved friends gather to remember their companion and share their loss. As Tennyson reads from some letters of the deceased, he is suddenly caught up in a sense of living communion with his departed friend:

> So word by word, and line by line,
>   The dead man touch'd me from the past,
>   And all at once it seem'd at last
> The living soul was flash'd on mine,

And mine in this was wound, and whirl'd
  About empyreal heights of thought,
  And came on that which is, and caught
The deep pulsations of the world . . .
                                    (186)

Though the poet's trance is presently "stricken thro' with doubt," it is on the strength of moments such as these that the faith of *In Memoriam* reposes.

The ending of the poem is consequently a bit of a shock—for it seems fundamentally incompatible with those moments of grace in which the poet's faith is kindled into incandescence by a love that endures beyond the limits of space and time. For in the last section, which is addressed to Tennyson's sister on the eve of her marriage to Edmund Lushington, the poet engages in a bit of philosophic sleight-of-hand. That is to say, he somehow contrives to smooth out the discrepancy between the biological myth of natural selection and the Christian hope of spiritual redemption. As the poet anticipates the birth of his sister's child, he is moved to reflect that Hallam was a premature example of the perfect human type into which the species is destined to evolve. Faith in the hereafter is thus replaced by faith in an evolutionary ameliorism, that "one, far-off, divine event / To which the whole creation moves" (198). Tennyson is thus unveiled as the quintessential child of his age—a poet who like many of his contemporaries confuses the issue of religious faith with belief in the inevitable progress of the human species. Chesterton, with his customary ability to pierce through the cant of philosophic fustian, summarizes the contradiction most tellingly: "When scientific evolution was announced, some feared it would encourage mere animality. It did worse: it encouraged mere spirituality. It taught men to think that so long as they were passing from the ape they were going to the angel. But you can pass from the ape and go to the Devil."[7]

But in despite of the egregious rationalization with which the poem concludes, *In Memoriam* as a whole is a profoundly moving record of the stages of bereavement, mourning, and renewal that are universal to human experience and a Victorian chronicle of the challenges to religious belief in an age of wavering and uncertain standards.

The poem that ratified Tennyson's fame following the publication of *In Memoriam* was *Idylls of the King*. Composed in orotund blank verse between 1856 and 1874, these jeweled frescoes of the Arthurian legends became a cultural touchstone of far-reaching significance to the Victorian age. One sees this not only in the poem's astonishing popularity but also in the number of Victorian artists who returned almost obsessively to these works for pictorial inspiration. The covering up of contemporary problems in medieval dress had, evidently, a universal appeal to an age that sought to hide its crass materialism behind the chain mail and flowing gowns of gothic romance. But Tennyson's poem is not purely escapist. Indeed, by the time Tennyson began to work on these legends in earnest he had come to recognize the truth of Chesterton's pronouncement: "You can come from the ape and go to the Devil." For Tennyson's Arthurian cycle is among other things a cultural diagnosis of those elements that can subvert a civilization and destroy its sense of purpose. The progressive deterioration of Camelot is symptomatic for Tennyson of the forces in modern England that imperiled Victoria's kingdom and threatened to unfix the foundations of Western Christendom.

The pessimism of the poem is, however, counterpoised by the aspiring heroism of Arthur's most exemplary knights. Tennyson's audience responded to their example in the same way that Shelley in *A Defence of Poetry* imagined the contemporaries of Homer responding to the heroic grandeur of Achilles, Hector, and Ulysses: "The sentiments of the auditors must have been refined and enlarged by a sympathy with such great and lovely impersonations, until from admiring they imitated, and from imitating they identified with the objects of their admiration."[8] In an age like our own, when the cynical process of downgrading and debunking has jettisoned the virtues of gratitude and admiration, Shelley's ideas about the value of heroic emulation fall on deaf ears. But this was not so to the really vast Victorian audience that enjoyed Tennyson's *Idylls*. Galahad, King Arthur, and Lancelot were authentic embodiments of courtesy, chivalry, heroic fortitude, and self-dedication that appealed to and transfigured the imaginations of Britain's youth. "Whatever may be felt about them now," Henry Newbolt, the Victorian barrister and novelist, wrote of Tennyson's tales, "these *Idylls* had an immense influence upon us as boys at the time. The contrasting knightly types, Galahad, Percivale, Lancelot, Bors, the sage Merlin, above all King Arthur himself, were very much to us. Side by side with Homer and Greek history, they gave us our standard."[9]

Despite the desultory nature of their composition, the *Idylls* as a whole display a coherent thematic pattern and sustain a consistent elevation of style. The opening dedication to the memory of Prince Albert reveals Tennyson's conscious awareness of the social message inherent in these ambitious poems. Albert is designated as a latter-day Arthur who exemplifies the virtues incarnate in Britain's legendary king—that is to say, a ruler "modest, kindly, all-accomplished, wise" who governs "with . . . sublime repression of himself" (303). Prince Albert expressed his admiration for the poem shortly before his death: "They quite rekindle the feeling with which the legends of King Arthur must have inspired the chivalry of old, whilst the graceful form in which they are presented blends those feelings with the softer tones of our present age."[10] Tennyson's softer tones were greeted with derision by less susceptible critics like Carlyle, who dismissed them as "lollipops." It is true that Tennyson's Arthur is more upright and virtuous in a storybook sense than earlier, more complex portrayals such as those of the fifteenth-century English romancer, Thomas Malory. But if Tennyson sometimes fails in bringing the king and his order to life, he invariably succeeds in bewitching us with all the magic intrinsical to the word "Camelot." In any case, the *Idylls* are one of the last examples in English poetry of a work that is uniformly inspired and completely accessible.

Tennyson's final arrangement of the *Idylls* highlights the central issue of civilization's decline that the poem explores. Not surprisingly, it provided both material and inspiration to T. S. Eliot in his own anatomy of cultural fragmentation, *The Wasteland* (1922). Both Tennyson and Eliot shared a common conviction that civilization was the by-product of a community that draws its sense of fellowship and solidarity from common adherence to a transcendent order. Deny, obfuscate, or abandon that order, and one by one all the dimensions of civilized activity—familial, social, aesthetic, economic, or martial—will suffer attrition, decline, confusion, and death. It is precisely this pattern of ineluctable decay that is born out by the *Idylls of the King*. In this regard, the arrangement of the *Idylls* illustrates a progressive contraction of narrative idiom, as the poem descends from a mythopoeic celebration of the founding of Arthur's kingdom to a level of increasing realism, both psychological and naturalistic, as the knights lose their original sense of purpose, deny the unconditional imperative behind their vows, and betray their commitment to an ideal order of conduct and beauty.

Thus "The Coming of Arthur," which initiates the cycle, describes the otherworldly origins of Camelot and the hieratic dignity of its proceedings. The king's birth is described by Merlin as a veritable theophany and the order of the Round Table as an act of providence:

> But when he spake and cheer'd his Table Round,
> With large, divine, and comfortable words,
> Beyond my tongue to tell thee—I beheld
> From eye to eye thro' all their Order flash
> A momentary likeness of the King:
> And ere it left their faces, thro' the cross
> And those around it and the Crucified,
> Down from our casement over Arthur, smote
> Flame-colour, vert and azure, in three rays,
> One falling upon each of three fair queens,
> Who stood in silence near his throne, the Friends
> Of Arthur, gazing on him, tall with bright
> Sweet faces, who will help him at his need.
>
> (307–308)

In this radiant altar piece, Arthur's legitimacy derives from the theological virtues of Faith, Hope, and Charity incarnate in the three Queens who gird his throne.

This primitive, mythical overture is immediately followed by a straightforward allegory that owes its inspiration to the medieval romance. "Gareth and Lynette" presents an aspiring young novice who, at his mother's request, undergoes a term of "kitchen vassalage" before he is assigned the first of his knightly quests. These quests involve freeing the imprisoned sister of the disdainful Lady Lynette, who regards the apparently lowborn Gareth with utter disdain. True to his chivalric pledge, he suffers her incivilities and dispatches with alacrity the three knights who hold Lynette's sister in thrall. Each of the knights represents a temptation indigenous to the three stages of human life: Youth (pleasure), Maturity (avarice), and Age (unrepentant insensibility). Having conquered all, Gareth last assays a knight who wears the image of a death's-head. After his defeat, this grim-visaged warrior turns out to be a child in forbidding armor. The allegory is simple and unambiguous. For the knight who successfully overcomes the temptations of a lifetime, death is not an unspeakable horror but the door to renewal and rebirth.

Beginning, however, with "The Marriage of Geraint" and ending with "The Passing of Arthur," the subsequent narratives become increasingly complex in the telling—a complexity that reflects the growing murkiness of the moral authority that animates the knights and the corrupting cross-purposes to which they cravenly yield. Thus Geraint's wrongful suspicion of his wife, Enid's, infidelity, almost destroys his marriage and precipitates his ruin. Were it not for the grace and loyalty of Enid, Geraint would have been destroyed by his own misguided passions. Enid's long-suffering fidelity may be commendable—and it does eventually prevail over the twisted hallucinations of her husband—but the distrust, self-doubt, and despair that bedevil Geraint's career in the wake of rumors regarding Guinevere's faithfulness to Arthur, is a premonition of worse things to come.

These worse things dominate the next *Idyll* in the series, "Balin and Balan." As their homophonic names underscore, these brothers are the divided halves of a single ego, torn by the contradictions of a world where the failings of Arthur's partisans travesty the imperial ideals of Camelot. This division manifests itself in the increasing dissociation of sexual appetite from personal responsibility and the concomitant emergence of an otherworldly asceticism of morbid and life-denying proportions. Each is seen to be a gross distortion of that harmonious equilibrium between the spirit and the senses which the King holds forth as a positive value. Of the two brothers, Balin is the one who suffers most from the conflict brought about by this polarization of human faculties. Vowing to defeat a monstrous apparition that guards the pass to King Pellam's castle, Balin's nerve is undermined by the discovery of Lancelot's illicit love for Guinevere. Though he penetrates King Pellam's castle—a realm of rarified religiosity of the kind that George Eliot contemptuously dismissed as "egoism turned heavenward"—Balin, in his progressive derangement, is at last destroyed by his own brother, whom he wrongly mistakes for King Pellam's brutal son. In this *Idyll* we hear for the first time of

Vivien—the enchantress who assumes a signal role in the undoing of Camelot. And it is the presence of Vivien that makes the next *Idyll,* "Merlin and Vivien," the most suggestive and complex.

Apart from her obvious role as femme fatale—an embodiment of all that is destructive and deliciously atavistic in the lure of the senses—Vivien represents on a more significant level what G. K. Chesterton describes as "the suicide of thought." Her purpose is to subvert the spiritual underpinnings of Camelot as personified in Merlin, the kingdom's prophetic sage and visionary. Merlin's lofty visions of moral excellence and mythopoeic beauty are deliberately undermined as Vivien preys upon the doubts and misgivings that attend any creative endeavor. For the uncertain glories and intangible benefits of Merlin's visionary faith, she offers the druglike fix of an instant gratification carried to an extreme of sensual refinement. If Camelot is the city that Merlin "built to music," then Vivien is "the little rift within the lute, / that by and by will make the music mute" (372). Vivien, in short, represents the rejection of what George A. Panichas describes as "a standard of excellence, moral and aesthetic," and the pursuit of "an excessive thrill in rendering man's diseased subjectivity." The idea of the holy is thus replaced by "blasphemies, profanations, and hedonisms" that paralyze the will and destroy the imagination.[11] Thus Merlin is imprisoned in a catatonic spell that signals the demise of Camelot. This is the "suicide of thought" that Chesterton describes as follows: "Human intellect is free to destroy itself. A set of thinkers can in some degree prevent further thinking by teaching the next generation that there is no validity in human thought. There is a thought which stops thought. That thought is the only thought which ought to be stopped. That is the ultimate end against which all religious authority was aimed. It only appears at the end of decadent ages like our own."[12] Clearly, the deconstruction of Merlin remains as relevant a warning to our age as it was to Tennyson's.

After "Merlin and Vivien," the curve dips steeply. The breakup of communal values and the disregard for first principles in "Lancelot and Elaine," "The Holy Grail," and "The Last Tournament" stun Arthur's knights into the equally invidious extremes of cultic fanaticism and sleazy sensationalism—both self-regarding in their respective obsessions and indifference to a sense of community. The revelation of Lancelot's affair with Guinevere is the beginning of the end of Arthur's court. Despite the cynicism, murder-ousness, and horror of these closing books, "The Passing of Arthur" bathes the *Idylls* as a whole in an elegiac mist of retrospec-tive pathos. As Sir Bedivere, the last remaining knight, bears the wounded Arthur "to a chapel nigh the field, / A broken chancel with a broken cross" (446), he is instructed by the dying king to re-turn the sword, Excalibur, to the Lady of the Lake. The entire scene with its "dark strait of barren land," flanked by the ocean on one side and "a great wide water" on the other, is perhaps the greatest instance of Tennyson's ability to create poetic settings that mirror the moods of his characters and echo the themes of his poems. This desolate seascape returns again in one of Tennyson's last poems, "Crossing the Bar," where the low moaning of the waves and the opposition of land and sea represent the point of intersection be-tween the temporal and eternal:

> Sunset and evening star
>   And one clear call for me
> And may be there be no moaning of the bar
>   When I put out to sea.
>
> But such a tide as moving seems asleep
>   Too full for sound or foam
> When that which turns from out the boundless deep
>   Turns again home.
>   (753)

So Arthur similarly returns to the great deep, borne by a barge into the distance where the three Queens of Faith, Hope, and Love conduct him to the threshold of eternity. In his valedictory words to Bedivere, Arthur muses on the fall of Camelot: "The old or-der changeth, yielding place to new, / And God fulfills himself in many ways, / Lest one good custom should corrupt the world" (449). Even the most august of creative achievements can betray its function as a conduit of the sacred and degenerate into a soulless self-reflection of human pride and skill. Thus Camelot must also pass so that paradoxically it may be born anew as an imperishable symbol of human aspiration toward a realm beyond the senses.

Tennyson's parting dedication, "To the Queen," is grave with warning and relates the decline of Camelot to the precarious state of Britain as a world power. Dismayed by the symptoms of spiri-

tual debasement and alarmed by the breakdown of traditional values, the poet concludes his exhortation with a summary of those
seditious forces that can sap the energy of the human spirit and
erode the confidence of a great culture:

> Take withal
> Thy poet's blessing, and his trust that Heaven
> Will blow the tempest in the distance back
> From thine and ours; for some are scared, who mark,
> Or wisely or unwisely, signs of storms,
> Waverings of every vane with every wind
> And wordy trucklings to the transient hour,
> And fierce or careless looseners of the faith,
> And softness breeding scorn of simple life,
> Or Cowardice, the child of lust for gold.
>
> (451)

The *Idylls of the King* is the capstone of Tennyson's poetic career
and the preeminent jewel in the crown of Victorian poetry. Its centrality not only to Tennyson's works but to the Victorian age
as a whole is summed up, both memorably and pertinaciously, in
the following passage from a study of the poem by George P.
Landow:

[The *Idylls of the King*] present what remain [Tennyson's] main concerns
throughout his poetic career: that both men and their societies must be
founded on Faith—or, more accurately, on many faiths, on faith between
ruler and ruled, man and woman, worshipper and God; and that such
faith, however essential, is necessarily a tenuous, subjective, non-rational
matter. *In Memoriam* appears optimistic because its overall movement
shows how one man, Tennyson, achieves faith after great trials, while the
Idylls of the King is most pessimistic because it dramatizes the destruction
of an ideal when men do not keep faith.[13]

Tennyson was perhaps the last poet in Western literary history
to enjoy the privilege of cultural pertinence and universal acclaim.
He was not only cited by the movers and shakers of imperial
power but venerated by the common reader and the English
schoolboy. The only other poet of the period who could possibly be
said to rival Tennyson for ownership of the prophetic mantle was
Robert Browning (1812–1889). As with Tennyson, Browning too

was destined to become a Victorian institution. But this election was less than salutary for his poetic output. The emergence of Browning Societies at the end of the century confirmed the poet in his worst habit: a tendency to preach in a kind of sanctimonious fustian to an audience that valued his ideas above his words. At his best, however, Browning was able to apply healing nostrums to human afflictions without violating the exigencies of his craft or flattening his poetry into philosophic paraphrase. Today, however, these nostrums tend among critics to be ignored or debunked.

It is presently fashionable to either denigrate or dismiss the philosophic preoccupations of this poet, and to concentrate instead upon his innovative techniques. The brilliant evocation of human personality, the rough-and-tumble of colloquial speech, those gruff and flinty verse rhythms that gave a new biting edge to the standard meters of English poetry—these are the elements of Browning's achievement that appeal most to contemporary critics. Moreover, Browning's awareness of the way in which our perceptions are conditioned and confined by the boundaries of our consciousness and the circumstances of our lives has a special appeal to postmodern critics who stress the relativistic and even solipsistic limits of human language and subjectivity. Despite the imbalance of this contemporary bias, Browning does, in fact, illustrate the peculiar dilemma of a Victorian poet who wished but was unable to follow his Romantic precursors—in Browning's case, most especially, Shelley—into regions of pure white light where the abiding verities repose, serene and absolute. In consequence, Browning's oracles are somewhat tongue-tied and diffident, hedged around with qualifications, projected onto dramatic personae, and therefore, limited by the wishful thinking or temperamental bias of the speaker.

Browning's first long poem, *Pauline* (1833), published when he was eighteen, is a Shelleyan excursion modeled on the example of *Alastor*. Stung by the asperity of a review by John Stuart Mill, who complained of the poet's morbid self-consciousness, Browning determined to write henceforth in a less personal or confessional vein. In any case, the attempt to emulate Shelley was misdirected, for as William Irvine notes, the Romantic poet's "intellectual atmosphere—that free heady ozone ... with its permanent sunset of Utopian vision—simply proved unbreathable."[14] Moreover, Browning was temperamentally a mingler. No reclusive visionary he: Browning loved the costume of history, the foibles of human personality, the racy catch of colloquial speech, the bustle and business of strong characters whose distinctive angles prick sharply against the world in an incessant war between human egotism and social restraint.

Hence, in a poem like "Up at a Villa, Down in the City," Browning's speaker expresses a characteristic preference for the color and swarm of the human ant-heap as opposed to the rustic delights of bucolic retreat:

All the year long at the villa, nothing to see though you linger,
Except yon cypress that points like death's lean lifted forefinger.
Some think fireflies pretty, when they mix i' the corn and mingle,

Or thrid the stinking hemp till the stalks of it seem a-tingle.
Late August or early September, the stunning cicala is shrill,
And the bees keep their tiresome whine round the resinous firs on the hill.
Enough of the seasons,—I spare you the months of the fever and chill.

Ere you open your eyes in the city, the blessed church-bells begin:
No sooner the bells leave off than the diligence rattles in:
You get the pick of the news, and it costs you never a pin.
By-and-by there's the travelling doctor gives pills, lets blood, draws teeth;

Or the Pulcinello-trumpet breaks up the market beneath.
At the post-office such a scene-picture—the new play piping hot!
And a notice how, only this morning, three liberal thieves were shot.
Above it, behold the Archbishop's most fatherly of rebukes,
And beneath, with his crown and his lion, some little new law of the
    Duke's.

(565–66)

And so the motley enumeration continues with an exhaustless relish for the hum and buzz of urban life. It is this aspect of Browning that Henry James expresses most tellingly in his witty observation on the poet and his peers: "Shelley . . . is a light and Swinburne, let us say, a sound; Browning alone of them all is a temperature."[15]

Given his delight in human bustle it is not surprising that Browning's interests should turn to the stage. But with the exception of *Pippa Passes* (1841)—an experimental closet-drama in which the naive songs of an exploited young heroine throw into relief the adult world of corruption—these attempts to follow the example of Elizabethan drama such as *Strafford* (1837), *The Return of the Druses*

(1843), and *A Blot in the 'Scutcheon* (1843), are generally regarded as but another example of nineteenth-century Shakespeareolatry, in which the superficial trademarks of the Bard are copied without a corresponding sense of theatrical tact. Browning's failures in this medium, however, were trial stages on the way to his true vocation as the principal exponent of the dramatic monologue—an idiom he developed to the height of its expressive capacity in his two most commanding volumes, *Men and Women* (1855) and *Dramatis Personae* (1864). "My interests," he wrote, "are in the incidents that go into the development of a soul." The stage with its external machinery and the exigencies of plot and action had been a hindrance to Browning's desire to create what Yeats calls "character isolated by a deed." The medium he needed was the dramatic monologue, which enabled him to explore the vagaries of individual character with the fine shading and nuance of a Renaissance portrait painter. Each monologue, addressed to a mute auditor, reveals the workings of an individual mind under the pressure of a dramatic event, a sudden confrontation, or an extended interview. The way in which the character is trapped into an involuntary confession, goaded to an act of self-betrayal, or lulled into a meandering maze of self-revelation is the distinctive feature of these poems. Browning's human types—deranged, grotesque, aspiring, equivocating, duplicitous, thwarted, obsessed, or heroic—are the most complex gallery of characters to be assembled in Victorian literature outside the novels of Dickens.

The monologues generally fall into three categories: those concerned almost exclusively with the complex, multiform levels of human character—what might be called psychology for psychology's sake; those that explore a moral or metaphysical dilemma in which the speaker's arguments with himself express an insoluble tangle of emotional ambiguities; and those in which the speaker himself is less important than the light his ruminations shed on matters of ultimate spiritual concern. These respective emphases often coalesce in any single poem, but there are some poems in which one of these elements clearly predominates over the others.

If technique is vision, and vision technique, then Browning's penchant for the monologue as a Victorian alternative to the Romantic lyric would suggest that the poet had become distressfully aware that critical assent to a pure rhapsodic utterance that transcends the ego of the speaker could no longer be sustained in an age so conscious of historical relativities. For Browning was very much aware that the Romantic fountains of unsullied lyricism had been muddied by the rock slides of contemporary thought. It would be wrong, however, to assume that Browning simply acquiesces in a kind of complacent skepticism or rejects the notion of an ideal toward which an individual may increasingly approximate. While an ultimate vision is not attainable on this side of paradise, Browning implicitly accepts the standards of Christian morality in his evaluation of human character even as he recognizes that the final word on the worth, the purity, or the value of any individual deed is necessarily limited to the partial perspectives of a finite being like man.

But this very uncertainty for Browning is the ground for growth, the indispensable stimulus that compels us to question our values, deepen our judgments, and transcend our present achievements for the sake of our future potential. Change is thus the principal law of human life. But change can mean either growth or corruption. For Browning, people are never stationary. They are either deepening, enhancing, and enriching their humanity through vital contact with one another and with God, or they are restricting, limiting, and arresting their development by retreating into a self-serving preoccupation with their own imagined importance. Moreover, the failures that attend human striving, the defects that diminish human work, the doubts that bedevil human faith, and the misunderstandings that plague human love are all unmistakable indications, for Browning, of an incompleteness in human affairs that he always construes in hopeful terms. That divine discontent which possesses all mortal achievements is a sign, for him, of man's supernatural destiny, of his being born to enjoy a felicity that no finite satisfaction can possibly sate. It is these considerations that compensate Browning's "Rabbi Ben Ezra" in his advancing years:

> For thence,—a paradox
> Which comforts while it mocks,—
> Shall life succeed in that it seems to fail:
> What I aspired to be
> And was not comforts me:
> A brute I might have been but would not sink i' the scale.
>
> (813)

Many of Browning's characters do, however, "sink i' the scale"—that is to say, glut themselves utterly with temporal luxuries as a way of escaping from the burden and glory of perpetually striving, failing, and humbly beginning again. Thus, in Browning's love poems, the speaker's level of enlightenment may be gauged by the grace with which he accepts the autonomy and self-determination of his beloved. Insofar as "Romantic" love deteriorates into a desire to possess one's partner, it becomes a grotesque caricature of itself. For couples, too, in Browning's universe, must perpetually grow in a dance of union and disunion if the relationship is not to petrify into the dead wood of complacency or subjection. Thus, in "Two in the Compagna," the speaker accepts the necessity of relinquishing a moment of supreme communion out of deference to his beloved's independence:

> I would I could adopt your will,
>   See with your eyes, and set my heart
> Beating by yours, and drink my fill
>   At your soul's springs—your part my part
> In life, for good and ill.
>
> No. I yearn upward, touch you close,
>   Then stand away. I kiss your cheek,
> Catch your soul's warmth,—I pluck the rose
>   And love it more than tongue can speak—
> Then the good minute goes.
>   (759)

Though yearning and wistful, Browning's speaker accepts the necessary tension between "Infinite passion, and the pain / Of finite hearts that yearn," as a dialectical element in any authentic expression of human love. When, however, Browning's characters demand a love that is perfect, final, unconditional, or absolute, it is a sure sign of potential derangement or abuse, as we see in "Porphyria's Lover" or "My Last Duchess." The latter poem is one of Browning's most accomplished creations—a concentrated monologue that distills the essence of the speaker's soul in a series of enjambed rhyming couplets of remarkable subtlety and suggestiveness. The duke's utterance is prompted by a desire to impress an emissary sent by an Italian count to determine the fitness of the duke as a potential husband for the count's daughter. What he reveals, however, under the pressure of imperious instincts, does not enhance his position. For the duke emerges as a patriarchal monster, a stunted monomaniac who has presumably destroyed his former wife in righteous indignation at her inability to place him first in all matters. The poem is full of marvelous psychological touches: the veiled portrait of the duchess, which only the duke can uncover as a sign of his posthumous control and possessiveness; the incriminating hints in the duke's words as he expatiates on the inability of any artist, however skilled, to reproduce the beauty of his wife's complexion: "Paint / Must never hope to reproduce the faint / Half-flush that dies along her throat . . ." (368); the way in which the warm, engaging, and lovable personality of the dead woman emerges between the lines of the duke's censorious memories; and the final self-entrapment of the duke when his hatred overwhelms his sense of prudence and discretion. Like the other objects in his collection—to whose beauty he is essentially dead—the duchess, too, was regarded by this unrepentant egotist as a mere extension of his power and authority.

The duke's distortion of both love and art is reflected, though on a somewhat less heinous level, in "The Bishop Orders His Tomb." Like the Bishop, many of Browning's characters are collectors or connoisseurs of beautiful objects. But Browning, who regards art as a medium of personal transformation and spiritual enlightenment, is acutely aware of the way in which a consumerist attitude toward aesthetic objects can betray or distort their essential purpose. Browning's bishop is a Renaissance worldling whose patronage of the arts precisely enacts such a betrayal. But it is not only art, it is also the church he has betrayed by using it to serve personal and selfish ends, while remaining blind to the values it enshrines. Nevertheless, one must not be entirely serious about the bishop. For, in many ways, this is a very funny poem; despite the old hypocrite's venality, he has some ameliorating virtues, not the least of which is an irrepressible gusto for life. Browning has marvelously captured the bundle of contradictions endemic not only to the bishop but to the Italian Renaissance as well. As the Victorian art critic John Ruskin observed of this poem: "I know of no other piece of modern English prose or poetry, in which there is so much told of the Renaissance spirit,—its worldliness, inconsistency, pride, hypocrisy, ignorance of itself, love of art, of luxury, and good Latin." Like the Pre-Raphaelites, Ruskin preferred the work of the

Middle Ages with its purity of intention and comparative lack of formal finish to the highly polished and anatomically correct productions of the Renaissance. Indeed, Ruskin's aesthetic philosophy is thoroughly compatible with Browning's poetry, as the following seminal excerpt from "The Nature of Gothic" underscores:

Imperfection is in some sort essential to all we know of life. It is the sign of life in a mortal body, that is to say, of a state of progress and change. Nothing that lives is, or can be, rigidly perfect; part of it is decaying, part nascent. The foxglove blossom,—a third part bud, a third part past, a third part in full bloom,—is a type of the life of this world. And in all things that live there are certain irregularities and deficiencies which are not only signs of life, but sources of beauty. No human face is exactly the same in its lines on each side, no leaf perfect in its lobes, no branch in its symmetry. All admit irregularity as they imply change; and to banish imperfection is to destroy perfection, to check exertion, to paralyze vitality. All things are literally better, lovelier, and more beloved for the imperfections which have been divinely appointed, that the law of human life may be Effort, and the law of human judgment, Mercy.[16]

Ruskin's defense of Gothic imperfection can be used as a yardstick to measure the shortcomings of Browning's bishop. Neither effort nor mercy are especially evident in this depraved ecclesiastic, though his love of sensuous beauty and his grudging acceptance of an undistinguished gritstone coffin endow him with a certain endearing honesty. For what the bishop wants, of course, is a sarcophagus of unprecedented splendor inwrought with an incongruous mixture of lecherous Pans and Christian saints; and it is this request that he tenders to his illicit sons as he lies, dying in state, in his own Church of St. Praxed. Realizing that his sons will squander their patrimony on selfish luxuries, he endeavors to bribe them with one last promise: when dead he shall intercede with St. Praxed herself—the virgin saint who preferred martyrdom to an illicit marriage—and win for his sons a healthy supply of mistresses with "great smoothe marbly limbs" (434). The preposterousness of this promise only underscores the bishop's inability to discern the application of those phrases he regularly mouths— "Vanity, saith the preacher, vanity!" (432)—to the demoralizing spectacle of his own life. Though deprived of the sepulcher he so earnestly covets, he is able to draw comfort from the thought that he at least deprived Gandolph, his arch ecclesiastic rival, of the mistress whom they both desired. Browning is very canny here about the way in which the machinery of a church can actually run counter to the values it purports to mediate. But despite his concupiscence, the bishop's garrulous good humor places him on a higher rung than the duke of "My Last Duchess" and infinitely higher than the hate-driven monk of "The Spanish Cloister," who so envies a monastic brother that his entire being is driven by a desire to see the fellow damned. Browning clearly understood that the temptations become greater as the professionally religious approaches the altar.

Two other Renaissance figures, "Fra Lippo Lippi" and "Andrea del Sarto," provide further examples of Ruskin's adage that "all things are literally better, lovelier, and more beloved for the imperfections which have been divinely appointed." Browning expressly contrasts two artists whose careers fall roughly at the beginning and end of the Renaissance in order to illustrate the interconnections between the growth and decline of an art, and the individual painter who is inescapably influenced by the spirit of his age. Thus, for all his imperfections and contradictions, Fra Lippo is an artist borne along by the early phase of cultural awakening that finds its counterpart in the painter's creative struggle with both himself and his art. Andrea del Sarto conversely reflects the exhaustion of the creative impulse in a period of polished mediocrity and moral self-complacence. These two monologues serve as pendants to one other, as their respective settings underscore. Fra Lippo holds forth on his life and art in the dawn of day and the spring of the year; Andrea ruminates in his studio at the end of an autumnal twilight.

Like Browning's bishop, Fra Lippo is torn between the antagonistic attractions of spirit and flesh, self-discipline and self-indulgence, Christianity and paganism, asceticism and dissipation. But he is conscious of the conflict and strives diligently to reconcile the warring parts of his divided nature. This translates into an art that dynamically reflects the moral crosscurrents and complex drives of wounded humanity. Browning's Andrea, however, has altogether ceased to struggle. His painting in its smooth but uninspired finish reflects the emptiness of a life that has lost its sense of purpose and value. The situation that has caused him to betray the nobler aspirations of Da Vinci, Michelangelo, Raphael—

There burns a truer light of God in them
In their vexed beating stuffed and stopped-up brain,
Heart, or whate'er else, than goes to prompt
This low-pulsed forthright craftsman's hand of mine . . .
(675)

—is his cringing attachment to Lucrezia, an unfaithful wife who exploits the uxoriousness of her husband by demanding that he accept commissions from her lovers according to their aesthetic requirements. Both Lucrezia's beauty and Andrea's painting are equally described as "perfect"—a telling Browningesque adjective for all that is icily regular and splendidly null. To support this woman in a style commensurate with her expectations, Andrea has stolen from the French king, allowed his parents to die in poverty, and betrayed the loftiest impulses of his own nature. It is thus singularly ironic that Andrea should articulate the line of Browning's that has attained the status of a proverb, and one that best distills the poet's overall philosophy: "Ah, but a man's reach should exceed his grasp, / Or what's a heaven for?" (675).

While love and art are central to the concerns of Browning's characters, there is a third area of consideration that equally commands this poet's attention: that quintessentially Victorian concern with matters of faith and doubt. The poems in this group are rather more uneven than some of Browning's other productions. The temptation that beset him in these poems was to ignore the complex shadings of human character and to turn his speaker into a mouthpiece for the airing of vapid pieties. At best, however, these monologues probe strenuously into the regions of religious conflict. The way in which the presence or absence of religious belief can enhance or diminish the characters of those who embrace its tenets or reject its conclusions is explored with uncommon delicacy and tact in poems like "An Epistle," "Cleon," "Caliban upon Setebos," and "Childe Roland to the Dark Tower Came" (though this latter poem is less of a monologue than a nightmare dream-sequence in which the topographical features of a blasted landscape translate into the harrowing doubts that beset an intrepid Knight-of-Faith).

Both "An Epistle" and "Cleon" express, as William Morris observed in a contemporary review for *The Oxford and Cambridge Magazine*, "the desires and doubts of men out of Christianity, in the days when Christianity was the true faith of a very few unknown men, not a mere decent form to all nations."[17] "An Epistle" is a letter from Karshish, an Arab physician on sabbatical to Jerusalem, to his mentor, Abib, regarding medical curiosities of interest in the region. Among these is the strange phenomenon of Lazarus, an apparently demented Hebrew who goes around in a state of seeming abstraction, indifferent to matters of life and death—such as the threat of a Roman scourge—and preoccupied instead with trivial irrelevancies such as the buzzing of flies or the "word, gesture, glance" of a child. Inquiring into his case, Karshish discovers that Lazarus suffers from the delusion of having died and been restored by a Hebrew "leech" or physician who was subsequently executed by Roman law. The interest of the monologue lies in the way in which the rational skepticism of Karshish imperceptibly yields to a burning fascination with Lazarus's account. Though inclined to dismiss the entire tale as a symptom of nervous disorder, he finds himself intrigued by the anomalous claim that the

> ... cured regards the curer, then,
> As—God forgive me! who but God himself,
> Creator and sustainer of the world,
> That came and dwelt in flesh on it awhile!
> (600)

Distrust and credulity war within Karshish as he relates these circumstances. But despite his fear of arousing the contempt of his sagacious correspondent, Karshish cannot forbear articulating the theological implications of this altogether unprecedented case history:

> The very God! think, Abib: dost thou think?
> So, the All-Great, were the all-loving too—
> So, through the thunder comes a human voice
> Saying, 'O heart I made, a heart beats here!
> 'Face, my hands fashioned, see it in myself!
> 'Thou hast no power nor mayst conceive of mine,
> 'But love I gave thee, with myself to love,
> 'And thou must love me who have died for thee!'
> The madman saith He said so: it is strange.
> (601–602)

If Karshish reveals a potential openness to those mysteries that lie beyond human ken, then his counterpart, the Greek Sophist, Cleon, expresses an attitude of mind that is at once enclosed, arrogant, puffed-up, stiff-necked, and, finally, self-contradictory. Like that of Karshish in "An Epistle," Cleon's condition unfolds by way of a letter. It is addressed to Protus, a Greek ruler during the age of the apostles. Protus has been Cleon's patron and student—for the Greek sage has distinguished himself as an artist, a thinker, and a poet. Both correspondents are aging, though Protus now envies Cleon his achievement as something of a stay to the inevitable dissolution that befalls all things human.

Cleon's response, however, is anything but consoling. The contrast between the enduring values of his cultural achievements and the progressive deterioration of his physical state only serves to embitter Cleon the more. As to the mention, by Proclus, of a Hebrew philosopher called Paulus, who is creating something of a stir in the ruler's kingdom, Cleon is convinced there is nothing of worth that could come from that quarter: "Thou canst not think a mere barbarian Jew / As Paulus proves to be, one circumcized, / Hath access to a secret shut from us?" (750). Cleon thus emerges as an ancient version of a Victorian phenomenon, the disabused intellectual who has grown increasingly sterile and self-regarding in a world where the so-called "Higher" biblical criticism has begun to deconstruct the foundations of religious belief. "Cleon," moreover, not only reflects the premise of the modern demythologist who assumes that all miraculous claims are bogus, it also alludes more specifically to Browning's contemporary, Matthew Arnold, whose verse drama *Empedocles on Aetna* similarly evokes a despairing Greek intellectual at the end of his spiritual tether.

Browning's preoccupation with love and faith achieves its richest and most complex fusion in *The Ring and the Book* (1869), perhaps the most demanding and formidable poem of the Victorian Age—a work that stretches the dramatic monologue to the limits of its expressive power. Not surprisingly, it had an enormous appeal for Henry James, whose essay "The Novel in *The Ring and the Book*" (1912) remains among the most pertinacious of commentaries on its structure and themes. Its affinity with the later novels of James is not only traceable to the convolution of its syntax. For, like James, Browning is concerned here with the psychological stratagems by which a character endeavors, either consciously or unconsciously, to avoid a disturbing revelation, to extenuate a base action, or to sidestep a crisis of self-knowledge. Furthermore, despite the apparent monumentality of *The Ring and the Book*, it is, if you will, the monumentality of miniaturism. For again, like James, Browning is fundamentally a micro-psychologist. The lengthy, patient, and considered circling about a small, pregnant center of human consciousness—examining its vagaries, weighing its responses, waiting upon its moments of self-disclosure or self-incrimination—is translated by Browning into a series of nervous, convoluted monologues that faithfully register the very pulse and pattern of the working mind. And, like an elaborate piece of musical counterpoint, each of these monologues represents one among a series of conflicting perspectives on a single unsavory subject: the question of whether or not one Guido Franceschini, a seventeenth-century Italian nobleman, should be found guilty of murdering his wife and in-laws.

Adapted from an actual murder case, Browning's story is told in the form of a trial in which the lawyers, the plaintiffs, the accused, the witnesses, and the judge—in this instance none other than Pope Innocent XII—each contributes his own perspective on the case. The circumstances of the trial are these: the thirteen-year-old Pompilia Comparini is forced by her parents into an arranged marriage with a covetous though impoverished count who subsequently mistreats his young bride on learning that her fortune is less than her parents had led him to suppose. To add insult to injury, he discovers that Pompilia is the illegitimate offspring of a prostitute adopted by the Comparinis and raised as their natural issue. Brutalized by her husband and in the last stages of pregnancy, she seeks help from Guiseppi Compansachi, a sympathetic priest, who helps her escape. Browning makes it clear that the average Italian assumes that the child is, in fact, the priest's and that Pompilia's temerity in leaving her husband threatens to dissolve the authority of those patriarchal institutions responsible for the stability of the social order. Not to be made a fool of, Guido hires some henchmen to murder his faithless wife and her parents. The parents are killed, but Pompilia survives long enough to depose evidence on her own behalf. Assuming that his defense of the patriarchal order will earn him an acquittal, Guido swaggers before the court but finds, to his astonishment, that he is condemned to death by the pope.

The multiplicity of issues raised by the drama is a recap of Browning's principal themes: the difficulty of judging clearly or accurately in an age of uncertain standards; the necessity of judging to stave off the onus of moral anarchy; the compromises of faith when faith is tied to the exigencies of a social order or a merely external institution; the distortion of love into a coercion made worse by the weight of social approval; and, above all, the necessity of establishing a balance of power between the sexes so that a woman like Pompilia could never again be subject to such unspeakable brutalization. In this regard, Browning's pope is remarkably iconoclastic, for in his condemnation of Guido, who among other things is a minor lay official of the church, he has deliberately placed himself on the side of a victim whose treatment had been, to some extent, excused by an institution too often tied to the conventions of patriarchy. *The Ring and the Book* is thus an important document in the history of feminism, for it implicitly asserts the importance of women's rights and self-determination as a vital constituent of any civilized culture.

Browning's feminism, as Ann P. Brady observes in a recent study, *Pompilia: A Feminist Reading of Robert Browning's* The Ring and the Book, is especially evident in the poet's sensitive portrayal of a young bride victimized by those patriarchal power-centers that flatter Franceschini in the belief that his wife's murder would not only be acceptable but exemplary to the majority of his male countrymen:

That a docile, passive, seventeen-year-old girl, married four years to a worldly aristocrat three times her age, would firmly resolve to run away from her husband; to make the decision in total isolation, without parental advice; to go directly contrary to counsel sought from the highest civil and ecclesiastical authority available, ... all this is a measure of Pompilia's courage, self-possession, self-direction.... It is a judgement against culture, going counter to a basic and deep rooted myth to which she will not assent: ... that a wife is a possession to be disposed of as a husband sees fit. She is instructed very bluntly in her marital duties not only by her husband, but by the archbishop and governor as well, and the youthful Pompilia rejects all their counsel.[18]

Browning's feminism is an unmistakable and recurrent element in his verse. But as the pope's lesson in consciousness-raising underscores, it is not indiscriminately drawn up against the whole of

Western culture. To the contrary, Browning's verse illustrates one of the salient attributes of Western society—its ability to change, grow, expand, and deepen the principles that give it identity. Thus, for Browning, the very justice that demands parity between the sexes is an extension and creative heightening of an incontestable moral law which requires that all human beings be treated not as a means to an end but as ends in themselves. This does not eventuate in a wholesale condemnation of the past, but rather in its fruitful extension and development into the present. Neither marriage nor the Christian promise are rendered invalid by this exercise; they are rather leavened by a more generous, comprehensive, and unbiased application of traditional morality. Such a leavening constitutes a real moral advance, for it grows organically and necessarily out of a principle without which the every idea of fairness would not exist. There is a difference, as C. S. Lewis remarks, between a "moral advance and a mere innovation." A mere innovation would deny the validity of the moral law and manufacture some wholly new ordinance without root in those living and, hence, growing values that speak to us of justice, temperance, love, or kindness.

Browning's feminist concerns have their counterpart, of course, in the equally tenacious manner with which the poet's wife, Elizabeth Barrett Browning, engaged these issues in her own prolific canon of poetic works. In her own lifetime (1806–1861), Elizabeth Barrett far outshone Robert Browning in both general popularity and critical esteem. Though posterity has correctly reversed this judgment, it is an historical truism that after Keble and Tennyson, Elizabeth Barrett was the most vaunted poet of her generation, outselling virtually every other poet of the age. Insofar as her writing, especially the enduring and remarkable verse novel *Aurora Leigh* (1857), were explicitly and programmatically feminist, the popularity of her poems says a lot about the receptivity of the Victorian public to the whole cluster of concerns associated with women's issues. John Ruskin, the foremost arbiter of Victorian taste, pronounced *Aurora Leigh* the "first perfect poetical experience of the age."[19]

Though fortunate in birth like her husband, Elizabeth Barrett was denied the parental support, the irrepressible health, and the ebullient spirits with which Robert was so abundantly blessed. Though her parents, Edward Moulton-Barrett and Mary Clarke, had inherited a substantial fortune, Elizabeth's childhood was shadowed by progressive ill health and the overbearing presence of a father of increasing megalomaniac disposition. This disposition became even more evident after the death of Elizabeth's mother in 1828–a death that exacerbated the constitutional nervousness that afflicted Elizabeth as early as 1821 when, under the care of a physician, she began to use opium and developed a lifelong addiction to this drug. Her health worsened following the death of her dearest brother in 1840, and she retired into what would become a valetudinarian existence in her father's home at Wimpole Street in London, where her communications with the outside world were largely confined to poetic missives. By 1844 her reputation had risen to such a pitch that an American editor of her poems appeared with an introduction by the most astute critic and accomplished poet yet to appear in the New World: Edgar Allan Poe. (It is notable that the singular stanza that Poe contrived for his celebrated and notorious poem, "The Raven," was in part modeled on Elizabeth Barrett's "Lady Geraldine's Courtship.")

Though a celebrated figure in the world of humane letters, Elizabeth led an increasingly cloistered life in the confines of Wimpole Street. From this living death she was redeemed—as she herself confessed in both letters and poems—by the unsubduable spirit of Robert Browning. Though Browning instigated Elizabeth's revaluation of her life and ultimately persuaded her to elope with him to Italy (where she enjoyed almost sixteen years of exceptional happiness), there was nothing clinging about this woman whose spirit, once restored, manifested itself in an outpouring of creative energy. Her *Sonnets from the Portuguese* (1845) were the first sonnets in the Petrarchan tradition in which a woman assumes the active role of extolling the virtues of her male paramour, while *Casa Guidi Windows* (1850) is the quintessential example of Elizabeth's passionate concern with the issues of freedom, democracy, and social justice. And in *Aurora Leigh* (1857), the feminist poem par excellance, Elizabeth proclaims both the importance of the visionary imagination in an age that weighed human progress exclusively in material and economic terms and also the need for women to break free of those stultifying male conventions and role models that have hitherto oppressed their native powers. With this poem, Elizabeth proclaims her right to enter the literary arena as a fully enfranchised exponent of the creative spirit.

Underlying all of Elizabeth's verse, however, is a profound commitment to the gospel of Christianity, a commitment apparent in her poems of social protest, such as "The Cry of the Children"—an unrelenting diatribe against the abusive, grinding wheels of a dehumanizing capitalist system—and in her assertions of sexual equality in the presence of a God who sees through the spurious authority of a male-centered culture. This is especially apparent in her sonnets to George Sand, the French woman novelist and sometime lover of Frederick Chopin, whose achievements shone forth like the serpent in the wilderness to the women of her generation.

As with Robert, however, Elizabeth's feminism is a creative extension and comprehensive application of principles derived from a belief in natural law—a belief which avers that each person, both male and female, is a free creative agent answerable to a higher power and, therefore, to be judged on the basis of character alone.

When it comes to the translation of these themes into her actual poetry however, Elizabeth was often carried away by her convictions to the point of artistic neglect. In this regard, her technical deficiencies are often conspicuous, and there are few of her poems that achieve a perfect balance between form and content. Even Poe, who venerated her "poetic inspiration" as "the highest," noted time and again her tendency to fall into "a mystical strain of ill-fitting and exaggerated allegory," and her habit of confusing "obscurity of expression with the expression of obscurity."[20]

Despite these shortcomings, poems like "The Cry of the Children," "A Musical Instrument," several of the *Sonnets from the Portuguese*, and much of *Aurora Leigh* are supreme examples of the way in which Elizabeth's concern with the inequities of the economic system, the peculiar burdens of the artist, the redeeming agency of love, and the self-determination of the female spirit are transformed into a poetry of exceptional strength and grace.

The *Sonnets from the Portuguese*, so named by Elizabeth out of a need to cover behind the mask of translation the extremely personal nature of these utterances, have enjoyed the widest popularity since their first appearance. Elizabeth's endeavor to overcome her longstanding isolation and respond to the love of Robert Browning expresses her conviction that short of the love of God, there is no higher or more ennobling experience than the mutual dedication of a man to a woman and a woman to a man. Like those other great sonnet sequences of the Victorian age, Dante Rossetti's *House of Life* and Christina Rossetti's *Monna Inominata*, Elizabeth's lyrics are informed by both Christian and Platonic principles. In his essay on *Romeo and Juliet*, Coleridge gives us the most compendious definition of these principles: "One infallible criterion in forming an opinion of a man is the reverence in which he holds women. Plato has said that in this way we rise from sensuality to affection, from affection to love, and from love to the pure intellectual delight, by which we become worthy to conceive the infinite in ourselves, without which it is impossible for a man to believe in a God. In a word, the grandest and most delightful of all promises has been expressed to us by this practical state—our marriage with the Redeemer of mankind" (651–52).

A disturbing essay by Sarah Paul entitled "Strategic Self-Centering and the Female Narrator," belabors the thesis that these sonnets mean exactly the opposite of what they say.[21] Love is really hate; gratitude, disdain; and humility, pride. The sonnets are described as "weapons in a struggle for power" in which "false modesty" functions as a "strategic" feint in order to subdue and overcome the enemy: in this case, Robert Browning. Beginning with a sweeping generalization that "neither Beatrice nor Laura nor any of the other heroines of sonnet tradition can be said to possess particular character or force beyond their beauty," and are thus deprived of "speech, intellect, feeling," the critic goes on to unearth those seditious undercurrents that fester beneath the surface of Elizabeth's sonnets.

Perhaps the first thing to observe is that this critic speaks of human love as if she were describing the clinical aberrations of an alien species that has not yet risen to the superior heights of ideological purity. If the first qualification of a critic, as Pope avers, is to "read each work of Wit / With the same spirit that its author writ" (70), then it is not surprising that this essay should begin on a false note and never recover the right key. The right key begins with an awareness that love is both a gift and a need. As C. S. Lewis observes, "Gift-Love" is akin to agape, that unconditional charity which reflects the love of God for his creation. In describing Robert's love for her in these terms, Elizabeth is drawing on precisely that Coleridgean formula which discerns the lower love of a man for a woman, or a woman for a man as mirror of that higher love of God for humanity. For Elizabeth this gift-love, which she

Tennyson and the Brownings

both gives to and receives from Robert, is counterpoised by "need-love," since mortals, unlike God, are not self-sufficient beings but creatures whose life is derivative and therefore dependent on the love of others.[22] For as C. S. Lewis cautions, the individual who professes his or her independence from "need-love" is in danger of congealing into a "cold egotist." Coleridge says it even more forcibly: "It is inevitable to every noble mind, whether man or woman, to feel itself, imperfect and insufficient, not as an animal only, but as a moral being. The Creator has ordained that one should possess qualities which the other has not, and the union of both is the most complete ideal of human character. In everything the blending of the similar with the dissimilar is the secret of all pure delight? Who shall dare to stand alone, and vaunt himself, in himself, sufficient?" (651).

Thus Elizabeth needs to feel Robert's love and approval, and like all lovers of either gender, is initially possessed by a sense of unworthiness in being the recipient of such a favor. In Sonnet XLI, describing Robert's delight in both her poetry and her character, Elizabeth expresses her gratitude that a man of his sensibility should respond so generously to her efforts:

> But, thou, who, in my voice's sink and fall,
> When the sob took it, thy divinest Art's
> Own instrument didst drop down at thy foot
> To hearken what I said between my tears, . . .
> Instruct me how to thank thee![23]

For Sarah Paul this is "sarcastic fawning," which hints at an "underlying resentment." I leave it to the reader to determine whether Elizabeth's simple declaration of her happiness at Robert's interest in her work and his impelling need to learn more about the woman who crafted that work is illustrative of resentment or gratitude. Any of us who has written a poem, planted a garden, painted a picture, or sung a song must surely have experienced that modest and altogether becoming pride that follows when a person we respect acknowledges the worth of our efforts. To be totally indifferent to the opinion of others borders on megalomania. Why should Elizabeth's simple gratitude for such notice be construed as unfeminist to the point that a critic needs to so thoroughly distort her meaning to overcome the apparent offense? Is this complete isolation in one's own self-approval to be understood as a moral advance over the humble confession of "need-love"?

In any case, one of the values central to Elizabeth's love for Robert is the parity and mutual self-esteem toward which it grows. Thus in Sonnet X, both Elizabeth and Robert are transformed by the fire of love—a fire that purifies their natures and purges them of those adventitious elements and man-made distinctions that obscure their essential equality. They behold one another with the same unconditional love with which God beholds the whole of creation:

> Yet love, mere love, is beautiful indeed
> And worthy of acceptance. Fire is bright,
> Let temple burn, or Flax. An equal light
> Leaps in the Flame from cedar-plank or weed:
> And love is Fire. And when I say at need
> *I love thee* . . . mark! . . . *I love thee*!—in thy sight
> I stand transfigured, glorified aright,
> With conscience of the new rays that proceed
> Out of my face toward thine. There's nothing low
> In love, when love the lowest: meanest creatures
> Who love God, God accepts while loving so.
> And what I *feel*, across the inferior features
> Of what I *am*, doth flash itself, and show
> How that great work of Love enhances Nature's.
>
> (216)

Here gift-love and need-love are the polarities that comprehend that double rhythm of abnegation and acceptance reflected in the mutual devotion of both lovers. The Platonic transfiguration that takes place in the last line prefigures the rapture of Sonnet XLIII, where Elizabeth proclaims that her love for Robert is sacramentally akin "to the depth and breadth and height / My soul can reach, when feeling out of sight / For the ends of Being and ideal Grace" (223). But this upward movement is counterbalanced by a downward movement that penetrates to the "level of every day's / Most quiet need" (223). And yet in this, the most celebrated of the forty-nine sonnets, Sarah Paul discerns nothing but "an orgy of self-reference," as if that were somehow a meritorious distinction. Genuine lovers of poetry may reflect, however, that despite such critical pronouncements, Elizabeth's sonnets shall remain in all their untarnished splendor.

In a "Poem of One's Own," the contemporary American poet Mary Jo Salter ruminates on the relations between the poet as woman and the woman as poet. Is a woman poet to be exclusively defined by her gender, or is she capable of expressing themes that transcend sexual differences? She concludes that whether a woman adheres, as Elizabeth Barrett did, to a Christian view of creation or endeavors to find meaning in other more secular forms of self-dedication, "the real point is that our personal desires and quests are always secondary, whether we are Christians or atheists. Is there a mature adult that honestly believes that he or she comes first? Even more to the point, has there ever been a great poet of any stripe who did not seek access to something greater than him or herself? And what if our desire *is* God? If that form of desire is to be disallowed, then the achievements of all sorts of women writers who put themselves second after God—writers from the twelfth-century Heloise to the twentieth-century Flannery O'Connor dissolve into nothingness."[24]

Inasmuch as Elizabeth is a part of that tradition which Mary Jo Salter cites, and insofar as her love for Robert and his for her uncovered a third ground, a holy ground "where the unfit / Contrarious moods of men recoil away / And isolate pure spirits" (219), her works may be said to "represent an effort to speak not only of being a woman, and not only to women." Judged by this standard of transexual value, which May Jo Salter aspires to in her own poetry, Elizabeth both anticipates and moves beyond many of the issues germane to women writers of the twentieth century.

These aspirations are most thoroughly enshrined in *Aurora Leigh.* Along with *Jane Eyre*, to which it is consciously indebted, *Aurora Leigh* is the indispensable feminist text of the Victorian age—a poem that explores the peculiar burdens of a woman whose dedication to poetry places her in opposition to conventional notions of femininity. In this novel of artistic growth and development, Aurora's difficulties are rendered more acute by dint of her struggles with sexism, but she also faces problems that any artist faces in a world where the bandwagons of a sometimes mindless activism are indiscriminately valued over the virtues of the contemplative life. In this regard, *Aurora Leigh* touches upon a universal Victorian dilemma: the tension between the social conscience of the altruistic reformer and the aesthetic consciousness of the introspective artist.

Aurora is the offspring of an English father and Florentine mother—a genetic mixture of Mediterranean sensuousness and northern austerity apparently conducive to the development of an artistic temperament. As a child in Florence, Aurora is much obsessed with the portrait of her mother, whose early death encumbered her with many questions about her mother's character. The portrait suggests a nature of tumultuous richness, complex, many-leveled, and inexhaustible:

> by turns
> Ghost, fiend, and angel, fairy, witch, and sprite
> A dauntless Muse who eyes a dreadful Fate,
> A loving Psyche who loses sight of love,
> A still Medusa with mild milky brows
>
> ... or anon
> Our Lady of the Passion, stabbed with swords
> Where the Babe sucked; or Lamia in first
> Moonlighted pallor.
>
> (256)

Aurora's mother is a compendium of goddesses, both sacred and profane, who anticipates Walter Pater's notorious description of the Mona Lisa in his study of 1869, *The Renaissance.* Both Aurora's description and Pater's echo of this passage are symptomatic of Victorian attempts to reexamine the goddesses of classical antiquity in the light of contemporary preoccupations with female power, identity, and creativeness. It is this portrait that awakens Aurora to the vitality and depth of the feminine psyche.

When her father dies, Aurora is sent to England, where she is cared for by a maiden aunt whose personal gifts have been stifled by the mind-forged manacles of patriarchy:

> She had lived
> A sort of cage-bird life, born in a cage,
> Accounting that to leap from perch to perch
> Was act and joy enough for any bird.
>
> (258)

The image of the caged bird is ubiquitous in feminist expressions, from Susan B. Anthony's famous adage, "the caged bird forgets how to build its nest," to the iconography of Victorian art. In Rossetti's painting of *Veronica Veronese*, for example, we see a woman flanked on either side by a violin—toward which she tentatively reaches in a gesture of half-resigned desire—and a caged songbird that represents the restraints imposed upon her wish to enter the world of imaginative creation. Thus, too, Aurora is constrained by her aunt to "cross-stitch" and "read a score of books on womanhood / To prove, if women do not think at all, / They may teach thinking" (260). Despite these onerous and meaningless tasks, Aurora contrives to read clandestinely in her father's library as a means of sustaining "the inner life with all its ample room / For heart and lungs, for will and intellect, / Inviolable by conventions" (261).

The principal drama of Aurora's life centers on her troublous relations with her aristocratic cousin, Romney Leigh, a liberal activist who dedicates his energies to the amelioration of social ills. His attitudes toward art are supercilious at best, and, in consequence, he regards both Aurora and her poetry as the vainest of diversions. However, he is also struck by his cousin's earnestness and idealism, and regards her as a being susceptible to improvement and instruction. His proposal to her, like that of St. John Rivers in Charlotte Brontë's *Jane Eyre*, is predicated on Aurora's willingness to efface herself as a fellow worker in the struggles of the proletariat. Her response is unequivocal: "You want a helpmate not a mistress sir / A wife to help your ends—in her no end" (276). (Aurora's relations with Romney clearly reflect a conflict central to Victorian poetry, from Tennyson's "The Lady of Shalott" to Arnold's "The Scholar Gipsy"—that troubling antagonism between the claims of withdrawal and engagement, action and contemplation, aesthetic detachment and moral commitment.)

In his work among England's slums, Romney meets Marian Erle, a young girl first abused and then abandoned by her parents. After assisting in her recovery, Romney proposes to Marian; but his intentions are thwarted by the schemes of Lady Waldemar, a disdainful socialite driven by her own designs on Romney and a conviction that he is squandering his inheritance on undeserving indigents. She convinces Marian that Romney's proposal is based on misdirected charity and that she would best serve the interests of her betrothed by withdrawing from the engagement. Accordingly, Marian flees to Paris, where she eventually becomes a prostitute. When Romney, who has opened his ancestral home to the needy and helpless, returns without his bride, the inmates of his house assume he has abandoned her and riot, destroying the priceless heirlooms of the Leighs, which include some first-rate pictures of Van Dyck. It is here that Elizabeth Barrett parts company with modern apostles of social equality. Despite her passionate repudiation of gender, racial, religious, or class discrimination, Elizabeth firmly believed in an aristocracy of spirit. The criteria of moral excellence, aesthetic worth, and spiritual beauty were not, in her estimation, subject to the laws of the marketplace or the untutored preferences of the working classes. In the gutting of Romney's ancestral home, Elizabeth anticipates the dangers of a leveling, one-dimensional socialism in which a herd mentality rises resentfully against the beauty and worth of a noble heritage that it can neither sympathize with nor understand.

In the meantime, Aurora, having come into her fortune, follows Marian to Paris, where she is now an impoverished single parent. Aurora convinces Marian to come with her child to Italy. It is there that Aurora establishes a benevolent sisterhood, rehabilitating the demoralized Marian and assisting in the education of her child.

Eventually Aurora learns of Lady Waldemar's involvement in Marian's downfall; she feels impelled to warn Romney but forbears because of a mistaken belief that Lady Waldemar and Romney have married. To Aurora's surprise, Romney appears at her doorstep, humbled and blind like Rochester in *Jane Eyre*. The concluding love duet between Aurora and Romney reveals that they have both been victims of pride, distorting both their attraction for one another and their rigid adherence to the respective claims of philanthropy or poetry into the prisons of sanctimonious self-righteousness. Mortified by the intransigence of their former selves, they come together in a marriage that ritualizes the need to build bridges, transcend pettiness, and restore equilibrium between the sexes.

Aurora Leigh thus rises at its conclusion above that "female literary tradition of rebelliousness, murderousness, and rage" which Sandra Gilbert and Susan Gubar bizarrely celebrate in their analyses of nineteenth-century women writers.[25] We are left instead with the idea of nurturant, loving female values as a necessary counterbalance to Aurora's initial search for artistic and personal emancipation.

The importance of *Aurora Leigh* in the history of women's literature cannot be overestimated. The search for female artistic precursors among women poets of the modern age begins with Elizabeth Barrett Browning; and it is *Aurora Leigh*—"one of the best-selling, most ambitious, most feminist, and longest poems in the English language," in the words of Mary Jo Salter[26]—in which female poets from the Victorian age to the present have perceived the dawning glow of a poetry that expresses woman's quest to know herself and emancipate her spirit.

· EIGHT ·

Four Oxonians

The Victorian age was a period when educational issues became matters of pressing and continuous concern. The radical transformation of old hierarchical ways of thinking generated by the methodologies of modern science resulted in the questioning of traditional curricula based on ancient texts, both classical and Christian. Symptomatic of these changes were the controversies and debates generated at Oxford University throughout the nineteenth century on the respective value of humane letters and scientific technique, and the weight that should be accorded to each in the university training of an undergraduate. Matthew Arnold's essay "Literature and Science" was thus expressly written to rebut Thomas Huxley, who disdained the inutility of the imaginative arts and programmatically endorsed a curriculum based on scientific method. The belief, in short, that a student's character and overall development could be ennobled and enhanced by living contact with those first principles whose effluence is transmitted through the poets, sages, and prophets of Athens and Jerusalem was gradually being superseded by a more pragmatic and utilitarian notion of instruction based on mechanical knowledge and its application to the workplace.

Matthew Arnold, Arthur Hugh Clough, Algernon Swinburne, and Gerard Manley Hopkins bore the unmistakable brunt of these changes and controversies. Their verse reflects either an adaptation to or a reaction against these changes and a lively awareness of the often bewildering choices that a growing relativism of thought and action opened up for an individual increasingly detached from any community of common belief. Notwithstanding the disparities among their final positions, Arnold, Clough, Swinburne, and Hopkins were all afflicted by the same cultural problems and metaphysical concerns. Their verse thus reveals a dialectic of far-reaching proportions, as they meditated on and endeavored to resolve the antagonisms and tensions of an age in which a sense of permanence was yielding implacably and irresistibly to a sense of uncertainty, indeterminacy, and loss.

Of all the Victorian poets, Matthew Arnold (1822–1888) is perhaps the figure most representative of his age and the writer most likely to appeal to our own. In his self-divisions he is, at once, quintessentially Victorian and peculiarly modern. He comprehended within himself the role of an optimistic school inspector who believed in the spiritual efficacy of cultural institutions, and an inconsolable poet consumed with a sense of human futility. He was an eloquent spokesman for the virtues of "sweetness and light"—that urbane tolerance of moral ambiguity and religious incertitude in an age of sometimes desperate evangelical zealotry—and at the same time an inveterate pessimist haunted by the "blankness" and "barrenness" of a life in which the figural imagination and "the last enchantments of the Middle Ages" were evaporating like mists under the desert light of a soulless empiricism. He is equally distinguished for his prose essays, which strenuously defend an "ideal order of conduct and beauty" and an adherence to strict aesthetic standards as a necessary counterweight to the fatuous banalities of a majoritarian taste, and for his elegiac poems, which bewail the spiritual drift and metaphysical anguish of an age in which the sober greyness of stoic resignation had replaced the stained-glass radiance of the Christian promise.

From an early age, Arnold was thrust into the center of these controversies. His father, Thomas Arnold, an eminent Victorian in his own right, was the headmaster of Rugby—a morally rigorous finishing school for the few college bound—and subsequently professor of history at Oriel College, Oxford. As a minister associated with the broad church wing of Anglicanism, he was John Henry Newman's principal opponent at Oxford during the years of Tractarianism. Unlike Newman, who emphasized the importance of the sacraments, the weight of tradition, the poetry of ritual, and the inwardness of the devotional life, Thomas Arnold was a matter-of-fact exponent of muscular Christianity as a source of social improvement, and thus was largely indifferent to matters of liturgy and dogma. When Matthew eventually matriculated at Oxford, he came out from under his father's intimidating shadow in a show of solidarity with Newman the wordsmith of poetic devotion, if not Newman the apostle of Anglo-Catholicism. It has been suggested

by A. L. Rowse that Arnold's character was forged in the war between the two sides of his nature respectively represented by his
father—the realist, the activist, the reformer—and his mother,
Mary Penrose, the dreamy poetic Celt whose tender, introspective
spirit was closer to the tact and reserve of Newman.[1] In any case, it
was Newman's magical cadences, "subtle, sweet, and mournful,"
as Arnold described them in a famous passage, which drew the
young poet weekly to the University Church, St. Mary the Virgin,
to hear those sermons that A. N. Wilson calls "the most superb
pieces of religious prose in the English language." For it was the
manner of Newman—restrained, aloof, slightly ironic, though
swept by undercurrents of poetic feeling—that Arnold chiefly
prized. To the *matter*, except insofar as the Anglican tradition could
be used to dignify the lives of the working masses, Arnold remained largely indifferent. And, of course, Arnold perceived Newman's eventual conversion to Catholicism as but another sign of
the moral desperation characteristic of the age.

When his faith lapsed, Arnold placed an increasingly higher pre-
mium on the role of culture as a means of counterbalancing the ap-
petency and self-centeredness of the Victorian middle classes. In
books and essays such as *Culture and Anarchy* (1869), "Literature
and Science" (1882), "The Study of Poetry" (1888), and "The Function of Criticism at the Present Time" (1865), Arnold extolled the
value of humanistic studies and endeavored to create an intellectual
climate favorable to the reception of "the best that has been thought
and known" in Western tradition. Moreover, Arnold proclaimed
the necessity of harmonizing the ethos of "Hebraism" (which he
designated as "strictness of conscience") with the spirit of Hellenism (or "spontaneity of consciousness") as a way of avoiding, on
the one hand, the extremes of an evangelical Protestantism based on
a narrow-minded and fundamentalist rigor inimical to the free play
of the creative spirit, and escaping, on the other hand, from the seductions of an unprincipled secularism devoted exclusively to the
pursuit of material satisfactions. Though Arnold questioned the supernatural claims of Christianity in books like *St. Paul and Protestantism* (1870) and *God and the Bible* (1875), he wished to preserve
both the aesthetic and ethical elements of the Christian message.

Arnold's substitute for religion was poetry—a substitution that
links him, ironically, with a growing phenomenon in Victorian letters: namely, the doctrine of art-for-art's-sake, in which the aes-

thetic experience is divorced from normal human preoccupations with how to live and the work of art is adjudged exclusively on the basis of its technical merit. Arnold would have no truck with the more flamboyant exponents of this view such as Swinburne, but it is a fine paradox that Arnold, the faithful husband, devoted father, and conscientious overseer of Britain's state schools, who eventually abandoned poetry for moral reasons, should be the progenitor of a view that was to terminate in the titillations, perversions, and sexual anarchy of the fin de siècle. To Arnold, however, the loss of traditional faith augmented the moral responsibility of the poet, and, hence, his critical standards for evaluating that art became more rigorous. In "The Study of Poetry," Arnold adduces certain critical "touchstones" that, he argues, will enable the reader to discriminate more sharply between poetry of secondary value (because of its merely "personal" or "historic" significance) and a poetry of "high seriousness," which was intrinsically vital or "real" by virtue of its perfect blending of verbal expression with a "criticism of life." Alternating between a theory of poetry that demanded the application of great or ennobling ideas to life and the recognition that as an art, with its own intrinsic virtues and requirements, poetry must not be treated simply as a vehicle for uplifting sentiments, Arnold was frequently involved in self-contradictory utterances. By the same token, in the "Preface" to the 1853 volume of his own *Poems*, Arnold rejected many of his most successful works—especially *Empedocles on Aetna* (1852)—precisely because they failed to inculcate tonic sentiments and expressed a morbid and irresolvable anxiety in the face of an ambiguous universe. Yet it is in *Empedocles* that Arnold achieved one of the high watermarks of his age. Browning, who recognized the poem's greatness, remonstrated with Arnold until he relented and the poem was reincorporated into the poet's canon. But nothing could be more remote from the resolute and unconquerable spirit of Browning. "Passive suffering is not a fit theme for poetry," Arnold averred, but it is precisely such suffering that characterizes Empedocles, Arnold's antihero of a bankrupt humanism.

The poem is a debate between youthful enchantment and disillusioned middle age, but insofar as these respective states are reflected in the poetic traditions of the nineteenth century, it is also a debate between the Romantic age and what Arnold called the "unpoetrylessness" of the modern world. Empedocles is an aging sage and poet ousted from cultural relevance by the arrival of a new school of sophists—the politically correct multiculturalists and relativists of classical Greece. For Callicles, the poet's admiring student who has not yet fully realized the havoc these fashionable ideosophers are going to wreak on traditional notions of the beautiful, the true, and the good, Empedocles's moral indignation is a mere fit of the blues. Insofar as Callicles represents the soul of the Romantic age, his inability to perceive the threat to the figural imagination as an organ of spiritual and poetic knowledge is a sign of his relative innocence and untroubled naïveté. Callicles's poetry is simple, sensuous, and passionate, rife with a Keatsian lushness and a Wordsworthian spirit of natural piety. As he tracks his mentor to the edge of Aetna, Callicles describes the verdant opulence of its lower slopes:

> ... the air
> Is freshen'd by the leaping stream, which throws
> Eternal showers of spray on the moss'd roots
> Of trees, and veins of turf, and long dark shoots
> Of ivy plants, and fragrant hanging bells
> Of hyacinths, and on late anemonies,
> That muffle its wet banks; but glade,
> And stream and sward, and chestnut-trees,
> End here; ...

> (414)

Beyond lies Aetna "without a shade." Thus Arnold implies that the sensuous, mythic worlds of youthful Romanticism have given way to the bare, inhospitable austerities of the modern age—an age in which careerists, opportunists, and academic power brokers have replaced the intuitive wisdom and ingenuous dedication of the authentic sage and aspiring enthusiast. No longer able to discern in the life of the mind or the word of the poet those healing agencies of wisdom or beauty or faith, he has succumbed to the demoralizing influence of those around him. Unlike Callicles, whose language still resonates with the poetic warmth of a more credulous age, Empedocles speaks in the spare, astringent accents of the modern skeptic:

> The sophist sneers: Fool, take
> Thy pleasure, right or wrong.

> The pious wail: Forsake
> A world of these sophists throng.
> Be neither saint nor sophist-led, but be a man!
>
> (416)

In his attempt to avoid the polar extremes of a soulless utilitarianism and a mindless religiosity, Empedocles reflects Arnold's own search for a middle way. But the poet here is more honest than the ideologue. The sense of loss and fragmentation and disinheritance is finally too much for the disabused sage who can bring himself to believe in nothing but the irremissive vacillations of his own divided will:

> But no, this heart will glow no more; thou art
> A living man no more, Empedocles!
> Nothing but a devouring flame of thought—
> But a naked, eternally restless mind!
>
> (438)

Empedocles's restlessness is an extreme consequence of that attitude which seeks on condition of never finding. The mind of the sage races itself without moving and inevitably breaks down—for it can acknowledge nothing greater or better than itself toward which to aspire and grow. When Empedocles leaps into Aetna to end his torment, the gracious song of Callicles rises from below in a spontaneous overflow of powerful feelings:

> Not here, O Apollo!
> Are haunts meet for thee.
> But where Helicon breaks down
> In cliff to the sea,
>
> . . . .
>
> First hymn they the Father
> Of all things, and then,
> The rest of immortals,
> The action of men.
>
> (441; 443)

As a remnant from the Romantic world of poetic myth, Callicles is still able to wring beauty from truth, redemption from suffering.

But Empedocles, the epitome of the modern intellectual, is a warning and a portent to an age that has lost its hold on the permanent things.

Urbane, assured, and even something of a dandy in his prose, Arnold is the opposite in his poetry. Like Tennyson, Arnold was a writer with "two voices"—one affirming the popular Victorian belief in human progress; the other lamenting the loss of a stable system of ordered and hierarchic values. His words from "Stanzas from the Grand Chartreuse" (1855), in which he describes himself as "Wandering between two worlds, one dead, / The other powerless to be born" (302), epitomize his self-division—his sense of having arrived too late to adhere with any conviction to the formulas of traditional Christianity and too early to embrace with any enthusiasm the demythicized system of ethics destined, in his mind, to take its place. Although Arnold's meditations center on the Alpine fastness of this famous Carthusian retreat, his debate with the spirit of monasticism reflects his own unresolved attitude toward Newman and the sacramental spirit of the Oxford Movement.

Though Arnold identifies with the withdrawn, contemplative life of these devout worshipers, he is ultimately unable to assent in their solution to the human dilemma:

> With nowhere yet to rest my head,
> Like these, on earth I wait forlorn.
> Their faith, my tears, the world deride—
> I come to shed them at their side.
>
> (302)

Though he is among them, Arnold is not of them—comparing himself instead to an ancient Greek translated to some northern clime where he puzzles over the indecipherable runes of Norse mythology. It has been observed that Newman's Christian sacramentalism was nourished by the spirit of Romantic poetry and the evolution of its surviving minions—Coleridge and Wordsworth—into the Anglican fold. Thus it is no surprise that as Arnold ponders over the lives of the solitary monks of Chartreuse, he is led to think of the Romantic poets and their early, doomed, and iridescent aspirations:

Four Oxonians

> What boots it, Shelley! that the breeze
> Carried thy lovely wail away,
> Musical through Italian trees
> Which fringe thy soft blue Spezzian bay?
> Inheritors of thy distress
> Have restless hearts one throb the less?
>
> (303)

The stanza recalls Arnold's famous designation of Shelley as a "beautiful and ineffectual angel, beating in the void his luminous wings in vain."[2] Neither the Christian hope of spiritual salvation nor the Shelleyan dream of human perfection can captivate Arnold more—despite their respective attractions.

What, then, is left? The poet's reflections are suddenly broken by a sound of clamor and movement—

> Pennon, and plume, and flashing lance!
> Forth to the world those soldiers fare,
> To life, to cities, and to war!
>
> (305)

These are the various apostles of modernity: captains of industry and soldiers of market capitalism who have engrossed the imaginations and dominated the minds of the contemporary world. But these are even less appealing in their getting and spending, their consumerist ethic of profit and loss, than the imaginary worlds of poet or believer that Arnold can bring himself to neither reject nor embrace. Confessing himself a child "rear'd in shade / Beneath some old-world abbey wall" (304)—that is to say, the Oxford of his youth, "home of lost causes and forsaken beliefs, and unpopular names, and impossible loyalties"[3]—Arnold retreats back to the simpler pieties of a believing age, not exactly for them but definitely not against them.

After a while the inconclusiveness of Arnold's position can get on a reader's nerves. In everything—love, art, and faith—the pros and cons are weighed to the point of weariness, until the only position left is the rejection of all positions. In consequence, Arnold's poetry is always resigned, always elegiac, always bewailing what might have been and always burdened with what can never be.

Yet it is the singular honesty and restraint with which he articulates this bafflement that makes him one of the most moving poets of his age. In this regard, "Dover Beach" (1867) is not only a concentrated extract of Arnold's poetic sensibility but perhaps *the* preeminent lyric of the Victorian period. Unburdened by the discursiveness of Tennyson's *In Memoriam* or the sometimes maddening prolixity of Browning, this most crisp, spare, yet haunting of lyrical poems is indeed a "touchstone" of the age—a poem whose extraliterary value lies in the consummate sweep with which it summarizes what Arnold spoke of as "the sickening consciousness of our difficulties." There are always difficulties—but for the Victorians these invariably shaped themselves into a nagging, inexpiable fear that life, consciousness, art, and religion were an accidental by-product of impersonal forces and biological laws. This fear is translated in the poem into a seascape that functions as a sounding board to the poet's anxieties.

Standing with his beloved by a window that overlooks the Straits of Dover, the poet with a few deft defining details evokes a marine world of utter desolation and unconsoling bleakness. The crepuscular light that glimmers in the first stanza lends a shadowy menace to those chalk cliffs that rise like an avatar of geologic time and throw into relief the transient, vulnerable humanity of the poet and his wife. "The grating roar of pebbles," with its ominous discordant undertow, further suggests the helpless, aimless drift of harried mortals subject to the eroding forces of time and tide. "The eternal note of sadness" discerned in the drifting spume carries the poet back to the world of Sophocles—a pre-Christian writer who can presumably speak authentically to a post-Christian age. For as the tide withdraws, the poet hears in its "melancholy, long, withdrawing roar" (211) an auditory equivalent to the progressive retreat of religious faith in a world now exposed to the dispassionate scrutiny of cold reason. This fatal recognition compels the poet to cling even more desperately to his only consolation—the fugitive stay of mutual love between mortals who can no longer detect a companionable presence behind the sensuous flux of existence.

And yet even human love for Arnold was of momentary duration, providing, at best, no more than an intermittent and tantalizing release from our customary state of alienated introspection. As he wrote in "To Marguerite" (1852): "Dotting the shoreless watery wild, / We mortal millions live *alone*" (182). This characteristic note of homesickness and disquietude is sustained in exquisite minor key in two of Arnold's most successful elegies: "The Scholar Gypsy" (1853) and "Thyrsis" (1866). Despite Arnold's ambivalence about the efficacy of Keats's influence on English poetry, in these lyrics Arnold relaxes those classical scruples that underpin his censure of the Elizabethans, Keats, and Tennyson, and reveals a strain of "natural magic," which he ascribed to the sensibility of the Celt and the lush, preternatural imagery of Keats. Arnold's attempt to emulate the austerity of Greek classical verse too often produced a poetry that reeked of the scholar's study—wooden, prosaic, and factitious. And while this austerity could be deeply moving in its dignified restraint, the infusion of poetic warmth that penetrates "The Scholar Gypsy" and "Thyrsis" is a welcome relief from the arid stretches of Arnold's more consciously high-minded verse. The warmth, of course, derives from Keats, after whose odes the stanza for these affiliated laments is clearly modeled.

Both "The Scholar Gypsy" and "Thyrsis" are pastoral elegies—a consecrated lyrical idiom traceable to the Greek bucolic poets Bion and Moschus, handed on to Virgil in the *Georgics,* and later rejuvenated in England by Milton in "Lycidas" and Shelley in "Adonais." The convention derives from the Greek myth of a golden age in which the poet as shepherd presides over a world of pastoral innocence and spiritual bliss. The elegiac strain is associated with the loss of this innocence and the uncovering of a new reality hostile to the inspiration of the poet or the pieties of the saint (for in its later incarnations the figure of the poet as pastor blends with images in the Psalms of the Lord as our Shepherd or Christ's injunction to his disciples: "Feed my sheep"). "The Scholar Gypsy" is thus a nostalgic backward glance from an age of spiritual confusion and intellectual aridity to an age characterized by a singleness of mind, a sense of permanence, and an ingenuous lyricism. While the subject of the poem derives from a seventeenth-century Oxford legend of a college dropout who sought for a wisdom superior to books, the shade of the scholar whose legendary ghost is still said to haunt the environs of Oxford becomes the personified image of a threefold ideal that Arnold associates, at once, with his own undergraduate illusions, the poetry of the Romantic period, and the great age of Anglican devotional piety when the church could boast such luminaries as Jeremy Taylor, Lancelot Andrews, George Herbert, Thomas Traherne, and Henry More.

Like so much of Arnold's verse, the poem dramatizes the poet's
struggle to escape from the regimented secularism of a collective
society indifferent to the vagaries of poetic vision. But Arnold's desire to escape is inevitably counterbalanced by an equal need to assume his responsibilities to that society through some program of
social improvement. Thus the poet's opening exhortation to the
shepherd to attend to his flock before joining the speaker in a midnight search for the elusive gypsy expresses Arnold's own misgivings about the potentially regressive nature of this search. But
these scruples do not last long. The first half of the poem is almost
entirely given over to a dream of wish fulfillment that expresses
Arnold's desire to lose himself in the greenwood, to escape from
the iron rule of history and embower himself among the floral luxuries of a mythic paradise. The poem has obvious points in comon
with Keats's odes—especially the "Ode to a Nightingale"—but
with one important difference. Keats's meditation evolves out of a
spontaneous response to a living songbird; Arnold's reveries are
excited by a legend in a book. The substitution of text for reality is a
telling indication of Arnold's distance from that first, fine, careless
rapture of the early Romantics. Moreover, it also suggests a typically Victorian misgiving that the natural magic of Romantic verse
may be nothing more than a necessary fiction existing only in the
dream worlds of poetic myth. The unmediated vision of the Romantics has thus given way to the dubious authority of a text that
relates a legend of questionable authenticity.[4]
Arnold's attempt to return to this natural magic is epitomized in
the gypsy's association with those annual spring rites that connect
humanity and nature in a life-dance of consecrated joys:

> Maidens, who from the distant hamlets come
>   To dance around the Fyfield elm in May,
> Oft through the darkening fields have seen thee roam
>   Or cross a stile into the public way.
>   Oft thou hast given them store
> Of flowers—the frail-leaf'd, white anemone,
>   Dark bluebells drench'd with dews ot summer eves,
>   And purple orchises with spotted leaves—
> But none have words she can report of thee.

(257)

But neither this nor the other scenes in which Arnold evokes the genial countryside of Oxford can forestall the realization that these natural pieties belong to an age that has long since fled. The gypsy, then, is a beautiful but ineffectual emblem of that traditional search for wisdom, or the beauty of holiness, or the good life that no longer appeals to those desanctifying enforcers of intellectual fashion who dismiss and debunk the past. The poet urges the scholar to sustain his quest remote from the acrimony of the modern ideologue whose draining, demoralizing cynicism would destroy his cherished ideals:

> But fly our paths, our feverish contact fly!
>   For strong the infection of our mental strife,
> Which, though it gives no bliss, yet spoils for rest;
>   And we should win thee from thy own fair life,
>   Like us distracted, and like us unblest.
>   Soon, soon thy cheer would die,
> Thy hopes grow timorous, and unfix'd thy powers,
>   And thy clear aims be cross and shifting made;
>   And then thy glad perennial youth would fade,
> Fade, and grow old at last, and die like ours.
>
> (261)

The lush pastoral diction of the earlier stanzas has here given way to the dry, abstract language of the modern cognoscenti—disillusioned, bleak, unedifying, and without hope.

"Thyrsis" further explores the inhospitable climate of the modern age in the context of a dirge for Arnold's longtime friend and fellow poet, Arthur Hugh Clough. Clough, who died in 1861—but a few months after Elizabeth Barrett Browning—had been associated with Arnold's family since childhood. As a boy, Clough had moved with his parents from Liverpool to South Carolina, where he was largely tutored by his scrupulously pious mother, whose maiden name was, significantly, "Perfect." On his return to England at the age of nine, Clough's perfectionist tendencies were reinforced at Rugby under the strenuous evangelical regimen of Thomas Arnold. Overburdened by a delicate conscience and a fastidious awareness of his own shortcomings, Clough was internally embattled throughout most of his life—a prey to divisive spiritual forces and warring psychological impulses that pulled him in opposing directions and gave to his verse an air of intellectual thorniness, spiritual enervation, and aesthetic fatigue. Though Thomas Arnold had unintentionally oppressed Clough with an ideal of perfection impossible to achieve, he was also the most kind and fatherly of schoolmasters—inviting the boy into his home where he became a virtual brother to Matthew Arnold. He subsequently followed Arnold to Oxford, but Clough, who was possessed of formidable scholarly credentials, became embroiled in Tractarian controversies.

The tracts, of course, were those written by J. H. Newman and his followers in an endeavor to prove that the 39 articles of the Church of England could be interpreted in a manner consistent with the doctrines of the pre-Reformational Catholic church—an endeavor regarded with alarm and suspicion by the more Protestant school of English divinity represented by Thomas Arnold. Torn between Thomas Arnold and John Henry Newman, Clough was a victim of his own divided loyalties—a division that upset the equilibrium of an already overwrought conscience. Despairing of answers to the imperious questions raised by the Christian catechism, Clough gave up the opportunity to teach at Oriel College—for he could not bring himself to assent to the Thirty-nine Articles of the Anglican Church to which all Oxford professors were then expected to subscribe. Arnold wondered why Clough made things so difficult for himself. After all, the articles were elastic enough to be interpreted in the broadest possible way. And Arnold himself had no difficulty recommending Christianity for the masses while touting in his essays and biblical commentaries a religion of high culture, stoic resignation, and moral probity.

It is perhaps to Clough's credit that he refused to temporize with these matters—especially when one considers that from Clough's day to the present there are professional clergy perfectly content to earn their living as "Christian" pastors while denying fundamental doctrines of the faith. At all events, Clough was a demythologist for whom Christ was only resurrected in the spirit of his disciples and those subsequent adherents who endeavored to live by his example. As for a literal resurrection, Clough, in the Easter Day chorus of his controversial poem, *Dipsychus*, made his position quite clear: "Christ is not risen." Clough's scruples, moreover, were such that he could not bring himself to profess what he did not in his heart believe. After a brief stay in Rome during the period of revolt against French hegemony, Clough was finally able to secure an educational post at University College, London. But here too he was forced to resign after a three-year tenure because he would not acquiesce in the religious component of the curriculum. In this life made up of perpetual conflicts, doubts, and misgivings on matters spiritual and moral, Clough was finally able to find some peace in his marriage to Blanche Smith and his subsequent dedication to the humanitarian work of Blanche's cousin, Florence Nightingale. Clough's happiness lasted only five years; and it was his premature death at the age of forty-two that prompted Arnold's somewhat ambivalent elegy, "Thyrsis."

In the first place the poem is not altogether fair to Clough, who is castigated for his inability to sustain the untroubled insouciance of their undergraduate role model, the scholar gypsy. Arnold, moreover, seems more concerned with the loss of his own youth than he is with the loss of Clough. And furthermore the Keatsian ideal of negative capability—of being content with half-knowledge and letting the mind be a thoroughfare for all thoughts—was no more achieved by Arnold than it was by Clough. Still, Arnold possessed what Clough did not: a sense of form and an ability, while crafting his verse, to set philosophical difficulties aside or incorporate them so thoroughly into his art that he could conscientiously attend to matters of aesthetic tact. Hence, there is some warrant to Arnold's implied criticism of his friend in the poem's penultimate stanza:

> What though the music of thy rustic flute
>   Kept not for long its happy, country tone;
>   Lost it too soon, and learnt a stormy note
> Of men contention-tost, of men who groan,
>   Which task'd thy pipe too sore, and tired thy throat—
> It failed, and thou wast mute!
>
> (269)

It is true that Clough's poetic voice is often rough and acidulous, as if grating against intractable themes that do not lend themselves to an expansive lyricism. Arnold complained of this in a letter to Clough in 1849:

If I were to say the real truth as to your poems in general, as they impress me—it would be this—that they are not *natural*. ... Naturalness ... an absolute propriety of form [is] the soul necessary of poetry as such: whereas the greatest wealth and depth of matter is merely a superfluity in the Poet *as such.* . . . I often think that even a slight gift of poetical expression which in a common person might have developed itself easily and naturally, is overlaid and crushed in a profound thinker so as to be of no use to him to help him to express himself.[5]

It is the preponderance of the reflective faculty, of distinctions multiplied to the point of tedium, and of qualifications made to the edge of exhaustion, that prevent Clough from being a poet of the first order. Yet, as an important figure in the history of ideas, Clough is indispensable to our understanding of the Victorian age and a vital link between the tremors of Victorian doubt and the uncompromising honesty and metaphysical anguish of Dostoyevski—or Tolstoy.

Especially Tolstoyan in its emphasis is Clough's verse chronicle of an undergraduate highland fling in the wilds of Scotland—the unpronounceable, somewhat unreadable, and largely unread *The Bothie of Tober-na-Vuolich* (1848). Among Oxonians in Scotland for a brief vacation is the oppressively cerebral Philip Hanson, pundit and socialist doctrinaire, who discovers that the peasantry is something more than an exploited labor force. For it is in a rustic *bothie,* or cottage, that he meets Elspie, a Scottish lass whose complex nature has lights and shades undreamt of by the exponents of dialectical materialism. Philip and Elspie marry and emigrate to New Zealand, where the erstwhile Oxford fop learns to dig with a spade, and like Tolstoy's Levin from *Anna Karenina,* he discovers that there is more to life than the theory of life. The poem is written in ponderous hexameters, which seem singularly inapposite to a subject of less than Homeric grandeur; but the realization that we are as plants that must root themselves in the earth if we are to bloom in the ether and bear fruit puts this poem among a group of nineteenth-century writings that, especially in Russia, warn of the emptiness and dessication of the detached intellect.

Dipsychus, which dates from 1850, is Clough's adaptation of the Faust legend and, as the title implies, an elaborate dialogue between the self and the soul. The Mephistophelian spirit of doubt argues on behalf of temporal joys and evanescent pleasures. Dipsychus is the emancipated intellectual who sees no harm in partaking of life's fruits and finding satisfactions within this brief interval of frost and sun. What this translates into, inevitably, is the seduction of a young girl by Dipsychus, who has determined to seize the day despite residual scruples:

> This lovely creature's glowing charms
> Are gross illusion, I don't doubt that;
> But when I pressed her in my arms
> I somehow didn't think about that.[6]

Dipsychus, the divided soul, goes on to become Lord Chief Justice; but an unexpected encounter with the woman he seduced years earlier precipitates him into an agony of remorse: "Once Pleasure and now Guilt—and after this / Guilt Evermore" (302–303). The "Evermore," perhaps a little too "Victorian" in the narrow and conventional understanding of that term, suggests a certain provinciality of mind that would be equally suspect to the traditional Christian or the emancipated hedonist. In any case, having embraced the spirit of denial, Dipsychus still remains dubious of its implication: namely, that the death of God means that everything is permissible. Though he remains a skeptic with regard to religion, he is equally conscious of the hollowness and self-deception intrinsic to an ethic that pursues self-interest and disregards the claims of others.

Of Clough's three extended poems, *Amours de Voyage* (1858) has perhaps the most interest for the modern reader—though its epistolary format is somewhat dated, being a series of letters generated between an Oxonian in Rome named Claude, the family of the Trevellans, and their correspondents in England. Claude emerges as perhaps the least likable character in English poetry—a self-regarding fop who sees through everything and in consequence lives in an invisible universe. He temporizes with the affections of Mary Trevellan but leaves Rome when the affair threatens to become serious. One by one he ticks off all the shortcomings of his Roman visit. He sees nothing to admire in the glorious inheritance of Renaissance architecture: "Rome disappoints me much" (177). In his apostasy, he has no feeling or reverence at all for the great cultural traditions of Catholic Christianity: "No, the Christian faith, as I, at least, understand it, / Is not here" (179). So much for Catholic Europe. In a fit of vituperative intolerance, he condemns the Jesuit order for vituperative intolerance. The Trevellans, for him, are the most boorish of English philistines: "Middle-class people these, bankers very likely, not wholly / Pure of the taint of the shop" (181). Perhaps his one saving grace is his awareness of being a pretentious, inflated, and, at bottom, insecure "coxcomb." G. K. Chesterton has observed that if you would make your universe large, you must make yourself small. But Claude's self-contempt continues to translate into a sneering condemnation of everything and everyone. Thus Mazzini's heroic uprising against French rule strikes him as inexpedient and self-destructive, and his flirtation with Mary Trevellan, who rightly perceives that he is "a little repulsive," simply evaporates into trifling inanity.

Claude, in brief, seems like a preliminary Victorian sketch for J. Alfred Prufrock—T. S. Eliot's dispossessed persona who cannot give himself to anything or anyone and whose life, in consequence, is superficially divided between a socially correct mask and an atavistic desire for primitive subhuman pleasures. Prufrock's wish to enter into the state of a crab that grasps its prey and ingests its meal without thought or deliberation is prefigured in Claude's estimation of himself as a "limpet": " . . . we open our shells to imbibe our / Nourishment, close them again, and are safe, fulfilling the purpose / Nature intended" (188). Clough's poem with its unpleasant antihero, alienating cerebrality, and drifting uncommitted lovers is a Victorian rough sketch of that intellectual type the twentieth century knows so well—the critical deconstructionist for whom, in the words of George A. Panichas, "there are no luminous moments, no fixed criterion, no truths of faith, no spiritual and moral equivalents, no permanent things, no fulfilling purpose, no redeeming experience."[7]

The trouble with Clough's poetry is that in depicting this state of aridity and dessication he has not found a way to avoid the impression of aridity and dessication in his own verse. There is not much in this poetry either tonic to the spirit or tuneful to the ear. There are, however, several of Clough's lyrics that strike deeper and more animating tones. The deeper tones are sounded in a poem that prefigures Dostoyevski's "Grand Inquisitor"—a story, written by the doubting Ivan in *The Brothers Karamazov*, that imagines the return of Christ and the dismay which that return would cause, not least among the members of his church. Like Ivan's story, Clough's hypothetical situation in "I dreamed a dream . . . " is wickedly satirical in capturing the effect a living Christ, as opposed to a safe, bland, and demythicized Christ, would have upon his worshipers.

Thus Peter, representing the church, is dismayed by Christ's disso-
ciating himself from teachings adventitious to a real Christianity.
In the same way, a middle-class Victorian patriarch expresses his
need for some cozy or comforting ritual—as long as it is not taken
too seriously. But the sting of Christ's return is double-edged. For
Clough imagines the shade of Christ as a specter bewildered and
confused by the doctrines that have grown up around him. The
ambiguity of the satire derives not only from the juxtaposition of
contemporary religion with the pure intentions of its founder, but
also from a sense that the claims of the founder, having proved
spurious in a strict supernatural sense, no longer exert—apart from
custom or convention—any binding authority on the men and
women of the modern age. There is, in short, an incoherence in the
poem that makes it representative of Clough's customary hesitations. A. O. J. Cockshut's observation that Clough was incapable of
forming any "coherent attitude toward religion, marriage, work, or
life itself" and that his poetry, as a consequence, invariably falls
short of a "grand central effect" is not altogether unjust.[8]

Indeed, the one poem of Clough's in which "a grand central effect" is achieved has made it the one indispensable and ubiquitous
anthology piece of this interesting but not quite major poet. "Say
not the struggle nought availeth" has rightly taken its place as the
salient expression of the Victorian urge to strive onward and upward despite the disheartening signs of the times. Though the
poem was written in 1849, it reads like a reply to Arnold's "Dover
Beach," written around 1851. Whether a conscious response or an
accidental palinode, the poem reads like a deliberate counterstate-
ment to Arnold's inconsolable dirge. The most obvious contrast is
the movement of the tide in either poem: Arnold's is going out,
Clough's is coming in. The imagery of the poem depicts an embattled warrior fighting against the forces of nihilism and despair. The
speaker urges the soldier to continue his campaign and employs
three images to suggest that, despite surrounding circumstances,
the smoke and battle of the present may obscure a promising future. Thus, if we look toward the east waiting for sunrise, we cannot see the western traces of light reflected from beneath the
horizon; and if we face the sea from the edge of the ocean, we are
less able to perceive the rising water level, which is apparent in the
creeks and shallows further inland. For once in Clough, image,
rhythm, diction, and rhyme grandly coalesce into a unified effect

that carries with it a ring of genuine conviction. To be sure, the hope is qualified by the understated phrase "it may be," which throws into doubt the assertion that the victory is coming despite our present woes, but this caveat only makes the concluding affirmation more plausible and more poignant:

> For while the tired waves, vainly breaking,
>   Seem here no painful inch to gain,
> Far back through creeks and inlets making
>   Comes, silent, flooding in, the main.
>
> And not by eastern windows only,
>   When daylight comes, comes in the light,
> In front the sun climbs slow, how slowly,
>   But westward, look, the land is bright.
>   (63)

Like many Victorians who had lost their faith in divine providence, Clough adhered to the ethical core of Christianity while repudiating its supernatural claims. In this regard, he illustrates the position advanced by Arnold in the opening paragraph of his seminal essay *The Study of Poetry* (1880). Arnold there prophesies that religion will decline as a decisive influence on human arrangements in proportion as it clings to a credulous faith in the literal truth of dogma or scripture. Conversely, in proportion as the poetry of Christianity is admitted as an expression of the human dilemma in its ethical and aesthetic dimensions, it will survive, along with other great imaginative creations, as an embodiment of impulses, hopes, and fears native to the human spirit. What is interesting and ambiguous about this formula is that it may be interpreted in two ways. One can choose, like Clough or Arnold, to emphasize the ethical value of poetry and religion, or one can choose, like Arnold's younger contemporary at Oxford, Algernon Charles Swinburne (1837–1909), to make poetry a religion in itself, emancipated from all considerations that are not purely aesthetic.

Along with D. G. Rossetti and William Morris, whom Swinburne met in 1856 when the poet-artist Rossetti accepted a commission from John Ruskin to paint the walls of Oxford Union with murals from the Arthurian Legends, Swinburne became the principal exponent of the art-for-art's-sake school of poetry that was to gradually supersede the Arnoldian notion of poetry as a criticism of life.

Swinburne's lineage was aristocratic, his mother being the daughter of an earl, and his father an admiral in the British navy. Following his graduation from Eton, Swinburne matriculated at Balliol College, Oxford, where he became, somewhat improbably, the favorite of the headmaster, Benjamin Jowett, the fastidious, austere, and professionally self-disciplined translator of Plato. Swinburne's linguistic abilities doubtless appealed to the professor, who saw in the youth a potential protégé in the line of classical languages and literatures. But Swinburne himself was anything but disciplined, fastidious, or austere. His dissipations at Oxford became legendary, and he was forced to leave without a degree in 1861. He spent some time with Rossetti at his studio in Cheyne Walk, London, but Swinburne's bohemianism became too much even for the irregular life of the Pre-Raphaelite artist. (Especially irksome to Rossetti was Swinburne's disconcerting habit, while in his cups, of sliding down the banisters naked.) By the age of forty Swinburne was so far gone in drink and sex that he suffered a severe breakdown. He was rehabilitated by Theodore Watts Dunton, a minor novelist of the period, who translated Swinburne to his country estate, where he watched over him for the next thirty years of his life.

Swinburne's contribution to Victorian poetry has been proverbially difficult to estimate. His haunting, drugged, liturgical rhythms, which rise and fall in oceanic swells like the lugubrious chant to some diabolic rite, have an almost hypnotic or hypnagogic effect. It is poetry that approximates to the condition of trance—a trance both fascinating and demoralizing in its seductive enchantment with the perverse, the moribund, and the deliquescent. His two big themes are Eros and Thanatos—for the two are inseparable in Swinburne's consciousness, love being a state that invariably terminates in a riot of torment and death. His rejection of Christianity is complete, utter, unequivocal. Like some pagan in the last days of Rome, he is a votary of the life-force, invariably personified in his poetry as an amoral goddess who bathes in blood and renews her charms through the sacrifice of her ravished minions. His severest shortcoming as a poet is the narrowness and repetitiousness of his themes. Over and over in a series of stanzas that can easily be changed about without any violation to the logic of his verse, he extols the seductions of oblivion as the only release from a life addicted to obsessive cravings, evanescent raptures, and residual disgusts. Surprisingly, he shared a mutual affection with his friend's sister, Christina Rossetti—the greatest Anglican devotional poet of the century. But the affinity is not perhaps as incongruous as at first appears. For the verse of both poets takes its point of departure from the vision of Ecclesiastes: life is vanity, dust and ashes all that is. It is in their prescriptions, however, that they differ.

Swinburne's goddess poems are all based on the assumption that the religion of nature, as personified in the worship of Prosperpine or Diana, is healthier than Christianity and closer to the facts of human existence. The cycles of the moon, the waxing and waning of the seasons as reflections of life and death in nature, stand, for Swinburne, in forcible contrast with the otherworldly aspirations and life-denying asceticism of the Judeo-Christian heritage. All of this sounds salubrious and remarkably contemporary—especially in its substitution of a female nature goddess for a patriarchal deity. The only problem with Swinburne's worship of nature is that, as G. K. Chesterton observed, "it somehow always becomes unnatural. A man loves nature in the morning for its innocence and amiability, and, at nightfall, if he is loving her still, it is for her darkness and cruelty. He washes at morning in clear water yet somehow at the dark end of day he is bathing in hot bull's blood as did Julian the Apostate."[9] Well, there was never anything innocent or amiable to begin with in Swinburne's nature worship, and it is precisely Julian the Apostate, the Roman emperor who repudiated Christianity on his deathbed, who utters the words of Swinburne's most notorious hymn to the goddess.

The supreme irony of the poem, of course, is that while Julian execrates Christianity as an anti-life religion, morbid in its espousal of self-mortification and suffering, the emperor's own paean to the goddess is characterized by a perverse fascination with transience, decay, and death. Still, the initial challenge to Christ sounds ebullient enough:

> Will thou yet take all, Galilean? But these thou shalt not take,
> The laurel, the palms and the paean, the breast of the nymphs in
>   the brake,
> Breasts more soft than a dove's that tremble with tenderer breath;
> And all the wings of the Loves, and all the joys before death . . .[10]

It is ironic that even the positive elements in this hymn to carnal pleasure should take their cue and much of their diction from the Song of Songs, which is Solomon's. Be that as it may, by the end of the poem Julian is resigned to the cycles of mutability and embraces death as the natural unredeeming complement to the life of the senses:

> Thou art more than the Gods who number the days
> of our temporal breath;
> For these give labor and slumber; but thou,
> Proserpina, death.
>
> (I, 205)

The dreary counterpart to this hymn is "The Garden of Proserpine," where death becomes even more alluring and seductive than the carnal delectations that precede it:

> Pale, beyond porch and portal,
>   Crowned with calm leaves she stands
> Who gathers all things mortal
>   With cold immortal hands;
> Her languid lips are sweeter
> Than love's who fears to greet her
> To men that mix and meet her
>   From many times and lands.
>
> She waits for each and other,
>   She waits for all men born;
> Forgets the earth her mother,
>   The life of fruits and corn;
> And spring and seed and swallow
> Take wing for her and follow
> Where summer song rings hollow
>   And flowers are put to scorn.
>
> (I, 300–301)

Unlike the goddess of classical antiquity who holds life and death in an equal balance of fruition and decay, Swinburne's idol shows no proclivity to leave the underworld of organic dissolution. The thrice-repeated polysyllabic rhymes at the end of each stanza are like a soft spot in a piece of overripe fruit, sweet to excess and inclining to decay.

It has been observed time out of mind that Swinburne's poetry is conspicuously deficient in color, shape, image, the hard wiry line of rectitude. Swinburne is indeed a "sound" and almost exclusively a sound, as Henry James averred. But if the technique of the artist inevitably brings us back to his metaphysics, then Swinburne's dissolving universe of decomposing forms and liquefying solids is the poetic counterpart of an evolutionary world in which the primeval flux of germinating matter takes precedence over any of its living but evanescent offshoots. The rippling liquidity of Swinburne's verse is a manifestation of this insensate and unremitting flux. Swinburne's fluency, in this regard, has been sometimes compared with the sound world of Shelley, but there is a vital difference: Shelley's poetry soars and sings, Swinburne's verse slithers and hisses.

This is apparent in Swinburne's greatest achievement, *Atalanta in Calydon* (1865), a Euripidean-styled tragedy on his usual theme of desire and destruction. Nothing could be more illustrative of Swinburne's pessimistic assessment of those betrayals and cross-purposes that estrange the human generations one from another and darken every desire with the concomitant of pain than this hopeless account of the love between a Greek Amazon and a Calydonian prince destroyed by his jealous mother. The presiding goddess of the play is Artemis or Diana, who is initially extolled in her threefold capacity as Luna, Diana, and Hecate, goddess of the moon, the hunt, and death—and thus a kind of female naturalistic counterpart to the Christian Trinity:

> Maiden, and mistress of the months and stars
> Now folded in the flowerless fields of heaven,
> Goddess who all gods love with threefold heart,
> Being treble in thy divided deity,
> A light for dead men and dark hours, a foot
> Swift on the hills as morning, and a hand
> To all things fierce and fleet that roar and range
> Mortal, with gentler shafts than snow or sleep;
> Hear now and help and lift no violent hand . . .
>
> (VII, 269)

And so the adjuration unfolds, coil by coil, like some exotically patterned snake of interminable length. Despite the chief huntsman's
attempt to avert the goddess's violent hand, the play is rife with violence—as the first principal chorus that celebrates the arrival of
spring heavily underscores:

> When the hounds of spring are on winter's traces,
> The mother of months in meadow or plain
> Fills the shadows and windy places
> With lisp of leaves and ripple of rain;
> And the brown bright nightingale amorous
> Is half assuaged for Itylus,
> For the Thracian ships and the foreign faces,
> The tongueless vigil, and all the pain.
>
> (VII, 271)

As the threefold goddess—experienced successively by men as
Mother, Mistress, and Death—Swinburne's deity is as busy at destruction as she is at creation. Her hounds pursue the spring as
they formerly pursued the hapless Actaeon, and the songbirds
who awake at the inception of the new season remind us of the
rape, murder, vengeance, and horror associated with the stories of
Philomela, who was turned by the gods into a nightingale after being raped by her brother-in-law, and of Procne, Philomela's sister,
who obtained revenge on her husband by killing their child Ity-
lus—subsequently reincarnated as a swallow. The whole ensuing
hymn to the goddess emphasizes the contradictory nature of the
spring as a season when the wolf follows the fawn, the god pursues
the maiden, and the satyr crushes the chestnut—in short, when life
and death, creation and destruction are inextricably intertwined.

The story that follows elaborates on the amoral impulse to procreation that turns generation against generation and kinsman
against kinsman. Because Althea, queen of Calydon, has failed to
propitiate the shrines of Artemis, the goddess of the hunt sends a
wild boar to ravish the countryside. None of Calydon's warriors
can slay the beast, and so a contest is held to attract and award a
huntsman up to the mark. But the victor is not a huntsman but a
huntress, the Amazon Atalanta, who conquers the boar and Meleager, Prince of Calydon, by the same stroke. When Meleager discovers that his uncles intend to slay Atalanta in male pique at having

been outshone by a woman, the young prince defends his beloved by murdering his own kinsman. And when the queen, Althea, discovers her son's familial treachery, she, in her turn, kills him as well. Thus human life is seen to be part of that same insensate universe in which "night [is] the shadow of light, / And life, the shadow of death" (VII, 280).

This amorphous, amoral goddess of life and death is extolled in the most orthodox of Swinburne's hymns to the principle of fertility, "Hertha." Like Shelley in "The Cloud," Swinburne has Hertha, the personified goddess of the life-force, utter forth her own identity in a series of stanzas that recall but parody the stanza Shelley contrived in "To a Skylark." Shelley's skylark stands equally for that unseen power which abides behind the shows of existence, but for Shelley this power is utterly transcendent and unapprehensible, even though its effects are apparent in the natural world which veils the spirit of its laws. Swinburne's Hertha is completely immanent, a goddess of chthonic powers, a cosmic female protoplasm that diffuses itself through space and time and has no existence apart from the protozoan that is shaped and reshaped through generations of Darwinian survival. She is, in short, the poetic counterpart to the theory of natural selection who defiantly repudiates the God of Moses by coopting his most consecrated line:

> First life on my sources
>   First drifted and swam;
> Out of me are the forces
>   That save it or damn;
> Out of me man and woman, and wild-beast and bird;
>   before God was I am.
>
> (II, 137)

The soup of this primeval slime dissolves solids and reconstitutes nature according to the flux of biological laws unredeemed by any saving purpose. Of course, the comfort of a goddess like Hertha is that she demands nothing of her votaries except that they give way to their own irrepressible instincts—for Hertha is nothing more than the evolutionary embodiment of those instincts and, hence, a cosmic rationalization for someone who wants a quasi-religious excuse for doing what he likes. The problem, of course, is not with evolution but with the way in which Swinburne interprets this phenomenon. As Chesterton observes,

Evolution is either an innocent scientific description of how certain earthly things came about; or, if it is anything more than this, it is an attack upon thought itself. If evolution destroys anything, it does not destroy religion but rationalism. If evolution simply means that a positive thing called an ape turned very slowly into a positive thing called a man, then it is stingless for the most orthodox; for a personal God might just as well do things slowly as quickly, especially if, like the Christian God, he were outside of time. But if it means anything more, it means there is no such thing as an ape to change, and no such thing as a man for him to change into. It means that there is no such thing as a thing. At best, there is only one thing, and that is a flux of everything and anything. This is an attack not upon the faith, but upon the mind; you cannot think if there are no things to think about.[11]

Perhaps the most serious shortcoming of Swinburne's verse, despite its inexhaustible lyricism, is not that he gets carried away by the sound of words to the point where his poetry becomes wearisome, repetitious, and monotonous, but that, in the last analysis, he leaves us in a world where there are no things to think about.

Such is not the case with the last Oxonian to be considered in this context; Gerard Manley Hopkins, underwent the most extensive, remarkable, and, perhaps, transfiguring pilgrimage of those poets who in their youth imbibed the spirit of Oxford.

Hopkins came up to Balliol College, Oxford, in 1863, when Matthew Arnold held the poetry lectureship. But the decisive influence on Hopkins was not Arnold, but Newman whose High Church legacy continued to inform the beliefs and practices of Oxford's Anglo-Catholics. If, for Arnold, Newman was principally revered as an accomplished and urbane master of English prose, for Hopkins he was very much more—a kindly light amid the encircling gloom of a world that had lost its hold on the permanent things.

Dissatisfied with Balliol's somewhat free-thinking atmosphere, Hopkins regularly attended services at Christ Church College, where Edward Pusey, one of Newman's original associates, sustained the values and beliefs of Tractarian worship. The appearance in 1864 of Newman's spiritual autobiography, *Apologia Pro*

Vita Sua, precipitated Hopkins into a crisis of faith. Despite the High Church affiliations of his family, Hopkins was persuaded that the Tractarian position was untenable and that the sacramentalism, ritualism, and sense of historical continuity it espoused was most fully incarnate in the Church of Rome. Accordingly, Hopkins wrote to Newman in August of 1866, declaring his intentions of becoming a Catholic: "I do not want to be helped to any conclusions of belief, for I am thankful to say my mind is made up[;] but the necessity of becoming a Catholic ... coming upon me suddenly has put me into painful confusion of mind about my immediate duty in my circumstances."[12] A month later Hopkins was invited to Newman's residence at Oak Hill, Hampstead. He described the interview to his friend and eventual literary executor, Robert Bridges: "Dr. Newman was most kind, I mean in the very best sense, for his manner is not that of solicitous kindness but genial and almost, so to speak, unserious ... he made sure I was acting deliberately and wished to hear my arguments; when I had given them and said I [could] see no way out of them, he laughed and said 'Nor can I.'"[13] A month later Hopkins wrote his mother describing his reception into the Catholic faith under the aegis of Newman. The extent of Hopkins's commitment became apparent two years later when he began an eight-year novitiate in the Jesuit order.

As priest and poet, Hopkins was sometimes divided by antagonistic demands, the lowliness and routine of his everyday duties proving something of an obstacle to the unfledging of his poetic powers. But it may be and has been argued that it was precisely this conflict that forged in the smithy of his soul a poetry more authentically real, solid, and untarnished than would otherwise have been the case. Indeed, so concentrated is this poetry, so exacting in its rejection of everything secondhand, uninspired, or incompletely wrought, that it poses peculiar problems for the reader accustomed to more conventional verse. In his own age, with the exception of a small circle of friends, Hopkins was entirely unknown. So daring and unprecedented were his techniques, that Robert Bridges waited thirty years after the poet's death to bring out a volume of his works in 1918. Yet the difficulty lies not in his themes, which are traditional, sacramental, and devotional, but in the diction, syntax, and form of the verse, which derive from Hopkins's experiments with poetic rhythm and conventional grammar.

As his early undergraduate verse demonstrates, the poet could write superlatively in traditional meters and was a master of English prosody. But like some of his contemporaries in the realm of painting who began, like Van Gogh for instance, to bypass the rules of representational accuracy for the purpose of seizing the indwelling essence of a perceived object, so Hopkins began to deliberately contravene the rules of standard English for the sake of seizing a poetic experience that eludes the customary requirements of verbal usage. He will thus do away with conjunctions, transitions, or whole trains of verbal slack for the purpose of grasping a reality in all its immediate, irreducible, and untranslatable uniqueness. Hopkins's tutor at Oxford, Walter Pater, noted in an important passage of Victorian aesthetics that "all art constantly aspires towards the condition of music,"[14] and that poetry, like music, should endeavor to free itself from discursive paraphrase and meld wholly with those words that are its essence and raison d'être. In this way, the poem "explodes," to use one of Hopkins's favorite words, in the consciousness of the reader with the sensuous immediacy of a musical air. Thus at the beginning of "The Windhover," the poet cries "I caught this morning morning's minion . . . ,"[15] leaving out phrases that would usually accompany the word "caught" when used in this context. To say, "I caught sight" or "I caught the meaning of"—for the poet is using "caught" here in both senses—would constitute a deflation of poetic excitement and perceptual shock into the pedestrian rules of ordinary speech. It would also unstring the line's rhythmic tautness and take away from the speaker's rapt and fairly breathless apperception of the windhover's unparalleled beauty.

The concentration and intensity of Hopkins's verse derives from two philosophic sources, one sacred and the other profane. The sacred source is the philosophy of Duns Scotus, the fourteenth-century Oxford theologian whom Hopkins celebrates in a sonnet to this "Towery city and branchy between towers" (40). Scotus was a medieval philosopher very much concerned with the principle of individuation: the particular and unrepeatable "thisness" of a created object that determines its unique characteristics and bespeaks an intrinsic and aboriginal virtue which distinguishes that object—animal, mineral, or vegetable—from the class of beings to which it belongs. For Scotus this essence as it is in itself is hidden from the world and known only to God, though its perceivable attributes give some tangible suggestion to its salient properties. Now for Hopkins, unlike Swinburne, the world is not just a flux of indeterminate matter, but the primal stuff that coalesces, as Scotus would have it, around the center of a unique, enduring, and individuated essence. If Swinburne's poetry is a mellifluous solvent that erodes the boundaries between distinctive objects, then Hopkins's poetry is a lyrical lodestone around which physical energies group in an abiding pattern.

Much of Hopkins's poetry is concerned with capturing the peculiar pattern, or what the poet habitually refers to as the "inscape," of things. In this regard, Hopkins is especially close to the spirit of St. Francis, for as G. K. Chesterton observes, "St. Francis was a mystic, but he believed in mysticism and not in mystification. As a mystic he was the mortal enemy of all those mystics who melt away the edges of things and dissolve an entity into its environment. He was a mystic of the daylight and the darkness; but not a mystic of the twilight."[16] The same could equally be said of Hopkins.

But if Scotus and St. Francis provide the philosophic underpinnings of Hopkins's search for sacramental essences, it was his tutor, Walter Pater, who taught him to wait upon those privileged moments "when some form grows perfect in hand or face; some tone on the hills or sea is choicer than the rest; some mood of passion or insight or intellectual excitement is irresistibly real and attractive for us,—for that moment only."[17] Pater's conclusion to that masterpiece of Victorian prose *The Renaissance* is an exhortation to cultivate exquisite and august sensations, to keep one's spirit as finely tuned as possible, and "to be present always at the focus where the greatest number of vital forces unite in their purest energy."[18] Pater's creed is hedonistic and necessitarian, for these moments of ecstatic discrimination take place in a world of centrifugal forces where the elements of existence are subject to incessant erosion and disintegration. Pater's position thus falls roughly between the opposing assumptions of Hopkins, the poet of abiding solids, and Swinburne, the songster of all that melts, thaws, and resolves itself into a dew—and it may well be Hopkins and Swinburne whom Pater respectively portrayed as Cornelius, the Christian soldier, and Flavian, the decadent aesthete, in that quintessentially Oxford novel *Marius the Epicurean* (1885). Be that as it may, Hopkins adapted Pater's urgent aestheticism to his own religious apprehension of the world, so that his moments of epiphanic intensity burn with that "hard gem-like flame" which Pater exhorted his disciples to cultivate.

In his second year at Oxford, Hopkins formulated the difference between what he perceived to be the highest class of poetry written in "the language of inspiration," by which he meant "a mood of great, abnormal in fact, mental acuteness, either energetic or receptive, according as the thoughts which arise from it seem generated by a stress and action of the brain or strike into it unasked," and that accomplished but rather pedestrian roll of elevated diction and and rhetorical flourish that Hopkins christened "Parnassian."[19] Hopkins's fastidious refusal to write in anything less than that "inspiration" which "raises [a poet] above himself" is thus the metrical counterpart to Pater's propitiation of the exceptional moment. But with Hopkins, Pater's "brief and wholly concrete moment which ... seems to absorb past and future in an intense consciousness of the present"[20] is endowed with a sacerdotal value, so that the Romantic "spot of time" which Pater has topped off with a Heracletian anxiety about the doom that attends all things mortal is transfigured into a moment of plenary grace and baptized into a gift of the Holy Spirit.

There is one other element of Hopkins's verse that needs to be broached before examining some lyrics representative of his genius: the notion, namely, of "sprung rhythm." Much of a highly technical and obfuscatory nature has been written by critics about this dimension of Hopkins's poetry. When we turn, however, to Hopkins's own observations we find that the subject is far more accessible than we are sometimes led to believe. Like his tutor, Walter Pater, Hopkins realized that poetry and prose were becoming far less distinct among contemporary practitioners of either art. The language had evolved, and the rhythms of everyday speech were no longer as readily amenable to the fixed patterns of the English metrical line. A poem written consistently in iambic pentameter was thus subject to a strain of artificiality inimical to that living catch of the speaking voice which Hopkins considered indispensable to the effects of an ingenuous lyricism. But this did not warrant the abolition of rhythm as a vital ingredient of poetic form.

Rhythm, after all, is one of the pleasures peculiar to verse and has its roots in those physiological rhythms that animate the human organism—the inhalation and exhalation of breath, the systole and diastole of the pulse, the recurrent measures of walking, running, swimming, or dancing. Poetry exploits rhythms for their expressive capacity, both those that uplift, like the rising sprint of the galloping anapest, or those that subdue, like the falling rhythm of the descending dactyl. Hopkins wished to retain these rhythms but to dispense with the necessity of writing an entire poem according to a prescribed number of iambics, dactylics, or anapests. Anarchy would be prevented by retaining a certain number of accentual beats per line, but these stresses would be determined not by the counting of syllables—as is commonly the case—but rather by the number of natural stresses as these occur in the inflections of ordinary speech. The rhythms are thus shaped more responsively to the actual events—be these physical or emotional—that the poem dramatizes.

It is not, therefore, surprising that "The Windhover," a poem that delineates the aerial ballet of a wheeling falcon, is Hopkins's first and most arresting experiment in this new form. "Why do I employ sprung rhythm at all?" Hopkins asked by way of response to Robert Bridges; "because it is the nearest to the rhythm of prose, that is the native and natural rhythm of speech, the least forced, the most rhetorical and emphatic of all possible rhythms, combining, as it seems to me, opposite and, one would have thought, incompatible excellences, markedness of rhythm ... and naturalness of expression."[21] As precedents for this practice Hopkins cited the choruses of Milton's *Samson Agonistes* (1671) and the classic English nursery rhyme. Thus "One two / Buckle my shoe" contains the same number of beats per line notwithstanding the discrepancy in the number of syllables. Hopkins simply expanded this practice into a complex and highly sophisticated musical fabric capable of the subtlest response to mood and feeling, as is apparent in "The Windhover, *To Christ Our Lord*":

> I caught this morning morning's minion, king-
> dom of daylight's dauphin, dapple-dawn-drawn Falcon,
> in his riding
> Of the rolling level underneath him steady air, and
> striding
> High there, how he rung upon the rein of a wimpling wing
> In his ecstasy! then off, off forth on swing,

As a skate's heel sweeps smooth on a bow-bend: the
                                 hurl and gliding
   Rebuffed the big wind. My heart in hiding
Stirred for a bird,—the achieve of, the mastery of the
      thing!

Brute beauty and valour and act, oh, air, pride, plume, here
         Buckle! AND the fire that breaks from thee then, a billion
Times told lovelier, more dangerous, O my chevalier!
      No wonder of it: sheer plod makes plough down sillion
      Shine, and blue-bleak embers, ah my dear,
         Fall, gall themselves, and gash gold-vermillion.

                                                          (29)

One can see at a glance that after an initial line of ten syllables, Hopkins's poem takes off in a syncopated series of rhythmic pulses that follow the wingbeats of the bird and awaken the poet to a rapt contemplation of the Christian mysteries. Thus, the second, third, and fourth lines contain, respectively, 16, 15, and 12 syllables—yet each may be scanned in a manner that produces five stresses. Moreover, each of these stresses falls in a pattern which accentuates the flight of the bird, as when in the fourth line, the word "High" carries a stress that gives rhythmic propulsion to the bird's ascent. The poem's dedication, "To Christ Our Lord," is carried through in the connotative diction that endows the falcon with the attributes of the Trinity. It is at once "King," "minion," and "dauphin," ruler, servant, and heir to the throne in the paradoxical language that denotes the hypostatic union of the Father and the Son.

Insofar as the whole of creation partakes of and proclaims for Hopkins the life and character of its Maker, the flight of the bird adumbrates the earthly pilgrimage of God the Son, whose fullness of identity was achieved through a series of renunciations, culminating in the crucifixion. Hence, while the falcon initially rides the wind, circles about a pocket of air, and then takes, off like a skater, in an acute and dexterous "bow-bend," the fullness of its essence or inscape is not ultimately revealed until it yields or "buckles" to the overpowering breath of the wind. The image here is presumably that of a bird climbing the air and then falling back with its wings outspread (in the shape of a cross) as the wind assumes control and carries it, like a kite, across the sky. Though the beauty of the bird had previously arrested the poet's attention, its final act of self-abnegation before the wind is "more dangerous" and "beautiful" than any of its former pyrotechnics. It is this that "stirs" the poet's heart and compels him to define the principle implicit in the falcon's self-effacing gesture.

The sestet enunciates this principle by appealing to other phenomena in nature that illustrate the same law—namely, that the essence of a thing is most fully revealed when it submits to a power greater than itself. Thus an unplowed field, dull and muddy-colored, reveals under the impact of the plow, a glowing band of "sillion" in that silvery shine which extends along a fresh-dug furrow. And in the same way a piece of coal-black kindling reveals, under the stress of a fire, a glowing interior of gold-vermillion. Despite the diversity of these phenomena, they are all illustrative of the law of "intress"—a Hopkinsian term that designates an act of spiritual transformation brought about by the pressure of the divine will on the myriad inscapes of the created universe. By surrendering to this will, these inscapes paradoxically reach their fullest potential of individual existence and illustrate in their several ways the all-embracing truth of the Gospel precept: "He that findeth his life shall lose it; and he that loseth his life for my sake shall find it."

The theological connotations in the sestet present this process as a copy or continuation of that law which is expressed most perspicuously in Christ's sacrifice. The coals "Fall, gall themselves," recalling the circumstance that necessitated the intervention of God in human affairs—namely, the *Fall*—and the ultimate consequence of that event for the Creator who foresaw, at the dawn of creation, the gall and wormwood of Calvary. The fact, moreover, that the coals "*gash* gold-vermillion" underscores the affinity between the light that breaks from the fire and the blood that gushed from Christ's wounds. The interjection "Ah, my dear" alludes to George Herbert's devotional lyric "Love," in which the penitent sinner in the full consciousness of his unworthiness diffidently approaches the Savior of humankind: "Ah my dear / I cannot look on thee."[22] Despite the innovativeness of Hopkins's techniques, the subject matter of his poetry is clearly traditional.

From his years at Oxford onward, Hopkins was much preoccupied with the relations between sensuous beauty and its supersensuous origins. A lover of Pre-Raphaelite painting, a musician with a keen ear for the felicities of Purcell, a draftsman of no mean skill, and a poet of Keatsian intensity, Hopkins, by dint of these very talents and susceptibilities, could be tyrannized over and oppressed by that sense of beauty which he was so adroit at creating and devout at extolling. The danger of such a tyranny was exacerbated, of course, by Hopkins's vocation as a priest and by his overwhelming sense that worship of the Creator involved an unwavering fidelity to the first and second commandments. Negotiating the relationship between the Paterian moment of sensuous beauty and the Christian apprehension of God's supreme and immaterial otherness could be a balancing act of some nicety. Thus "Elected Silence," an early poem of 1866, heralds a theme that surfaces again and again in Hopkins's verse. Ostensibly a poem of renunciation, it employs the diction and movement of Keats's verse to express a most un-Keatsian penchant for the ascetic life. Yet this very asceticism somehow seems more satisfying than any indulgence of taste or touch, sound, or sight. The ideal Hopkins here pursues is not less than the senses but more—a trans-sensuality that goes beyond rather than falls below any physical ravishment:

> Elected Silence, sing to me
> And beat upon my whorlèd ear,
> Pipe me to pastures still and be
> The music that I care to hear.
>
> . . . .
>
> Palate, the hutch of tasty lust,
> Desire not to be rinsed with wine.
> The can must be so sweet, the crust
> So fresh that comes in fasts divine!
>
> (8–9)

The first stanza recalls Keats's "unheard melodies" that "Pipe to the spirit ditties of no tone" in the "Ode on a Grecian Urn," but more than Keats, it paradoxically contrives to suggest a felicity greater and more ultimately satisfying than any delectation available to the mere sensualist.

"To what serves mortal beauty" and "The Leaden Echo and the Golden Echo," play variations on the theme of "Elected Silence," though the context has changed and the sense of temptation has become more acute. In "To what serves mortal beauty," Hopkins recognizes that the distinctive, irreducible inscapes of things reach

their highest pitch of beauty and individuation in a human being—
and that, accordingly, the dangers of concupiscence are most alive
in the presence of a supremely beautiful person:

> Self flashes off frame and face,
> What do then? How meet beauty? Merely meet it; own,
> Home at heart, heaven's sweet gift; then leave, let that alone.
> Yea, wish that though, wish all, God's better beauty, grace.
>
> (60)

As the last line underscores, the only orthodox way of comporting
oneself to this beauty for Hopkins is by seeing it as a manifestation
of divine beauty and commending it back to the giver.

"The Leaden Echo and the Golden Echo" is a poem of remarkable verbal richness, complex wordplay, bold experimentation,
and aching tenderness. In the first place, it carries to an extreme
Hopkins's experiments with sprung rhythm. Whole phrases are
treated, prosodically, as if they were a single word and the entire
poem alliteratively unfolds in the melismatic rise and fall of a liturgical chant:

> How to keep—is there any any, is there nonsuch, nowhere,
>   known some, bow or broach or braid or brace, lace,
>   latch or catch or key to keep
> Back beauty, keep it, beauty, beauty, beauty, . . . from
>   vanishing away?
>
> (54)

Both Swinburne and Hopkins, as the above passage clearly demonstrates, were excessively fond of internal rhyme and alliteration,
but there is a vital difference that Charles Williams noted. Of Swinburne's alliteration "all that can really be felt," observes Williams,
"is that they do begin with the same letter." With Hopkins, however, "it is as if the imagination, seeking for expression, had found
both verb and substantive at one rush, had begun almost to say
them at once, and had separated them only because the intellect
had reduced the original unity into divided but related sounds."[23]

In any case, the related sounds of the leaden echo are resonant
with mortal dismay at the inevitable wasting of youth and beauty.
Significantly, ending with the word "despair," four times repeated

in a diminuendo of utter hopelessness, the first section of the poem is at length answered by an echo that iterates the last syllable of the preceding section. "Despair" is thus superseded by the saving word "Spare!" For the consoling strains of the golden echo asseverate that all we love and cherish is ultimately spared from "death's worst, winding sheets, tombs and worms and tumbling to decay" (54).

In the first section the speaker searches for a "key" to lock beauty away, to arrest its brief perfection, and preserve its transitory bloom. But the second section provides the "key," or the answer that will unlock the speaker (who is presumably a young girl) from the self-regarding fear of her own mortality. Instead of holding to the gifts of youth and beauty, one must gladly and lavishly let them go. The act of genuflection before the power of time becomes an act of human generosity and self-acceptance—an ecstatic acquiescence in one's mortality and, in consequence, an act of trust that the giver of life will preserve our transient graces with greater solicitude than we would be capable of ourselves.

Hopkins's preoccupation with the theme of mortal transience is signally distinct from that of the other poets of his generation for whom the so Victorian theme of loss was equally central. It is a difference best summarized by F. R. Leavis: "The Victorian-romantic addicts of beauty and transience cherish the pang as a kind of religiose-poetic sanction for defeatism in the face of an alien actual world—defeatism offering itself as a spiritual superiority. Hopkins embraces transience as a necessary condition of any grasp of the real."[24] There is, in short, in Hopkins a kind of no-nonsense supernatural realism that enabled the poet to see both art and beauty from the perspective of that ultimate source from which they derive and toward which they point. Given the portentous solemnities and pretentious affectations with which the disciples of art-for-art's-sake genuflected before the work of their own hands, it is with a sense of relief that we attend to Father Hopkins's observations on these matters:

Art and its fame do not really matter, spiritually they are nothing, virtue is the only good; but it is only by bringing in the infinite that to a just judgment they can be made to look infinitesimal or less than vastly great; and in this ordinary view I apply to them, and it is the only true rule for dealing with them, what Christ our Lord said of virtue, Let your light shine before men that they may see your good works (say, of art) and glorify your Father in heaven (that is, acknowledge that they have an absolute excellence in them and are steps in a scale of infinite and inexhaustible excellence)....[25]

It is arguable that the seven years of poetic silence to which Hopkins vowed himself during his training as a Jesuit gave him precisely the distance, perspective, and spiritual tact necessary for the execution of one of the major poems of the Victorian era, "The Wreck of the Deutschland" (1876). Pater may have exhorted his followers to "burn with a hard gem-like flame," but the cultivation of beauty for beauty's sake rarely conveys in the poetry of a Swinburne or a Morris or the decadents who followed them, anything more than a kind of wistful nostalgia or forced hyperbole. But Hopkins's poetry is genuinely hard and gemlike because it bears witness to an actual encounter—an encounter so overpowering and real in its supreme otherness that it leaves no room for the kind of self-conscious embroideries with which Hopkins's peers sometimes decked out their lives and sensations. It is, indeed, a terrible thing to fall into the hands of the living God:

> Thou mastering me
> God! giver of breath and bread;
> World's strand, sway of the sea
> Lord of living and dead;
> Thou hast found bones and veins in me, fastened me flesh,
> And after it almost unmade, what with dread,
> Thy doing: and dost thou touch me afresh?
> Over again I feel thy finger and find thee.
>
> (11)

So begins "The Wreck of the Deutschland," an extended elegy that Hopkins wrote during the term of his novitiate to commemorate the deaths of five nuns and their fellow voyagers in a shipwreck off the coast of England. The first part of the poem is a retrospective survey of Hopkins's conversion, during which he was both torn asunder and reconstituted by the God who governs both the affairs of men and the tides of the sea. Describing his attempts to circumvent the worship and obeisance he owes to God, Hopkins describes the breakdown that preceded the revaluation of his life and rededication of his powers. He describes the revelation of his utter dependence on God as a perception that suffused his entire being in the way that the bittersweet plum of the blackthorn suffuses the palate with its tart and unmistakable taste:

> How a lush-kept, plush-capped sloe
> Will, mouthed to flesh-burst,
> Gush!—flush the man, the being with it, sour or sweet,
> Brim, in a flash, full!—Hither then, last or first,
> To hero of Calvary, Christ's feet—
> Never asked if meaning it, wanting it, warned of it—men go.
>
> (14)

The imagery owes something to Keats's grape burst against the palate fine, but the overtones here are explicitly eucharistic and Christian. At all events, the spiritual convulsions that preceded Hopkins's conversion link up in part two with the convulsions of wave and wind that brought the *Deutschland* to its demise.

The theme of the poem is central to any religious apprehension of the world and reposes on the belief that mortal accidents are more than mere contingency—or rather that mere contingency can be transformed into an event of providential significance insofar as it is accepted and suffered as the occasion for spiritual growth. George MacDonald, the Victorian poet, preacher, and fabulist expresses it most succinctly:

> When thou dost send out whirlwinds on thy seas,
> Alternatest thy lightning with its roar,
> Thy night with morning, and thy clouds with stars
> Or, mightier force unseen in midst of these
> Orderest the life in every airy pore;
> Guidest men's efforts, rul'st mishaps and jars—
> 'Tis only for their hearts, and nothing more.[26]

For the nonbeliever such a notion may seem like a supreme rationalization. Hopkins, however, forestalls objections by dwelling with extreme pertinacity on the physical sufferings of the crew members. The superficial faith that worships a God of saccharine wish fulfillment could not be further removed from the blunt realism with which Hopkins depicts the sufferings of those on board. In one especially vivid scene, a sailor with a rope about his waist leaps into the waves to rescue a woman, but the waves are so severe that he is dashed immediately to death while his body, broken and battered, continues, to the horror of the onlookers, to beat against the side of the ship. These vivid depictions of brute force give authenticity and credence to the words of a nun whose "virginal tongue" summons the survivors to prayer and presumably to conversion. The sinking of the ship becomes, in consequence, the ransoming of a flock for whom this catastrophe provided the occasion of a turning toward God. This realization so overpowers the poet that in formulating it he incorporates into the very texture of his verse the elisions and syntactical breakdowns of a consciousness beseiged by a daring and august truth that defies verbal transcription:

> But how shall I . . . make me room there:
> Reach me a . . . Fancy, come faster—
> Strike you the sight of it? look at it loom there,
> Thing that she . . . there then! the Master,
> Ipse, the only one, Christ, King, Head:
> He was to cure the extremity where he had cast her;
> Do deal, lord it with living and dead;
> Let him ride, her pride, in his triumph, despatch and have done
> with his doom there.
>
> (20)

As the poet comes to the realization that, at the back of this dire north wind, "lovely felicitous providence" was at work for the salvation of the crew, the poem itself devolves into a more even, conventional syntax that verbally echoes the subsidence of the retreating storm and the return of calmer seas.

Yet these epiphanies, which enabled Hopkins to ecstatically perceive that "Christ plays in ten thousand places, / Lovely in limbs and lovely in eyes not his" (53), were mysteriously withdrawn from the poet in his later years. A dark night of the soul enveloped him so that he was obliged, in the extremity of abandonment, to cling to the perceptions that had formerly directed his life but that now seemed nebulous, uncertain, and doubtful. Dialectically, this experience of "dryness" or "acedia" is a not uncommon stage in the life of a believer—a kind of testing that forces the disciple to bear witness in the dark to that which he had formerly perceived in the light. In the wake, then, of those hallowed moments in which the poet knew that "The world is charged with the grandeur of God," Hopkins was visited by a host of harrowing fears regarding his life, his work, and his faith. The result was a series of excruciating sonnets in which the sense of spiritual abandonment echoes the cry of Christ in Gethsemane—"the cry which confessed," as G. K. Chesterton observes, "that God was forsaken of God."[27]

In a sonnet like "Carrion Comfort," the thew and sinew of the verse replicates in its staccato of sharp consonants and halting syntax the poet's sense of being physically engaged in a fight for survival with the demon of despair:

> Not, I'll not, carrion comfort, Despair, not feast on thee,
> Not untwist—slack they may be—these last strands of man
> In me or, most weary, cry *I can do no more.* I can; . . .
>
> (61)

The struggle eventuates, however, in a resolution that affirms the poet's triumph over that dread which almost unmans him, for he realizes in retrospect that he has been wrestling with God himself: "That night, that year / Of now done darkness I wretch lay wrestling with (my God!) my God" (62). Especially effective is that twice-repeated exclamation, which on its second utterance evolves from a conventional expression of dismay into a searingly vivid realization that his antagonist has been the Lion of Judah. For all its dread and horror, the sonnet ends on a redemptive note inasmuch as the poet realizes that his struggle has raised him to a higher level of spiritual awareness.

Such is not the case, however, in sonnets like "No worst, there is none," "To seem the stranger lies my lot," or, most harrowing of all, "I wake and feel the fell of dark." Into the dense imagery, broken syntax, and sophisticated metrics of these compelling lyrics, Hopkins will frequently interject a demotic expression so simple and straightforward in its confession of anguish that the reader is almost inclined, in human modesty, to glance away from a grief so profoundly real and sincere:

> I wake and feel the fell of dark, not day.
> What hours, O what black hours we have spent

This night! What sights, you, heart, saw; ways you went!
And more must, in yet longer light's delay.
    With witness I speak this. But where I say
Hours I mean years, mean life. And my lament
Is cries countless, cries like dead letters sent
To dearest him that lives alas! away.

                            (65)

To compare the above utterance with a poem like Tennyson's *In Memoriam*, in which the issue of doubt and faith is equally engaged, is to realize the distance between Hopkins and his contemporaries. Hopkins stretches the language to its expressive limits for the purpose of dramatizing an event that is imperiously immediate and uncomfortably actual. Arnold, Tennyson, and Swinburne too often diffuse their griefs in a wash of Parnassian eloquence that falsifies or obscures the darker realities from which they shy away. But Hopkins places our hands right on the sore spot, "the fell of dark, not day," so that the horror of spiritual abandonment translates into the fell, or pelt, of a carnivorous beast that threatens the poet's life (as Dante's in the *Inferno* is threatened on the *fell* of an obscure wood by the *fell* or life-threatening proximity of wolf, leopard, and lion). After this sophisticated verbal punning, the stark declaration "With witness I speak this" is all the more poignant in its confessional candor and personal pathos. The final comparison of prayer to a series of letters sent to an addressee who has presumably moved residence or died is the most extreme expression in Hopkins's poetry of that dark night cruelly and paradoxically reserved for the most elect of Christ's disciples. It is a paradox best described by C. S. Lewis in his reflections on the agony in the garden. The pertinence of this passage to Hopkins's own situation, especially insofar as it illumines those necessary and inescapable connections between the poet of sacred fervors and the poet of God's silence, should be readily apparent:

As for the last dereliction of all, how can we either understand or endure it? Is it that God Himself cannot be Man unless God seems to vanish at his greatest need? And if so, why? I sometimes wonder if we have begun to understand what is involved in the very concept of creation. If God will create, He will make something to be, and yet to be not Himself. To be created is, in some sense to be ejected or separated. Can it be that the more perfect the creature is, the further this separation must at some point be pushed? It is saints, not common people, who experience the "dark night." It is men and angels, not beasts who rebel. Inanimate matter sleeps in the bosom of the Father. The "hiddenness" of God perhaps presses most painfully on those who are in another way nearest to Him, and therefore, God Himself, made man, will of all men be by God most forsaken?[28]

· NINE ·

The Pre-Raphaelite Circle

In the middle of the nineteenth century, England was graced with a school of artists whose influence on public taste and sensibility was perceptible not only in the domains of fine art and poetry but also in the more practical and applied realms of interior design, church ornament, bookbinding, and household furnishings. Though they began as rebels, decrying the sober finish, dull conventionality, and saccharine subject matter of much academic art, their rebellion was animated by a stance even more reactionary than that of those artists—largely followers of Sir Joshua Reynolds—whose works they so strenuously condemned. Among these, genre painters of domestic trivia, such as Sir David Wilke (1785–1841) in *The First Ear-Ring,* and historical painters of inflated pretensions, such as William Etty (1787–1849) in *Sleeping Nymph and Satyr* were especially reprobated. Christening themselves "Pre-Raphaelites," they wished to return, both theologically and aesthetically, to the heraldic world of medieval Christendom and the stained-glass radiance of medieval iconography. In this regard, they were an artistic counterpart to the Oxford Movement and shared with the young Newman a keen interest in the work of the Nazarenes—that youthful group of Romantic German artists who traveled to Italy and endeavored to resuscitate the tradition of biblical and sacred portraiture from Giotto to Perugino. Among these, Overbeck's chaste, cool, marmoreal images of the Madonna were held in especial esteem. But the roots of the Pre-Raphaelites were equally fixed in the world of post-Enlightenment science, especially as this was expressed in the theoretical work of Ruskin, for whom the austere grandeur of mountain crag, the delicate tracery of tendril and vine, or the ever-shifting patterns of cloud and wave were all signatures of an unsearchable essence expressed in the manifold and microscopically distinct profiles of great creating nature. To reproduce this Bible of nature with painstaking fidelity to its laws and effects was to reveal, according to Ruskin, that indwelling divinity whose hand the artist's brush imperfectly aspires to copy.

"All great art is Praise," wrote Ruskin, who subsequently came to the defense of the Pre-Raphaelites with the same ardor with which he had formerly championed the works of Turner. But there was nothing inarticulate about these daubers who were possessed of tongues as eloquent as Ruskin's. Indeed, their commitment to literature was commensurate with their devotion to painting, and in 1848 they founded a journal entitled *The Germ* as a vehicle for the propagation of their aesthetic principles and a venue for the dissemination of their poetry. The ringleader of the movement was an impassioned young man of twenty, of mixed Italian and English descent, by the name of Dante Gabriel Rossetti (1828–1882). Equally distinguished as poet and painter, and possessed of a personality, by all accounts, of magnetic and mesmerizing intensity, he became the center of a group of artists who saw in him the inspired hierophant of an art that would redeem the modern age from its dreary secularism and free Victorian painting from the bleak shadows, brown-hued finish, and factitious certified look of the "old masters" from Raphael to Rembrandt, who, paradoxically, were not old enough for the taste of these backward-looking iconoclasts. Their motto could easily have been that of Blake's inspired pupil, Samuel Palmer, who defiantly observed, "the past is for poets, the present for pigs."

In addition to Rossetti, the brotherhood initially consisted of John Everett Millais, William Holman Hunt, James Collinson, and Ford Madox Brown. But insofar as it is the poetry with which we are concerned, it is the second stage of Pre-Raphaelitism, as manifest at Oxford in 1856, that compels our attention. For then, to Dante Gabriel's and his sister, Christina's (1830–1894), were added the poetic voices of William Morris and Algernon Swinburne, although Swinburne's unabashed paganism and paucity of visual detail make him a less pure disciple of this school, despite his strange affinity to the verse of Christina.

Though Dante, or Gabriel, as he was more familiarly called by family and friends, and Christina were the most distinguished of the Rossettis, their entire family was exceptionally gifted and perhaps second only to the Brontës in the alarming genius of its progeny. The other two Rossetti children were equally accomplished: William Michael, as a critic and man of letters; and Maria, who became an Anglican nun, as the author of a still readable introduction to the foremost poet of medieval Christendom, Dante Alighieri (1265–1321). Maria, in this regard, continued the scholarly investigations of her father, an Italian expatriate who fled to England to escape political persecution, secured a position as Professor of Romance Languages at the University of London, and married Frances Polidori, the sister of Byron's personal physician, John Polidori, who penned the gothic thriller *The Vampyr* (1816) and whose romantic life ended in suicide at the age of twenty-six. The exotic background of the Rossetti children was reinforced by frequent visits of Italian exiles who fulminated against the Bourbon occupation of their homeland and preached revolution. Despite these diatribes, the household remained, under the watchful eye of the mother, Frances Rossetti, devoutly Anglican.

But the combination of Anglican piety and Italian impetuosity created a less than easy mix in the temperaments of Christina and Gabriel, whose verse bears the strain of an incessant conflict between Mediterranean sensuousness and High Church austerity. The sensuousness ultimately triumphed in Gabriel, though not without pangs of conscience that made his later years a continual struggle with the demon of remorse. Christina's renunciatory faith (for though she did not follow her sister into the convent, her imagination was entirely possessed by the ethos of Anglicanism) was an equally turbid mixture of religious resolution and earthly regret. Gabriel's passionate pursuit of beauty led to entanglements that belied the devout ideals which he initially reverenced; Christina's austere search for perfection was equally troubled by many back glances at the mortal happiness she deliberately renounced.

Gabriel's poetic career began in a spirit of humility and homage to his great Italian namesake, Dante Alighieri. The poet was fully conscious of his spiritual affinity to the medieval master, who was the subject of an extensive study by Rossetti's father. When the elder Rossetti passed away, his son commemorated his relationship to the author of *The Divine Comedy* in a sonnet on his father's death:

> And did'st thou know indeed, when at the font
> Together with thy name thou gav'st me his,
> That also on thy son must Beatrice
> Decline her eyes according to her wont

> Accepting me to be of those that haunt
> The vale of magical dark mysteries.
>   (145)

Rossetti's Beatrice was Elizabeth Elinor Siddal, a cockney milliner who soon became the principal model for the brotherhood. There are, moreover, some remarkable parallels between Rossetti's drawings of Elizabeth Siddal and his sonnets from *Dante and His Circle,* which belong to the first phase of the poet's career. Both are characterized by a self-effacing homage to the spirit of the model— whether the living woman or the Italian poet—in which the features of the original are tactfully reproduced, shorn of ornament or exaggeration. In a word, both the artist's pencil and the poet's pen trace in lines of sparing and unswerving simplicity and unadorned beauty of their respective prototypes.

Ruskin, who frequently complained of Rossetti's excesses, was entirely correct when he wrote to the painter, "I think [Miss Siddal] should be very happy to see how much more beautifully, perfectly and tenderly you draw when you are drawing *her* than when you are drawing anybody else. She cures you of all your worst faults when you only look at her."[1] Rossetti's dexterous fidelity to the soul of his model and the spirit of his namesake is best revealed in a "Ballata" of Dante's appended to Rossetti's translation of the *New Life.* The words Dante here addresses to Beatrice are in perfect accord with Rossetti's devotion to Elizabeth and the spirit in which his drawings of her were executed.

> Because mine eyes can never have their fill
> Of looking at my lady's lovely face,
>   I will so fix my gaze
> That I may become blessed, beholding her.
>
> Even as an angel, up at his great height
> Standing amid the light,
>   Becometh blest by only seeing God:—
> So, though I be a simple earthly wight,
> Yet not the less I might
>   Beholding her who is my heart's dear load,
>   Be blessed, and in the spirit soar abroad.
> Such power abideth in that gracious one,

Albeit felt of none
Save of him who, desiring, honours her.[2]

The tremulous transparency of the verse—like a cup of cold water—perfectly suggests the sober, somewhat archaic purity of the Italian original. Stripped of unnecessary frills or indulgent mannerisms, Rossetti's chaste utterance at this period parallels the delicacy and charm with which he memorialized the features of Elizabeth Siddal in that series of pen-and-ink drawings which are presently regarded as the preeminent masterpieces of Pre-Raphaelite draftsmanship.

Both Rossetti and Elizabeth endeavored to sustain, in the early stages of their relationship, the spirit of Dante in *La Vita Nuova*. A brief comparison, then, of Dante Alighieri and Dante Rossetti is necessary for an understanding of the Victorian poet's work. *La Vita Nuova* is, perhaps, the consummate expression of the courtly love ideal, though in Dante the process of imaginative and spiritual refinement removes this love from the illicit passions into which it frequently devolved. In this autobiographical record of his love for Beatrice, Dante goes through a series of stages that roughly correspond to the medieval notion of the soul's approach to God. At first, Dante is plunged into a state of dereliction at the sight of Beatrice. The distance that separates him from his beloved testifies to his own unworthiness. He becomes obsessed with his own feelings, moods, desires, and is cut off from normal, healthy relations with his fellow men. For the medieval mystic, such a recognition of the soul's unworthiness was a salutary stage in the direction of spiritual growth. Still, it was a stage beset with dangers, not the least of which is that despair which doubts the exhaustlessness of divine grace. But Dante transcends these self-tormentings and rises to a higher stage of spiritual illumination in which the virtues of the beloved are celebrated notwithstanding the distance that places her beyond his possession. In the third and final stage, love has fully expanded beyond desire. Beatrice is the chosen vessel through whom the poet is able to rise to a contemplation of God himself. In consequence, his obsession with the mortal Beatrice gives way to a freedom from will and desire in which through her he is granted an ultimate vision of reality. Dante's passage through the stages of dereliction, purgation, and enlightenment finally enables him to recognize that, in the words of Simone Weil, "the longing to love the beauty of the world in a human being is essentially the longing for the Incarnation. It is mistaken if it thinks it is anything else. The Incarnation alone can satisfy it. It is therefore wrong to reproach the mystics, as has been done sometimes, because they use love's language. It is theirs by right, others only borrow it."[3]

Both Dante and Christina Rossetti use love's language in their poetry to describe what was otherwise ineffable. But if Christina uses this language "by right," the question remains whether Gabriel has only borrowed it to serve ends that are somewhat less than theocentric. The fact is that Rossetti, contrary to his medieval alter ego, illustrates a kind of inversion of those three stages of spiritual development heretofore traced in Dante. For with Rossetti, love gradually disengages itself from that broader spiritual universe in which it assumes its full significance for the medieval poet. Thus, the mystical raptures of Rossetti's youth first give way to an increasing absorption in the physical charms of his beloved, and then finally devolve into a barren and futile brooding over the poet's misdirected powers, his failure to live up to his ideal, and his dereliction in the pursuit of more tangible compensations. But if Rossetti ends where Dante begins, it is important to remember that unlike Dante, Rossetti lived in an age when faith had withdrawn into the realm of subjective feeling, while the world of Victorian industry and thought seemed increasingly indifferent, if not hostile, to the needs of the human spirit.

Two early poems of Rossetti, "The Blessed Damozel" and "My Sister's Sleep," are nominally Dantesque in inspiration but reveal, on closer inspection, a sizable rift between what Jacques Maritain described as the medieval poet's "absolute firmness in a consistent universe of thought rooted in reason and faith"[4] and what may be described as the Victorian poet's contradictory attempt to reconcile competing realities and antagonistic ideals.

"The Blessed Damozel" was originally written in 1848, but Rossetti revised it throughout his life—not only to improve its diction and rhythm, but to bring it into closer proximity with the actual events of the poet's life (for after Elizabeth's death in 1862, Rossetti virtually became the haunted and sometimes hallucinating speaker of his youthful poem). The Dantesque situation—for the poem is ostensibly uttered by the departed yet very tangible spirit of a young woman yearning from the ramparts of heaven for her bereaved lover on earth—is complemented by reminiscences of another Pre-Raphaelite artist-hero, Edgar Allan Poe. As Rossetti wrote apropos of "The Raven," "I saw that Poe had done the utmost it was possible to do with the grief of the lover on earth, and I determined to reverse the conditions, and give utterance to the yearning of the loved one in heaven."[5] Like Tennyson, then, in *In Memoriam*, Rossetti expresses a typically Victorian anxiety about post-mortal survival—an anxiety apparent on a popular level in the rise of seances, mediums, and parapsychology. The attempt, however, to commune with the dead is in some ways at the farthest remove from what is traditionally designated as prayer. For instead of surrendering to the will of God or accepting the laws of providence, traffickers in the occult are intent upon controlling destiny or manipulating the divine will. But as it ultimately transpires, "The Blessed Damozel" is a complete hoax. For the foundations of Rossetti's hereafter are rooted in the fears and anxieties of the poem's bereaved lover whose grief, as the parenthetical stanzas in the poem underscore, has so disrupted his sense of reality that he is unable to distinguish between psychological projection and empirical fact. Moreover, the image of the beloved he projects is in conspicuous conflict with the Christian trappings that cling to his conception of heaven. Indifferent to saints, angels, the Virgin, and even Christ—except insofar as he can broker a reunion between herself and her paramour—Rossetti's damozel shows a certain lack of ordonnance in her priorities that would disturb most professing Christians.

Moreover, unlike Dante, who humbly accepts Beatrice's admonition that God is not only to be found in her eyes, Rossetti's lover, who has duped himself into a belief that the leaves which fall about his head are nothing less than the disentwined tresses of his beloved, has no inkling of a paradise that exists apart from the passionate breast of his departed lady. And although the jewel-like imagery and archaic diction have something in common with the radiant icons of a Fra Angelico—

> Herself shall bring us, hand in hand,
>   To Him round whom all souls
> Kneel, the clear-ranged unnumbered heads
>   Bowed with their aureoles;

> And the angels meeting us shall sing
>> To their citherns and citoles—
>
> (6)

the spiritual atmosphere is strangely troubled by an earthy turbulence that seems singularly out of place in this distinctly sacrosanct setting.

If the Pre-Raphaelites endeavored to achieve, in poetry and painting, the ingenuous piety of that Christian art which predated Raphael, then "My Sister's Sleep," another of Rossetti's early poems, is a telling indication of how difficult this evangel was to sustain. The poem apparently turns on the Christian premise that death is the door to rebirth, while the dramatic situation involves a poor widow in a cold boardinghouse keeping vigil, with her son, by the side of her dying daughter. Having gone sleepless for days, their senses, under the duress of fatigue and anxiety, are preternaturally alert. The poem's details are, in consequence, uncannily vivid, almost surreal, and seem to cry out for symbolic interpretation—but ironically these details stand for nothing beyond themselves.[6] At one point the speaker confesses:

> I had been sitting up some nights,
>> And my tired mind felt weak and blank;
>> Like a sharp strengthening wine it drank
> The stillness and the broken lights.
>
> (97)

But unlike the cup of salvation, this cluster of unrelated and imperiously vivid impressions, which the speaker imbibes "like a sharp strengthening wine" offers nothing in the way of solace or redemption.

> Just then in the room over us
>> There was a pushing back of chairs,
>> As some who had sat unawares
> So late, now heard the hour, and rose.
>
> (97)

The movement upstairs coincides with a midnight bell heralding the arrival of Christmas day. Within moments, the mourners, discovering that their loved one has died, fall on their knees and wearily declare "Christ's blessing on the newly born." But this final, somewhat feeble attempt to transform a demoralizing vigil into a situation of faith seems lame at best and only serves to throw into even starker relief those sharply etched inhospitable details that surround a family shrunken by poverty and mortal sickness. The rustle of the mother's gown, the click of her knitting needles, the grating of the chair leg, the pure facticity of the bare cold room, and the wan moon whose "hollow halo" is like an "icy crystal cup" offer no consolation, despite the teasing reference to a halo whose appearance, here, is an effect of atmosphere rather than a sign of grace.

Rossetti's abandonment or modification of his early ideals coincided with the death of Elizabeth Siddal. His posthumous painting of Elizabeth as the *Beata Beatrix* of Dante is a moving testimonial both to the woman he loved and the vision she inspired. Rossetti's declared intention was to capture that moment in the *Vita Nuova* when "through her shut lids" Beatrice is "conscious of a new world, as expressed in the last words" of Dante's autobiographical poem: "That blessed Beatrice who now gazeth continually on His Countenance who is blessed throughout all ages."[7] There is, however, a lugubrious, almost spectral aura to this painting which suggests a less edifying interpretation and which Swinburne, who cherished a deep affection for Elizabeth, describes as follows: "Her beautiful head lies back, sad and sweet, with fast-shut eyes in a death-like trance that is not death; over it the shadow of death seems to impend, making sombre the splendor of her ample hair and tender faultless features."[8] The fact is, tragically, that Elizabeth was a victim of her own hand.

Rossetti first met Elizabeth in the house of his fellow painter, John Everett Millais. Dressed in a Renaissance gown, she was lying flat in a tub full of water as Millais painted her in the posture of the hapless Ophelia. It was a prophetic pose. After a tempestuous courtship, she and Rossetti were married, but Rossetti, unable to maintain in the usages of daily life the spirit of reverence with which he first approached Elizabeth, began to neglect the real Elizabeth out of deference to the ideal Elizabeth of his art. After the delivery of a stillborn child, Lizzie succumbed to despair and took her life with an overdose of laudanum.

The long courtship and troubled marriage of Rossetti and Elizabeth have occasioned numerous critical pronouncements. But historical judgments—especially when they involve the domestic arena—are notoriously tricky. Elizabeth's chronic ill health and Rossetti's irrepressible libido doubtless contributed to their difficulties, but it must also be noted that Rossetti was as solicitous and supportive of Elizabeth's artistic growth as she was of his. Jan Marsh, the principal English authority on Pre-Raphaelitism, has recently said that "Siddal and Rossetti had a much more collaborative artistic partnership than has recently been thought. . . . [Even] during the period when Rossetti's affections had cooled for Lizzie . . . he continued to admire and defend her work and, more significantly, continued what was to him an important artistic collaboration."[9] Moreover, in her book *The Pre-Raphaelite Sisterhood,* Marsh further notes that

. . . within the Pre-Raphaelite circle the women found many encouraging, supportive, loving men, who were notable for their freedom from the overbearing chauvinism of their time. The women were offered opportunities denied to most members of their sex and class, and were in many ways liberated from what would have been far more oppressive positions, whether as working women or idle wives. . . . In the atmosphere of the artistic world they were freed from some restricting conventions imposed on their less fortunate sisters. They were able to pursue their own interests, developed friendships and participated in a wide range of activities.[10]

For years during their chaste courtship, Rossetti remained faithful and devoted to his Dantesque vision of love. But Rossetti's chivalrous ideals were deeply compromised in his relationship with Jane Burden—the eventual wife of his friend, William Morris, and principal model to Rossetti following the death of Lizzie. If the *Beata Beatrix* represents the culmination of Rossetti's early painting, then it is precisely through his portrait of Janey as *Proserpine* that we witness an inversion of those values we have traced in Dante's *Vita Nuova*. The Romantic pitfall that Dante adroitly avoids in that work, namely, the longing for an ideal union with the beloved in a mounting and inexhaustible passion whose only fulfillment lies in the mutual extinction of the two lovers—that seductive mingling of love and death which finds its musical counterpart in that other nineteenth-century expression of courtly love, Wagner's *Tristan*—is crystallized most fully in Rossetti's portrait of Janey on the threshold of the underworld. Holding a ripe pomegranate with an oval gash extending along its skin, she is on the point of entering those "Tartarean" halls where she will perpetually lament, in the words Rossetti etched in the upper right-hand corner, "how far away / The nights that shall be from the days that were" (261). Prosperpine's obligation to return to Pluto, king of the underworld, for six months out of the year is, perhaps, a tacit biographical allusion to Jane's obligatory return to William Morris following her periodic visitations to Rossetti. In any case, in this painting Eros is virtually indistinguishable from Thanatos, and the "dire fruit" that, once tasted, enthralls its victims into that mystic, sensuous longing for night and the void, became for Rossetti an increasing temptation.

Rossetti's poetry, like his painting, also reverses that expansion and deepening of spiritual vision characteristic of Dante. Three early sonnets in Rossetti's major work—*The House of Life*—crystallize, for a brief luminous moment, those Platonic heights the poet was to abandon for the "sloping shades" and "bewildered tracts of night" (120).

In the first of these, "Bridal Birth," Rossetti conjoins Eros and Agape—in this case, Cupid and Christ—into a single composite image. In the octet of the poem the two lovers imagine the growth of their love in terms of the conception of a symbolic child. With the physical consummation of their love, this child—an embodiment of their passion—grows into manhood. The child, however, does not expire with the expiration of his parents' physical love; he remains to conduct them through the night of death into an eternity of bliss, where they, in turn, shall be born again, baptized into the religion of love that they first conceived in their hearts and that now, in turn, conceives them anew:

> Now, shielded by his wings, our faces yearn
> > Together, as his full-grown feet now range
> The grove, and his warm hands our couch prepare:
> Till to his song our bodiless souls in turn
> > Be born his children, when Death's nuptial change
> Leaves us for light the halo of his hair.
>
> (105)

Yet this child, who redeems his parents, differs from Christ in an important respect. Instead of being a God-man, that is to say, a being whose ontological origin is divine, the Word made flesh, this child is a man-god, that is to say, a being who is born of mortal passion and becomes the means, not of transcending that passion, but of preserving it indefinitely in a realm unhindered by the restraints of finite existence: the flesh made word.

Rossetti's tendency to conceive of a finite, sensuous experience as if it were an absolute value is given unequivocal expression in another early sonnet, "Love's Testament." Here Rossetti actually speaks of the sexual act itself in terms of a sacrament in which the bodies of the two lovers are transubstantiated into a new body of incorruptible life:

> O thou who at Love's hour ecstatically
>   Unto my heart does evermore present,
>   The body and blood of Love in sacrament;
> Whom I have neared and felt thy breath to be
> The inmost incense of his sanctuary . . .
>
> (105)

Moreover, the woman in this sonnet intercedes on behalf of her lover and, like Christ harrowing hell, becomes the means of his redemption:

> O what from thee the grace, to me the prize,
>   And what to Love the glory—when the whole
>   Of the deep stair thou tread'st to the dim shoal
> And weary water of the place of sighs,
> And there dost work deliverance, as thine eyes
>   Draw up my prisoned spirit to thy soul!
>
> (106)

But as early as "The Kiss," the sixth sonnet in the collection, Rossetti's vision of deal love begins to be troubled by a presentiment of those mortal accidents—"death's sick delay / Or seizure of malign vicissitude"—that the poet has hitherto kept at bay. Accordingly, the apotheosis of human passion into a quasi-Dantesque vision of enduring splendor gives way to a tenebrous lament whose deepening pathos makes up the bulk of Rossetti's figurative "House." In this regard, T. E. Hulme's remarks on the limits of Romantic love are of special pertinence. As Hulme observes:

You don't believe in Heaven, so you begin to believe in a heaven on earth ... and as there is always a bitter contrast between what you think you ought to do and what man actually can do, Romanticism always tends, in its later stages at any rate, to be gloomy.[11]

Rossetti's confusion of sexual fantasies with spiritual potentialities takes its toll in the increasing morbidity of the poet's desire to hold on to a moment of supreme passion foredoomed to decay by virtue of its own evanescence.

"Silent Noon," the nineteenth sonnet in the series, still preserves a sense of spiritual and physical equipoise; but it is surrounded by forces that threaten to destroy its short-lived serenity. Rossetti traces a magic circle around his beloved, bounded by "golden kingcup-fields with silver edge" (216) and bastioned by a circum-ambient breadth of clouds shot through with a dizzying inter-change of light and shade. But the purity of this vision is already held in suspense, not only by the alternate "gleams and glooms" of the "billowing skies," but also by a principle of disintegration that is implicit in the moment itself. The "silence" of the lover's mutual rapture is ominously compared to the stillness of an hourglass, and the dragonfly that hangs like a visible emblem of the intersection of eternity with time is, after all, as susceptible of sudden and erratic flight as the moment it symbolizes.

It is no wonder that Rossetti's self-conscious absorption in the mutability of passion becomes thematically more central to him than the celebration of passion itself, as is apparent in the eighty-third sonnet, "Barren Spring." The octet of this poem presents a Fragonard-like scene in which the season is personified as a young girl balanced on a swing that sweeps her delightedly back and forth. Her joy in the exercise evokes no equivalent response from the poet, who is still obsessed with the "dead boughs" of the past "winter." Moreover, the season itself is unable to charm him from his gloom; having tasted of the fruit of the tree of knowledge, the poet is not to be deceived. The flame-like crocus irradiates a con-suming fire; the snowdrop is seen as less durable than the snow through which it issues; and the biblically resonant "apple-blos-som" maliciously turns into an overripe fruit that "breeds the serpent's art." The lilies, roses, and carnations with which Rossetti decked his house and surrounded his models have begun to fade: ". . . on the year's last lily stem / The white cup shrivels round the golden heart" (121).

But the nadir of Rossetti's despair is not reached until "A Superscription," perhaps the most enigmatic of the sonnets and, when fully understood, the most lacerating. The title presumably refers to the imposition of one name on top of another and may very well allude to the covering or obscuration of Elizabeth Siddal's finely penciled beauty by the smoky Titianesque brushwork of Rossetti's later portraits of Jane Morris. The speaker in the poem can be identified in two ways: he is either the lost, bankrupt wraith of the poet's youth, forlorn and dispossessed of his original idealism, or she is the image of the poet's deceased wife addressing him from the grave he recently exhumed. Neither interpretation cancels the other, since Rossetti almost regarded Lizzie herself as an incarnation of his youthful ideals. But the exhumed grave needs some explanation. At the death of Lizzie, Rossetti seized by a fit of remorse, placed the only copy of his early poems in her coffin. Ten years later, after the poet had won success as a painter, his business associate, Charles Augustus Howell, suggested that his growing fame would ensure the successful sale of his poems. Rossetti agreed, and the poems were retrieved. The sonnet, then, may be interpreted as a threnody not only of the poet's neglect of his wife but also for his infidelity to that vision of love which she represented.

But the haunting reemergence of his wife's spirit does not signal a recommitment to vanished ideals; at most, the sumptuous language and rolling periods sound nothing more than the last attempt of a shattered pilgrim, stricken with the futility of his search, to remember who he was through a painful recollection of his first vows:

> Look in my face; my name is Might-have-been;
>   I am also called No-more, Too-late, Farewell;
>   Unto thine ear I hold the dead sea shell
> Cast up thy Life's foam-fretted feet between;
> Unto thine eyes the glass where that is seen
>   Which had Life's form and Love's but by my spell
>   Is now a shaken shadow intolerable,
> Of ultimate things unuttered the frail screen.

Mark he how still I am! But should there dart
  One moment through thy soul the soft surprise
  Of that winged Peace which lulls the breath of sighs,—
Then shalt thou see me smile, and turn apart
Thy visage to my ambush at thy heart
  Sleepless with cold commemorative eyes.

                      (127)

In the disfiguring glass of death that Lizzie holds up for him to contemplate, the poet is brought face to face with his deepest fears, that beyond the "frail screen" of life there is nothingness. Furthermore, should the poet seek solace or comfort in the realm of physical passion—"that winged Peace which lulls the breath of sighs"—he is again forestalled by the image of his wife, whose smile—the immutable grin of a death's-head—keeps him "sleepless" in dreadful commemoration of their past together.

One might parenthetically add that Rossetti was literally "sleepless" at this point in his life—the victim of a relentless insomnia that drove him deeper and deeper into a debilitating dependence on chloral—a mixture containing the same drug with which Lizzie had taken her life.

The concluding sonnet from *The House of Life* thematically sums up one of the salient elements in Rossetti's art, the adaptation of medieval typology to personal history. Typology is a mode of biblical analysis that interprets events in the Old Testament as prefigurative of events in the New Testament, where their ultimate meaning and significance is more fully revealed. Thus in an early sonnet to one of his own drawings, "On the Passover of the Holy Family," Rossetti interprets the Jewish feast as a foreshadowing of events that are fully consummated in the Last Supper of Christ. But, as we have seen, despite his youthful orthodoxy, Rossetti was unable to sustain these beliefs in his later years. The typological reading of sacred history based on the authority of scriptural evidence thus gives way to a personal and idiosyncratic typology in which moments of exceptional value or intensity in the poet's life are transfigured into epiphanies of almost occult significance. Moreover, these moments—almost invariably involving an interchange of mutual raptures between the poet and his beloved—are subsequently read as dim prefigurations of a future bliss in which the transports of earthly love are caught up in a beatitude of endless duration. Unlike Dante, who suffers a crucifixion of the natural man as he turns his gaze from Beatrice to God (for Dante is constantly goaded by his paramour to lift his gaze beyond her undeniable beauty), Rossetti's wistful suspension between heaven and earth is finally undercut by the one inescapable fact of which the poet is most certain: the heartbreaking brevity and irretrievable intensity of youth, passion, love, and romance. Thus the tremulous, almost resigned despair of the final question in *The House of Life*:

> When vain desire at last and vain regret
>   Go hand in hand to death, and all is vain,
>   What shall assuage the unforgotten pain
> And teach the unforgetful to forget?
> Shall Peace be still a sunk stream long unmet,—
>   Or may the soul at once in a green plain
>   Stoop through the spray of some sweet life-fountain
> And cull the dew-drenched flowering amulet?
>
> (128)

But whether that "sweet life-fountain" will drench and reawaken the withered petals of those luminous moments in the poet's past remains an excruciatingly open question.

Unlike Gabriel's attitude toward medieval Christendom, which was much like that of Keats toward classical antiquity—a seedbed for poetic cultivation, not a bedrock for religious faith—there was nothing spurious or decorative in Christina's utter surrender to the Gospel of Christianity. Living in the place and time she did, Christina's faith was far more troubled and turbulent than that of George Herbert, the seventeenth-century devotional poet to whom she is most frequently compared. Her limpid style, however, is the perfect expression of her sincerity. This is most apparent in her sonnets, which read as if her dialogue with God fell naturally and unself-consciously into the exacting measures of this demanding form. The artlessness and transparency of her faith translates into a diction that never calls attention to itself or distracts us from the concentrated stillness of her devotion:

> Lord, thou Thyself art Love and only Thou;
>   Yet I who am not love would fain love Thee;
>   But Thou alone being Love canst furnish me
> With that same love my heart is craving now.

> Allow my plea! for if thou disallow,
>> No second fountain can I find but Thee;
>> No second hope or help is left to me,
> No second anything, but only Thou . . .
>
> (74)

Her sonnets present an obvious contrast to her brother's, whose lavish polysyllables and swelling sonorities become more portentous and opulent in inverse ratio to the poet's doubts regarding his role as inspired soothsayer and oracle. Christina's subtle cadences and crystalline form were rightly extolled by Virginia Woolf in her discriminating appreciation of this poet: "Your instinct," she writes, "was so sure, so direct, so intense that it produced poems that sing like music in one's ears—like a melody by Mozart or an air of Gluck."[12]

It has been objected that Christina's verse is monothematic—that, like the insistent long-voweled rhyme in the following lyric, it comes back again and again to the same doleful burden of renunciation, resignation, and regret:

> Passing away, saith the World, passing away:
> Chances, beauty, and youth, sapped day by day:
> Thy life never continueth in one stay.
> Is the eye waxen dim, is the dark hair turning to grey
> That hath won neither laurel nor bay?
> I shall clothe myself in Spring and bud in May:
> Thou, root-stricken, shalt not rebuild thy decay
> On my bosom for aye.
> Then I answered: Yea.
>
> (191)

To be sure, the religious hope that acts as a counterpoise to the cruel realities of the sublunar world is too often in Christina a distant hope whose compensatory value is virtually annulled by the fears and misgivings that attend it. But if her faith, unlike George Herbert's, is frequently faint and brokenhearted and her sense of the divine almost Manichean in its withdrawal from natural ties, there is something peculiarly apposite about Christina's poetic witness to an age in which the devotional life had become increasingly anachronistic:

> We are of those who tremble at Thy word;
>> Who faltering walk in darkness toward our close
> Of mortal life, by terrors curbed and spurred:
>> We are of those.
>
> (196)

Hers was a philosophy of Christian disillusion that T. S. Eliot stated perhaps most compendiously: "not to expect more from *life* than it can give or more from *human* beings than they can give; to look to *death* for what life cannot give."[13] But, Eliot notwithstanding, the uncomfortable suspicion sometimes arises that Christina looked to death a little too eagerly and in doing so lost sight of the fact that, as Herbert well knew, Christianity is an incarnational religion that implicitly hallows human relations and consecrates those natural elements of existence that are adjusted to human needs. The Catholic philosopher Jacques Maritain once argued that human beings are faced by two basic temptations, to reject the human condition purely and simply or to accept the human condition purely and simply. The first temptation leads us away from the world that demands our active participation and caring concern; the second temptation immerses us in the world at the price of stifling our higher faculties and obscuring our spiritual needs. As a volunteer who devoted her energies to the rehabilitation of women prisoners, Christina did not scant her temporal obligations to the world—but in her poetry the desire to rise above the pull of sorrow frequently devolves into a scarcely veiled death wish:

> When I am dead, my dearest,
>> Sing no sad songs for me;
> Plant thou no roses at my head,
>> Nor shady cypress tree:
> Be the green grass above me
>> With showers and dewdrops wet:
> And if thou wilt, remember,
>> And if thou wilt, forget.
>
> (290)

Even here, however, the apparent morbidity is offset by the poet's characteristic tenderness and empathy; rather than have her beloved suffer, she would much rather be forgotten to spare him the pangs of memory.

If Christina's verse is more than commonly rueful, this is traceable, in part, to the difficult circumstances of her life. She was twice disappointed in love and less than edified at the fate of Elizabeth Siddal and the bohemian antics of the Pre-Raphaelite Brotherhood. Her personal struggles to conform to Gospel values translated into tolerance and forbearance toward others, and while she possessed a keen sense of wrong regarding human nature, she was incapable of reproaching or condemning the behavior of others. Still, she could not but find her beloved Gabriel less than exemplary in his relations with women. Her satire on "The Sleeping Beauty," entitled "The Prince's Progress" (1865), is a clear indictment of a male temporizer whose uncommitted affections contribute to the decline of his paramour:

> Too late for love, too late for joy,
> > Too late, too late!
> You loitered on the road too long,
> > You trifled at the gate:
> The enchanted dove upon her branch
> > Died without a mate;
> The enchanted princess in her tower
> > Slept, died, behind the grate;
> Her heart was starving all this while
> > You made it wait.
>
> (34)

Christina superintended the funeral arrangements for Elizabeth, whom Gabriel habitually referred to as "Dove," and, therefore, one may surmise that this poem, like Christina's sonnet "In an artist's studio" is a tacit censure of the brother by a woman poet who shared a sense of sisterhood with those female models whose lives were entwined with the Pre-Raphaelites.

Christina herself posed for many of her brother's pictures, twice as the Virgin Mary and several times as herself. She shared with Lizzie Siddal the somewhat incongruous honor of posing as Christ (complete with fake beard) for one of the most famous of Pre-Raphaelite icons, William Holman Hunt's "The Light of the World." The image of Christ holding a lantern as he knocks at the door of the heart subsequently inspired one of Christina's lyrical dialogues between her Lord and the human soul, the poem "Despised and Rejected":

> "Friend open to Me."—"Who is this that calls?
> Nay, I am deaf as are my walls:
> Cease crying, for I will not hear
> Thy cry of hope or fear.
> Others were dear,
> Others forsook me: what art thou indeed
> That I should heed
> Thy lamentable need?
> Hungry should feed,
> Or stranger lodge thee here?"
>
> (241)

Inspired presumably by George Herbert, whose lyric "Love" presents a dialogue between the soul and Christ, Christina often used the device of a colloquy to communicate her internal struggles between divine grace and human self-will:

> My Lord, when Thou didst love me, didst thou know
>   How weak my efforts were, how few,
> Tepid to love and impotent to do,
>   Envious to reap awhile, slack to sow?
> —"Yea, I knew"—
>
> (219)

By the age of eighteen Christina had virtually renounced the possibility of earthly bliss. A broken engagement to the Pre-Raphaelite painter James Collinson, whose portrait of Christina nearly matches the features of Saint Elizabeth in his prodigious historical painting "The Renunciation of Queen Elizabeth of Hungary," left her, as her brother William Michael confessed, in a state of extreme despondency—a state exacerbated by her subsequent affliction with Graves' disease.

As a model to the Brotherhood, who yet possessed an autonomous creative life of her own, Christina found in the very image her brother popularized—a woman's face sadly veiled in tinted half-lights, with unsearchable eyes wistfully yearning for something or someone unseen and unheard—a kind of protective pose behind which she could develop her spirit unmolested by male importunities:

> Somewhere or other there must surely be
>   The face not seen, the voice not heard,
> The heart that not yet—never yet—ah me!
>   Made answer to my word.
>
> (362)

These words are a verbal equivalent to Gabriel's portraits of Christina and seem to express that Platonism which was indigenous to the poet's character and implicit in the model's gaze as she looks through the counterfeit joys of earth to their prototype in eternity.

Moreover, Christina's voice—discrete, reserved, unemphatic—is the poetic counterpart to the Tractarian doctrine of "reserve" as it was preached from the pulpit by Newman, Keble, and Edward Pusey—the sometime vicar at Christ Church, Albany Street, which Christina attended in childhood with her mother. As a doctrine, "reserve" is an application of biblical events to the spiritual growth of the believer. Because, according to scripture, God's self-disclosure was gradual and incremental—appearing first in the long historical travails of Israel in its growth and decline as an earthly kingdom, and second during the years of Christ's pilgrimage on earth when his full identity was revealed by slow degrees to his disciples—so, according to this formula, the effect of God's pressure upon the soul is not something that happens at once and forever in a triumphalist outburst that calls attention to itself, but rather something that proceeds slowly and almost unconsciously through a process that is hidden from the world and invisible to the eyes of the unresponsive. Simone Weil, who is in some ways a twentieth-century counterpart to Christina Rossetti, describes it as follows: "God could create only by hiding himself. Holiness should be hidden too, even from consciousness in a certain measure. And it should be hidden from the world." Christina's poetry is characterized by this hiddenness, or reserve, so that her relationship to her reader is somewhat analogous to that of the female model in her poem "Day-Dreams," whose character remains an enigma to the artist who has faithfully captured her spiritual essence without understanding the significance of the image he has painted:

> Who can guess or read the spirit
>> Shrined within her eyes,
> Part a longing, part a langour,
>> Part a mere surprise,
> While slow mists do rise and rise?
>
> Is it love she looks and longs for,
>> Is it rest or peace,
> Is it slumber self-forgetful
>> In its utter ease,
> Is it one or all of these?
>
> (332)

So the artist, like many of Christina's commentators, remains in the dark with regard to that inconsolable secret at the heart of Christina's poetry. Yet the secret does slip out in the form of longings that have their origin in mortal objects but that crave their completion in a kingdom not of this world:

> I never watch the scattered fire
>> Of stars, or sun's far-trailing train,
> But all my heart is one desire,
>> And all in vain.
>
> For I am bound with fleshly bands,
>> Joy, beauty, lie beyond my scope,
> I strain my heart, I stretch my hands,
>> And catch at hope.
>
> (398)

Even in a poem as deceptively obvious as "A Birthday," the poet's use of the language of love can be easily misconstrued. Her desire to proclaim her joy from a platform of Pre-Raphaelite design can easily obscure the motive for her celebration:

> Raise me a dais of silk and down;
>> Hang it with vair and purple dyes;
> Carve it in doves and pomegranates,
>> And peacocks with a hundred eyes;

Work it in gold and silver grapes,
   In leaves and silver fleurs-de-lys;
Because the birthday of my life
   Is come, my love is come to me.

(335)

But this is no ordinary love. The dais from which she enunciates her joy is the scene of a marriage with the Bridegroom himself, whose relations to the church is the type and emblem of human marriage. Christina's birthday is the new birth of which Dante speaks and for whose sake she remained aloof from her mortal wooers. In middle age, Christina was again courted, this time by her father's former student, Charles Bagot Cayley, who, in addition to translating *The Divine Comedy*, taught languages at Cambridge and translated the New Testament into Iroquois. These attainments notwithstanding, Christina's rejection of her suitor was consistent with her former break with Collinson; both men were found wanting in the depth of their religious commitments. Though she remained a life-long friend of Cayley's, her position was summed up most emphatically in "The Heart Knoweth Its Own Bitterness": "Of all my past this is the sum— / I will not lean on child of man" (192).

In the last analysis, Christina's verse bears witness again and again to that spiritual principle which Simone Weil articulates most clearly: "all that man vainly desires here below is perfectly realized in God. We have all those impossible desires within us as a mark of our distinction, and they are good for us provided we no longer hope to fulfill them."[14] Critics who react indifferently to these sentiments find it difficult to see Christina's stance as anything more than an unhealthy and neurotic disdain for the pleasures of the flesh. But in Christina's case, this abstention is richer than any possible indulgence, this unconsummated longing more to be cherished than any ephemeral pleasure.

It is difficult in the present age to sympathize with this posture or with the humility expressed in a poem like "The Lowest Place," which Dolores Rosenblum describes as "infamous" from a feminist perspective. For in this poem, as in "A Better Resurrection," the question of rights for women, or any other group, virtually disappears in the contemplation of realities that go beyond any claims that human beings can advance for themselves. Christina does not reject these claims as they operate in the realm of human relations, but for her the whole fabric of those relations dwindles into pettiness when compared to the overwhelming otherness of God's claim upon the human worshiper. From the perspective of that claim, Christina can do nothing but confess the nothingness of human self-importance. This confession, moreover, contrasts forcibly with the weltschmerz of the Romantic poet who wears his melancholia like a badge of distinction and, therefore, remains to some extent superior to his metaphysical wounds. But the wound of nothingness Christina undergoes again and again in her poetry becomes, paradoxically, the joyous mark of her reliance on divine charity.

Thus, in "A Better Resurrection," the poet confesses her destitution as a being whose existence is wholly derivative:

> My life is like a broken bowl,
>   A broken bowl that cannot hold
> One drop of water for my soul
>   Or cordial in the searching cold.
>   (191)

This confession, however, is not an end in itself, but a preliminary stage in her prostration before her maker:

> Cast in the fire the perished thing;
>   Melt and remold it, till it be
> A royal cup for Him my King:
>   O Jesus, drink of me.
>   (192)

The last line appears somewhat paradoxical insofar as it seems to reverse the customary stance of the communicant toward the eucharistic cup. Instead of draining the cup of salvation, the poet asks her Lord to drink of her. The situation, however, is only apparently heterodox and can be explained by again appealing to Simone Weil, whose spirit, like Christina's, was uncommonly attuned to the niceties of the spiritual life: "Just as Christ emptied himself of his divinity, we should empty ourselves of the false divinity with which we were born. Insofar as I become nothing, God loves himself through me."[15]

Christina's abnegation before her Creator did not, however, translate into an attitude of subservience to her male counterparts in the Pre-Raphaelite circle. In this regard, "Goblin Market," one of the central poems in her canon, takes issue with the attitudes and assumptions of male artists while subtly insinuating a feminist poetics. But while sexual politics play an important role in "Goblin Market," it is, finally, of less significance than that Christian poetic which Christina opposes to the traditions of secular verse as these are reflected in the history of English poetry.

Despite its fairytale trappings, "Goblin Market" is anything but childlike in its themes and images. Written in irregular verse paragraphs of mixed meter and rhyme, the poem describes the temptation of two sisters whose cottage by the woods stands in close proximity to a sinister world of goblin men. The appearance of these creatures seems modeled on that menagerie of exotic animals which Dante Gabriel kept, to the dismay of his neighbors, in his studio garden in Cheyne Walk, London:

> One had a cat's face,
> One whisked a tail,
> One tramped at a rat's pace,
> One crawled like a snail,
> One like a wombat prowled obtuse and furry,
> One like a ratel tumbled hurry skurry.
>
> (2)

The goblins sell magical fruits whose properties are addictive and ultimately fatal—especially to women. Notwithstanding the danger, Laura—the more inquisitive of the two sisters—cannot resist a taste. The goblins demand a lock of her hair in payment and then disappear as Laura sinks into a decline for want of their produce. Alarmed by her sister's condition, Lizzie determines to find the goblins and obtain their fruit without, however, bartering any of her bodily excrescences for the desired victuals. When she refuses to give up a lock of her hair (a virtual token in Pre-Raphaelite art of the female spirit),[16] Lizzie is cruelly beset by the uncouth beasts:

> White and golden Lizzie stood
> Like a lily in the flood
>
> . . . .

Like a fruit-crowned orange-tree
Sore beset by wasp and bee,—
Like a royal virgin town
Topped with gilded dome and spire . . .

(6)

In their rage, the goblins obscenely smear her with their dubious produce: "Of juice that syruped all her face, / And lodged in dimples of her chin, / And streaked her neck which quaked like curd." Withstanding their assault, Lizzie returns home to Laura, whose decline is arrested and reversed by the medicinal procedure of licking the pulp from her juice-stained sister:

Come and kiss me.
Never mind by bruises,
Hug me, kiss me, suck my juices
Squeezed from goblin fruits for you,
Goblin pulp and goblin dew.
Eat me, drink me, love me,
Laura, make much of me.

(7)

As a result of this homeopathic cure, Laura is restored and released from desire for the debilitating fruits.

What does one make this peculiar and, from a post-Freudian perspective, strangely erotic allegory? On one level, of course, the poem is a straightforward warning to Victorian girls about the suspect motives of male wooers. Christina's charity work with London's prostitutes would certainly have some relevance here. But these goblin fruits evoke literary echoes that have an equal if not more pressing significance. One thinks, for example, of Coleridge's inspired bard in "Kubla Khan," whose visionary pronouncements are nourished by "honey dew" washed down with "milk of paradise." The goblin condiments are akin to these delicacies and may be construed as the fruits of art that fall outside the scheme of generation. (Laura cannot, for example, grow another crop of these fruits from the leftover pits.)[17] Lizzie's subsequent refusal to buy these fruits on the goblin's terms is parallel, then, to Christina's refusal to emulate a poetry conditioned by the secular and especially Pre-Raphaelite themes of seduction and betrayal. When Lizzie offers herself to her declining sister as a kind of eucharistic meal, she at once calls up the sacrifice of Christ and affirms that artistically inclined women, like Laura, must evolve an aesthetic that is not merely a reflection of the profane world of male-centered poetry but rather an expression of those Christian ideals that transcend gender distinctions (as when St. Paul argues that in Christ there is neither male nor female, Jew or gentile, for all are equal and one).

Lizzie, then, expresses a poetics in which the Gospel values of sacrifice, service, and praise are preeminent over the worldly values of pride, lust, or avarice. In short, like her favorite devotional poet, Christina expresses the same theme found in George Herbert's "Jordan." Repudiating the conventions of courtly love, its dubious "fictions" and "false hair," Herbert concludes his lyric with a spirited defense of his own sources of inspiration:

> I envy no man's nightingale or spring;
> Nor let them punish me with loss of rhyme,
> Who plainly say, *My God, My King*.[18]

In the same way, Christina's "Goblin Market" makes a qualitative distinction between the profane sources of much Pre-Raphaelite verse and her own poetics of the sacred. The fundamental difference between Christina and her brother's friends is best summarized by Arthur Waugh in an article that appeared in 1930 to commemorate the centenary of the poet's birth:

[Dante Rossetti and William Morris] chose [the Middle Ages] to typify the world of the soul, a garden full of flowers and fruits, of fountains and of music. What they did not realize was the shattering fact that all these consolations were purely artificial, joys of the eye and ear, with no lasting appeal to the heart. Christina Rossetti alone of the little company was swept off her feet by the conviction that the palace of peace, like the Kingdom of God, was within, and not without.[19]

Unlike Christina, whose nostalgia for the absolute inspired her with a certain mistrust for all that lies within the spatio-temporal boundaries of mortal life, William Morris (1834–1896) shared with Dante Gabriel an exhaustless relish for the finite world of eye and ear. His poetry, like his life, is torn with contradictions. After a brief undergraduate flirtation with High Anglicanism, Morris became the most doctrinaire of socialists. And yet, like Ruskin before him, his tirades against the industrial exploitation of the working masses were rife with a craftsman's love of the medieval guild. Moreover, Morris believed that the whole of a laborer's powers should be engaged in the creation of beautiful or at least necessary objects, which could adorn and ennoble the tragic brevity of mortal life. His hatred of mass-produced objects that require a labor force reduced to the level of mechanical drudges was based on a Ruskinian belief in the creative capacities of the human spirit and a concern at the plunder of natural resources for the satisfaction of human greed. Despite his Marxist leanings, Morris's indefatigable energy was chiefly directed at the refashioning of life in the image of a medieval dream-world—an effort that involved a marriage between fine art and applied art.

With Morris, then, the Pre-Raphaelite movement entered a realm of domestic manufacture and church decoration. Even more of a polymath than Rossetti, Morris developed a firm that produced upholstery, wallpaper, furniture, tapestry, fine books, and poetry for the purpose of transforming the English household. Even the most common objects of everyday use should contribute to a conception of life as a ritual in which the sense of beauty and the spirit of humanity were visibly expressed. Much of this immense effort—for Morris was a classic workaholic—enabled the poet to suppress the great sorrow of his life, the growing realization that the Pre-Raphaelite model Jane Burden has married him chiefly to remain in close proximity to Rossetti. Morris's acceptance of this situation was either uncommonly magnanimous or abjectly uxorious—depending on one's point of view. In any case, he found Platonic consolation in the friendship of Georgina Burne-Jones, wife of the Pre-Raphaelite artist Burne-Jones, who was otherwise engaged in obsessively painting portrait after portrait of the Greek stunner Maria Zambaco—a situation Rossetti summed up in a wicked limerick:

> There is a young artist named Jones
> Whose conduct no genius atones:
> His behaviour in life
> Is a pang to the wife
> And a plague to the neighbors of Jones.[20]

When Maria tried to arrange a suicide pact with her love by leaping into the Thames, Jones endeavored to restrain his overwrought mistress. He was collared in front of Browning's house by bobbies who mistakenly thought he intended the girl some harm. It is no wonder that Christina Rossetti had become less than sanguine about the prospects of married bliss, or that Morris spent most of his time working at his loom and dictating poetry with the same alacrity as a shuttle weaving between multicolored threads.

Morris's poetry falls roughly into three periods. His early poems, including "The Defense of Guinevere" (1858), are inspired, like Rossetti's, by the romance of the Middle Ages. The prototype, however, is not Dante, but Malory and Froissart. Morris was a burly, boisterous, physically energetic man, and his early poetry rings with the sound of chain mail and the clash of swords. The atmosphere is vigorous, violent, and dramatic. Thus in "The Haystack and the Floods," Morris describes in grim and vivid detail the fate of a knight beheaded by his mortal enemy as his lady, bound to a tree, is compelled to watch:

> . . . the blow told well,
> Right backward the knight Robert fell,
> And moaned as dogs do, being half dead,
> Unwitting, as I deem: so then
> Godmar turn'd grinning to his men,
> Who ran, some five or six, and beat
> His head to pieces at their feet . . .[21]

"The Defense of Guinevere" is a spirited account of the queen's rescue by Lancelot just at the point where Arthur's knights are about to burn her at the stake. Her defiant defense of the liaison contrasts forcibly with Tennyson's Guinevere, who cowers remorsefully in the *Idylls* at Arthur's feet. Morris's queen, to the contrary, is unrepentant to the last and utters some of the most sultry verse Morris ever wrote:

> . . In that garden fair
>
> Came Launcelot walking; this is true, the kiss
> Wherewith we kissed in meeting that spring day,
> I scarce dare talk of the remember'd bliss,

When both our mouths went wandering in one way,
And aching sorely, met among the leaves . . .

(I, 5)

It is a matter of some irony that both Rossetti in the Oxford frescoes and Morris in the only oil painting he essayed chose to portray Janey as Queen Guinevere. In both instances there is a tacit allusion to the real-life triangle in which Rossetti played Launcelot to Morris's King Arthur.

Morris's major work, which came in the second phase of his career as a poet, is the voluminous *Earthly Paradise* (1868–1870), though the title is something of a misnomer, inasmuch as the poem as a whole demonstrates the hollowness of all earthly bliss. Morris is caught in a quandary here, for although he acknowledged no other world besides our own in which to satisfy the longings of the human heart, his poem is saturated with a constant sense of the world's insufficiency. C. S. Lewis, who along with W. B. Yeats was Morris's most ardent critical partisan in the first half of the twentieth century, summed up the contradiction by observing that for Morris, "Love of the world and earth must tempt desire to sail beyond the frontier of the earth and world. Those who sail must look back from shoreless seas to find that they have abandoned their sole happiness. Those who return must find their happiness once more embittered by its mortality, must long again." Lewis concludes that Morris was "an imaginative Positivist—an animal man flawed by the longing for a colored cloudland—a potential mystic inhibited by a too-convinced love of the material world."[22]

Lewis's formula especially applies to *The Earthly Paradise*—a series of verse tales based on Greek and Norse mythology told by a wandering cadre of disillusioned elders seeking respite in foreign lands from the plagues of fourteenth-century Europe. Readers of Bulfinch's *Mythology* would be familiar with the heft of these, though it is arguable that "The Story of Cupid and Psyche" or "The Love of Alcestis"—Yeats's favorite—has never been told with greater delicacy, charm, or metrical accomplishment. For Morris is the most adroit of craftsman, and his narratives—whether they be told in heroic couplets, octosyllabic couplets, or ottava rima—are invariably felicitous in their rhythmic pace and ductile phrasing. For this reason, some readers, wearied by too much of a good thing, have found these stories somewhat anesthesizing. But Morris's dependable and conscientious workmanship is and has always been a virtue evidenced by very few.

Still, *The Earthly Paradise* is almost uniformly wistful—a state of mind difficult to sustain without tedium over such lengthy narrative stretches. Moreover, the characters in these tales have that sad dreaminess, faraway look, and anemic pallor that one associates with the figures of Burne-Jones and seem incapable, as Yeats wryly observed, of losing their placidity or good manners even under the most trying circumstances. Savored, however, at discrete intervals, their magic does cast its spell—a spell that is provisionally struck and gracefully prolonged in those lyrical prologues and epilogues that mark the passage of the seasons and suggest a story, for those familiar with Morris's biography, of unreciprocated love and long-suffering affection:

> Peace and content without us, love within
> That hour there was, now thunder and wild rain
> Have wrapped the cowering world, and foolish sin
> And nameless pride have made us wise in vain;
> Ah, love! although the morn shall come again,
> And on new rose-buds the new sun shall smile,
> Can we regain what we have lost meanwhile?
>
> (IV, 143)

The prefatory lyric to *The Earthly Paradise* is an "Apology" that has achieved independent status as one of those watershed poems that mark the passage from one literary epoch to another:

> Of Heaven or Hell I have no power to sing,
> I cannot ease the burden of your fears,
> Or make quick-coming death a little thing,
> Or bring again the pleasure of past years.
> Nor for my words shall ye forget your tears,
> Or hope again for aught that I can say,
> The idle singer of an empty day.
>
> (III, 1)

Morris's diffident disavowal of prophetic purpose crystallizes the essential difference between the Pre-Raphaelites and the Romantics. The Romantics were visionaries whose poems had their source in an immediate experience of nature, art, or humanity; the Pre-Raphaelites were dreamers who self-consciously withdrew from the mechanical character of modern civilization in order to cultivate the refined and exquisite sensations of a bygone age. Morris's unpretentious aesthetic is not, however, as devoid of inner substance as the poet himself suggests. The dexterous weaving of those elegant gold-threaded lines subserves a theme somewhat larger than that of entertainment or mild distraction—a theme Walter Pater cannily summarized as follows: "It is [the] grace of Hellenism relieved against the sorrow of the Middle Age, which forms the chief thread of *The Earthy Paradise* . . . on its surface [there is] the continual suggestion, pensive or passionate of the shortness of life. This is contrasted with the bloom of the world, and gives new seduction to it—the sense of death and the desire of beauty: the desire of beauty quickened by the sense of death."[23]

The last phase of Morris's poetic career was marked, however, by a stoic withdrawal from the cultivated sensibilities and refined aestheticism of *The Earthly Paradise*. The bitterness and impersonal epic scope of *Sigurd the Volsung* (1876), which Morris began during his visit to Iceland and which is based on the same complex of Nordic myths which Richard Wagner tapped in the *Ring* cycle, is not only influenced by the rocky stretches and barren peaks of the Icelandic landscape but also by the poet's mournful acceptance of domestic failure. For Morris's arrival in Iceland coincided with Rossetti's arrival at Kelmscott, the sixteenth-century manor house where Morris lived with his wife and two daughters. While Rossetti enjoyed Janey's company, Morris toiled through the desolate wastes of the north chanting his forlorn hexameters with frosted breath:

And they sat on the side of Hindfell, and their fain eyes looked and loved,
As she told of the hidden matters whereby the world is moved:
And she told of the framing of all things, and the houses of the heaven;
And she told of the star-worlds' courses, and how the winds be driven;
And she told of the Norns and their names, and the fate that abideth the
  earth;
And she told of the ways of the King-folk in their anger and their mirth;
And she spake of the love of women, and told of the flame that burns,

And the fall of mighty houses, and the friend that falters and turns,
And the lurking blinded vengeance, and the wrong that amendeth wrong,
And the hand that repenteth its stroke, and the grief that endureth for
  long.

(XII, 128)

It is difficult to excerpt a passage from this atmospheric and inexorably fatalistic poem that follows several generations of warring Nordic tribes to their bloody demise. At the center of Morris's poem, as in Wagner's opera, stands, of course, the love of the mortal Sigurd for the Nordic goddess Brynhild (one of Odin's Valkyries who bears the souls of the slain from the battlefield to Valhalla). The foregoing citation from Book II is spoken by Brynhild after being released by Sigurd from the circle of fire in which she was imprisoned by Odin. Its impersonal pathos is one with the granitic grandeur, pulsing march, and icy uncouth northernness of this grim and ruthless legend. Morris's domestic sorrows doubtless drove him farther away from personal expression into the sublime vastness of historical cycles where individual needs could be forgotten in contemplation of implacable forces or heroic ideals. After *Sigurd,* Morris, to the dismay of his Pre-Raphaelite brethren, busied himself almost exclusively with working-class Marxists and visions of a socialist utopia.

There are two other poets who, during their respective careers, passed briefly but significantly through the wizard circle of the Pre-Raphaelite Brotherhood—Coventry Patmore (1823–1896) and George Meredith (1828–1909). Patmore is a poet of mystical pretenses adapted somewhat incongruously to the bathetic details of married life. To be sure, marriage is considered a sacrament by the church, but Patmore's principal work, *The Angel in the House* (1854–1862), mixes the trivial and the portentous in an unctuously fluent verse that is repelling in its patronizing attitude toward women. It details with homely circumstance the fulsome longueurs of a poet named Vaughn, who is enamored of Honoria, daughter of the dean of Salisbury Cathedral. Not only feminists have rightly balked at the poem's stereotypical portraiture of Honoria, who has no existence apart from the role she plays as muse to her versifying husband. There are some moments of genuine beauty in the poem, such as the following description of Honoria at a county ball:

Her ball-dress seem'd a breathing mist,
   From the fair form exhaled and shed,
Raised in the dance with arm and wrist
   All warmth and light, unbraceleted.[24]

This lovely quatrain seems a pure verbal equivalent of a ball scene by Renoir, but the monotony of the quatrains combined with the cringing homage the poet pays a little too glibly to his beloved, has more in common with the oily obsequiousness of Uriah Heap—the excessively humble but scheming sycophant in Dickens's *David Copperfield*—than it does with the restrained ardors of Dante, whose grave but sweet cadences ring unmistakably true or, for that matter, of Rossetti, whose attempted accommodations of the spirit and the flesh express a genuine and heartfelt struggle. But in Patmore the "nasty mixture of piety and concupiscence," as it was described by A. E. Housman, seems forced, mincing, and unreal. It repelled Cardinal Newman, despite its aura of Catholic piety, and contrasts forcibly with the genuine piety of Christina Rossetti, whose yearning for a Heavenly Bridegroom is at one with the austerity and reserve of the poet's life.

Patmore, however, was married three times, inherited a large fortune from his second wife, brought up his children with the strictness of a Tartar, was politically illiberal and religiously intolerant. His combination of prurience and prayer is less than convincing, especially in that series of putatively mystical odes *The Unknown Eros* (1877), where he descends into unforgivable and gratuitous attacks on Jews and women who do not accept his notions of subservience. Hopkins was appalled by the anti-Semitism of Patmore's ode "1867," in which an attack on Disraeli's policies deteriorates into a vicious comment on the prime minister's Jewish background. To his credit, Hopkins reminded Patmore that Christians not only owe an immense debt to the Jews but should regard them with a special love inasmuch as Christ descended from their ancestors and was nurtured in their traditions. The combined effect of Patmore's bigotry and sexist blather is even less excusable when one considers how he contorts language for the sake of rhyme or meter.

Still, Patmore's poetry is not wholly unredeemable. When he is honest enough to face his own shortcomings, Patmore can write a poetry more moving in its penitential truth that the high-flown mixture of bathos and mysticism that disfigures his other verse. Thus, in "The Toys" the poet stands self-condemned after having struck his child for some minor infraction of house rule:

> My little Son, who look'd from thoughtful eyes
> And moved and spoke in quiet grown-up wise,
> Having my law the seventh time disobey'd,
> I struck him, and dismiss'd
> With hard words and unkiss'd,
> His Mother, who was patient, being dead.
>
> (365)

The poet's memory of his deceased wife throws into relief the invidious gap between her forbearing patience and his undisciplined temper. Moreover, his personal dereliction is further underscored by his implicit violation of Christ's gracious injunction regarding the necessity of forgiving offenses not just seven times, but seventy times seven. When the poet enters his son's room, he finds the boy asleep, surrounded by his favorite toys and treasures. In a cry of contrition, the poet ashamedly realizes that he is far more culpable in the eyes of God than the sleeping child whom he intemperately reproved. This is certainly one poem of Patmore's that deserves to live.

At the opposite extreme from Patmore's *The Angel in the House* stands George Meredith's iconoclastic sonnet sequence *Modern Love* (1862). Distinguished as both poet and novelist, Meredith was nevertheless a little too labored in his style and emphatic in his philosophy to convey, in either prose or verse, the true voice of human feeling. His expressiveness, in short, is somewhat vitiated by the preponderance of his theories about life—theories that may best be described as a kind of evolutionary ameliorism in which the tragic elements in Darwin's theory are comically applied to human professions of disinterested virtue. We are all egotists according to Meredith—a thesis clearly demonstrated in *Modern Love*, which describes the failure of a marriage brought about by the extreme self-will of both partners. Neither husband nor wife seems to learn much from decay of their alliance; there are few poems in the English sonnet tradition as detachedly ironic and grimly disenchanted as these versified slices of domestic life on the verge of dissolution. At a dinner party, for example, the poet and his wife carry on the correct motions while cordially despising each other's presence:

> At dinner, she is hostess, I am host.
> Went the feast ever cheerfuller? She keeps
> The topic over intellectual deeps
> In buoyancy afloat. They see no ghost.
> With sparkling surface-eyes we play the ball.
> It is in truth a most contagious game:
> HIDING THE SKELETON, shall be its name.[25]

The poem concludes with an acidulous but heartbroken sneer that distills the tone of much of the sequence: "Dear guests, you now have seen Love's corpse-light shine."

When he is not writing about interpersonal matters, Meredith is usually quite positive. He is the complete naturalist for whom the world is a self-contained ecosystem without the need of a divine intercessor. Irrepressibly healthy, he found his brief stay at Rossetti's studio at Cheyne Walk somewhat demoralizing. A discussion of aesthetics over breakfast with Rossetti and Swinburne ended in a food fight in which Meredith ended up being covered with poached egg and tepid tea. But it was not only the domestic habits of the Pre-Raphaelites that he found unpalatable; he was equally unenchanted by Rossetti's medievalism and Swinburne's morbidity, especially in matters of love. As a natural instinct, love, for Meredith, needs no justification from the Platonizers or distorted homage by the libertines. His most popular poem, "Love in the Valley," a frankly sensual celebration of the mating game, gallops along in rollicking anapests like a hunter in chase of his fox. Indeed, the speaker's pursuit of the full-blooded maiden whose charms he relishes reminds us of Oscar Wilde's description of the English foxhunter: the unspeakable in pursuit of the uneatable. In any case, the sexual urge that tingles in the poet's veins is one with the tree that sweats sap as it burgeons in the spring—a simple and naturalistic part of the procreative scheme.

Perhaps Meredith's best poem is "The Lark Ascending," a lyric whose octosyllabic couplets flow with such lithesome grace that they inspired the British composer Ralph Vaughan Williams to compose a tone poem in their honor. No Victorian poet could write about a lark without alluding, however discreetly, to the lark that Shelley heard. But unlike Shelley's lark, "a scorner of the ground," whose song is a conduit of transcendental meaning, Meredith's lark is a brief embodiment of a wholly immanent life-force, which gushes forth in an unconscious hymn to the powers of earthly procreation.

Finally, it is worthy of note that Meredith's short but arresting lyric "Dirge in the Woods" was signalized by Jacques Maritain in his magisterial philosophy of aesthetics, *Creative Intuition in Art and Poetry* (1954). Maritain regards the exercise of poetry as a means of attaining intuitive knowledge about ourselves and the world—a knowledge based not on the operations of reason but rather on a species of "affective union" with the natural world in a flash of exceptional insight. Such a flash is apparent for Maritain in Meredith's "Dirge"—a lyric that like Hopkins's "Spring and Fall," expresses with the utmost verbal economy a perception of abiding and universal significance:

> A wind sways the pines,
>   And below
> Not a breath of wild air;
> Still as the mosses that glow
> On the flooring and over the lines
> Of the roots here and there.
> The pine tree drops its dead;
> They are quiet, as under the sea.
> Overhead, overhead
> Rushes life in a race,
> As the clouds the clouds chase;
> And we go,
> And we drop like the fruit of the tree,
>   Even we,
>   *Even so.*

(I, 427–28)

· TEN ·

Hardy, Housman, and the Nineties

Although two major poets—Thomas Hardy and W. B. Yeats—whose verse was nurtured in the atmosphere of the 1890s, emerged from the last decade of the nineteenth century to set the standard and chart the direction for the poetry of our own age, the period known as the fin de siècle is chiefly characterized by a heterogeneous mix of minor poets who, within the limits of their somewhat diminished practice, achieved a rare perfection in the refinement of lyrical form and a subtle distinction in the development of a poetry that approximates to the condition of pure song.

The term "aestheticism," which has been previously discussed in relation to the Pre-Raphaelites and certain poems of Tennyson, here reaches its apogee in the attainment of an art that has virtually loosed all connection with the ordinary spheres of human struggle, achievement, and aspiration. But as Browning would warn of all perfection—of all work, that is to say, which aspires to a complete, self-contained, and isolated purity remote from any sphere of sensibility or action outside of itself—it is a perfection that contains the seeds of its own decadence. And, hence, the poets of this period are known as "decadents" by dint of the supreme polish they bring to a subject matter of increasingly narrow and even morbid compass. With the exception of a poet like W. H. Henley (1849–1903), whose collection *In Hospital* constitutes "the first resolute attempt in English to use ugliness, meanness and pain as subjects of poetry,"[1] the principal poets of this period are characterized by a withdrawal from the moral strenuousness of the high Victorian age and the cultivation of a pessimism deeply beautiful in expression but profoundly demoralizing in effect.

Their aesthetics and philosophy derive from the work of Walter Pater, whose modest, withdrawn, and delicately nuanced spirit was inherited and modified in the flagrant histrionics of Oscar Wilde. As a poet, Wilde is derivative; his verse, with the exception perhaps of "The Ballad of Reading Gaol," is an egregious mixture of pastiche. The best of these poets—Ernest Dowson (1867–1900), Lionel Johnson (1867–1902), and Arthur Symons (1865–1945)—belonged to what Yeats denominated in his *Autobiography* as "the tragic generation." And there is no better point of departure or standard of reference for this period than the chapter of Yeats's reminiscences which deals with that hapless crew of poets who gathered at "The Cheshire Cheese" in London; who published in the *Yellow Book* (made notorious by Beardsley's erotically obsessed drawings of famishing aesthetes and lust-drained hermaphrodites); and who all came, with the exception of Yeats himself, to an early, usually sordid, and sadly self-destructive end.

Prosodically, one of the distinguishing features of the period is the creation of a poetic line that eschews the steady pulse of the metronome and incorporates, within the recurrent patterns of a skillfully modulated stanza, an utterance that is "not speech but perfect song, though song," as Yeats describes it, "for the speaking voice."[2] The boundaries, moreover, between poetry and prose were beginning to erode, as we can see in the flexible, sinuous, and subtly insinuating syntax of Pater, whose description of the Mona Lisa from his study of Da Vinci in *The Renaissance* (1878) became, for Yeats the seminal expression of that new, wavering, eloquently pliable music that the poets of the nineties took as their model and inspiration. In fact, in his edition of *The Oxford Book of Modern Verse* (1936), Yeats breaks up Pater's fluid description into a vers libre that sets the tone for the volume's subsequent citations and stands as a watershed between the poetry of the Victorians and the poetry of modernism. Its importance to Yeats no less than its impact on his contemporaries makes it worth quoting in full:

> She is older than the rocks among which she sits;
> Like the Vampire,
> She has been dead many times,
> And learned the secrets of the grave;
> And has been a diver in deep seas,
> And keeps their fallen day about her;
> And trafficked for strange webs with Eastern merchants;
> And, as Leda,
> Was the mother of Helen of Troy,
> And, as St. Anne,
> Was the mother of Mary;

And all this has been to her but as the sound of lyres and flutes,
And lives
Only in the delicacy
With which it was molded the changing lineaments,
And tinged the eyelids and the hands.[3]

Pater's Mona Lisa is the personified spirit of aestheticism, the goddess who presides impassively over the historical cycles of paganism and Christianity, using each for her own artistic purposes and deriving from each, equally, the inspiration for an art that reflects the tragic antinomies which were expressed, respectively, in ancient Greece, by Dionysus—god of procreation, wine, and natural ecstasy—and Apollo, the god of harmony, order, and aesthetic repose. She is the perfect decadent artist: a mere detached spectator for whom the rise and fall of civilizations, the respective appeals of spirit and flesh, and the whole moral struggle of humanity consumed in purblind cross-purposes, provide nothing more than the pretext for the manufacture of art, myth, and ritual. Her smile, like that of the Cheshire cat in *Alice in Wonderland,* is the smile of someone who looks on at the human dilemma with studied indifference, and suffers the human tragedy by transforming it into an aesthetic pattern that has no end beyond the perfect elaboration of its own constituent elements and sensuous properties. Her smile is the smile of someone who has seen through the vain search for moral absolutes and who has therefore come to embrace art as a way of distancing, dramatizing, and defusing the explosive impact of historical existence into the hurtless, impartial, and imperturbable designs of a perfectly realized art. Life for her, as for Nietzsche, is only justifiable as an aesthetic phenomenon.

Yet the poets of this period who cultivated the attitude of art-for-art's-sake bear witness, in their shortcomings and limitations, to the deficiencies of such an attitude. Their poetry now strikes us as effete, overly perfumed, and officiously artificial—and this is largely due to their indifference to that moral desideratum which Simone Weil recalls with such unassailable good sense: "Writers do not have to be professors of morals, but they do have to express the human condition. And nothing concerns human life so essentially, for everyone at every moment as good and evil. When literature becomes deliberately indifferent to good and evil it betrays its function and forfeits all claim to excellence."[4]

Still, it would be ungenerous to sweepingly blame these poets for an attitude whose shortcomings both their verse and their lives ultimately reveal. For their dilemma was a genuine one, exacerbated by an age in which the march of progress had pretty much banished the artist from a world obsessed with material advancement. The aspirations of the human spirit, were, in consequence, privatized into a realm increasingly remote from the public arenas of competitive capitalism, majoritarian politics, and popular culture. Like the French symbolists—Baudelaire, Verlaine, Mallarmé—the English poets of the nineties endeavored to escape from "mere literature" insofar as it had been corrupted by commercialism, politics, and the daily newspaper. Their search for an untainted verbal music led, however, to a split between art and socially recognized values; an indifference to the real world; and the poetic pursuit of a chimerical aesthetic purity in which everything, including morality, is a branch of aesthetics.

Yet one must not minimize the heroic struggle these poets underwent, or the opposing moral pressures by which they were divided. On the one hand, Dowson, Johnson, and Symons were possessed of an artistic conscience in relation to the demands of their verse, even when these demands were in conflict with prudential considerations of worldly self-adjustment or public success. On the other hand, because each poet is "a man before being an artist," he must equally recognize, as Jacques Maritain reminds us, that "the autonomous world of morality is simply superior to (and more inclusive than) the autonomous world of art." Yet if, for prudential reasons, the poet censors his work out of deference to a conventional public morality, he may, as Maritain equally observes, "betray his own singular truth as an artist" and "break ... one of the springs, the sacred springs, of human conscience and, to that extent, wound moral conscience itself." Conversely, if the artist remains "indifferent to the good of human life," he restricts the breadth of his subject matter and renders himself liable to forces that a Mona Lisa may be able to contemplate with equanimity but that no mortal can sustain without self-destruction. It need hardly be said that "once a man is through, his art is through also."[5] There is no satisfactory solution, perhaps, to this dilemma which Yeats, reflecting on those "Poets with whom [he] learned [his] trade / Companions of the Cheshire Cheese,"[6] described as the choice between perfection of the life or of the art; but to understand this dilemma enables one to reach a dimension that transcends the mechanical application of a generalized maxim or a ready-made appeal to an extrinsic morality. The key to an understanding of these poets is charity—a necessary key for anyone who wishes to appreciate their art.

Among this ill-fated group, Ernest Dowson stands out as the most distinguished and most representative. Dying at the age of thirty-one from tub rculosis exacerbated by dependency on alcohol and drugs, Dowson spent a brief two years at Queens College, Oxford, where he fell under the spell of Pater, returned to this family's dock house on the East End of London, watched his father die of the disease that would ultimately claim himself, discovered his mother hanging by a rope shortly after her husband's death, and suffered an unrequited passion for Adelaide Foltinowitz—the pubescent daughter of a Polish immigrant who worked in her father's London pub as a waitress. Despite the many poems wafted in her direction by the adoring poet who quietly sipped his pint in the corner while chiseling his sentiments into an English equivalent of his favorite French and Latin models—Verlaine, Catullus, and Propertius—Adelaide was unmoved and ran off eventually with a dish boy.

Dowson's peculiar note resolves itself into a strange combination of decadence and classicism in which the poem's ultimate significance is inseparable from the faint rhythms, decorous rhymes, and chastely restricted diction that are its sole purpose and raison d'être. In an essay that is itself a consummate prose-poem and elegiac tribute to Dowson and the spirit of the nineties, Arthur Symons describes the theory, such as it was, behind Dowson's fastidious and exacting verse:

I remember his saying to me that his ideal of a line of verse was the line of Poe: "The viol, the violet, and the vine," and the gracious, not remote or unreal beauty which clings about such words and such images as these, was always to him the true poetical beauty. There never was a poet to whom verse came more naturally, for the song's sake; his theories were all aesthetic, almost technical ones, such as a theory, indicated by his preference for the line of Poe, that the letter "V" was the most beautiful of letters, and could never be brought into verse too often.... He had the pure lyric gift, unweighted or unballasted by any other quality of mind or emotion; and a song, for him, was music first, and then whatever you please afterwards, so long as it suggested, never told, some delicate sentiment, a sigh or a caress.[7]

The influence of the French symbolists is paramount here, but it must be confessed that Dowson falls far short of a poet like Verlaine, who somehow contrives to create a verse of delicately nuanced music devoid of apparent statement or message while setting off a train of associations more far-reaching in their spiritual suggestiveness and psychological depth than anything of which Dowson was capable. Still, Dowson is the closest approximation we have in English to the diaphanous tonalities of Verlaine, and it is no less a poet than Yeats who pronounced that "Dowson's best verse [is] immortal, bound, that is, to outlive famous plays and learned histories and other discursive things...."[8] There is, moreover, an inevitability about some of Dowson's lines that is the hallmark of great art. Though few people would be able to trace the origin of proverbial phrases like "gone with the wind" or "the days of wine and roses," which have gained currency through the popular media, these lines are, in fact, by this reclusive doomed poet of the eighteen-nineties.

Beyond a few detachable phrases, however, Dowson's poetry has been largely forgotten except by those students of the nineties who prize its circumspect craftsmanship and savor the dead-leaf musk of its period charm. For although Poe first articulated the theory of art-for-art's-sake, considering beauty of phrase a sufficient end and a long poem, by dint of its adventitious discursiveness, a contradiction in terms, it was Poe who also recognized that the undue brevity of a concentrated lyric may militate against its wider renown by creating an effect too evanescent and impalpable to sustain a poet's reputation. Such has been, in part, the fate of Dowson. The lugubrious Latin titles, like a mournful drum-roll, with which Dowson sonorously announces the brief lyrics that follow, are often as lengthy in their scholarly loquaciousness as the English verse they usher in with stately preamble. Thus *Vitae summa brevis spem nos incohare loqam* ("How should a mortal's hopes be long, when short his being's date") gives us about as much thematic substance as the fugitive poem that follows:

> They are not long, the weeping and the laughter,
> Love and desire and hate:

I think they have no portion in us after
> We pass the gate.

They are not long, the days of wine and roses:
> Out of a misty dream
Our path emerges for a while, then closes
> Within a dream.

(32)

As Desmond Flower, the poet's editor, cannily observes, Dowson's poetry is the "quintessence of a quintessence"—a definition clearly apposite to the preceding stanzas. These stanzas, moreover, encapsulate virtually the whole of Dowson's thematic range—a wistful acquiescence in the transitoriness of life, the futility of hope, the vanity of love, the premature decay of innocence, the nothingness of ambition—and, surprisingly, the distant uncertain compensations of the Christian faith. For despite the attempt to justify life as an aesthetic phenomenon, Dowson could not imperturbably sustain the ironic detachment of the Mona Lisa smile. Indeed, to this friend Arthur Symons, Dowson would always be remembered in the Polish restaurant with its "narrow room" and "rough tables" for the most part empty, except in the innermost corner, where "[the poet] would sit with that singularly sweet and singularly pathetic smile on his lips (a smile which seemed afraid of its right to be there, as if always dreading a rebuff)."[9] And it was in this restaurant that Dowson conceived the one poem that, like a sachet of dried but aromatic flowers, has the power of evoking the heady, overripe, and self-consciously disillusioned bouquet that characterized the final decade of Victoria's reign:

Last night, ah, yesternight, betwixt her lips and mine
There fell thy shadow, Cynara! Thy breath was shed
Upon my soul between the kisses and the wine;
And I was desolate and sick of an old passion,
> Yea, I was desolate and bowed by head:
I have been faithful to thee, Cynara, in my fashion.

. . . .

I have forgot much, Cynara! gone with the wind,
> Flung roses, roses riotously with the throng,
Dancing to put thy pale, lost lilies out of mind;

> But I was desolate and sick of an old passion,
> Yea, all the time, because the dance was long:
> I have been faithful to thee, Cynara! in my fashion.
>
> (52)

These first and penultimate stanzas of the poem popularly known as "Cynara" are a poetic redaction of Wilde's notorious formula in his "aphorisms for the young": "To cure the soul by means of the senses and the senses by means of the soul." The use of the alexandrine is a example of Dowson's distinctive and French-flavored music, and his skill as a poet is illustrated in the perfectly timed pauses and artful hesitations that prevent this exotically patterned line from falling into the monotony that the six regular beats too often create in the measures of English prosody. For unlike the English alexandrine, where the pacing of accents is determined by a fixed number of syllables, the French alexandrine relies on the grouping of words, the lengthening of vowels, and the rising of pitch to determine the stress of the verse. Dowson, in a way that defies the laws of translation, has somehow managed to reproduce the effects of French prosody in a line that remains idiomatically English.

But accomplished metrics notwithstanding, Dowson could not cure the soul through the means of the senses. The "madder music and stronger wine" that the poet summons to obscure the unsleeping despair of those lost illusions led Dowson, like many a poet of his generation, to embrace the Christian faith. The attractions of Catholicism and Catholic ritual to Dowson, Johnson, and other poets of the nineties, strike us, however, as somewhat factitious and unreal. The effect produced by Dowson's religious poetry is diametrically opposed to that of Hopkins, for example, where the swinging of a thurible, the rising of the incense, or the euphonious roll of the old Latin service seems incidental—even extraneous—to a faith too solid and central to dally overmuch among these excrescences. In matters as delicate as these, however, judgment must be to some extent suspended—and it is serviceable, in any estimate of this period, to recollect Simone Weil's judicious observations on the function of beauty in the economy of the spiritual life:

In everything which gives us the pure authentic feeling of beauty, there is really the presence of God. There is, as it were, an incarnation of God in the world, and it is indicated by beauty. The beautiful is the experimental proof that the incarnation is possible ... a Gregorian melody is as power-ful a witness as the death of a martyr.[10]

Still, in poems such as *Benedictus Domini*, Dowson's embrace of religion seems somewhat regressive and escapist. The function of Holy Communion is not to leaven his spirit so that it can go forth among his fellow mortals, transfigured by contact with the second person of the Trinity and empowered, by that contact, to minister faithfully to others. To the contrary, for Dowson the gap between the sacred and the profane remains unbridgeable, and the church an aesthetic refuge from a world unamenable to the spirit of Christ:

> Without, the sullen noises of the street!
> The voice of London, inarticulate,
> Hoarse and blaspheming, surges in to meet
> The silent blessing of the Immaculate.
> (48)

This same attitude is also evident in "Nuns of the Perpetual Adora-tion," whose hermetically remote existence seems an end in itself, rather than a mode of intercession for a world written off as irre-trievably unredeemable:

> Calm, sad, secure; with faces worn and mild:
> Surely their choice of vigil is the best?
> Yea! for our roses fade, the world is wild;
> But there, beside the altar, there is rest.
> (37)

Given, however, the tragic circumstances of Dowson's life, there is something to be said for a poetry that recognizes, among other things, that "The Church," as Newman wrote in one of his Oxford sermons, "is a Home for the Lonely." For despite the foregoing qualifications, Dowson's religious poetry is not at all that far re-moved from the spirit of Newman when he writes: "Let us turn from the world, let us hide ourselves in His dwelling place, let us shroud ourselves from the earth, and disappear in the spiritual Kingdom of God."[11] In this regard, Dowson's religious poems, like Newman's sermons, will always, perhaps, appeal to a very few and not at all to the popular imagination.

Dowson, in the estimate of his friend Arthur Symons, "had exquisite sensibility, he vibrated in harmony with every delicate emotion . . . but he had no outlook, he had not the escape of intellect."[12] The same cannot be said of Lionel Johnson—the poet whom Yeats described as "stern by nature, strong by intellect."[13] But the intellect is, perhaps, no less liable than the emotions to distortion or misuse—as is evident to some degree in the life and poetry of Johnson. For Johnson lived almost exclusively in the confines of his library, piecing together occult traditions, Catholic mysticism, and the search for an ideal of purity and grace in what the French poet Rimbaud would call "a long, immense and reasoned out distraction of all the senses." This distraction was exacerbated by two afflictions from which Johnson suffered until his premature death at thirty-five, alcoholism and ateliosis. But his intellect, which was formidable, and the hard-edged clarity of his verse, were greatly admired by Yeats, who was already endeavoring to escape from the rosy mists and artificial langors of the nineties by sleeping on hard boards and cultivating a style of greater pith and sinew. Yeats's evocation of Johnson from the retrospect of middle life has become one of the famous verse-portraits of the period:

> Lionel Johnson comes the first to mind,
> That loved his learning better than mankind,
> Though courteous to the worst; much falling he
> Brooded upon sanctity
> Till all his Greek and Latin learning seemed
> A long blast upon the horn that brought
> A little nearer to his thought
> A measureless consummation that he dreamed.
>
> (130)

As this stanza underscores, Johnson lived the life of an ascetic, the self-conscious celebrant of an arcane ritual withering in the icy air of his own monologues. While there is no doubt that his conversion was sincere, there is a hectic, overwrought element in his cultivation of Catholic ritual that places him at a far remove from the ingenuous candor of a Hopkins or the self-effacing equanimity of a Newman. In Johnson's presence, Yeats confessed that he could not forbear repeating those disdainful, supercilious words of the French symbolist Villiers de L'isle Adam: "As for living—our servants will do that for us." Johnson's aristocracy of spirit was symptomatic of a profound split in the European psyche at the turn of the century—a split characterized by a spiritual inwardness opposed to the mechanized rhythms of the modern industrial state and an impoverished activism obsessed with material expansion at the price of those delicate shades, immortal longings, and secret wounds which the human spirit—exiled from any communal order of inherited beliefs—was now fated to suffer in lonely isolation.

T. S. Eliot was the first poet to develop a poetic idiom responsive to this anomalous state, but already in Johnson one can detect the first inchoate sketch of that quintessentially modern type who walks in interior exile across the pages of *The Wasteland*. Thus, in "A Stranger" Johnson describes a denizen of the London streets who is at once Maeterlinck's Melisande or perhaps the Lady of Shalott evicted from her medieval tower, and at the same time one among the many blank faces that vainly search the crowded thoroughfares of contemporary London in a state of spiritual estrangement:

> Her face was like sad things: was like the lights
> Of a great city, seen from far off fields,
> Or seen from sea: sad things, as are the fires
> Lit in a land of furnaces by night:
> Sad things, as are the reaches of a stream
> Flowing beneath a golden moon alone.
>
> . . . .
>
>   And those eyes,
> What saw they of long ago, that now they dreamed
> Along the busy street, blind but to dreams?
> Her white lips mocked the world, and all therein:
> She had known more than this; she wanted not
> This, who had known the past so great a thing.
> Moving about our ways, herself she moved
> In things done, years remembered, places gone.
> Lonely, amid the living crowds, as dead,
> She walked with wonderful and sad regard:
> With us, her passing image: but herself
> Far over the dark hills and the long sea.[14]

For Johnson, this stranger is the human soul divided from itself and forced to dwell among those for whom its very existence is a scandal.

As his addictions became more imperious, Johnson began to report conversations that he had had with great men—including Newman—which were purely hallucinatory, though the conviction with which he described these imaginary encounters gave them an air of credence that belied, for a while, their delusional origins. Hence, an entirely imaginary statement of Newman's, which Johnson said he picked up in conversation with the great man, became accepted as one of the venerable churchman's authentic utterances: "I have always considered the profession of a man of letters to be a third order of priesthood."[15] The difference, in this regard, between the Christianity of a Johnson and a Hopkins may be illustrated by the fact that while Hopkins actually met and received baptism from Newman, Johnson only conversed with Oxford's greatest theologian in an alcoholic fantasy. Johnson's religion, in consequence, takes places, to cite the title of a representative poem, in "The Church of a Dream":

> Sadly the dead leaves rustle in the whistling wind,
> Around the weather-worn, gray church, low down the vale:
> The Saints in golden vesture shake before the gale;
> The glorious windows shake, where still they dwell enshrined;
> Old saints, by long dead, shrivelled hands, long since designed:
> There still, although the world autumnal be, and pale,
> Still in their golden vesture the old saints prevail;
> Alone with Christ, desolate else, left by mankind.
>
> (82–83)

The above lines have obvious affinities with the neo-Gothic dream worlds of the Pre-Raphaelites. But is is a supreme irony that Rossetti, Burne-Jones, and Morris, whose faith in the doctrines of Christianity was either nebulous or nonexistent, should have a more direct and triumphant connection with the real world of religious worship than Johnson. For the Pre-Raphaelites had the strength of their convictions and were, to a large extent, able to impose their medieval dream worlds on the Victorian public through their connection with the solid and more socially functional arts of architecture, church ornament, and ecclesiastical decoration. Johnson's religion seems comparatively a thing of the mind alone, disconnected from any congregational body or living community. The poet's inability to abide the tensions of the religious life, as his poem "Dark Angel" underscores—

> Dark angel with thine aching lust
> To rid the world of penitence;
> Malicious Angel, who still dost
> My soul such subtile violence!—
>
> (65)

was doubtless a factor in his premature decline, which, according to Yeats, Johnson seemed to contemplate with a fascinated relish. Like his seventeenth-century hero, King Charles, who found solace in the poetry of Herbert as he awaited, in prison, his execution at the hand of Cromwell's parliamentarians, Johnson, who denominated himself both "Mystic and Cavalier," pathetically prefigured his own end in the poem that has become indissolubly associated with his death:

> Go from me: I am one of those who fall.
> What! hath no cold wind swept your heart at all,
> In my sad company? Before the end,
> Go from me, dear my friend!
>
> (29)

Yeats, indeed, went from Johnson before the end, feeling that his sympathetic presence perversely encouraged the poet's all-night vigils of debilitating drink and silver-tongued discourse. Johnson died as he anticipated in the first line of "Mystic and Cavalier," falling, in drunken stupor, from a stool in a pub and suffering a fatal concussion.

The last poet to be considered in the context of "The Tragic Generation" is Arthur Symons, for whom the music hall and ballet stage were shrines of worship every bit as sacrosanct as the dim naves and stained glass of Johnson's medieval churches. Johnson was disdainful of Symons's penchant for this milieu and of the impressionism—derived, at once, from Whistler, Degas, and Toulouse-Lautrec—that broke up the hierarchies of a coherently structured universe into the shifting, primastic hues of a world limited to the kaleidoscopic circle of fleeting sensation. "A London fog, the blurred tawny lamplight, the red omnibus, the dreary rain, the depressing mud, the glaring gin shop, the slatternly women, three dextrous stanzas telling you that and nothing more"[16]—this, according to Yeats, was Johnson's dismissive summary of Symons's poems and the broken world of flickering images to which Symons was constitutionally attuned.

Yet by a curious paradox, both poets endeavored to find, in their respective worlds of music hall and sanctuary, a symbol of that lost wholeness, that "unity of being," as Yeats described it, which could telescope the dichotomous worlds of intellect and emotion, spirit and flesh, life and art, imagination and reality into an ecstatic and life-enhancing synthesis. What the eucharist was to Johnson, the dance was to Symons, a point of connection and incarnation in which mind and body, spirit and matter completely coalesce. Thus in his evocation of "Javanese Dancers," whose exotic Asian rhythms and pentatonic scale the French composer Debussy was beginning to tap in his own music, Symons describes a world of trance-like ritual in which the movements of the dancers choreograph a world in which the duality between thought and gesture, the body's vital energies and the mind's cunning designs, is completely overcome:

> Smiling between her painted lids a smile,
> Motionless, unintelligible, she twines
> Her fingers into mazy lines;
> The scarves across her fingers twine the while.
>
> . . . .
>
> Still, with fixed eyes, monotonously still,
> Mysteriously, with smiles inanimate,
> With lingering feet that undulate,
> With sinuous fingers, spectral hands that thrill
>
> In measure while the gnats of music whirr,
> The little amber-colored dancers move,
> Like painted idols seen to stir
> By the idolators in a magic grove.[17]

Despite the apparent discrepancy between Symons's pagan idolators and Johnson's "one ancient Priest ... Murmuring holy Latin immemorial" in the church of a dream, both celebrants are emblematic of a spiritual wholeness, an incarnate presence capable of transfiguring the mechanized nature of modern life and reestablishing a vital link between the individual lost in the bureaucratized labyrinths of a mass society and a transcendent order of sacral presences and primordial energies disclosed in the rituals of art and religion. The extent to which this enterprise failed, however, is apparent in the poetry of the nineties itself—for Johnson's priest and Symons's dancer only survive by dint of their conspicuous detachment from a desanctified world whose slightest touch would violate their healing reveries.

Despite their heroic resolve to overcome this anomalous split, which T. S. Eliot would memorably designate as a "dissociation of sensibility," the poets of the nineties were incapable of moving beyond the solipsistic circle of their own nebulous impressions. In his "Conclusion" to *The Renaissance*, Pater declares that "experience, already reduced to a group of impressions, is ringed round for each one of us by that thick wall of personality through which no real voice has ever pierced on its way to us, or from us to that which we can only conjecture to be without. Every one of those impressions is the impression of the individual in his isolation, each mind keeping as a solitary prisoner its own dream of a world."[18] The history of modern poetry may be described as an attempt, first initiated by the poets of the nineties, to break out of that prison. When Symons wrote

> I have loved colours, and not flowers;
> Their motion, not the swallow's wings;
> And wasted more than half my hours
> Without the comradeship of things
> (887)

he was confessing the deficiencies of an impressionist art in which sensations are fleetingly savored in a world that no longer provides a bridge between a moment of isolated vision and a communion of common beliefs. Indeed, Symons's "Credo" echoes Pater's conclusion even as it anticipates the last lines of T. S. Eliot's *The Wasteland*:

> Each, in himself, his hour to be and cease
> Endures alone, yet few there be who dare,

Sole with themselves, their single burden bear,
All day long until the night's release.

(884)

In the same way, Eliot describes the psychological legacy of a fragmented culture in which the individual remains a solitary prisoner
in a dream of a world:

I have heard the key
Turn in the door once only;
We think of the key, each in his prison
Thinking of the key, each confirms a prison
Only at nightfall.[19]

The quests of the twentieth century's two greatest poets to transcend the limits of individual consciousness and to find some
objective and impersonal order of traditional beliefs—either Christian and communal, as in the case of Eliot, or occult and esoteric, as
in the case of Yeats—have their roots in the dilemmas of the
nineties. Yeats's ideal of the dance—"O body swayed to music, O
brightening glance, / How can we know the dancer from the
dance" (214)—like Eliot's embrace of Anglicanism, are the respective but complementary ways in which the two greatest poets of
our age endeavored to heal the split between the solipsistic worlds
of poet and artist and the exhausted dregs of a European culture
plagued by turn-of-the-century doubts about its direction and survival.

At least one poet of the nineties was able, in an arresting ode of
classic stature, to break out of this house of mirrors and convinc-
ingly dramatize an encounter with a power whose otherness is
made poetically real and imperiously actual. The poet is Francis
Thompson (1859–1907), whose "Hound of Heaven" was once regarded as an anthology piece of indispensable importance. In the
most recent anthologies of Victorian poetry from the Oxford University Press and the Everyman series, it has, significantly, vanished. That it is no longer a reference point either in survey courses
of the period or studies in Victorian literature says as much about
the present historical moment in the discussion of English letters as
the former enthusiasm this poem was accorded, despite its minor
blemishes, tells us about the sensibilities of preceding generations.

For the silent death which has befallen this considerable work is not exclusively traceable to matters of taste. To be sure, its richly brocaded textures, romantic sweep, and opulent imagery are very much at variance with the diminished postmodern worlds we presently inhabit; but our embarrassment in its presence has more to do with a disloyalty so deep that the very suggestion of an ultimate reality independent of the human mind inspires us with a defensive panic to uphold the frontiers within which we have restricted our sights. For Thompson's ode is the one poem of the period that shatters the artificial hothouses of aesthete or decadent and makes us aware that one of the principal but hidden motives behind the conflicted range of human endeavor is the flight from God. The poem deftly weaves together a panoply of theological traditions and poetic influences from St. Augustine, the Psalms, the English metaphysical poets, and the Romantics to give majestic utterance to a theme that has preoccupied the finest spirits of each succeeding generation—the relentless pursuit of the soul by God:

> I fled Him, down the nights and down the days;
> I fled Him, down the arches of the years;
> I fled Him, down the labyrinthine ways
> Of my own mind; and in the mist of tears
> I hid from Him, and under running laughter.
> Up vistaed hopes I sped;
> And shot, precipitated,
> Adown Titanic glooms of chasmed fears,
> From those strong Feet that followed, followed after.
> But with unhurrying chase,
> And unperturbed pace,
> Deliberate speed, majestic instancy,
> They beat—and a Voice beat
> More instant than the Feet—
> "All things betray thee who betrayest Me."[20]

The various strategems whereby the individual soul endeavors to evade the acknowledgment of this holy mystery, fleeing from that presence which exposes the pretense and hollowness of our habitual preoccupations and avoiding that act of contrition which our indifference has rendered a necessity, is captured by Thompson in a poem whose energy, pace, and dramatic power ultimately triumph over the poet's tendency to pile up images in a surfeit of metaphysical conceits or to exploit language for its purely euphonius effects. The "labyrinthine ways" that the poet threads in an insensate flight from that presence which literally dogs his heels are not only the rationalizations of a mind that wishes to sustain its own self-regarding autonomy, they are also the tunnels and arches of the Thames embankment where the poet, following his expulsion from medical school, spent many years as a street person and opium addict until rescued by a prostitute and rehabilitated by the Meynells, a Catholic literary family.

The poem unwinds in a series of capricious and refractory rhythms that record the poet's search for an ultimate happiness among the things of the finite world. In romantic love, the idealization of childhood, and the worship of nature, the poet vainly seeks to appease those nameless longings that can only be satisfied at the poem's end by the power from which these goods derive their existence. Thompson does not reject these goods but comes to recognize that they betray us when treated as ends in themselves and pursued as idols that obscure their dependency on the power that made them. The divine words that clash about the poet "like a bursting sea" in the poem's final lines underscore the necessity of confessing that all mortal gifts have their root and being in the grace of an immortal giver:

> "All which I took from thee I did but take,
>   Not for thy harms,
> But just that thou might'st seek it in My arms.
>   All which thy child's mistake
> Fancies as lost, I have stored for thee at home:
>   Rise, clasp My hand, and come!"
>
>   Halts by me that footfall:
>   Is my gloom, after all,
> Shade of His hand, outstretched caressingly?
>   "Ah fondest, blindest, weakest
>   I am He Whom thou seekest.
> Thou dravest love from thee, who dravest Me."
>   (112–13)

In its combination of baroque grandeur and Romantic spontaneity, Thompson's ode rises above the ethos of the nineties and takes its place among the great odes in the English poetic tradition, from Milton and Crashaw to Wordsworth and Shelley. The drawbacks of aesthetic religion, as epitomized in Pater's Mona Lisa, are, moreover, implicitly revealed in the success of this poem. For even from a purely literary perspective, it is apparent that the attitude of passive spectator—looking with detached indifference at the human situation, except insofar as it lends itself to artistic treatment—both restricts and vitiates the expressive capacities of the poet. The ability to grasp and give poetic conviction to certain experiences evidently requires that the attitude of spectator give way to that of witness. For there are some things that must be suffered, undergone, and lived through with the full participation of the poet's being if he is to seize their inmost essence and translate their impact into a poetry that sustains the weight of its dramatic convictions. The validity of Thompson's experience is not the question here— for the purpose of religious poetry is not to convey religious beliefs, but as T. S. Eliot sagely observes, to communicate what it feels like to hold certain beliefs. As long as such beliefs continue to engross the human imagination, Thompson's ode will continue to be valued as a testimony to an experience central to the Christian humanism that has shaped Western civilization from the Middle Ages to the near present. Of course, the time may arrive, and for some may already have arrived, when such an experience seems anachronistic and marginal to a society that has so thoroughly standardized its conception of human personality and so programmatically curtailed its sense of human possibility to the realm of secular aims and goals, that experiences such as those to which Thompson gives utterance will be regarded as a temporary aberration in the delivery of the mind from all loyalties and inklings unworthy of notice by the social engineer.

The last and greatest of the poets to be discussed in the context of this transitional phase in the evolution of English poetry are A. E. Housman (1859–1936) and Thomas Hardy (1840–1928). Neither poet fits neatly into our estimate of this period—though Housman is more certainly a product of his age than Hardy. Both are pessimists—but it is a pessimism, paradoxically, dependent on the religious traditions they interrogate or reject. Both poets, moreover, are steeped in the biblical tradition or Christian assumptions to which their verse frequently though ironically alludes. Finally, both poets were able by luck of circumstance and breadth of imagination to create a verse rooted in the homely soil of England's rural classes and attuned to the sensibilities of yeoman and commoner. In this way, they successfully avoided the chief pitfall of their contemporaries, that is, the rarefaction of verse into a private mythology or privatized kingdom of exquisite sensations remote from the concernsof average humanity. The combination of peasant vigor and classical precision that informs Housman's poems was the supreme imaginative achievement of a poet who had little or no contact with the rustic worlds of laborers, lovers, athletes, young conscripts, and malt-sodden misfits who inhabit the rural stretches of Ludlow and Teme, the places in which his poems are mainly set. Indeed, though he lies in Ludlow cemetery, Housman was actually born in Worcestershire—though the Shropshire hills on the edge of that shire evidently made a strong appeal to his imagination. Like Hardy's, Housman's is an imagination steeped in the prevailing melancholy of the nineties, but like Hardy, too, though he was very much in the world of the nineties, he was not altogether of it. To a request by Arthur Symons for permission to include Housman's poems in an anthology of the Rhymer's Club, Housman's response was unequivocal and derisive: "To include me in the anthology of the Nineties would be just as technically correct, and just as essentially inappropriate, as to include Lot in a book on Sodomites."[21]

The unflattering terms of Housman's comparison may be lacking in civility, but the fact is that his verse does have stoic detachment and impersonal authority that distinguishes it, qualitatively, from the often effete world of the Rhymers. A lapidary concision of style and a sharp eye for the evocative detail are virtues that place Housman above and beyond many of his contemporaries.

After graduating from St. John's College, Oxford, he worked as a clerk in the Patent Office and wrote poetry of a mawkish and self-pitying turn. But after his appointment as professor of Latin at University College, London, he was able to distance himself from his private sorrows, and by 1895 he produced one of the classic volumes of English poetry, *The Shropshire Lad*. That turn-of-the-century lassitude Housman shared with his contemporaries is here counterbalanced by a stony resolve to maintain one's character in the face of a hostile universe and by an ability to transform sensationalistic stories of rural mayhem—of the kind one reads in the

tabloids—into a plangent but self-possessed lament on the bitterness of passing beauty and the isolation of the human heart:

> There sleeps in Shrewsbury jail to-night,
>   Or wakes, as may betide,
> A better lad, if things went right,
>   Than most that sleep outside.
>
> And naked to the hangman's noose
>   The morning clocks will ring,
> A neck God made for other use
>   Than strangling on a string.[22]

Housman's poems are exquisitely double-edged—breathtak-
ingly poised between the opposing pitfalls of cheap irony and
maudlin sentiment. But it is precisely this poise that keeps the sentiment from deteriorating into sentimentality or the irony from becoming glib and automatic. The volume opens with the lyric
"1887," in commemoration of Victoria's jubilee. The village celebrations, lit with bonfires and reverberant with regiments singing
"God Save the Queen," are at once a testimonial to Britain's undisputed preeminence among the nations and an indication of the ex-
ploitable credulity of those patriots who accept their role as cannon
fodder for the empire from one generation to another. The poem is
so delicately balanced that both readings flash stereoscopically into
view without obscuring or displacing one another:

> "God save the Queen," we living sing,
>   From height to height 'tis heard;
> And with the rest your voices ring,
>   Lads of the Fifty-third.
> Oh, God will save her, fear you not:
>   Be you the men you've been,
> Get you the sons your father's got,
>   And God will save the Queen.
>
>   (10)

Despite the ambiguity of those last lines, Housman apparently
took umbrage at the suggestion that his words were anything less
than patriotic.

The volume as a whole is not, however, in the main concerned with the rise and fall of empires, but rather with the haunting, idiosyncratic sorrows of obscure villagers whose loves, hates, and fears are suffered without comprehension or recompense and whose lives are threatened by inevitable and usually premature extinction. As with Pater, Housman's only consolation is found in the short and precarious interval of mortal beauty that is all the more heartbreaking for its cruel brevity. The hackneyed image of life as a transient spray of bloom is, however, completely transformed by Housman in "Loveliest of Trees"—a poem "as graceful as flowers and as hard as gems" which rings a crisp and crystalline change on the consecrated theme of carpe diem. The last stanza sums up the theme:

> And since to look at things in bloom
> Fifty springs are little room,
> About the woodland I will go
> To see the cherry hung with snow.
> (11)

In the poem's second stanza, Housman has surely given us the most poetically resonant example of simple arithmetic ever done up in octosyllabic couplets:

> Now, of my three score years and ten,
> Twenty will not come again,
> And take from seventy springs a score,
> It only leaves me fifty more.
> (11)

It is astonishing how this act of artless computation, worked out without explicit comment or regret, is transformed utterly by the dexterous addition of rhyme and rhythm into a bitter sweet commentary on the fugitive span of human life. The understated, almost offhand insertion of the word "only" is all the more eloquent in its discrete but poignant dismay that "fifty years leave little room" for the harvest of a quiet eye. It is worth noting, too, that the penal connotations of the work "hung" in the last line of the poem and the equation of bloom with "snow" are further examples of the way in which Housman's poems work stereoscopically—here, to suggest, that the "bloom along the bough" is already condemned to premature execution by the snows that inevitably strangle the "white" of "Eastertide" (as presumably, by a further extension of the poem's imagery, the Easter story with its hopeful answer to the poet's despair is also, for Housman, in its last gasp).

Subsequent poems describe, with retrospective irony and pathos, the delusions of glory or happiness that young men cherish to their inescapable frustration. Thus "The Recruit" leaves the village of Ludlow to "make the foes of England / Be sorry you were born" (12) and to win thereby an everlasting fame. The concluding stanza sums up the indifference of the universe to such far-flung heroics, as Ludlow tower—symbol of historical continuity and memory—is contraposed with a cosmological awareness of time in which all things human are forgotten:

> Leave your home behind you
>   Your friends by field and town:
> Oh, town and field will mind you
>   Till Ludlow tower is down.
>
>   (13)

But as other poems in the volume, which advert to the ruins of the Roman settlements near Ludlow, make us aware, Ludlow tower is as transitory as the civilizations that preceded it.

Much of the volume stoically describes the impermanent nature of human love and the way in which vows are broken by irrational fits of hate or the sudden death of a lover. The most famous instance of this is the twenty-seventh lyric, "Is my team plowing," written in the form of a dialogue between the spirit of a dead youth and the living friend who has supplanted him in the affections of his sweetheart:

> "Is my friend hearty
>   Now I am thin and pine,
> And has he found to sleep in
>   A better bed than mine?"
>
> Yes, lad, I lie easy,
>   I lie as lads would choose;
> I cheer a dead man's sweetheart,
>   Never ask me whose.
>
>   (43)

"To an Athlete Dying Young" reflects on the vainglory of another human impulse—the need to distinguish ourselves in some paramount way from our fellow mortals. Here the burial of a village athlete is compared to the procession that formerly carried him in honor of his victory. The speaker reflects that the youth's early death has at least spared him the humiliations of outliving his success and declining into age and sickness. The brawn and energy of the dead athlete are now seen to be as vulnerable and precarious as a young girl's beauty.

The fortieth lyric pungently distills the pervading melancholy of the volume. Reflecting on the "blue remembered hills" of his childhood, the speaker realizes that his nostalgia is, in part, a falsification of a rural life that had abundant measure of sorrows, losses, frustrations, and disappointments. But despite his clear-eyed perception of the distant past, the speaker is nevertheless unable to find anything in his present maturity to compare with the early illusions that he now sees through without ceasing to cherish them still:

> Into my heart an air that kills
> From yon far country blows:
> Where are those blue remembered hills,
> What spires, what farms are those?
>
> That is the land of lost content,
> I see it shining plain,
> The happy highways where I went
> And cannot come again.
>
> (58)

The poem repudiates the Wordsworthian myth of childhood recaptured and memory triumphant in a late Victorian lamentation on the limits of nostalgia and the futility of regret.

The volume concludes with an apologia uttered by "Terrence," the volume's fictitious poet, by way of response to a group of pub mates who upbraid the bard for the morbidity of his subject matter and the lugubriousness of his themes: "But, oh, good Lord, the verse you make, / It gives a chap the belly-ache" (88). Terrence responds that if they want a good time they had best order up another round of malt; its effect, he argues, is far more potent than Milton's in justifying the ways of God to man. The only trouble is that Terrence himself has tried that approach to life's ills only to end up cold, sodden, and hung over in a ditch. The brief solace of intoxication only exacerbates the human situation once the fumes have worn off and the same grim realities return with undiminished force. For his money, then, Terrence finds there is more to be gained in facing down those ills that are part and parcel of the human situation:

> Luck's a chance, but trouble's sure,
> I'd face it as a wise man would,
> And train for ill and not for good.
>
> (89)

Wordsworth proclaimed in his "Preface" to *Lyrical Ballads* that the practice of poetry is therapeutic: through rhythmic cadence and recurrent rhyme the poet is able to subdue hurtful experiences and transform even the most painful of subjects into a soothing nostrum for the human mind. Terrence compares this practice to the sagacity of a king who frustrates a treasonous plot to have him poisoned. By building up his tolerance for the poison by slow degrees, the king can at last drain an entire cup of deadly brew without suffering any untoward effects. So, Terrence implies, the accumulated sorrows of *The Shropshire Lad* when admixed with the palliatives of rhyme and rhythm not only lose their power to hurt but become instead a fortifying cordial that triggers an immune defense within the human spirit.

Apart from *A Shropshire Lad*, which came and went in an unprecedented outburst of creative energy, Housman's poetic output is extremely sparse. Such is not the case with Thomas Hardy, one of the major and most prolific of Victorian writers. He was also a polymath of diverse gifts and talents, who excelled not only as poet, but as a novelist, architect, stonemason, and violinist—in which capacity he played at many a village wedding. Moreover, he achieved works of the first and major rank in both prose and verse, creating novels brimful of lyricism, balladic sweep, and poetic atmosphere and poems all the more moving in their rough-cut, unadorned, and sometimes prosaic imitation of a countryman's halting, deliberate, and carefully weighted speech. Though he was capable of writing in a strain of fluent lyricism, Hardy's best poems are those that seem like the verbal counterpart of a village craft fair where unpretentious artifacts with uneven surfaces, bearing the trace of mallet, jigsaw, or chisel, are all the more precious for retaining the impress of the artisan's thumb.

Even more than Housman's, Hardy's poetry is as remote as can be imagined from the cloistral confines of the Rhymers—though he does share their penchant for the dying fall, the wistful back-glance, the sense of human futility, the deceptions of romantic love, and the homelessness of the human spirit in a world that mocks our need for comfort, companionship, and spiritual consolation. Indeed, the poetry that is most frequently cited or anthologized is that which declares most starkly Hardy's doctrinal conviction that all things are governed by chance. The bare statement of this belief does not, however, always make for the best verse, and poems like "Hap" 'or "The Subalterns," in which Hardy pushes his point most explicitly, are quickly assimilated and soon exhausted. Hardy's "philosophy," when stated abstractly, becomes as unpalatable as poetry as does religious verse whose principal purpose is the formulation of doctrine. There is, moreover, a contradiction in Hardy's "Heroic Pessimism," as it is described by C. S. Lewis, in that

... if a Brute and Blackguard made the world, then he also made our minds. If he made our minds, he also made that very standard in them whereby we judge him to be a Brute and Blackguard. And how can we trust a standard which comes from such a brutal and blackguardly source? If we reject him, we ought also to reject all his works. But one of his works is the very moral standard by which we reject him. If we accept this standard then we are really implying that he is not a Brute and Blackguard. If we reject it, then we have thrown away the only instrument by which we can condemn him. Heroic antitheism thus has a contradiction in its centre. You must trust the universe in one respect even in order to condemn it in every other.[23]

C. S. Lewis's logic may be sound as logic and perhaps should give us pause when estimating Hardy's abilities as a thinker, but Hardy as a poet does not merely express the doctrine of blind chance in abstract and formulaic terms. His best verse is precisely that in which the putative arbitrariness of human life is examined in the context of personal relationships between men and women—and the apparently accidental way in which chance meetings between the sexes, occurring either too late or too soon, leads to relationships that cannot live up to the expectations people bring to them. The theme of these poems is best summarized by Ifor Evans: "a man and a woman are thrown together by the irony of circumstance and from their union arises a moment of passion which they call love, only to discover that its aftermath is a dreary record of semblance and deceit."

Two phrases from Hardy's most poetic novel, *Tess of the D'Urbervilles,* crystallize the essential tensions in Hardy's verse—namely, the antagonism between "the ache of modernism" and the "appetite for joy." The ache is a post-Darwinian anxiety that the coupling of the sexes is merely the means through which the gene pool renews itself through subsequent generations, each to be disposed of as grist for the reproductive mill. As Hardy says in "Heredity,"

> I am the family face;
> Flesh perishes, I live on,
> Projecting trait and trace
> Through time to times anon,
> And leaping from place to place
> Over oblivion—
>
> The years-heired feature that can
> In curve and voice and eye
> Despise the human span
> Of durance—that is I;
> The eternal thing in man,
> That heeds no call to die.
>
> (434)

Overriding, however, the pessimistic conclusions that may be drawn from such a premise, is the "appetite for joy" that impels each created being to believe that the fulfillment of natural instinct is not incompatible with the pursuit of personal happiness. The expression of joy, however, did not come easily to Hardy; and it is significant that his most ebullient lyric was activated by the imagination of another artist—Mozart—to whom Hardy responded in one of his most rhapsodic poems, "To a Movement in Mozart's E-Flat Symphony":

> Show me again the time
> When in the Junetide's prime
> We flew by meads and mountains northerly!—
> Yea, to such freshness, fairness, fulness, fineness, freeness,
> Love lures life on.
>
> . . . .
>
> Show me again the hour
> When by the pinnacled tower
> We eyed each other and feared futurity!—
> Yea, to such bodings, broodings, beatings, blanchings, blessings
> Love lures life on.
>
> Show me again just this:
> The moment of that kiss
> Away from the prancing folk, by the strawberry tree!—
> Yea, to such rashness, ratheness, rareness, ripeness, richness,
> Love lures life on.
>
> (458–59)

This poem strikes an unusual balance in Hardy, and has an engaging lightness of touch that, if it is viable to draw comparisons between the sister arts, owes something to the balance and buoyancy of Mozart, in whose music the ache of mortality and the appetite for joy seem held in perfect balance. This equipoise often eluded Hardy, whose verse rhythms seem so often to trudge along in exaggerated complaint as if weighed down and overcaked with the mire of mortal existence. For whatever joys are snatched by the strawberry tree for this poet are almost inevitably overshadowed, if not traduced, by those "bodings and blanchings" that Mozart economized into his music with a tact and perspective that Hardy never quite achieves. For it is the long dreary aftermath of love rather than its quickening or consummation that most activates Hardy's rueful and elegiac lyricism.

The specter, for example, of a departed lover addressing his surviving paramour from the grave, descanting on the tragic waste of lost opportunities, unreciprocated tenderness, and a lifetime of indifference or neglect is a common mise-en-scène of Hardy's verse. Among these the most poignant perhaps is "An Upbraiding":

Now I am dead you sing to me
　　The songs we used to know,
But while I lived you had no wish
　　Or care for doing so.

Now I am dead you come to me
　　In the moonlight, comfortless;
Ah, what would I have given alive
　　To win such tenderness!

When you are dead, and stand to me
　　Not differenced, as now,
But like again, will you be cold
　　As when we lived, or how?

　　　　　　　　　　　　　(532)

In the last stanza, the ghost is presumably resigned to the fact that years of a living emotional coldness will be succeeded by the physical coldness of death, in which all sense and feeling are frozen to the core. The fact, however, that a question remains as to whether death will provide an opportunity to make up for the missed chances of earthly life implies that the speaker here is really the living survivor for whom the "appetite for joy" has awakened too late. The speaker's self-reproach is, thus, projected onto the imagined ghost of the departed. That the speaker here is really the remorseful survivor may be assumed on the basis of Hardy's other poems in which a bereaved lover imagines a dialogue between himself and the departed.

Thus in "Her Immortality" a lover contemplates suicide as a way of rejoining his dead sweetheart. He is forestalled, however, by the imaginary voice of the dead woman protesting that his death would not lead to post-mortal reunion, but rather to her irretrievable extinction, for she exists now only as a subjective impression in the mind of the living, and will abide only as long as those who once loved her remain in existence to sustain that memory:

"A Shade but in its mindful ones
　　Has immortality;
By living, me you keep alive,
　　By dying you slay me.

"In you resides my single power
　　Of sweet continuance here;

> On your fidelity I count
> Through many a coming year."
> (55–56)

As a result of this adjuration the lover determines to go on living:

> "I will not die, my One of all!—
> To lengthen out thy days
> I'll guard me from minutest harms
> That may invest my ways."
> (56)

The pathos of the poem's conclusion is rendered even more intensely poignant by the lover's concern that his death, sometime in the future, will be harder to bear, not for his own sake but for the sake of her who survives exclusively in his consciousness.

> ... When I surcease,
> Through whom alone lives she,
> Her spirit ends its living lease,
> Never again to be!
> (56)

Further dialogues between the living and the dead that ring variations on this theme are apparent in "Woman in the Rye," "The Workbox," and "Are you digging on my grave," though this latter most frequently anthologized of Hardy's poems goes over the top from pathos to the pathetic—even the bathetic—when the shade of the dead speaker, hearing some movement on the turf of her grave, goes through a series of mistaken conjectures as to the identity of the living loiterer. For it is neither her lover (who has found another bride), nor her kin (for whom her memory is becoming dimmer), nor her enemy (who has forgotten her completely), but rather her dog. The irony becomes even more heavy-handed and meretricious, however, when the speaker's delight in discovering at least one survivor by whom she is not utterly forsaken is rudely disappointed as she learns that the dog is oblivious of her burial spot and has only come to unearth a bone.

If Hardy pours it on a little too thickly here, his customary tact is again apparent in "Woman in the Rye" and "The Workbox." In the former poem, a widow wanders in aimless self-reproach among

sodden fields of rye, recalling an exchange of bitter words between
herself and her husband. Her husband's death shortly thereafter
has intensified her awareness that her love for him is unabated, despite the momentary aberration of a curse in which she wished him
dead—a curse that now seems horribly fulfilled:

> . . . And I hate the sun,
> And stand here lonely, aching, chill;
>
> Stand waiting, waiting under skies
> That blow reproach, the while I see
> The rooks sheer off to where he lies
> Wrapt in a peace withheld from me!
> (360)

Many of these colloquies between the dead and the living read like
novels from which every extraneous detail has been burnt away, so
that the master passion of an entire lifetime seems distilled down
to its unalloyed essence. If Hardy's novels often read like folk ballads spun out in naturalistic detail, then his poems by a kind of reverse process, read like the concentrated extract of a prose
narrative in which lyrical emotion has been disengaged from its
workaday context and charged with a heightened sense of human
tragedy.

In a poem like "The Workbox," Hardy evokes the tragedy of love
in a domestic ballad rife with multiple ironies. The poem begins
with a carpenter presenting a sewing box as a present to his wife—
a box he has planed from the same wood used for a coffin in which
a local villager, John Wayward, was recently buried. The carpenter
cannot forbear dilating on the manifold and contradictory ways in
which objects fashioned from the same material reflect the vagaries
of life and fate. Thus the pattern on the rim of the sewing box "continues right on in the piece / That's underground with him" (398).
The wife turns white on hearing of this, and her husband assumes
that she may have known Wayward and the mysterious cause of
which he died. She disowns any knowledge of the man and further
adds that her husband has misread her reaction:

> "Don't, dear, despise my intellect,
> Mere accidental things

Of that sort never have effect
On my imaginings."
(398)

But her disclaimer is immediately undercut in the last stanza, where the narrator comments, in tones at once rueful and bitter, on the wife's true emotional condition:

Yet still her lips were limp and wan,
Her face still held aside,
As if she had known not only John,
But known of what he died.
(398)

In forty lines of this compact, suggestive ballad, Hardy evokes the tangled and melancholy cross-purposes of love in a way that a fiction writer like Joyce in "The Dead" or Hardy himself in any of his major novels can do only in as many pages—or chapters. For as the last stanza of "The Workbox" insinuates, the dead John Wayward was in fact well-known by the wife—his death being a consequence of her presumed rejection.

Hardy's rather bleak assessment of human relations has its theoretical counterpart in the philosophy of Schopenhauer, for whom this poet felt a special affinity. In brief, Schopenhauer sees the world as either "will" or "idea." The will, whose representative organ is the genitals and whose manifestation lies in the urge to procreate, and the "idea," whose organ is the imagination and whose manifestation lies in the creation of art, are, for Schopenhauer, the two antinomian impulses that divide human existence. The only way to escape from the ultimately deceptive and self-destructive urges of the will for Schopenhauer is by attaining the pure contemplation and aesthetic distance that art is able to provide. This secular version of beatitude reposes quite clearly upon a notion of human life that is irredeemably bleak and pessimistic. But poets, unlike philosophers, have a way of transcending even those schematizations of human life to which they are nominally committed. Hardy is, thus, never more appealing than when his irrepressible appetite for joy overturns the rather arid and austere convictions of his conscious mind. This debate between living impulse and demoralizing idea is apparent in two of Hardy's most compelling poems, "He Abjures Love" and "To an Unborn Pauper Child."

In the first of these, the poet repudiates the illusions to which love is prone in the hope of circumventing the heartache that inevitably attends the worship of eros:

> No more will now rate I
> The common rare,
> The midnight drizzle dew,
> The grey hour golden,
> The wind a yearning cry,
> The faulty fair,
> Things dream't, of comelier hue
> Than things beholden! . . .
>
> (237)

Most poets would have ended with this penultimate stanza, stoically embracing the state of disenchantment as a kind of achieved wisdom. But Hardy almost always provides a further turn of the screw in which the poet reflexively sees through his own cynical tendency to see through the very things he formerly cherished. In endeavoring to make himself invulnerable to pain, the poet realizes he has also made himself impervious to love. Note how in the first four lines of the last stanza the poet initially congratulates himself on his own superior wisdom—a stance with which many a lesser poet would end in a kind of pat resolution. But Hardy's afterthoughts pull the rug from beneath this secure position, as the poet acknowledges that there is nothing left to believe in or hope for other than that very love that the poet, in resentful self-defense, has summarily rejected:

> I speak as one who plumbs
> Life's dim profound,
> One who at length can sound
> Clear views and certain.
> But—after love what comes?
> A scene that lours,
> A few sad vacant hours,
> And then, the Curtain.
>
> (237)

In the same way, Hardy's stoical determinism evanesces into a mere abstraction when faced with the pathos of a fetal life about to enter a world of poverty and hardship. Logically, Hardy's position in "To An Unborn Pauper Child" should be more in accordance with those who approve of abortion on demand—especially since in Hardy's official estimate human beings are nothing but by-products of the evolutionary drive. But, once again, Hardy the poet—for whom human life is intrinsically precious despite its apparent subjection to impersonal forces and mechanistic laws—triumphs over the bleak conclusions of Hardy the philosopher, and the poem concludes, despite misgivings, with an involuntary benediction on the womb-life of this prenatal specimen of humanity. To be sure, the poet's initial reckonings of the child's chances for mortal happiness are so unencouraging that he cannot suppress a morbid death wish as the sole anodyne to those ills which the unborn is doomed to inherit:

> Breathe not, hid Heart: cease silently,
> And though thy birth-hour beckons thee,
>> Sleep the long sleep:
>> The Doomsters heap
> Travails and teens around us here,
> And time-wraiths turn our songsingings to fear.
>> (127)

A catalog of the sufferings the child may expect in his post-uterine life mournfully follows, as the poet proclaims his helplessness in the face of those accidents and antagonisms that his compassion is incapable of preventing. The poem cannily illustrates the way in which pity and compassion—commendable in themselves—can be ultimately destructive if our sole notion of human good is restricted purely to the alleviation of suffering. For there is something finally dehumanizing about a compassion that is so concentrated on protecting an individual from all pain and hardship, that it would prefer to abort an unborn fetus rather than allow it the challenge of growing in a world often haphazard and cruel. In consequence, the poet's compassion evolves into a resigned acceptance of the inevitable expressed in crisply tight-lipped syntax: "Must come and bide." But once again the apparent resolution—which could seem so pat—is but a preliminary stage in

the evolution of the poet's full attitude, which ultimately efflo-
resces in an irrepressible and full-throated affirmation of life's potential blessings and the hope that these—despite all evidence to
the contrary—will yet be portions of the child's earthly pilgrimage.
The sudden turn from despair to hope in the last stanza makes it
one of Hardy's most deeply moving and fully human poems:

> Must come and bide. And such are we—
> Unreasoning, sanguine, visionary—
> That I can hope
> Health, love, friends, scope
> In full for thee, can dream thou'lt find
> Joys seldom yet attained by humankind!
>
> (128)

As with all the poets considered in this survey of English verse,
Hardy shares a conviction in the ultimate efficacy of art as a means
of bearing with and making endurable the pathos of the human lot.
It is perhaps salutary to conclude our discussion of this phase of
English letters with Hardy's grateful acknowledgement of those
poetic traditions that nurtured his own literary genius—traditions
that take us back to the burgeoning of that cultural force with
which our survey began, namely, the Romantic movement. It was
observed at the beginning of this volume that the publication of
Lyrical Ballads in 1789 marked a watershed in the evolution of English poetry. And certainly Hardy's poems of rural tragedy among
the average English commoner, written in adaptations of the traditional ballad form, bear everywhere the impress of Wordsworth
and Coleridge's first assays in this folk idiom.

Moreover, Hardy's poems on the Keats House at Hampstead
and Shelley's skylark, as well as his notable elegy on the Protestant
Cemetery in Rome, where both of these poets lie buried, bear witness to his continued engagement with the art of the Romantics.
His mediations in "At the Pyramid of Cestius near the Graves of
Shelley and Keats" not only underscore the continuity in English
poetry that this volume as a whole has endeavored to trace, they
also reaffirm one of the salient ingredients in any poet's achieved
success—a conscious tribute to the traditions of a native language
honed into a tool of artistic expression by those few rare and gifted
spirits to whom any genuine creator remains deeply indebted.

Thus, the tomb of Rome's forgotten centurion, Cestius, which marks the spot where Hardy's countrymen are buried, no longer testifies to the self-regarding pomp of those who worship power for its own sake. Cestius and his policies, for good or ill, are forgotten; but the poets whose modest graves his pyramid oversoars continue to speak to the fundamental needs and aspirations of humanity—and still constitute a standard of reference and an ideal of art to which Hardy pays tribute:

> Cestius in life, maybe,
> Slew, breathed out threatening;
> I know not. This I know: in death all silently
> He does a finer thing.
>
> In beckoning pilgrim feet
> With marble finger high
> To where, by shadowy wall and history-haunted street,
> Those matchless singers lie . . .
>
> —Say, then, he lived and died
> That stones which bear his name
> Should mark, through Time, where two immortal Shades abide;
> It is an ample fame.
>
> (105)

The immoral shades of those matchless singers to whom Hardy here pays conscious reverence and debt preside as well over the poem that casts a retrospective light on the poetry of the nineteenth century. This, of course, is the "The Darkling Thrush"—a lyric that pays conscious homage to Hardy's poetic forebears even as it anticipates the challenge of a new uncertain age. For the very title of "The Darkling Thrush" discreetly alludes to a pair of seminal lyrics that respectively epitomize the contrasting sensibilities of the Romantic and Victorian periods. "Darkling, I listen," observes Keats in the "Ode to a Nightingale," as the music of another world penetrates and illumines the embowered glooms of a beechen grove. But the leafy bowers of Keats's ode are stripped bare in Arnold's "Dover Beach," where "a darkling plain / Swept with confused alarms" has drowned the music of the Romantic spirit. Hardy's thrush summons up the perspective of both worlds as the speaker leans in the twilit eve of the twentieth century on a "coppice gate," observing the barren vastness of a frozen landscape locked in frost and devoid of comfort. The bare trees remind him of the "strings of broken lyres" (150), recalling the stonework of the broken lyre on Keats's grave—a symbol of the poet's premature death transformed by Hardy's allusion into the unfulfilled promise of the Romantic period.[24]

The second stanza evokes more particularly the gaunt-featured landscape that the poet construes as the nineteenth "Century's corpse" and the end of an era. In this anti-bower, which contrasts forcibly with those deciduous havens of the Romantic imagination, the poet is arrested by the sound of a thrush whose "full-throated evensong" simultaneously sums up the worlds of faith and hope respectively embodied in Keats's nightingale, which sings in "full-throated ease" of a world beyond the temporal boundaries of mortal life, and the rituals of the Anglican church, whose nightly evensongs enunciate the immemorial promise of the Christian faith. The song here represents for Hardy those irrational and presumably exploded hopes that the poet still cherishes even in a world where evidence for their support is as attenuated as the landscape, "shrunken hard and dry." The "aged thrush," like Hardy himself, is a belated wanderer at the century's end recalling the visions that make life bearable despite their apparent groundlessness. But once again, as in "The Pauper's Child" or "He abjures Love," the poet, despite the disillusions of time and the dearth of empirical evidence, cannot forbear expressing his hope that "the appetite for joy" bears witness to a reality that transcends "the ache of modernism." Though his poetry as a whole casts doubt on such a hope, Hardy would still discern in the few notes of this blast-beruffled songster the inklings of a spiritual order immune to time and process, and alive to human need:

> So little cause for carolings
>   Of such ecstatic sound
> Was written on terrestrial things
>   Afar or nigh around,
> That I could think there trembled through
>   His happy good-night air
> Some blessed Hope, whereof he knew
>   And I was unaware.
>
> (150)

· *Notes and References* ·

Chapter One

1. William K. Wimsatt Jr., ed., *Alexander Pope: Selected Poetry and Prose* (New York: Holt, Rinehart and Winston, 1951), 99–100; hereafter cited in text.

2. Bertrand H. Bronson, ed., *Samuel Johnson: Rasselas, Poems, and Selected Prose* (New York: Holt, Rinehart and Winston, 1971), 52 (hereafter cited in text).

3. Irving Babbit, *Rousseau and Romanticism* (New York: Meridian Books, 1955), 32 (hereafter cited in text).

4. Arthur Johnston, ed., *Selected Poems of Thomas Gray and William Collins* (Columbia: University of South Carolina Press, 1970), 187–90.

5. H. W. Garrod, ed., *Keats's Poetical Works* (Oxford: Oxford University Press, 1958), 57 (hereafter cited in text).

6. Geoffrey Keynes, ed., *The Complete Writings of William Blake* (London: Oxford University Press, 1966), 11 (hereafter cited in text).

7. H. J. Jackson, ed., *The Oxford Authors: Samuel Taylor Coleridge* (Oxford: Oxford University Press, 1985), 68 (hereafter cited in text).

8. Robert Gittings, ed., *Letters of John Keats* (London: Oxford University Press, 1971), 70 (hereafter cited in text).

9. Carlos Baker, ed., *Selected Poetry and Prose of Shelley* (New York: Random House, 1951), 518.

10. Walter Pater, *Appreciations* (London: Macmillan, 1900), 274.

11. Matthew Arnold, *Essays in Criticism: Second Series* (London: Macmillan, 1941), 68.

12. Andrew J. George, ed., *The Complete Poetical Works of Wordsworth* (Boston: Houghton Mifflin, 1932), 231 (hereafter cited in text).

13. Thomas Hutchinson, ed., *The Complete Poetical Works of Percy Bysshe Shelley* (London: Oxford University Press, 1923), 436 (hereafter cited in text).

14. Despite some important differences in approach and interpretation, my reading here is strongly influenced by Geoffrey Durrant's perceptive commentary in *William Wordsworth* (Cambridge: Cambridge University Press, 1969), 18–24. See also David Perkins, ed., *English Romantic Writers* (San Diego: Harcourt, Brace, Jovanovich, Inc., 1967), 390.

15. D. G. James, *The Romantic Comedy* (London: Oxford University Press, 1963), 161.

Notes and References

Chapter Two

1. T. S. Eliot, *Selected Essays* (New York: Harcourt, Brace, 1950), 279.
2. Alexander Gilchrist, *Life of William Blake* (New York: Phaeton Press, 1969), I. 343.
3. Northrop Frye, *Fearful Symmetry* (Boston: Beacon Press, 1962), 38.
4. See G. K. Chesterton, *William Blake* (New York: E. P. Dutton, 1914). See also Harold Bloom, *The Visionary Company* (Garden City: Doubleday and Company, Inc., 1961), 1. Bloom writes, "The divine is the human released from every limitation that impedes desire."
5. James Boswell, *Life of Johnson* (London: Oxford University Press, 1970), 280.
6. Jacques Maritain, *Creative Intuition in Art and Poetry* (Cleveland: Meridian Books, 1953), 318.
7. Martin Buber, *Eclipse of God* (New York: Harper and Row, 1952), 14.

Chapter Three

1. C. B. Tinker and H. F. Lowry, eds., *The Poetical Works of Matthew Arnold* (London: Oxford University Press, 1963), 308 (hereafter cited in text).
2. Cited in Stephen Gill's *William Wordsworth: A Life* (Oxford: Oxford University Press, 1989), 397.
3. William E. Buckler, ed., *Prose of the Victorian Period* (Boston: Houghton Mifflin, 1958), 296.
4. Much has been written on this subject; see, in especial, D. G. James, *The Romantic Comedy* (London: Oxford University Press, 1963), 155–275.
5. A similar comparison also occurred to Richard Holmes in his brief but important study *Coleridge* (Oxford: Oxford University Press, 1982), 94: "What resonances does it stir in the modern reader—what groups of 'undead' men standing with glittering, accusing eyes beneath towers, behind barbed wire, in compounds, in courtyards, behind bolts and bars?"

Chapter Four

1. Byron, *Poetical Works* (London: Oxford University Press, 1967), 90 (hereafter cited in text).
2. Cited by Elizabeth Longsford in *The Life of Byron* (Boston: Little Brown, 1976), 210. Yet after this expression of defiance, Byron apparently muttered, "I fancy myself a Jew, a Mahomedan, and a Christian of every profession of faith. Eternity and space are before me; but on this subject, thank God, I am happy and at ease. The thought of living eternally, of again reviving, is a great pleasure."

Notes and References

3. Matthew Arnold, *Essays in Criticism: Second Series* (London: Macmillan, 1941), 136.

4. T. S. Eliot, *On Poetry and Poets* (New York: Farrar, Straus, and Giroux, 1970), 239.

5. George A. Panichas, ed., *The Simone Weil Reader* (New York: David McKay, 1977), 433.

6. Perhaps the most pertinacious of commentaries on this commanding poem may be found in Robert Gleckner's *Byron and the Ruins of Paradise* (Baltimore: Johns Hopkins Press, 1967). For Arnold reference, see P. J. Keating, ed., *Matthew Arnold: Selected Prose* (Harmondsworth: Penguin, 1987), 404. For Knight reference, see G. Wilson Knight, *Byron and Shakespeare* (New York: Barnes & Noble, 1966), 1.

7. George Santayana, *Winds of Doctrine and Platonism and The Spiritual Life* (Gloucester: Peter Smith, 1971), 180.

8. C. S. Lewis, *Christian Reflections* (Grand Rapids: William B. Eerdmans, 1967), 70.

9. Søren Kierkegaard, *Edifying Discourses: A Selection* (New York: Harper & Row, 1958), 186.

10. For a brilliant discussion of Asia's significance in *Prometheus Unbound*, see F. A. Pottle "The Role of Asia in the Dramatic Action of Shelley's *Prometheus Unbound*" in *Shelley: A Collection of Critical Essays* ed., by George M. Ridenour (Englewood Cliffs: Prentice-Hall, 1965), 133–43.

11. C. S. Lewis, *Literary Essays* (Cambridge: Cambridge University Press, 1969), 204.

12. Santayana, *Winds of Doctrine*, 163.

13. Carlos Baker, ed., *Selected Poetry and Prose of Shelley* (New York: Random House, 1951), 317.

14. My reading of this poem is profoundly indebted to Earl Wasserman's magisterial discussion in *Shelley: A Critical Reading* (Baltimore: Johns Hopkins University Press, 1971), 462–502.

15. Santayana, *Winds of Doctrine*, 16. Ibid., 172.

Chapter Five

1. For an insightful and appreciative discussion of Keats's imagery, see R. H. Fogle, *The Imagery of Keats and Shelley* (Chapel Hill: University of North Carolina Press, 1949).

2. The comparison of Keats with Shakespeare was initially made by Matthew Arnold in his *Essays on Criticism: Second Series*. It remained to John Middleton Murry in his indispensable study *Keats and Shakespeare* (London: Oxford University Press, 1964) to develop this comparison to the full.

3. The most canny discussion of this poem is found in Tilottama Rajan's *Dark Interpreter: The Discourse of Romanticism* (Ithaca: Cornell University Press, 1980), 129–33.

4. My reading here owes much to Earl Wasserman in *The Finer Tone* (Baltimore: Johns Hopkins University Press, 1967), 13–62; and Cleanth Brooks in *The Well-Wrought Urn* (New York: Harcourt, Brace, 1947), 151–66.

5. For a detailed discussion of this poem, see my article "Finite Transcendence in the 'Ode to a Nightingale,'" *Soundings* 66, no. 1 (Spring 1983): 46–69.

6. The significance of Moneta's unveiled countenance is discussed at length by D. G. James in *The Romantic Comedy* (London: Oxford University Press, 1963), 147–51; see also Stuart Sperry, *Keats the Poet* (Princeton: Princeton University Press, 1973), 329–33.

7. Helen Vendler, *The Odes of Keats* (Cambridge: Harvard University Press, 1983), 14.

8. Walter E. Houghton, *The Victorian Frame of Mind* (New Haven: Yale University Press, 1966), xiv. For a further discussion of Keats's relationship to the next generation of poets see George H. Ford, *Keats and the Victorians* (New Haven: Yale University Press, 1944). See also my article "Between Two Worlds: Keats's 'Hyperion' and Browning's 'Saul,'" in *Studies in Browning and His Circle* 8, no. 2 (Fall 1980): 57–74.

Chapter Six

1. John Henry Newman, *Essays and Sketches* (New York: Longmans, Green, 1948), I, 76.

2. J. R. Watson, ed., *Everyman's Book of Victorian Verse* (London: J.M. Dent and Sons, 1982), XIV.

3. Walter Pater, *Appreciations* (New York: Macmillan, 1900), 105–106.

4. Noted by G. B. Tennyson in *Victorian Devotional Poetry* (Cambridge: Harvard University Press, 1981), 227. See also Tennyson's invaluable discussion of *The Christian Year*, 72–113.

5. Joseph H. Summers, ed., *The Selected Poetry of George Herbert* (New York: New American Library, 1967), 255.

6. Lewis Carroll, *Alice's Adventures in Wonderland and Through the Looking Glass* (Oxford: Oxford University Press, 1986), 19 (hereafter cited in text).

7. Martin Gardner, ed., *The Annotated Snark* (New York: Simon and Schuster, 1962), 56.

8. The phrase is from Arnold's critically important "Preface" to *Poems, 1853*. See P. J. Keating, ed., *Matthew Arnold: Selected Prose* (Harmondsworth: Penguin, 1987), 41.

9. Barbara G. Walker, *The Woman's Encyclopedia of Myths and Secrets* (San Francisco: Harper & Row, 1983), 70. See also Christine Downing, *The Goddess* (New York: Crossroad, 1987), 13–15.

10. Rollo May, *Love and Will* (New York: Dell, 1969), 45.

11. Alicia Craig Faxton, *Dante Gabriel Rossetti* (New York: Abbeville Press, 1989), 67.

12. Oswald Doughty, ed., *Rossetti's Poems* (London: J.M. Dent and Sons, 1968), 70 (hereafter cited in text).

13. Cited in Faxton, *Dante Gabriel Rossetti*, 67.

14. George A. Panichas, ed., *The Simone Weil Reader*, 446.

15. William Michael Rossetti, ed., *The Poetical Works of Christina Georgina Rossetti* (London: Macmillan, 1924), 63 (hereafter cited in text). See also Betty S. Flowers, "The Kingly Self: Rossetti as Woman Artist," in *The Achievement of Christine Rossetti* (Ithaca: Cornell University Press, 1987), 174; In same volume, see Rosenblum, 144.

16. Ian Jack, ed., Browning: *Poetical Works: 1833–1864* (London: Oxford University Press, 1970), 582 (hereafter cited in text).

17. Carol T. Christ, *The Finer Optic* (New Haven: Yale University Press, 1975), 12–13.

18. James Gibson, ed., *The Complete Poems of Thomas Hardy* (New York: Macmillan, 1976), 101 (hereafter cited in text).

19. Virgil Nemoianu, *The Taming of Romanticism* (Cambridge: Harvard University Press, 1984), 85. This book is especially helpful in defining the shift in sensibility that took place in Europe between the Romantic and Victorian periods.

20. Desmond Flower, ed., *The Poetical Works of Ernest Christopher Dowson* (London: Cassell, 1950), 113 (hereafter cited in text).

21. W. J. Rolfe, ed., *The Poetic and Dramatic Works of Alfred Lord Tennyson* (Boston: Houghton Mifflin, 1898), 520–21 (hereafter cited in text).

22. G. K. Chesterton, *The Victorian Age in Literature* (Notre Dame: University of Nortre Dame Press, 1963), 31.

23. Charles Dickens, *Hard Times* (New York: New American Library, 1961), 11.

24. John Kelley and Eric Domville, eds., *The Collected Letters of W. B. Yeats* (Oxford: Clarendon Press, 1986), I, 23.

25. T. S. Eliot, *Selected Essays*, 294.

26. George A. Panichas, ed., *The Simone Weil Reader*, 380.

Chapter Seven

1. Max Beerbohm, *Rossetti and His Circle* (New Haven: Yale University Press, 1987), 9.

2. Virgil Nemoianu, *The Taming of Romanticism*, 77.

3. My discussion of this poem is deeply indebted to the classic analysis of Cleanth Brooks in *The Well-Wrought Urn*, 167–77.

4. T. S. Eliot, *Selected Essays*, 291.

5. For a discussion of this tactic in *In Memoriam*, see Marion Shaw, *"In Memoriam* and Popular Religious Poetry," *Victorian Poetry* 15, no. 1 (Spring 1977): 1–8.

6. For this insight I am indebted to Bernard Richards, *English Poetry of the Victorian Period: 1830–1890* (London: Longman Group UK, 1988), 34.

7. G. K. Chesterton, *Orthodoxy* (New York: Doubleday, n.d.), 153.

8. Carlos Baker, ed., *Selected Poetry and Prose of Shelley*, 501.

9. Cited in Mark Girouard, *The Return of Camelot* (New Haven: Yale University Press, 1981), 172–73.

10. Cited by Clyde de L. Ryals in *From the Great Deep: Essays on* Idylls of the King (Athens: Ohio University Press, 1967), 41.

11. George A. Panichas, "The Critic as Conservator," *Modern Age* 26 (Summer/Fall 1982): 335.

12. G. K. Chesterton, *Orthodoxy*, 33.

13. George P. Landow, "Closing the Frame: Having Faith and Keeping Faith in Tennyson's 'The Passing of Arthur,'" *Bulletin of the John Rylands University Library* 56 (1974); 442.

14. William Irvine and Park Honan, *The Book, The Ring, and the Poet* (New York: McGraw Hill, 1974), 35.

15. Henry James, *Literary Criticism: Essays, American and English Writers* (New York: Library of America, 1984), 803.

16. William E. Buckler, ed., *Prose of the Victorian Period*, 376. See also John Ruskin, *Modern Painters,* (New York: John Wiley & Sons, 1886), IV, 369.

17. William Morris, "Men and Women: A Review," In *The Bibelot* (New York: William H. Wise, 1898), IV, 89.

18. Ann P. Brady, *Pompilia* (Athens: Ohio University Press, 1988), 14–15.

19. Quoted by Gardiner B. Taplin in his introduction to *Aurora Leigh* (Chicago: Academy Chicago Limited, 1979), xix.

20. Edgar Allan Poe, *Essays and Reviews* (New York: The Library of America, 1984), 141, 121, 119.

21. Sarah Paul, "Strategic Self-Centering and the Female Narrator," *Browning Institute Studies* 17 (1989): 75–90.

22. C. S. Lewis's discussion of these terms may be found in *Four Loves* (New York: Harcourt Brace Jovanovich, 1960), 11–21.

23. Harriet Waters Preston, ed. *The Complete Poetical Works of Elizabeth Barrett Browning* (Boston: Houghton Mifflin Company, 1900), 233 (hereafter cited in text).

Notes and References

24. Mary Jo Salter, "A Poem of One's Own," *New Republic*, 4 March 1991, 33.

25. The epithets that to this writer seem entirely accurate are those of Carol Ianone in "The Barbarism of Feminist Scholarship," *Intercollegiate Review* 23, no. 1 (Fall 1987): 38.

26. Mary Jo Salter, "A Poem of One's Own," 31.

Chapter Eight

1. See A. L. Rowse, *Matthew Arnold: Poet and Prophet* (London: Thames and Hudson, 1976).

2. Matthew Arnold, *Essays in Criticism: Second Series*, 177.

3. P. J. Keating ed., *Matthew Arnold: Selected Prose*, 130.

4. This distinction is discussed with great insight by David Reide in *Matthew Arnold and The Betrayal of Language* (Charlottesville: University Press of Virginia, 1988), 134–47.

5. P. J. Keating, ed., *Matthew Arnold: Selected Prose*, 412.

6. H. F. Lowry, A. L. P. Norrington, and F. L. Mulhauser, eds., *The Poems of Arthur Hugh Clough* (Oxford: Oxford University Press, 1951), 241 (hereafter cited in text).

7. George A. Panichas, "The Critic as Conservator," 334.

8. A. O. J. Cockshut, "Clough: The Real Doubter," in *The Unbelievers: English Agnostic Thought 1840–1890* (New York: New York University Press, 1966), 41.

9. G. K. Chesterton, *Orthodoxy*, 77.

10. Sir Edmund Gorse and Thomas James Wise, eds., *The Complete Works of Algernon Charles Swinburne* (London: William Heinemann, 1925), I, 201 (hereafter cited in text).

11. G. K. Chesterton, *Orthodoxy*, 34–35.

12. Gerald Roberts, ed., *Gerard Manley Hopkins: Selected Prose* (Oxford: Oxford University Press, 1980), 25.

13. Ibid., 25–26.

14. Walter Pater, *The Renaissance* (Oxford: Oxford University Press, 1986), 86.

15. Robert Bridges, ed., *Poems of Gerard Manley Hopkins* (London: Oxford University Press, 1933), 29 (hereafter cited in text).

16. G. K. Chesterton, *St. Francis of Assisi* (New York: George H. Doran, 1924), 128–29.

17. Walter Pater, *The Renaissance*, 152.

18. Ibid., 152.

19. Hopkins, *Selected Prose*, 19.

20. Pater, *The Renaissance*, 94.

21. Hopkins, *Selected Prose*, 66.

Notes and References

22. Joseph H. Summers, ed., *George Herbert: Selected Prose* (New York: New American Library, 1967), 255.

23. From his introduction to the Bridges edition of Hopkins's *Poems* as cited in text x–xi.

24. F. R. Leavis, "Metaphysical Isolation," in *Gerard Manley Hopkins: The Kenyon Critics* (New York: New Directions, 1945), 122–23.

25. Hopkins, *Selected Prose*, 143.

26. George MacDonald, *Diary of an Old Soul* (Minneapolis: Augsburg Publishing House, 1975), 59.

27. G. K. Chesterton, *Orthodoxy*, 138.

28. C. S. Lewis, *Letters to Malcolm: Chiefly on Prayer* (New York: Harcourt Brace Jovanovich, 1964), 43–44.

Chapter Nine

1. Cited by Ronald W. Johnson in "Dante Rossetti's *Beata Beatrix* and the *New Life*," *The Art Bulletin* 57, no. 4 (December 1975): 548.

2. The Everyman edition of Rossetti's poems used throughout this text does not include the poet's translations from the Italian: *The Early Italian Poets from Ciullo D'Alcumo to Dante Alighieri* (1861). The citation here is from *Poems and Translations: 1850–1879* (London: Oxford University Press, 1925), 396.

3. George A. Panichas, ed., *The Simone Weil Reader*, 479.

4. Jacques Maritain, *Creative Intuition in Art and Poetry* (Ohio: Meridian Books, 1954), 277.

5. Reported by Hall Caine, *Recollections of Dante Gabriel Rossetti* (Boston: Roberts Brothers, 1883), 284.

6. My reading is strongly influenced by Carol T. Christ in *The Finer Optic*, 41–42.

7. D. G. Rossetti, *Poems and Translations*, 393.

8. Derek Stanford, ed., *Pre-Raphaelite Writing* (London: J.M. Dent & Sons, 1973), 160.

9. *Pre-Raphaelite Society Newsletter*, Autumn 1990, 1.

10. Jan Marsh, *The Pre-Raphaelite Sisterhood* (New York: St. Martin's Press, 1985), 358.

11. T. E. Hulme, "Romanticism and Classicism," in *Critical Theory Since Plato*, ed. Hazard Adams (New York: Harcourt Brace Jovanovich, 1971), 768.

12. Virginia Woolf, "'I Am Christina Rossetti,'" *The Nation and the Atheneum 48* (6 December 1930): 324.

13. T. S. Eliot, *Selected Essays*, 235.

14. George A. Panichas, ed., *Simone Weil Reader*, 446.

15. Ibid., 352.

16. Many feminist scholars of Victorian literature have noted the significance of hair as a symbol of a woman's essense, creativity, or sexuality.

Notes and References

See, for example, Nina Auerbach, *Romantic Imprisonment* (New York: Columbia University Press, 1985), 235–61.

17. Dolores Rosenblum in *Christina Rossetti: The Poetry of Endurance* (Carbondale and Edwardsville: Southern Illinois University Press, 1986) is very canny about the significance of these fruits. But although her analysis of "Goblin Market" (63–108) is rife with insights, she generally distorts the tone, the themes, and the spirit of Christina Rossetti.

18. Joseph H. Summers, ed., *Selected Poetry of George Herbert*, 97.

19. Arthur Waugh, "Christina Rossetti," *The Nineteenth Century and After* 108 (December 1930): 788.

20. Cited by Jan Marsh in *The Pre-Raphaelite Sisterhood*, 273.

21. William Morris, *The Collected Works of William Morris* (New York: Russell & Russell, 1966), I, 128 (hereafter cited in text).

22. C. S. Lewis, *Literary Essays*, 229.

23. Walter Pater, *Sketches and Reviews* (New York: Boni and Liveright, 1919), 18–19.

24. Frederick Page, ed., *The Poems of Coventry Patmore* (London: Oxford University Press, 1949), 156 (hereafter cited in text).

25. Phyllis B. Bartlett, ed., *The Poems of George Meredith* (New Haven and London: Yale University Press, 1978), I, 126 (hereafter cited in text).

Chapter Ten

1. Vivian de Sola Pinto, *Crisis in English Poetry: 1880–1940* (London: Hutchinson, 1965), 28.

2. William Butler Yeats, *The Autobiography of William Butler Yeats* (New York: Macmillan, 1965), 200.

3. W. B. Yeats, ed., *The Oxford Book of Modern Verse* (New York: Oxford University Press, 1937), 1.

4. George A. Panichas, ed., *The Simone Weil Reader*, 265.

5. Jacques Maritain, *The Responsibility of the Artist* (New York: Charles Scribner's Sons, 1960), 41.

6. William Butler Yeats, *The Collected Poems of W. B. Yeats* (New York: Macmillan, 1964), 101.

7. Arthur Symons, "Ernest Dowson," in *The Bibelot* (New York: W.H. Wise, 1900), VI, 356–57.

8. Yeats, *The Autobiography*, 208.

9. Arthur Symons, "Ernest Dowson," 345.

10. George A. Panichas, ed., *The Simone Weil Reader*, 379.

11. John Henry Newman, *Parochial and Plain Sermons* (San Francisco: Ignatius Press, 1987), 849.

12. Arthur Symons, "Ernest Dowson," 349.

13. Yeats, *The Autobiography*, 207. For Villiers quotation, see page 203.

14. Ian Fletcher, ed., *The Complete Poems of Lionel Johnson* (London: Unicorn Press, 1953), 190 (hereafter cited in text).

15. Ibid., 204.

16. Jerome Buckley and George Woods, eds., *Poetry of the Victorian Period* (Glenview: Scott, Forsman 1965), 883. Symons's works are hard to come by. This copious anthology of Victorian poetry contains a generous sampling of Symons's verse (hereafter cited in text).

17. Walter Pater, *The Renaissance*, 151.

18. Wilfred Meynell, ed., *The Collected Works of Francis Thompson* (Westminster: The Newman Bookshop, 1947), 107 (hereafter cited in text).

19. Cited by Christopher Ricks in his introduction to *The New Oxford Book of Victorian Verse* (Oxford: Oxford University Press, 1987), xxiv.

20. A. E. Housman, *The Collected Poems of A. E. Housman* (New York: Holt, Rinehart and Winston, 1965), 21 (hereafter cited in text).

21. C. S. Lewis, *Christian Reflections* (Grand Rapids: William B. Eerdmans, 1967), 66–67.

22. My reading is indebted to David Perkins's erudite analysis "Hardy and the Poetry of Isolation," in *Hardy: A Collection of Critical Essays* ed. by Albert J. Guerard (Englewood Cliffs: Prentice-Hall, 1963), 150–54.

· Selected Bibliography ·

PRIMARY WORKS

Arnold, Matthew, *The Poetical Works of Matthew Arnold*. Ed. C. B. Tinker and H. F. Lowry. London: Oxford University Press, 1963.

Blake, William, *The Complete Writings of William Blake*. Ed. Geoffrey Keynes. London: Oxford University Press, 1958.

Browning, Elizabeth Barrett. *The Complete Poetical Works of Elizabeth Barrett Browning*. Ed. Harriet Waters Preston. Boston: Houghton Mifflin, 1900.

Browning, Robert. *Poetical Works: 1833–1864*. Ed. Ian Jack. London: Oxford University Press, 1970.

Byron. *Poetical Works*. London: Oxford University Press, 1967.

Clough, Arthur Hugh. *The Poems of A. H. Clough*. Ed. H. F. Lowry, A. L. P. Norrington, and F. L. Mulhauer. Oxford: Oxford University Press, 1951.

Coleridge, Samuel Taylor. *The Oxford Authors: Samuel Taylor Coleridge*. Ed. H. J. Jackson. London: Oxford University Press, 1985.

Dowson, Ernest Christopher. *The Poetical Works of Ernest Christopher Dowson*. Ed. Desmond Flower. London: Cassell, 1950.

Gray, Thomas, and William Collins. *Selected Poems of Thomas Gray and William Collins*. Ed. Arthur Johnston. Columbia: University of South Carolina Press, 1970.

Hardy, Thomas. *The Complete Poems of Thomas Hardy*. Ed. James Gibson. New York: Macmillan, 1976.

Hopkins, Gerard Manley. *Poems of Gerard Manley Hopkins*. Ed. Robert Bridges. London: Oxford University Press, 1933.

Gerard Manley Hopkins: Selected Prose. Ed. Gerald Roberts. Oxford: Oxford University Press, 1980.

Housman, A. E. *The Collected Poems of A. E. Housman*. New York: Holt, Rinehart and Winston, 1965.

Johnson, Lionel. *The Complete Poems of Lionel Johnson*. Ed. Ian Fletcher. London: Unicorn Press, 1953.

Johnson, Samuel. *Samuel Johnson: Rasselas, Poems, and Selected Prose*. Ed. Bertrand H. Bronson. New York: Holt, Rinehart and Winston, 1971.

Keats, John. *Keats's Poetical Works*. Ed. H. W. Garrod. Oxford: Oxford University Press, 1958.

———. *Letters of John Keats*. Ed. Robert Gittings. London: Oxford University Press, 1971.

Meredith, George. *The Poems of George Meredith*, 2 vols. Ed. Phyllis B. Bartlett. New Haven and London: Yale University Press, 1978.

Morris, William. *The Collected Works of William Morris*, 24 vols. New York: Russell and Russell, 1966.

Patmore, Coventry. *The Poems of Coventry Patmore*. Ed. Frederick Page. London: Oxford University Press, 1949.

Pope, Alexander. *Alexander Pope: Selected Poetry and Prose*. Ed. William K. Winsatt, Jr. New York: Holt, Rinehart and Winston, 1951.

Rossetti, Christina Georgina. *The Poetical Works of Christina Georgina Rossetti*. Ed. William Michael Rossetti. London: Macmillan, 1924.

Rossetti, Dante Gabriel. *Poems and Translations: 1850–1870*. London: Oxford University Press, 1925.

———. *Rossetti's Poems*. Ed. Oswald Doughty. London: J.M. Dent and Sons, 1968.

Shelley, Percy Bysshe. *The Complete Poetical Works of Percy Bysshe Shelley*. Ed. Thomas Hutchinson. London: Oxford University Press, 1923.

———. *Selected Poetry and Prose of Shelley*. Ed. Carlos Baker. New York: Random House, 1951.

Swinburne, Algernon Charles. *The Complete Works of Algernon Charles Swinburne*, 20 vols. Ed. Sir Edmund Gosse and Thomas Wise. London: William Heinemann, 1925.

Tennyson, Alfred Lord. *The Poetic and Dramatic Works of Alfred Lord Tennyson*. Ed. W. J. Rolfe. Boston: Houghton Mifflin, 1898.

Thompson, Francis. *The Collected Works of Francis Thompson*. Ed Wilfred Meynell. Westminster: The Newman Bookshop, 1947.

Wordsworth, William. *The Complete Poetical Works of Wordsworth*. Ed. Andrew J. George. Boston: Houghton Mifflin Company, 1932.

Yeats, William Butler. *The Collected Poems of W. B. Yeats*. New York: Macmillan, 1964.

SECONDARY WORKS

Abrams, M. H. *The Mirror and the Lamp*. New York: W.W. Norton, 1958. Comprehensively examines the theoretical underpinnings of Romantic verse in both England and Germany. A classic in the history of ideas.

———. *Natural Supernaturalism*. New York: W.W. Norton, 1973. For Abrams, the Romantics adapted biblical themes and Christian ideals to the secularized idioms of post-Napoleonic Europe; hence the "natural" is invested with a "supernatural" value. One of the best studies of the period—especially good on Wordsworth, Coleridge, Keats, and Shelley.

Babbit, Irving. *Rousseau and Romanticism.* New York: Meridian Books, 1955. An adversarial but also astute and insightful analysis of Romantic excess as typified in "the ascendency of imagination over judgment."

Baker, Carlos. *Shelley's Major Poetry.* Princeton: Princeton University Press, 1948. The single best synoptic treatment of Shelley's growth and development as a poet.

Bate, Walter Jackson. *John Keats.* New York: Oxford University Press, 1966. The Pulitzer Prize–winning biography that explores both the life and art of a major poet with the grace and understanding of a genuine humanist.

Bloom, Harold. *The Visionary Company.* New York: Anchor Books, 1963. A comprehensive overview of Romantic poetry in one of the first and still one of the best of Bloom's authoritative works.

Brooks, Cleanth. *The Well-Wrought Urn.* New York: Harcourt, Brace, 1947. The classic of textual analysis that includes four indispensable studies of Gray, Wordsworth, Keats, and Tennyson.

Buckley, Jerome. *Tennyson: The Growth of a Poet.* Cambridge: Harvard University Press, 1960. The best single overview of Tennyson's poetic development.

Christ, Carol T. *The Finer Optic.* New Haven and London: Yale University Press, 1975. An intellectual tour de force that provides one of the best possible handles on the sometimes bewildering diversity of Victorian verse. Christ explores a wide-ranging corpus of Victorian poetry from the perspective of the poet's concern with the relations between the particular and the universal, the one and the many, the finite and the infinite. A basic work in any study of the period.

Cockshut, A. O. J. *The Unbelievers.* New York: New York University Press, 1966. Contains an excellent chapter on Arthur Hugh Clough.

Davie, Donald. *Thomas Hardy and British Poetry.* New York: Oxford University Press, 1972. A rich appreciation by a contemporary poet of Hardy's achievement and his influence on modern verse.

Eliot, T. S. *Selected Essays.* New York: Harcourt, Brace, 1950. Among the essays collected here, the four on Tennyson, Arnold, Blake, and Swinburne are among the most valuable ever written on these poets.

Faxton, Alicia Craig. *Dante Gabriel Rossetti.* New York: Abbeville Press, 1989. The coffee-table book par excellence. A sumptuously illustrated and judiciously balanced discussion of Rossetti the painter, which also throws light on Rossetti the poet.

Fogle, Richard Harter. *The Imagery of Keats and Shelley*. Chapel Hill: University of North Carolina Press, 1949. Sensitively attunes the reader to the peculiar image-worlds of both poets and the relation of these images to the themes and ideals each poet cherished.

Ford, G. H. *Keats and the Victorians*. New Haven: Yale University Press, 1944. An erudite analysis of Keats's stylistic legacy to the Victorian poets.

Frye, Northrop. *Fearful Symmetry*. Boston. Beacon Press, 1967. The most learned, exhaustive, canny, and, at times, controversial study of Blake to appear in the twentieth century.

Gaunt, William. *The Pre-Raphaelite Dream*. London: Reprint Society, 1943. A novelist's evocation of the Pre-Raphaelite circle, coupled with a critic's discernment of their artistic and poetic achievement.

Gilbert, Sandra, and Susan Gubar. *The Madwoman in the Attic*. New Haven: Yale University Press, 1979. A mixed bag of willful distortion and genuine insight that explores nineteenth-century women poets from a feminist point of view. Especially helpful on Elizabeth Barrett Browning; less so on Christina Rossetti.

Gill, Stephen. *William Wordsworth: A Life*. Oxford: Oxford University Press, 1989. An evocative and compelling biography that sheds light on Wordsworth's life and work.

Gleckner, Robert. *Byron and the Ruins of Paradise*. Baltimore: Johns Hopkins University Press, 1967. Explores Byron's Romantic pessimism with uncommon sensitivity. One of the few superlative studies in which the craft of Byron the poet takes precedence over the foibles of Byron the man.

Grob, Alan. *The Philosophical Mind*. Columbus: Ohio State University Press, 1973. A chronological commentary on Wordsworth's poetic development with special attention to his philosophic conversion from a natural to a supernatural understanding of reality.

Holms, Richard. *Coleridge: Early Visions*. New York: Viking Penguin, 1989. The first part of a projected two-part biography told with a novelist's art and poet's insight into the workings of the creative process.

———. *Shelley: The Pursuit*. New York: E.P. Dutton, 1975. Holmes almost invariably assumes that allegations of Shelley's improprieties are to be taken at face value. Debunks "the beautiful but ineffectual angel" image of the poet, erring too much on the side of cynicism. Still, a compelling read with many arresting insights into the man and poet.

Houghton, Walter E. *The Victorian Frame of Mind*. New Haven: Yale University Press, 1957. The classic study of the social, intellectual, and cultural climate of the Victorian age.

Irvine, William, and Park Honan. *The Book, The Ring, and The Poet*. New York: McGraw Hill, 1974. The standard biography of Browning—thorough, judicious, humane.

Jack, Ian. *English Literature: 1815–1832.* Oxford: Clarendon Press, 1963. Contains valuable essays on the second generation of Romantic poets: Byron, Shelley, Keats.

James, D. G. *Matthew Arnold and the Decline of English Romanticism.* Oxford: Oxford University Press, 1961. Examines Arnold against the legacy of English Romanticism and the controversies associated with the Oxford Movement. Deftly exposes the contradictions between Arnold the critic and Arnold the poet.

———. *The Romantic Comedy.* London: Oxford University Press, 1963. Among the top critical books on the Romantic period. Follows the evolution of Romanticism from Blake through Keats and its eventual absorption, through the theological writings of Coleridge, into the historical continuity of the Anglican Church.

Johnson, E. D. H. *The Alien Vision of Victorian Poetry.* Hamden: Anchor Books, 1963. One of the best introductions to the poetry of Arnold, Tennyson, and Browning. Explores the respective ways in which each of these poets responded to the increasingly agnostic and materialist atmosphere of Victorian England.

Johnson, Wendell Stacy. *Cerard Manley Hopkins: The Poet as Victorian.* Ithaca: Cornell University Press, 1968. A painstaking study of Hopkins's poetry in the context of the aesthetic, religious, and philosophic controversies germane to the Victorian Age. Adroit, clear, and illuminating readings of individual poems.

King, Jr., Roma A. *The Focusing Artifice.* Ohio: Ohio University Press, 1968. The single best overview of Browning's poetry from *Pauline* to *Asolando.* Exhaustive, but not superficial; wide-ranging, yet detailed and profound.

Knight, G. Wilson. *The Starlit Dome.* Oxford: Oxford University Press, 1971. The uncanny feel for poetic images and the ability to grasp the spirit of an author's work that Wilson demonstrated in his studies of Shakespeare is here matched by an equally penetrating discussion of the major Romantic poets.

Leggett, B. J. *Housman's Land of Lost Content.* Knoxville: University of Tennessee Press, 1970. A close, perceptive examination of theme and structure in Housman's poetry; extraordinarily sensitive in the analysis of diction and imagery.

Lewis, C. S. *Selected Literary Essays.* London: Cambridge University Press, 1969. Everything Lewis wrote is worth reading; of special relevance here are two essays on Morris and Shelley, respectively, which defend the achievement of both poets against their early modernist detractors.

Lucas, F. L. *Ten Victorian Poets.* Hamden: Archon Books, 1966. These essays were originally radio talks for the B.B.C.; genial, infectious, and distilled discussions of Victorian poets, which wear their learning lightly without being superficial or patronizing. Highly recommended.

Marsh, Jan. *The Pre-Raphaelite Sisterhood.* New York: St. Martin's Press, 1985. A feminist who writes with discernment and grace, Marsh looks at the lives of the women associated with the Pre-Raphaelite circle and finds much to commend in the work of the poets and painters whom they inspired.

Murry, John Middleton. *Keats and Shakespeare.* London: Oxford University Press, 1964. Going beyond stylistic resemblances between Keats and Shakespeare, Murry notes the sympathy of vision and poetic tact that make this Romantic poet one of the few writers to whom the epithet "Shakespearian" legitimately applies.

Nemoianu, Virgil. *The Taming of Romanticism.* Cambridge: Harvard University Press, 1984. This broad historical survey discusses the adaptation of English and European Romanticism to the more comfortable perspectives and limited expectations of the bourgeoisie in post-Napoleonic Europe.

Pater, Walter. *Appreciations.* London: Macmillan, 1900. The essays here on Wordsworth, Coleridge, Rossetti, and the concluding postscript on Romanticism are necessary reading for any student of nineteenth-century poetry.

———. *The Renaissance.* Oxford: Oxford University Press, 1986. The single most important text for understanding the sensibility and ethos of late Victorian poetry. Pater's aesthetic stance was the principal influence on the poets of "the tragic generation."

Perkins, David. *The Quest for Permanence.* Cambridge: Harvard University Press, 1959. Perkins's comparative study of Wordsworth, Shelley, and Keats from the perspective of their need to place the world of change and flux in the context of a reality that is permanent and abiding greatly enhances our understanding of these poets.

Pick, John. *Gerard Manley Hopkins: Priest and Poet.* New York: Oxford University Press, 1966. This short, brisk biography is uncommonly successful in tracing the relationship between the poetry and the life—and in exploring the tensions between Hopkins's dual vocations as poet and priest.

Pinto, Vivian De Sola. *Crisis in English Poetry.* London: Hutchinson, 1965. The indispensable study of English poetry in transition between the late Victorian and early modernist periods.

Rajan, Tilottama. *Dark Interpreter.* Ithaca and London: Cornell University Press, 1980. A self-proclaimed "deconstructionist," Rajan focuses on the ambiguities implicit in the Romantics' attitude toward the imagination. Explores with extreme pertinacity the poetry of Shelley, Keats, and other Romantics (both German and English) as "necessary fictions" self-consciously constructed to stave off the destructive forces of an alien universe that eventually undermines the poet's visionary faith. Too doctrinaire by far, but rich in detailed analysis and insight.

Reide, David. *Dante Gabriel Rossetti and the Limits of Victorian Vision.* Ithaca and London: Cornell University Press, 1983. Traces Rossetti's progressive doubts about the Christian and Romantic sources of his art, his growing skepticism regarding the role of the poet as soothsayer or witness, and his increasing emphasis on the subjectivity of language and experience. An excellent book.

———. *Matthew Arnold and the Betrayal of Language.* Charlottesville: University Press of Virginia, 1988. A softly deconstructive analysis of Arnold's poetry that explores the dismay and skepticism of a Victorian poet who can no longer trust language as the medium of a higher revelation.

Richards, Bernard. *English Poetry of the Victorian Period.* London and New York: Longman Group UK, 1988. A genial, urbane commentary on Victorian poetry that highlights poets and works customarily neglected or accorded scant attention. A refreshing book that extends the range of the subject and helps to rectify imbalances in previous treatments of Victorian verse. Emphasis on genre, diction, versification, image, and theme as opposed to individual poets.

Rosenblum, Dolores. *Christina Rossetti: The Poetry of Endurance.* Carbondale and Edwardsville: Southern Illinois University Press, 1986. Rosenblum's study is unyieldingly partisan in a way that distorts Rossetti by remaking her in the image of a postmodern feminist. The reading offered here of "Goblin Market" is, however, one of the best and most thought-provoking to appear in recent years.

Rowse, A. L. *Matthew Arnold: Poet and Prophet.* London: Thames and Hudson, 1976. Always outspoken in his biases, Rouse nevertheless offers a handy, readable overview of Arnold's life and work.

Ryals, Clyde de L. *From the Great Deep.* Athens: Ohio University Press, 1967. A thorough, coherent exposition of Tennyson's *Idylls of the King,* which explores the unity of the series and the persistence of the poet's thematic preoccupations. Good on theme, character, and imagery.

Santayana, George. *Winds of Doctrine and Platonism and the Spiritual Life.* Gloucester: Peter Smith, 1971. Santayana's essay on Shelley in this volume is a tribute from one literary genius to another. The style here is a model of grace, and the insights into Shelley's poetry and character are of rare and arresting depth.

Sperry, Stuart. *Keats the Poet.* Princeton: Princeton University Press, 1973. Sperry's complete survey of Keats's poetry is among the most balanced and perspicuous of commentaries on this poet. An introductory chapter discusses the influence of Keats's medical studies and scientific training on the poet's conception of the creative process.

Tennyson, G. B. *Victorian Devotional Poetry.* Cambridge: Harvard University Press, 1981. An important volume that explores the unjustly neglected poetry of Oxford's Tractarians: Newman, Keble, and Isaac Williams. The legacy of Tractarian aesthetics is also discussed in relation to Gerard Manley Hopkins and Christina Rossetti.

Trilling, Lionel. *Matthew Arnold.* New York: Columbia University Press, 1958. A measured and penetrating discussion of Arnold as poet and cultural critic, which emphasizes the social dimension of Arnold's criticism and the poet's protest against the materialism of his age.

Wasserman, Earl. *The Finer Tone.* Baltimore: Johns Hopkins Press, 1967. Wasserman's grasp of the philosophic dimensions of Keats's poetry is formidable indeed—as is his ability to detect thematic relationships between the poet's letters and his more consciously crafted work. His analyses of the major odes, "The Eve of St. Agnes." and "La Belle Dame" are nothing short of dazzling. The only drawback here is a too systematic approach to a poet whose mind was less rigid and more subtly toned than Wasserman suggests.

———. *Shelley: A Critical Reading.* Baltimore: Johns Hopkins University Press, 1971. Wasserman's philosophic system-building sometimes betrays the ambiguities, contradictions, and unassertive suggestiveness of Keats's verse. With Shelley, however, Wasserman finds a poet as metaphysically inclined as himself. His expositons of Shelley's major poems are unchallenged in their erudition, exhaustiveness, and detailed analysis. The discussion of "Adonais" is almost as breathtaking as the poem itself.

Willey, Basil. *More Nineteenth-Century Studies.* New York: Columbia University Press, 1977. Willey continues his exploration of the Victorian ethos as expressed in the biographical writings of Christian apostates and intellectual skeptics. Of supreme merit here is the long discussion of Tennyson, whose life and works (especially *In Memoriam*) are illuminated in an engaging style and interpreted by an empathetic mind.

———. *Nineteenth-Century Studies.* New York: Columbia University Press, 1977. A study of the history of ideas in the nineteenth century, beginning with Coleridge's aesthetic and theological thought and ending with a study of Matthew Arnold. Points between include Newman, Carlyle, Mill, and George Eliot. Indispensable for an understanding of the period.

Yeats, William Butler. *An Autobiography of William Butler Yeats.* New York: Macmillan, 1965. Yeats's recollections of Morris and the poets of the nineties bear valuable witness to the influence of the Pre-Raphaelites and the decadents on one of the twentieth century's greatest poets.

· *Index* ·

Abrams, M. H., 13
Aligheri, Dante, 27, 84, 86, 93, 97, 98, 125, 126, 244–45, 247, 248, 275; *"Divine Comedy, The,"* 97, 240, 264; *Vita Nuova, La (The New Life)*, 92, 246–47, 250, 251
Aristotle, 120–21, 132
Arnold, Matthew, 52, 81, 127, 131, 134, 136, 137, 139, 150, *200–212*, 225, 240; *Culture and Anarchy*, 202; "Dover Beach," 208, 217; *Empedocles on Aetna*, 186, 203–6; *Essays in Criticism*, 10–11, 69, 75; "Function of Criticism at the Present Time, The," 202; *God and the Bible*, 202; "Literature and Science," 200, 202; *St. Paul and Protestantism*, 202; "Scholar Gipsy, The," 197, 209–11; "Shelley," 207; "Stanzas from the Grand Chartreuse," 146, 206–7; "Stanzas in Memory of the Author of *Obermann*," 43, 152; "Thyrsis," 209, 211–13; "Tristran and Iseult," 148; "To Marguerite," 208

Babbit, Irving: *Rousseau and Romanticism*, 4, 20, 23
Baudelaire, Charles, 282
Beardsley, Aubrey, 280
Beattie, James, 4
Beckett, Samuel, 154
Beddoes, Thomas, 131
Beerbohm, Max: *Rossetti and His Circle*, 154
Bion, 94, 209
Blake, William, 10, 16–17, 21, 22, 26–41, 42, 100, 147, 243; "Auguries of Innocence," 13–14; *Book of Thel, The*, 34; *Book of Urizen, The*, 39; *Four Zoas, The*, 10, 39; *Jerusalem*, 28, 39; *Marriage of Heaven and Hell, The*, 36–37; *Milton*, 26, 28, 39–41; "Mock On, Mock On, Voltaire, Rousseau," 26; *Poetical Sketches*, 31–32; *Songs of Experience*, 34–36; *Songs of Innocence*, 19, 32–34; "To the Muses," 7–8; "Vision of the Last Judgment," 18
Bloom, Harold, 29
Brontë, Charlotte: *Jane Eyre*, 195, 197

Browning, Elizabeth Barrett, 143, 144, *189–99*, 211; *Aurora Leigh*, 143, 189, 190, 191, 195–99; *Casa Guidi Windows*, 190; "Cry of the Children, The," 191; "Lady Geraldine's Courtship," 190; "Musical Instrument, A," 191; *Sonnets from the Portuguese*, 144, 190, 191–95
Browning, Robert, 136, 137, 140, 148, 150, *175–89*, 191–95, 203, 208, 279; "Andrea del Sarto," 183–84, "Bishop Orders His Bomb, The," 181–83; "Blot in the 'Scutcheon, The," 178; "By the Fireside," 144–45; "Caliban upon Setebos," 184; "Childe Roland to the Dark Tower Came," 184; "Cleon," 184, 186; *Dramatis Personae*, 178; "Epistle, An," 184–86; "Fra Lippo Lippi," 183–84; *Men and Women*, 178; "My Last Duchess," 180–81, 183; *Pauline*, 176; *Pippa Passes*, 177; "Porphyria's Lover," 180; "Rabbi Ben Ezra," 179; *Return of the Druses, The*, 177; *Ring and the Book, The*, 186–188; "Saul," 146–147; "Spanish Cloister, The," 183; *Strafford*, 177; "Two in the Compagna," 180; "Up at a Villa, Down in the City," 177
Buber, Martin, 40
Burke, Edmund, 148; *Reflections on the Revolution in France*, 23
Byron, George Gordon, Lord, 10, 16, 70–84, 93, 100, 131; *Childe Harold's Pilgrimage*, 18, 24, 73, 75–79, 81, 84; *Don Juan*, 75, 81–84, 132; *English Bards and Scotch Reviewers*, 74; "Epistle to Augusta," 76, 80; *Giaour, The*, 75; *Hebrew Melodies*, 80; *Hours of Idleness*, 74; *Island, The*, 75; *Manfred*, 76, 79–80; *Prisoner of Chillon, The*, 80–81; "She Walks in Beauty," 80

Camus, Albert, 79, 81, 100
Carlyle, Thomas, 131, 135, 136, 148, 170
Carroll, Lewis: *Alice in Wonderland*, 137–39; 281; *Hunting of the Snark, The*, 138–39
Catullus, 283
Chapman, George, 102

Index

Index

Index

"Tithonous," 159–60; "Two Voices, The," 139, "Ulysses," 158–59
Thompson, Francis: "The Hound of Heaven," 294–97
Thomson, James: *Seasons, The,* 4
Tolstoy, Leo, 214
Typology, 256–57

Utilitarianism, 134–35, 157

Vendler, Helen, 128
Verlaine, Paul, 282, 283, 284
Virgil, 85, 97, 209

Watts, Isaac, 137–38
Weil, Simone, 79, 141–42, 153, 158, 246–47, 262, 265, 281, 286–87
Wilberforce, Bishop, 138
Wilde, Oscar, 279–80, 286
Williams, Isaac, 132
Wollstonecraft, Mary, 37, 92; *Vindication of the Rights of Woman, The,* 21
Woolf, Virginia, 258
Wordsworth, Dorothy, 49, 55, 65, 66–67; *Journals,* 67
Wordsworth, William, 1, 21, *42–53,* 55, *64–69,* 70, 77, 78, 80, 82, 100, 108, 126, 131, 132, 206, 297, 313; "Earth has not anything to show more fair," 68; "Elegiac Stanzas," *Excursion, The,* 12, 43–44; "I wandered lonely as a cloud," 14–16, 81, 162; "Idiot Boy, The," 50; "It is a beauteous evening, calm and free," 68; "Lines composed a few miles above Tintern Abbey," 43, 49–50, 52, 57, 65, 80, 156; *Lyrical Ballads,* 52, 61, 313; *Michael,* 50–52; "Ode: Intimations of Immortality," 6, 18, 52, 65–68, 97; "Poet's Epitaph, A," 52; "Preface" to *Lyrical Ballads,* 7, 16, 46, 53; *Prelude, The,* 12, 22–24, 42, 45–49, 52; "Resolution and Independence," 4, 19, 50; "Simon Lee," 50; "Thorn, The," 50; "To the Cuckoo," 65; "We Are Seven," 19, 50; "World is too much with us, The," 68

Yeats, William Butler, 148, 151–52; 271, 279; "Among School Children," 294; *Autobiography,* 280, 288–89; "Grey Rock, The," 282; "In Memory of Major Robert Gregory," 288
Young, Edward, 1

· *About the Author* ·

Dr. Stephen Gurney is a member of the faculty at Emmanuel College, Oxford, and professor of English at Bemidji State University in Minnesota. He has contributed seven articles to other books and has written numerous articles and reviews in professional journals. His poetry has recently appeared in the United States in *The Formalist* and is due to appear in a British anthology edited by the Cambridge Poetry Group. He is an editorial adviser for *Modern Age*, a publication of the Intercollegiate Institute at Bryn Mawr. His critical study *Alain-Fournier* (1987) was extolled in *French Studies* as "a detailed reading... all the more invigorating for having been written by a specialist in English literature." Dr. Gurney has lived and studied in Oxford.